Revealing Cumbria's

150 Years of the Cumberland and Westmorland Antiquarian and Archaeological Society

Revealing Cumbria's Past

150 Years of the Cumberland and Westmorland Antiquarian and Archaeological Society

Edited by
Michael Winstanley
Assisted by Rob David and Ian Whyte

CUMBERLAND AND WESTMORLAND
ANTIQUARIAN AND ARCHAEOLOGICAL SOCIETY
2016

Cumberland and Westmorland
Antiquarian and Archaeological Society
Hon. General Editor
Professor Colin Richards

Revealing Cumbria's Past

150 Years of the Cumberland and Westmorland Antiquarian and Archaeological Society

EXTRA SERIES NO. 45

ISBN 9781873 124734

Printed by
Titus Wilson & Son, Kendal
2016

The publication of this book has been made possible through
a generous bequest left to the Society by its member
Thomas William Whinn Jones (1924-2013).

Contents

List of Contributors

Adrian Allan studied Modern History at Durham University. He joined Liverpool University's staff in 1970, retiring, as University Archivist, in 2008. A member of CWAAS since 1972, he has served as Membership Secretary since April 2013.

David Breeze is a past President of the Society. He is an honorary professor at four UK universities and has written extensively about the Roman army and Roman frontiers.

Ian Caruana, archaeologist, now retired, formerly with the Carlisle Archaeology Unit. Society Librarian and stock holder. Active with the Senhouse Museum Trust. Main research interest currently paranumismatics.

Alan Crosby is one of Britain's best-known local historians. Editor of *The Local Historian* since 2001 he has published extensively on the history of north-west England and taught for several universities, specialising in social history and landscape history.

Rob David is a retired lecturer. He has been Chair of the Publications Committee and is currently a Vice-President of the Society and co-ordinator of the 150th Anniversary events programme.

Antony Dickson works for Oxford Archaeology North as their lithic specialist. He is currently involved in the publication of the results of a technological analysis of a large Mesolithic lithic assemblage recovered during excavations at Stainton West, Carlisle.

Rachel Newman has worked in the North West for over 30 years, after studying at Durham University. She is now responsible for the post-excavation programme and publications at Oxford Archaeology North and is currently President of the Society.

Ian Whyte is Emeritus Professor of Historical Geography in the Lancaster University Environment Centre. His research focuses on landscape, and economic and social change in upland Britain in the post-medieval period. He is currently editor of *Transactions*.

Angus Winchester is Professor of Local & Landscape History at Lancaster University and is a Past President of CWAAS. He joined the Society as a schoolboy in its centenary year.

Michael Winstanley was Senior Lecturer in History at Lancaster University until 2010 with particular interests in the history of north-west England which he continues to pursue in 'retirement'.

W.G. (Bill) Wiseman moved to the county in 1971 and joined the Society the following year. He was elected Joint Editor of *Transactions* in 1983, with Bruce Copley Jones, and continued in that office until 2008.

Fiona Wooler is a north Cumbrian who has been interested in vernacular buildings from an early age. She is a qualified buildings archaeologist, with a particular interest in traditional farm buildings, industrial structures and landscapes.

List of Figures

Acknowledgements

The Society's archive is deposited with the Cumbria Archive Service, and we are grateful to the archivists for making it available to a number of the authors who have contributed to this volume. The staff at the Local Studies Libraries in Carlisle and Kendal, and at Carlisle Archive Centre have been particularly helpful in finding and scanning illustrations.

As readers of this volume will discover, Titus Wilson & Son of Kendal have printed nearly all of the Society's publications over the last 150 years. It is therefore particularly appropriate that this volume should have been designed and published by the company, and the Society would like to acknowledge the professional skill and help so readily shown by those who have worked there over the years. Our anniversary year has also been marked by the digitization of the complete run of *Transactions* and we would like to thank all the team involved in that, particularly Pat Garside and John Steel, since it has greatly facilitated the editorial process. Colin Richards, the General Editor of the Cumberland and Westmorland Antiquarian and Archaeological Society, and Bryan Harper of Titus Wilson's have steered this volume through the publishing process.

We should like to thank the contributors for their readiness to respond to questions and requests. We are also very grateful to the Society's General Secretary, Marion McClintock, who read through, and commented on, an earlier draft of the complete text.

We are equally grateful to all those individuals and institutions who have supplied images and given permission for them to be reproduced. We have taken all reasonable steps to obtain this permission but apologise for any omissions or errors where owners could not been traced or have been incorrectly identified.

Foreword

In 1916, at the time of the Society's golden jubilee, the world was at war, and the event was limited to a dinner, a 'lantern lecture' by the President and a visit to Hadrian's Wall. At the time of the Centenary in 1966, the Society sponsored an excavation at the Roman fort at Maryport and organized an ambitious celebratory three-day meeting based in Carlisle. This involved a dinner at the Crown and Mitre Hotel, and a series of visits to Tullie House Museum, Carlisle Cathedral and Castle, Maryport Roman Fort (to examine the excavations), Birdoswald Roman Fort, Naworth Castle and Lanercost Priory. For the 150th anniversary in 2016, the Society planned a series of celebratory events, completed a project to digitize *Transactions*, and commissioned this book, the first full history.

For 150 years the Society has tried to remain true to the vision of the founders despite the disappearance in 1974 of the counties of 'Cumberland and Westmorland' and significant changes to the concepts 'antiquarian and archaeological' and to the methodologies underlying the study of the past. From the beginning the area of Lancashire North of the Sands was considered part of the region covered by the Society's interests, so with the local government reorganization of 1974 which created Cumbria County Council covering Cumberland, Westmorland, Lancashire North of the Sands and the area around Sedbergh and Dent the administrative boundaries in effect caught up with the area traditionally covered by the Society.

Part 1 begins with a chapter which charts the history of the Society in the context of changes in how the past has been studied and the role of county societies in the development of regional history. Perhaps the most significant contribution of the Society to an understanding of Cumbria's past has been as a publisher both of *Transactions* and of a diverse range of books. This is explored in Chapter 2. The focus of all the chapters in Part 2 is the role the Society has played in developing our understanding of Cumbria's past. Given the timespan and the range of publications this is necessarily selective. Archaeology has been a significant part of the Society's activities since it was founded. Chapter 3 explores the varied interests of archaeologists, alongside the use of changing methodologies, that have characterised Cumbrian archaeology during the Society's lifetime. Some of the sub-disciplines of local history over the 150 years are explored in chapters 4-8. These include longstanding areas of interest such as political, religious and social history as well as more recent contributions on industrial history/archaeology and the development of vernacular buildings. As an illustration of the antiquarianism of the early years we have included a chapter exploring the nature of the

Society's early interest in customs and folklore, but for reasons of space we have had to exclude studies of the early enthusiasm for genealogy, manorial descents and ecclesiastical buildings. The concluding chapter (Chapter 9) considers the significance of the Society, both regionally and nationally, over its first 150 years. Biographical summaries of the Presidents and a complete list of publications are incorporated as appendices as is a short history of the Society's Library. A major anniversary project has been the complete calendaring of the Society's records including the archives of CWAAS, the affiliated groups and key members of the Society. A brief summary of what exists is set out in a further appendix and a detailed list can be consulted on the Society's website.

Michael Winstanley
Rob David
Ian Whyte

Part 1

The History of the Society

Chapter 1
The Society's First 150 Years

Angus J. L. Winchester

> ... such societies serve many useful purposes. They cultivate a knowledge of local history, they act as a check upon that tendency of the age which holds nothing sacred that is not useful, they form a common ground of meeting for men and women of kindred tastes, and present through the pleasant medium of excursions into the country an interesting study which many of us are too apt to associate with the unattractive researches of Dryasdust.[1]

So wrote an anonymous journalist in the *Carlisle Journal*, reporting a meeting of the Society in Keswick on 12 July 1871, at a time when the fledgling society was emerging from a period of crisis during which its future was far from clear. 'We should have very much regretted to see it pass away', he wrote, before penning the endorsement quoted above.[2] But survive it did, fulfilling the functions he described across 150 years of changing circumstances. This chapter charts the foundation of the Society and sketches its history across the succeeding century and a half as a preface to the more detailed accounts of the different aspects of the Society's activities and contributions to the understanding of Cumbria's past, provided in subsequent chapters.

One of the major developments in historical and archaeological study across England in the nineteenth century was the establishment of clubs and associations to bring together those with an interest in the local past. The earliest provincial society of that kind was the Society's elder sibling, the Society of Antiquaries of Newcastle upon Tyne, founded in 1813. The 1840s and 1850s saw the foundation of county associations to foster either the tangible legacies of the past by focusing on archaeological and architectural remains, or the documentary record by undertaking record publication (represented in northern England by the Surtees Society (1834) and the Chetham Society (1843)). During the middle decades of the nineteenth century a more wide-ranging form of society came to prominence, concerned with all aspects of the local past and sometimes including the study of natural history as well. These were generally county-wide in their scope, based in the county town and drawing together a membership which embraced both the gentry and clergy (the traditional proponents of antiquarian study) and the rising urban middle classes. By holding excursions and meetings at which papers were read and subsequently published, they fostered serious research – largely undertaken by amateurs – as well as generating a constituency of informed and influential individuals who were concerned to protect what would now be termed the local 'heritage'.[3] Among such groups was the Cumberland and Westmorland Antiquarian and Archaeological Society, founded in 1866.

The establishment of the Society was not, of course, the beginning of antiquarian and archaeological study in Cumbria. Like most other English counties, Cumberland and Westmorland had an antiquarian tradition stretching back to the reign of Elizabeth I. The pioneers, gathering remains in the period when William Camden was preparing the first English edition of *Britannia* (which appeared in 1610), were Reginald Bainbrigg, the Appleby schoolmaster and collector of Roman inscriptions, who was Camden's principal local contact, and John Denton, the Cumberland lawyer who attempted the first manorial history of the county *c.*1600.[4] The later seventeenth century saw a flowering of antiquarian study, much of it documentary rather than archaeological, spearheaded by clerics: Thomas Machell, vicar of Kirkby Thore, who gathered voluminous notes on the history of the two counties; Hugh Todd, who prepared a history of the diocese of Carlisle in the 1680s and Bishop William Nicolson, a scholar of note who preserved Machell's manuscripts for future generations.[5] The first printed account of the antiquities of the two sister counties appeared in 1777 when Joseph Nicolson and Richard Burn published their *History and Antiquities of the Counties of Westmorland and Cumberland* in two volumes, drawing heavily on their seventeenth-century predecessors. This joined the growing body of county histories of the later eighteenth century and became the standard work for many decades. Other works followed, notably Hutchinson's history of Cumberland (1794) and Samuel Jefferson's freshly-researched but incomplete history of the county, of which volumes on Carlisle, Leath Ward and Allerdale above Derwent appeared between 1838 and 1842.[6] The richness of the region's antiquities had been demonstrated by these early works, whetting the appetite of those who formed the new society.

Victorian origins and early years (to 1900)

The Cumberland and Westmorland Antiquarian and Archaeological Society was established at a meeting held at the Crown Hotel, Penrith, on 11 September 1866, called by five members of the moneyed middle classes of the two counties (fig. 1.1).

The promoters came from a range of backgrounds. George Gill Mounsey (1797-1874) of Castletown, Rockcliffe, near Carlisle, was a lawyer (deputy registrar of Carlisle diocese and secretary to the bishop) and a published

Fig. 1.1. Crown Hotel, Penrith *(reproduced by permission of Cumbria County Council, Carlisle Library)*

historian, his *Carlisle in 1745* having appeared in 1846. The Revd James Simpson (1819-1886), vicar of Kirkby Stephen, was 'an all round antiquary' who was to become the leading light in the newly-formed Society. Robert Ferguson (1817-1898) of Morton, Carlisle, was a cotton mill owner, who had been mayor of Carlisle twice in the 1850s and would later serve as MP for the city. His counterpart in Westmorland was John Whitwell (1811-1880), a Kendal carpet manufacturer, six times mayor of Kendal and MP for the borough from 1868 to 1880. The fifth, and by some years the youngest, member of the group was the Revd Alfred Francis Curwen (1835-1920), rector of Harrington and a younger son of the Curwens of Workington Hall (fig. 1.2). In geographical spread, they provided good coverage of the twin counties: two, Whitwell and Simpson, were Westmorland men; two, Mounsey and Ferguson, were from Carlisle; and the fifth, Curwen, was from west Cumberland. In representing the establishment in mid-Victorian provincial society, the scholarship and ecclesiastical links of Mounsey and Simpson were balanced by the wealth and public prominence of Ferguson and Whitwell. It is striking that most of the promoters were drawn from the business and professional classes, rather than the old county families: only Curwen was a scion of an ancient gentry lineage.

The meeting at Penrith, attended by around 50 gentlemen and 'several ladies' and chaired by William Browne of Tallentire, adopted a constitution and appointed officers. The Society's purpose was defined as 'investigating, describing and preserving the Antiquities of Cumberland and Westmorland'. Membership was to be at an annual subscription of one guinea, ladies having 'the privilege of membership' for 10s. per year. New members would be admitted by vote on nomination by two existing members (fig. 1.3). The inaugural meeting appointed a 14-man Council, a Treasurer and three Honorary Secretaries (one of whom was Alfred F. Curwen). The founding Council included the other four promoters – led by Simpson, who soon assumed the chairmanship – and drew in several members of the gentry (F.L.B. Dykes of Dovenby, Philip Howard of Corby, J.P. Senhouse of Netherhall) as well as scholarly clerics (Dr G.H. Ainger, principal of St Bees Theological College, Henry Ware, vicar of Kirkby Lonsdale and later suffragan bishop of Barrow-in-Furness, and George F. Weston, vicar of Crosby Ravensworth).

Fig. 1.2. The promoters of the Society. Clockwise from top left: George Gill Mounsey; James Simpson; Robert Ferguson; John Whitwell; Alfred Francis Curwen. *(Mounsey, Ferguson and Curwen reproduced by permission of Cumbria County Council, Carlisle Library; Simpson reproduced by permission of Cumbria County Council, Kendal Library; Whitwell reproduced by courtesy of Kendal Town Council)*

The Presidency was initially titular and filled by members of the aristocracy, the Earl of Lonsdale being the founding President.

Fig. 1.3. Member's ticket and ladies' admission ticket, 1866 (DSO/1/1) *(image: Cumbria County Council, Carlisle Archive Centre)*

Founding members numbered 84 men; by the end of 1866 the Society could list 115 members, including three ladies, drawn from across the two counties, with a handful coming from further afield. Many were from the sections of society traditionally associated with antiquarian study, the landed gentry and the clergy. Indeed, more than one quarter (30 of the 112 male members) were clergymen, reflecting the passion for antiquarian matters among Victorian country parsons and cathedral dignitaries. Yet, from the very beginning, the urban middle classes were attracted to the Society: 36 per cent of those who joined the Society in 1866 lived in either Carlisle or Kendal.

The constitution also allowed for the appointment of honorary members and four were elected at the inaugural meeting, including the two leading antiquaries from the North East, William Greenwell of Durham, the barrow-excavating cleric (and inventor of the 'Greenwell's Glory' trout fly), and Dr John Collingwood Bruce, secretary to the Society of Antiquaries of Newcastle upon Tyne, famed for his guide to Hadrian's Wall.[7] Both played active parts in the early meetings of the newly-formed Society, reflecting the inspiration the new Society sought and gained from across the Pennines, particularly from its elder sibling, the Society of Antiquaries of Newcastle upon Tyne.

Launching the new Society amid great enthusiasm, James Simpson's inaugural address on 'The present state of antiquarian research in Cumberland and Westmorland' cast the net wide. It ranged from prehistoric monuments ('remains of the Celtic period') and Roman antiquities, through 'The Northmen – Runic Inscriptions' to 'Old Documents – Churches – Castles' and 'Old Customs'. Simpson ended with a flourish: local knowledge was more useful than 'great ability or great learning', he claimed, urging the Society to work together in collecting facts in the established antiquarian manner:

> If only we labour diligently and examine carefully; gather up facts as they present themselves, and place on record our experience as it grows; if only we speak that we know and testify to that we have seen, bearing with each other and helping each other, we shall gradually unfold the pages from which may be read the history of our counties.[8]

He was followed by William Greenwell, who read a paper on 'Recently opened tumuli in Westmorland and Cumberland', generating enthusiastic discussion of barrow-opening among the assembled members before they proceeded to dinner in the Assembly Rooms. In discussion at the meeting, several crucial questions surfaced, which have resonated down the decades in the history of the Society. One was the inherent tension between archaeological and historical approaches to the past. In responding to Simpson's address, Greenwell had championed the study of Anglo-Saxon remains, a suggestion welcomed by repeated cries of 'Hear, hear!' from the audience. This led the young Richard S. Ferguson, who was to play such a major role in the Society later in the nineteenth century, to enquire whether 'this society was to devote itself exclusively to Anglo-Saxon remains'; he urged the need for documentary research, which could be undertaken particularly by members, such as himself, who lived in London. The Society should not devote itself exclusively to any one branch of antiquarian study (more cheers of 'Hear, hear!'). In response, Greenwell and John Whitwell encouraged Ferguson to embark on documentary research. The relationship between the fledgling society and the established antiquarian bodies across the Pennines was also raised by Greenwell, who noted that both the Society of Antiquaries of Newcastle upon Tyne and the Surtees Society envisaged Cumberland and Westmorland as falling within their spheres of interest. The close links between the Society and these bodies which continue today – notably in organising decennial pilgrimages to Hadrian's Wall and in joint record publications – thus stretch back to the very beginning.

Initiated in an atmosphere of such enthusiastic anticipation, the Society set to work. Its core activities were spelt out in a resolution passed at the inaugural meeting:

> 6. That the Society shall hold two or more Meetings in each year at some place of interest, at which papers on Antiquarian or Architectural subjects shall be read, to be printed, if approved, by the Council as part of the transactions of the Society. The publications of the Society shall be edited by the Printing Committee, to consist of three Members, to be elected by the Council.

The momentum gained at Penrith was built on by a second meeting, held at Carlisle on 7 November 1866. Attended by around 100 members, including 'many ladies', the second meeting set a pattern. The day was led by John A. Cory, the architect and county surveyor of Cumberland, who read papers on the Cathedral and conventual buildings and led an excursion to the sites. Members were given an opportunity to show exhibits: at that meeting these included antique maps from Corby Castle, examples of Roman pottery and fragments of medieval stalls from St Cuthbert's church, Carlisle. The meeting was followed by dinner at the County Hotel and a 'conversazione' at Morton, hosted by Robert Ferguson.

Four meetings were planned for 1867 (though it appears that only three took place) and the AGM at Kendal Museum in August agreed to a reduction in subscriptions to half a guinea for men and 5*s*. for ladies. A Printing Committee was established, consisting of James Simpson, Robert Ferguson and John Whitwell, while Simpson, Whitwell and John Cory were appointed to act as 'a sub-committee for general arrangements'. In 1867 the Society also fired its first salvo in protecting archaeological remains: the secretary at Kendal was asked to write to the county surveyor for Westmorland 'drawing attention to the recent carrying away of stones from the Cairn in Dunmail raise' (figs. 1.4 and 1.5).[9]

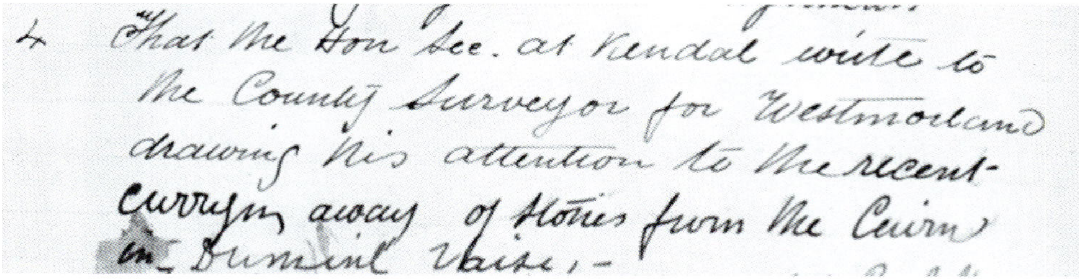
4 That the Hon Sec. at Kendal write to the County Surveyor for Westmorland drawing his attention to the recent carrying away of stones from the Cairn in Dunmail Raise,-

Fig. 1.4. Minute relating to the Society's action over damage to the cairn on Dunmail Raise (DSO/1/1 Minutes of General Meeting 29 August 1867) *(image: Cumbria County Council, Carlisle Archive Centre)*

Fig. 1.5. The cairn on Dunmail Raise *(photograph by courtesy of Pat Rowland)*

The following year saw the beginnings of systematic attempts to record and explore archaeological remains. Council agreed that an outline map of Cumberland and Westmorland – including, significantly, 'the border of Yorkshire and North Lonsdale' – should be prepared, on which to mark all known Roman roads and other 'well ascertained Antiquarian remains which may be from time to time examined by the Society'. It also sought permission from Lord Lonsdale to carry out its first excavation, an investigation of the Roman fort at Low Borrow Bridge, which had the clear objectives of ascertaining 'its exact form and arrangement and by what Legions it was occupied' (figs. 1.6 and 1.7).[10]

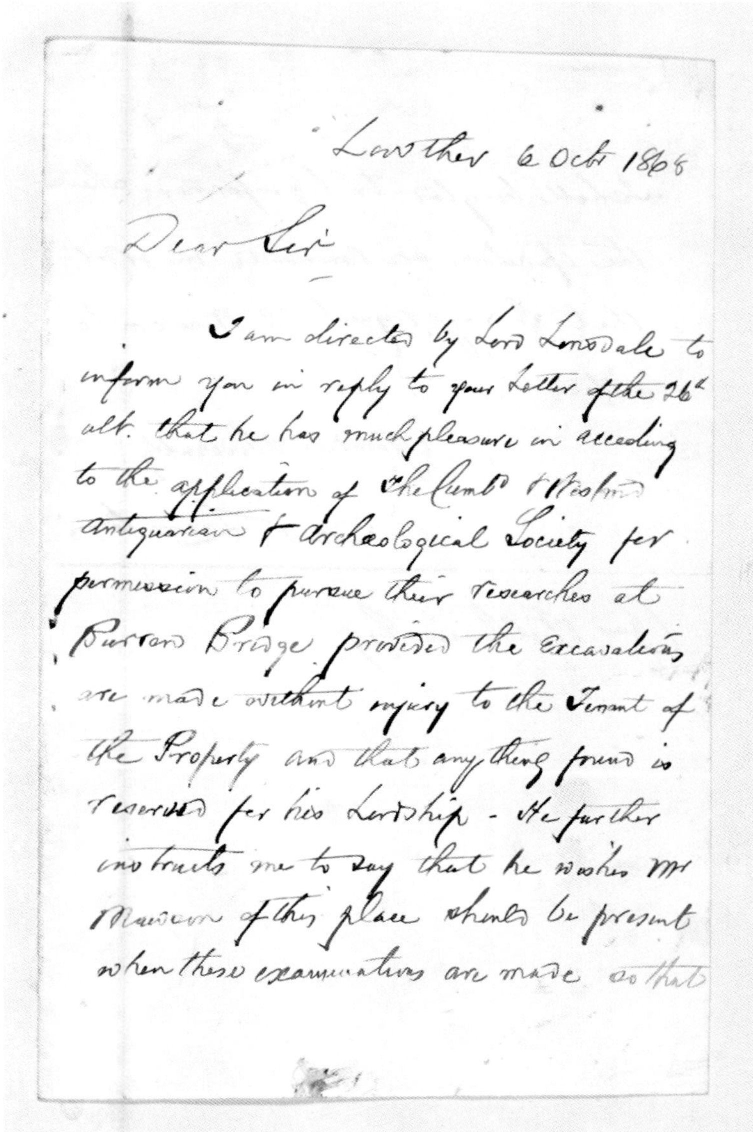

Lowther 6 Octr 1868

Dear Sir

I am directed by Lord Lonsdale to inform you in reply to your Letter of the 26th ult. that he has much pleasure in acceding to the application of the Cumbd & Westmd Antiquarian & Archaeological Society for permission to pursue their researches at Burrow Bridge provided the excavations are made without injury to the Tenant of the Property and that any thing found is reserved for his Lordship - He further instructs me to say that he wishes Mr Mawson of this place should be present when these examinations are made so that

Fig. 1.6. The first page of the letter from the Earl of Lonsdale granting the Society permission to excavate at Low Borrow Bridge Roman fort, 6 October 1868 (DSO/1/1 Minutes of meeting at Penrith 23 September 1868) *(image: Cumbria County Council, Carlisle Archive Centre)*

Fig. 1.7. Low Borrow Bridge: foundation of the Eastern Gateway; from R.S. Ferguson, 'The Roman Camp at Low Borrow Bridge: report of the Committee appointed Aug. 22, 1883', *CW1*, 8 (1886), 1-6 *(image: Cumbria County Council, Kendal Library)*

The energy of the initial three years was difficult to sustain, however. No meetings were held during 1869 (the explanation given was that there were no papers to be read); in consequence, membership subscriptions were waived for the year. A concerted effort was made in 1870-71, under the leadership of James Simpson and Charles Ferguson, to revive the fledgling society's fortunes. Part of the problem seems to have stemmed from the secretarial arrangements. The triumvirate appointed in 1866 did not work. Tellingly, it was said in 1871 that the 'combined – or, perhaps it would be more accurate to say, independent – exertions of three honorary secretaries' had failed to provide a sound administrative basis.[11] Simpson determined that a single secretary was needed and in 1871 Titus Wilson (1834-1917), the Kendal printer who had prepared the Society's first *Transactions* the previous year, was appointed Honorary Secretary, a position he held until 1911.

Wilson's appointment seems to have given a fresh impulse to the Society, which was given a further boost by the energetic presence of Richard S. Ferguson, who returned to Cumberland three years later. A regular pattern of meetings was re-established, though attendance in the early 1870s was sometimes so small that costs could not be covered. From 1873 two two-day meetings were normally held each year,[12] usually in opposite corners of Cumbria, to enable members from across the region to participate. The young society soon ventured further afield – to Melrose in 1873 and to Hexham three years later, in a joint meeting with the Durham and Northumberland Archaeological and Architectural Society. It is striking that Lancashire North of the Sands (implicitly omitted from the Society's area of interest in its title) soon came to be considered 'home' territory. An excursion to Arnside in 1875 overlapped the county boundary to take in Cartmel as well and 1877 saw the first of several excursions to Low Furness, including a visit to Furness Abbey (fig. 1.8).

More adventurous excursions took place as the century progressed: a week-long meeting in Carlisle with the Royal Archaeological Institute in 1882, the first two of the decennial pilgrimages to Hadrian's Wall with the Society of Antiquaries of Newcastle upon Tyne in 1886 and 1896, and a residential visit across the water to the Isle of Man in 1894.[13] The notorious Cumbrian weather sometimes dampened spirits but seems rarely to have deterred the hardy antiquaries: for example, the weather for the excursion to the Brampton area in August 1879 was reported to have been 'that usually experienced on these occasions. A brisk breeze was blowing, and as it drove a heavy rain before it, and the sky was quite leaden-coloured, things looked hopeless enough to discourage anybody but antiquaries'.[14]

From the mid-1870s, the Society's energy was directed once again towards systematic study and recording. In 1874 Simpson sent a circular to the Anglican clergy, asking for a list of all pre-seventeenth-century

Fig. 1.8. The Society visit to Furness Abbey in September 1895 *(image: Cumbria County Council: Barrow Archive Centre)*

sepulchral slabs, brasses, effigies and crosses in churches and churchyards.[15] The following year small committees were appointed in each of the wards of Cumberland and Westmorland (and, significantly, in 'Lonsdale-over-Sands', reinforcing the area's status as part of the Society's region) to examine the objects reported by the clergy in their returns.[16] A further impetus came in 1886 when the Society of Antiquaries of London wrote to all county societies seeking recommendations for monuments which might be scheduled under the Ancient Monuments Protection Act 1882. Only five prehistoric monuments (the stone circles at Long Meg, Castlerigg and on Burn Moor, together with the henges at Mayburgh and King Arthur's Round Table) had been scheduled by then and the Society appointed a committee to make recommendations.[17] In the event, the Society was the only county society to respond.[18] In 1890, again under the aegis of the Society of Antiquaries, the Society revived its plan to draw up an archaeological map of Cumbria.

A sustained programme of excavation was initiated in 1894 with the establishment of the Cumberland Excavation Committee, to investigate the Cumberland section of Hadrian's Wall. The key player in this was Francis Haverfield of Oxford University, one of the pioneers of scientific archaeology and the leading Romanist of the day.[19] An annual programme of excavation began, funded in roughly equal parts by a grant from the Society and subscriptions raised in Oxford by Haverfield. Results were published in *Transactions*, accompanied by sophisticated colour illustrations of stratigraphical sections and plans.[20]

Meanwhile, the Society was also beginning to open up the region's documentary record. The first record publication, Ferguson's edition of Bishop Nicolson's *Miscellany Accounts of the Diocese of Carlile*, was published in 1877 (fig. 1.9) and *Transactions* were published with increasing regularity. While the first volume, covering the years up to 1873, had been published in stages,[21] Richard Ferguson's editorship resulted in regular biennial publication, the second volume, published in 1876 and covering the Society's activities in 1874 and 1875, established the pattern which continued until 1900. Under Ferguson's drive, a systematic programme of record publication was also conceived. In 1887 and 1888 the Society voted funds for transcribing episcopal registers and the major monastic cartularies. In the event, only one cartulary, that of Wetheral Priory, was published during Ferguson's lifetime and that was edited and, significantly, funded privately by Archdeacon (later Chancellor) J.E. Prescott (1832-1920) in 1897. On the back of its publication, however, a 'chartulary publication account' was opened, to which £50 had been subscribed within a few months.[22]

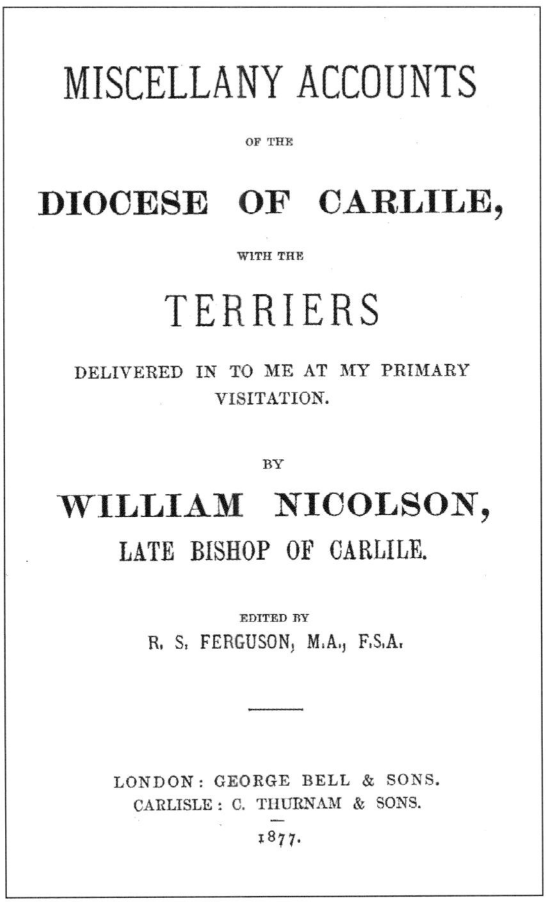
MISCELLANY ACCOUNTS

OF THE

DIOCESE OF CARLILE,

WITH THE

TERRIERS

DELIVERED IN TO ME AT MY PRIMARY VISITATION.

BY

WILLIAM NICOLSON,

LATE BISHOP OF CARLILE.

EDITED BY

R. S. FERGUSON, M.A., F.S.A.

LONDON: GEORGE BELL & SONS.
CARLISLE: C. THURNAM & SONS.
1877.

Fig. 1.9. The title page of Bishop Nicolson's *Miscellany Accounts of the Diocese of Carlile*, edited by R.S. Ferguson (1877). This was the first volume published by the Society (see also p.74)

As with so many voluntary bodies, leadership of the Society in the years after its initial enthusiastic foundation came to be concentrated into the hands of a few key players, who drove the Society forward. Only two of the original promoters, John Whitwell and James Simpson, continued to shoulder the weight of the Society after its inaugural year. Others who sustained the Society at this time included Charles John Ferguson (1840-1904), the Carlisle architect and brother of Richard S. Ferguson. He appears to have been the most effective of the Society's three original secretaries and continued to be an active member of Council and leader of excursions.

James Simpson remained the driving force behind the Society across its first 20 years. He was a Westmorland man from Crosthwaite and Lyth, educated at the University of Durham, who returned to his native county, serving successively as curate of Morland, vicar of Shap and, from 1863, vicar of Kirkby Stephen. He was an energetic public servant – a well-known educationalist, a Poor Law guardian and magistrate (serving as chairman of Westmorland Quarter Sessions) – as well as a keen antiquary. He chaired Council as 'President of Council' almost from the outset and, when the Society's President, St George Lowther, 4th Earl of Lonsdale, died in 1882, the titular presidency was, in effect, abolished and Simpson became President of the Society. He seems to have been the right man to nurture the young Society, possessing 'boundless energy ... shrewd common sense, great local knowledge, and [a] keen sense of humour [which] made him a genial check upon the eccentricities antiquaries are liable to fall into when they have imbibed a little too much learning'.[23]

On Simpson's death in 1886, the Society's Editor, Richard Saul Ferguson (1837-1900), became President, thus vesting the two key offices in one individual. Ferguson was the 'heart and soul of the Society' in the late-Victorian years, regularly taking the leading role in excursions as well as editing *Transactions*.[24] A member of the Carlisle cotton dynasty, he trained as a lawyer and returned to his native city in 1874 after the breakdown of his marriage. He became prominent in the public life of the city, served as a councillor and mayor and was instrumental in establishing Tullie House as a museum, public library and art gallery. In 1887 he was appointed chancellor of the diocese, the first layman to fill the position. His huge energy and 'enthusiastic affection' for the twin counties were directed towards antiquarian study. He and his brother Charles had contributed a substantial paper on Lanercost Priory to the Society's 1868 visit to the site[25] and, immediately he returned to Cumberland, his presence was felt. He contributed papers (his first was a pioneering, analytical study of the heraldry of Cumberland and Westmorland, read to the Society in 1873)[26] and under his skilful editorship, from 1874, *Transactions* became the primary repository of archaeological and historical knowledge about the region. His editions of a series of important manuscripts were published as extra volumes by the Society (see Chapter 2 and Appendix 2), leading the way in the Society's proud tradition of record publication, which continues to this day. Towards the end of his life he was appointed county editor for the Victoria County History of Cumberland, but his sudden death in March 1900 prevented him from seeing even the first volume to fruition. Having the means and the leisure to devote himself to antiquarian matters, Chancellor Ferguson made a major contribution to the flowering of historical scholarship in Cumberland and Westmorland, channelling much of his energy through the Society.

Simpson and Ferguson, the two leading lights in the Society's first 30 years, encapsulated the different constituencies it sought to hold together. Both were distinctive figures with long, untamed Ruskinian beards and both were passionate about the region's past, but Simpson was the outdoor man (his obituary had noted that 'walking over a fell he could leave younger men far in the rear'), whereas Ferguson was portly and struggled with asthma. Simpson was genial and a kindly critic, while Ferguson was a man of 'strong feelings though few words'. Each represented different facets of the Society's interests: Simpson the proud Westmerian and Ferguson the Carlisle-based Cumbrian; Simpson the archaeological fieldworker and excavator and Ferguson the historical record searcher and editor. By the 1890s, under Ferguson's leadership, the Society's intellectual power house was based in the cathedral city, yet this was balanced by its administrative affairs being squarely located in Kendal, under the experienced hand of the Secretary, Titus Wilson, and the Kendal-based treasurer, the banker William Dilworth Crewdson.

The Collingwood years and the Second World War (1900 to 1945)

With the death of Chancellor Ferguson, the new century ushered in a new era for the Society As Ferguson had dominated the Society's affairs in the latter decades of the old century, so the Collingwoods, father and son, were at the core of its life for most of the first four decades of the twentieth century.

William Gershom Collingwood (1854-1932) was a polymath – 'artist, author and antiquary' in the shorthand of his biographer.[27] He is often described as 'Ruskin's secretary' (a term which does not do justice to his much wider role as a member of the sage's inner circle) and as Professor of Fine Art at University College, Reading. But neither description fully portrays the sheer diversity of his interests or the range of his contributions to the study of Cumbria's past. His deep fascination with the region led not only to historical novels set in Norse Lakeland (*Thorstein of the Mere* (1895) and *The Bondwoman* (1896)), but also to non-fiction: his comprehensive guidebook, *The Lake Counties* (1902; 2nd edition 1932) and the shorter *Lake District History* (1925; 2nd edition 1928) were both widely read. He was the authority on pre-Norman sculpture, publishing numerous articles on the subject, culminating in the definitive survey of its generation, *Northumbrian Crosses of the Pre-Norman Age* (1927). His publications, particularly in the pages of *Transactions*, spanned a huge breadth: prehistory, medieval buildings, sixteenth- and seventeenth-century mining (notably *Elizabethan Keswick* (1912), published as a – particularly hefty – Tract Series volume), and a pioneering study (with T.H.B. Graham) of the patron saints of parish churches in Cumbria. Equally pioneering were his inventories of ancient monuments in Cumberland (1923) and Westmorland and Lancashire North of the Sands (1926).[28]

From the Society's perspective, Collingwood was a towering figure, the fulcrum around which its activities turned. A vigorous outdoor man, short and broad-shouldered with 'bright and piercingly blue' eyes, he was a charismatic leader.[29] From his base at Coniston, Collingwood had been a dominant figure in the Society, long before becoming President, not least in his role as Editor of *Transactions* for a quarter of a century from 1900. He had served on Council since 1896 and replaced Ferguson at the heart of the Society's meetings and excursions from 1900. He regularly served on the committees 'for local arrangements' which organised excursions and was elected Chairman of Council in 1912, eight years before he became President. Since he continued to chair Council when he became President, the two roles were effectively merged.

One of Collingwood's lasting gifts to the Society was the seal which he designed in 1901 and which emblazoned the cover of *Transactions* until 2000 and still graces the *Newsletter* (fig. 1.10). Taking the shape of a medieval vesica seal, it shows two figures, a male standing and digging, facing a seated female who is earnestly writing, presumably representing the Society's twin concerns of archaeological and antiquarian endeavour. The figures are set in a field of antiquities: medieval tracery, a Viking-age hammerhead cross (based loosely on that at Addingham) and, at the bottom, in the act of being excavated, a Roman altar, inscribed 'DISCIPULINAE' ('learning; knowledge') – appropriately in the plural. This was no abstract altar but that (inscribed in the singular 'DISCIPULINA') excavated at Castlesteads, north of Brampton.[30]

It is clear that Collingwood evoked not only respect but affection from those with whom he worked on the Council. When he had been Editor of *Transactions* for a decade, Council marked the occasion by making him a gift of 50 guineas, a substantial sum in 1910. Collingwood accepted it gracefully and reported that he had 'already made full use of the cheque in a way that had pleased him best' by climbing up Latrigg, the fell behind Keswick, on a glorious evening, where he 'offered it as a burnt sacrifice to the elder deities of the place'.[31] When he resigned as Editor after 25 years, several members suggested that the Society should recognise his service 'in some tangible form' but, at his own request, 'the matter was allowed to remain with that feeling of individual love and gratitude'.[32] A stroke in 1929 prevented him from continuing to play an active role in the Society. The following year, as illness closed in on him, he sent a simple message ('his love') to the General Meeting of the Society by his son, Robin, and when he resigned as President in June 1932, three months before his death, the General Meeting resolved that Robin should 'convey personally a message of love to him from the Society'.[33] It is rare for such terms of endearment to appear in the dry minutes of serious antiquarian societies. Collingwood made clear his affection for the Society in the revised edition of his *Lake Counties* (1932), which he dedicated to the Society and the Lake Artists Society: 'may they flourish and long survive their faithful servant', he wrote. His energy and unwavering commitment – and his status as a scholar – did much to enhance the Society's reputation. Council was exaggerating neither his pivotal role nor the standing of the Society in the first half of the twentieth century when it praised him for raising the Society 'to a high position among the learned societies of the country'.[34]

Fig. 1.10. The Collingwood Seal

It would be wrong, however, to see Collingwood as the sole driver behind the wheel of the Society during the first three decades of the twentieth century. Responsibility for different aspects of work was shared among an increasing number of officers. At first, as we have seen, the chairmanship of Council had been distinct from the presidency: on Ferguson's death, Thomas Hesketh Hodgson became chairman of Council, while Henry Ware, suffragan bishop of Barrow-in-Furness, was elected President. The two offices were combined briefly when Hodgson became President in 1909 but from 1911 Collingwood, chaired Council. His role as chairman no doubt became more central when the Society elected the eminent archaeologist, Francis Haverfield, professor of Ancient History at Oxford, as President in 1915. Haverfield was the first President to be drawn from the wider academic community and the first to be based outside Cumbria.

The Secretaryship provided continuity but also evolved across the early decades of the century. Titus Wilson was succeeded by his son Edward Wilson in 1911, who served for 16 years until his death in 1927. His successor was Gertrude Ainsley, his secretary at the printing works, who was appointed General and Financial Secretary of the Society, with an honorarium of £10 a year (increased to £20 in 1935). The Secretary was supported by others who took on specific roles. Perhaps the most prominent in the life of the Society was John F. Curwen (1860-1932), the Kendal architect, who had served as Secretary jointly with Titus Wilson from 1898 and became 'Hon. Secretary for Antiquarian Correspondence' from 1911. A scholar in his own right (notably for his authoritative *Castles and Fortified Towers of Cumberland, Westmorland and Lancashire North of the Sands* (1913)), Curwen had a hand in the majority of the Society's excursions for many years, he and Collingwood regularly leading the sub-committees for local arrangements which planned and organised each excursion.[35]

A handful of other figures feature prominently, their social status and antiquarian interests reflecting the character of the Society in the early twentieth century. Dr Henry Barnes (1842-1921), a member of a leading medical family in Carlisle, frequently chaired Council in the second decade of the century; T.H.B. Graham (1857-1937), a barrister from the landed family of Edmond Castle, contributed a profusion of manorial histories to *Transactions*, which he edited 1926-34; Henry Swainson Cowper (1865-1941), with deep family roots in Hawkshead, of which he was the pioneering local historian, was an active Vice-President and frequent speaker on the Society's excursions.[36]

The life of the Society in the early twentieth century

The number of members remained fairly stable across the earlier decades of the twentieth century. Standing at 565 in 1914, it fell slightly, to around 550 in the mid-1930s. But the nature of the membership and, hence, the character of the Society was beginning to change. An analysis of individuals elected to membership at the beginning of the second and fourth decades of the century (tables 1.1 and 1.2) shows some significant differences. The number of women joining, running at around one quarter of the new members in the five years 1910-14, had risen to over 40 per cent by the early 1930s. Although, like most other societies, the Society had the character of a gentlemen's club in its early days, women came to play an important part in its work from the early twentieth century. The first female member of

Council was Mrs Hesketh Hodgson, elected in 1916, and the Society gained its first lady Vice-President, Lady Henley, in 1930.[37]

As women became more prominent, the number of clergy was falling, from around one-sixth of all new members on the eve of the First World War to under five per cent in the early 1930s. There were also changes in the geographical distribution of new members. The proportion of members joining from outside Cumbria rose, to stand at one-fifth in the early 1930s, while, within the Society's region, the centre of gravity was shifting. Taken together, those whose addresses are given as Kendal, the Lake District (Keswick, Ambleside, Windermere etc) and Lancashire North of the Sands, rose from around one-fifth of all new members in 1910-14 to almost one-third 20 years later. The rise almost certainly reflects the growing middle-class population of the Lake District in the inter-war years, reinforced, we may suppose, by Collingwood's role in opening up the history of that part of the county. Meanwhile, new members from the industrial towns of West Cumberland dwindled as economic depression settled on that area.

Period	Total new members	No. (%) of women	No. (%) of clergy
1910-14	214	59 (27.5%)	35 (16%)
1930-4	216	90 (42%)	9 (4%)

Table 1.1: Members joining the Society during the quinquennia 1910-14 and 1930-34: women and clergy.

Period	Total new members	No. (%) West Cumb.	No. (%) Carlisle and elsewhere	No. (%) Southern Cumbria	No. (%) from outside Cumbria
1910-14	214	17 (8%)	119 (56%)	47 (22%)	31 (14%)
1930-4	216	1 (0.5%)	102 (47%)	67 (31%)	46 (21%)

Table 1.2: Members joining the Society during the quinquennia 1910-14 and 1930-34: regional breakdown.*

Source: records of admissions to membership at General Meetings in Minute Books 4 and 5, CAS (Carlisle), DSO/1/4 and DSO/1/5. Note: * areas are based on post towns of the addresses as given in the minutes. 'Southern Cumbria' incorporates Kendal area, the Lake District and Lancashire North of the Sands; 'West Cumberland' incorporates Whitehaven, Maryport and Workington area.

Members continued overwhelmingly to come from the leisured and moneyed classes – the number of titled men and women (including men with military rank) is striking. The doubling of the annual subscription, to one guinea, in 1920 does not seem to have interrupted the flow of new members.

The regular pattern of meetings established by the Victorians continued to form the basis of the Society's life. The year began with a Spring meeting 'for the reading of papers', almost invariably held in Carlisle, normally at Tullie House. This was followed by two two-day excursions in June or July and in September. At each gathering, Council met in advance of a General Meeting which received its report and at which new members were elected. The General Meeting at the Summer Excursion in June or July served as the AGM at which the Society's officers were elected and the Treasurer's statement was received. Meetings and excursions continued to be held on weekdays, reinforcing the socially self-selecting nature of the membership: few office workers or working men would have been able to attend. When, in 1913, a member suggested that Thursdays and Fridays were 'not the most suitable days' for excursions, Council rebuffed the idea, since those days were 'convenient to the majority'.[38]

A flavour of excursions in the Edwardian period can be gained from the first summer excursion in 1907. This was held on Thursday 11 and Friday 12 July in the Crosby Ravensworth and Kendal districts. The committee making the arrangements consisted of Collingwood and Curwen (who, between them, acted as guides to almost all the sites visited during the two days), assisted by Harvey Goodwin of Orton Hall and two clergymen, Joseph Whiteside, formerly vicar of Shap, and Sidney Swann, vicar of Crosby Ravensworth. Curwen dealt with the bookings. Members met at Shap railway station at 11.05 a.m. on the Thursday, leaving their luggage (addressed to the 'Archaeological Meeting') with the station master, for conveyance, free of charge, to Kendal. The party, numbering more than 40, then departed in horse-drawn coaches on an itinerary which included earthworks on Wickerslack Moor, Maulds Meaburn Hall, Crosby Ravensworth church and the 'British settlement' at Woodfoot, nearby (fig. 1.11). 'Two fine days, after the rain and cold of a late summer, had brought the moors into good condition for walking, and the weather on this occasion was all that could be desired'.[39] A cold lunch was provided at 1s. 6d. per head at Flass House, home of R.W. Dent, who had been high sheriff of Westmorland the previous year – the sum collected, amounting to over £5, was then sent to the Church Missionary Society. Drinks were provided free of charge by Harvey Goodwin. After a cup of tea at Tebay station, the party then took the train to Kendal (had it been very wet, LNWR had 'courteously consented to have the ... train from Penrith stopped at Shap by signal' but the sun shone and this was not required). Council met before dinner at the Commercial Hotel, Kendal, after which the Annual General Meeting was held, at which six papers were presented to the Society. The following morning (having left their luggage 'in the charge of the Hotel Boots, who will see to its conveyance to the Oxenholme Railway Station'), the party departed by coach to visit sites around Kendal: the motte on Castle How, Watercrook Roman fort, Kendal Castle and the 'British camp' at Castlesteads near Oxenholme.[40] The total cost was 19s. 6d., made up of coach tickets at 4s. 6d. for the Thursday and 2s. 6d. for the Friday, 9s. 0d. for dinner, bed, breakfast, luggage and attendance, and 3s. 6d. in total for the two lunches.

Fig. 1.11. The summer excursion in 1907. Clockwise from top left: Shap station; Crosby Ravensworth church; The Commercial Hotel, Kendal; Kendal Castle; Flass, Maulds Meaburn; *(Crosby Ravensworth church reproduced by courtesy of Chester Forster; others reproduced by permission of Cumbria County Council, Carlisle Library)*

The practical tasks involved in arranging excursions could be a heavy burden and across these decades the Society tried out various solutions. In 1909, Collingwood, Titus Wilson and Curwen interviewed Anthony Barnes of Kendal, who was appointed 'Excursion Agent' on the basis of a ten per cent commission on the price of every ticket. How long the arrangement lasted is not clear.

From the beginning of the century, the pattern of excursions had become more ambitious. In most years the first and second two-day meetings were held in different parts of Cumbria (Gosforth and Penrith in 1902, south Westmorland and Maryport in 1903, for example), to ensure a balance between the centres of population. Excursions to adjacent counties became more frequent: to Durham in 1901, Teesdale and Richmond in 1905, Liddesdale and Dumfries in 1909. Bolder excursions were also tried in the Edwardian era, notably the special excursion to the Hebrides in 1904, when the Society chartered the S.S. Princess Beatrice (with state room accommodation for over 70 passengers) for a voyage from Oban to the principal archaeological sites on the Inner and Outer Isles. Participants numbered 74 for all or part of the voyage, many coming as part of a family group – it was clearly a social and sociable occasion.[41]

Unsurprisingly, the life of the Society was disturbed by the First World War. The meeting planned for Ambleside in September 1914, to view the Society's excavations at the Roman fort, did not take place and summer excursions were abandoned for the duration of the war. But the Spring meetings continued to be held, as did one-day meetings each autumn. Publication of *Transactions* for 1915-16 was delayed because of 'War difficulties' and the Pilgrimage to Hadrian's Wall, scheduled for 1916, was postponed. The Society's golden jubilee in the same year was a muted affair. The 'Jubilee Meeting of the Society' on 7 September 1916 was appended to a joint visit to the Wall with members of the British Association and took the form of a dinner in Carlisle followed by an illustrated 'lantern lecture' by the President, Francis Haverfield, on the history of the Roman Wall.

Under Collingwood's steady chairmanship, the business of the Society was sustained across the war years and the pre-war pattern of meetings was quickly revived in 1919. In 1925 another attempt was made to put the onerous task of organising meetings on a sustainable footing. Major R.E. Porter, land agent for the Rydal estate, was appointed 'Hon. Secretary for Excursions', a position he held for 20 years.[42] By 1934 he was assisted by George Aitchison, his colleague at the Rydal estate office, in a role variously described as 'Transport Officer' (1934), 'Traffic Director' (1935) and 'Route Marshall' (1937). By the 1930s one of the two meetings, usually that in September, was held out of Cumbria, normally in northern England or southern Scotland though the Isle of Man was revisited in 1931 (fig. 1.12), and, on the eve of the Second World War, the Society ventured further afield, to Wiltshire in 1939.

Fig. 1.12. Canon Quine addressing archaeologists, Isle of Man, July 1931. Drawn by Katherine Fell, the sister of Clare Fell (WDX/1408/2/3) *(image: Cumbria County Council, Kendal Archive Centre)*

Excavation and protection of ancient monuments

The Society's role in archaeological study became more formalised under Collingwood's leadership. A Research Fund was established in 1907, its first grant, of £15, being for work on native settlements near Crosby Ravensworth under Collingwood's direction. Further grants in 1909 for excavations at Stainton Stone Closes near Dalton-in-Furness and at Bannisdale Moor, Coniston, and in 1911 for work on the caves on Warton Crag and at Leck, both across the county boundary in Lancashire, reflect the shift in focus towards the south of the region and also brought to a head the question of the Society's boundaries in relation to its southern neighbour, the Lancashire and Cheshire Antiquarian Society (LCAS). The Society entered into negotiations with its sister society in an attempt to formalise a take-over of Lancashire North of the Sands and a working compromise was reached in 1911. LCAS was unwilling formally to accept 'any curtailment of the area defined by [its] title' but agreed that CWAAS might include Furness and Cartmel in its area of study and could control unauthorised excavations in the area – it was an annexation by the Cumberland and Westmorland in all but name. But by funding activities at Warton, near Carnforth, and Leck, the Society was also trespassing on to 'mainland' Lancashire. The situation was not resolved until over 20 years later when, in 1933, it was suggested that the Society's area of activity might be extended formally to include the Lune Valley. Further discussions took place with LCAS, who again were unwilling to relinquish territory but hoped for cooperation and (presumably recognising that they could not prevent antiquarian encroachments) recorded that they were willing to accept accounts of discoveries made by members of the Society on their side of the frontier.

The Society also sponsored systematic excavations on some of the major Roman sites in the years immediately before the First World War, presaging the larger campaigns of the 1930s. The driving force in the early years was the combined influence of Francis Haverfield, the pioneer of scientific study of Roman sites in Britain and the Society's President from 1915, and his pupil, Robin Collingwood, W.G. Collingwood's son. In 1912 Council granted £25 from the Research Fund for experimental excavations at Papcastle Roman fort under expert supervision, to be identified by Haverfield, who nominated Robin Collingwood. On the eve of war, a programme of excavations began at the fort at Ambleside, under the auspices of a committee set up by Council in 1913 (fig. 1.13). They continued under Robin Collingwood's direction until 1915 and were the destination for the Society's only excursion that year, a single day visit in September.

Fig. 1.13. Ambleside Roman fort: a view of the piers of East Gate, looking west, from the 1914 excavation *CW2*, 15 (1915), 11 *(image: Cumbria County Council, Kendal Library)*

The Society's role as guardian of historic and archaeological sites within its region became increasingly important as the statutory framework of ancient monuments protection developed in the years leading up to the First World War. The Royal Commissions on Historical Monuments began their work in 1908; the role of Inspector of Ancient Monuments, in abeyance since 1900, was revived in 1910; and the Ancient Monuments Consolidation and Amendment Act 1913 strengthened the systems of protection.[43] Increasingly, the Society's role was to keep a watching brief on Cumbria's tangible heritage, attempting to protect individual sites from damage, at a time when national protection of historic monuments was in its infancy. It minuted concerns and, where possible, acted on threats and damage to monuments, both major and minor. In 1910 Lord Lonsdale's 'vandalism' at Shap Abbey in carting off large quantities of 'interesting abbey stones' to Lowther Castle seems to have caused the Society some embarrassment, as two prominent members of the Lowther family were Vice-Presidents; the following year when the farmer at Hartley Castle was pulling down the medieval fabric, Council asked Dr Haswell to interview the estate's agent; in 1920 it was reported that building work at Wharton Hall, undertaken 'without responsible supervision', had resulted in the destruction of part of the historic remains. Cracks in the Bewcastle cross and damage to the base of the cross by boys were noted in 1921 and solutions proposed (Council rejected Revd F.L.H. Millard's suggestion of filling the cracks and placing a light railing around the base, recommending instead that 'the cross be covered with preservative solution'). Threats to lesser antiquities were also recorded and pursued, such as the re-setting and protection of the Greystoke sanctuary stone in 1909, and the removal of an heraldic stone on a bridge at St Bees to St Bees School for safekeeping in 1910. When it was proposed to use the Langbar stone on White Lyne Common at Bewcastle as a war memorial in 1921, Council noted that, as it was regarded as an antiquity, 'it is considered inadvisable to remove it'. Prompted by a general concern to preserve ancient monuments, the Society published a leaflet in 1916, 'to send where occasion required', pointing out the dangers of allowing trees and ivy to grow on 'ancient walls'.

The large-scale road improvements which accompanied the increasing volume of motor traffic in these decades also threatened historic sites. In 1908 Council expressed its concern over plans to widen the Nether Bridge at Kendal and were reassured to learn that the north parapet would be rebuilt to the same design as before 'so as to preserve as far as possible its present picturesque appearance'. The same road improvements also yielded an object of antiquarian interest, which was exhibited to members in July 1908; the stump of Kendal's ancient maypole, discovered 'standing erect in the centre of Kirkland opposite to the Parish church gates' when the road was dug up. When it was proposed in 1912 to build a motor road from Ambleside to

Ravenglass over Wrynose and Hardknott, the Society was concerned that no damage should be done to Hardknott Roman fort. The Rey Cross (or Rere Cross), the ancient boundary marker on Stainmore, was repeatedly in danger of damage, lying beside a bleak and increasingly busy trunk road. Railings, which had been placed around the cross by the Society in partnership with Yorkshire Archaeological Society, were in need of repainting by 1908 and in 1928 the Society agreed to bear the cost of a notice to be attached, drawing attention to its historical importance.

The Society's contribution to the national protection of ancient monuments expanded after 1911 when it was asked by H.M. Office of Works to provide a 'list of Monuments within our sphere of action which by the co-operation of their owners, might be handed over to the custody of the Office'. At the same time the county councils were asked to draw up lists of monuments for scheduling and Council appointed a sub-committee, consisting of Collingwood, Haverfield and Curwen, who rapidly drew up a list of monuments for protection in Cumberland and Westmorland. In 1921, H.M. Inspector of Ancient Monuments invited the Society to nominate correspondents to act as his eyes and ears, keeping scheduled monuments under 'effective supervision'. Curwen was appointed chief correspondent for Westmorland and Lancashire North of the Sands, while his fellow architect, James Henry Martindale (1855-1931) of Wetheral, the diocesan surveyor, was named to act in the same capacity for Cumberland. This established a formal link with the inspectorate which continued, with some permutations, until the 1980s.

The Society thus took its role in the protection of ancient monuments very seriously in the 1920s and 1930s. Some of its suggestions might cause modern conservators to blanch, particularly the idea that the Bewcastle and Gosforth crosses should be covered with 'preservative liquid', but in one instance it exhibited forward thinking, far ahead of its time. This was in response to proposed quarrying close to Hadrian's Wall in 1930. H.S. Cowper and Robin Collingwood drafted a resolution expressing the Society's concern, which asked central government to act to prevent the quarrying on the grounds that 'this unique site ... depends for its educational and historical value not on the Wall alone, but on the whole complex of works in their topographical setting'.[44] In adopting the resolution, the Society was anticipating by 40 years the concept of an archaeological landscape and the need to view and protect it in its entirety.

The Documentary Record

Preserving and publishing the region's documentary heritage also went forward, though not in such an ordered manner. Record publishing continued,

Collingwood, like Ferguson before him, editing several manuscripts. As the list of the Society's publications shows (see Chapter 2 and Appendix 2), the first three decades of the twentieth century saw a steady accumulation of volumes, if not the flood that had occurred in the 1890s, the titles split with little obvious rationale between three series (the Extra, Tract and Record Series). Under the prompting of the scholarly clerical patriarch, Chancellor J.E. Prescott, a Record Publication Fund was established in 1912, Collingwood playfully urging members to contribute annually 'the other half guinea they owed to the Society in return for a volume of Transactions worth a guinea'. Within a year, the fund had a balance of over £54. Its purpose, spelt out in 1916, was to fund the publication of 'ancient records, such as Episcopal Registers etc., hitherto unpublished, but not suitable for inclusion in the Transactions'.[45] Some volumes were subsidised (in September 1922, for example, William Farrer offered to put up half the costs of printing the *Records of Kendale* volumes) or were joint ventures with other publishers, such as the collaborations in 1915 with the Surtees Society over James Wilson's edition of the St Bees cartulary and with Manchester University Press over Sedgefield's *Place-Names of Cumberland and Westmorland*.

Transcribing and printing parish registers formed a distinct area of record publishing. After withdrawing from the genealogical publisher Phillimore's scheme to transcribe marriages from parish registers, the Society set up its own Parish Register Section in 1911 to transcribe and publish registers in their entirety. The Section retained a semi-autonomous status, reporting its progress to Council but maintaining its own accounts. Between 1912 and 1939 it published 27 volumes, an average of one per year, and it remained active into the 1950s. The leading light in the 1920s and 1930s, who also played a very active role in the Society's wider affairs, was Col. John Francis Haswell (1864-1949), a Penrith doctor, for many years the town's Medical Officer of Health as well as a soldier who commanded the 2/4th Border Regiment in India during the First World War. Over a 20-year period from 1925 he prepared editions of no fewer than 19 registers for publication in the series.

One project which wove in and out of the Society's consciousness was the abortive attempt to complete Victoria County Histories (VCH) for Cumberland and Westmorland. Only two general volumes for Cumberland were published (in 1901 and 1905), edited by James Wilson, the scholarly vicar of Dalston.[46] As the project failed after the First World War, the Society attempted to save such work as had been completed. Although no editor had been appointed for Westmorland, it is likely that William Farrer's two volumes of *Records Relating to the Barony of Kendale* (published in the Record Series in 1923-4) and F.W. Ragg's deeply researched studies of manorial history in north Westmorland, which appeared as substantial papers in *Transactions* between 1911 and 1928, represent materials that had been gathered in anticipation of the VCH for Westmorland. In Cumberland, James Wilson had completed the two volumes of parish histories intended to form volumes III and IV of the history. At his death a protracted dispute with the publishers of the VCH had left these unpublished and in limbo. In 1923 William Page, the general editor of the VCH, invited the Society to take 150 copies of Cumberland Volume III 'if proceeded with, no guarantee given'. In the event nothing happened and, in 1932, Council agreed to approach Wilson's widow asking whether she would be willing to sell what was described as 'the MS of Volume 3'. Mrs Scott-Nicholson of Carlisle had offered £100 towards printing the volume and she was to be asked whether the sum might be used to purchase the manuscript instead. In the event, no progress could be made, either with Mrs Wilson or through William Page, the publisher of the VCH, and the matter was dropped in 1934. It appears that Wilson's parish histories were consigned to the fire.[47]

By the early decades of the twentieth century, the scale and range of the Society's activities were generating a considerable body of material: archaeological finds, plans and other excavation records, maps and an accumulating library, not least of other societies' journals received in exchange for *Transactions*. Tullie House Library and Museum in Carlisle became the repository for the Society's library and other collections, probably as a natural outcome of the close involvement of Chancellor Ferguson in both bodies. How formal the initial arrangements were is unclear but the Society's 'Exchange Library' was in the care of Tullie House by 1902 and by 1912 there are references to the Society's 'chest' or 'cabinet' there, housing maps and plans.[48] Members of the Society had access to the cabinet on application to the museum curator but could not remove material without explicit written permission from the President or chairman of Council. In 1924 the Society's rules were amended to add the posts of Librarian and Curator to the Society's officers, positions which were held *ex officio* by the librarian and the curator at Tullie House. In the absence of a base of its own, the Society took advantage of the opportunity to use Tullie House as its repository, with the result that the holdings of the Museum and Library included much material belonging to the Society. At this stage the arrangement seems not to have caused problems, though the potential for difficulty seems to have been recognised by 1929 when, on the resignation of the curator, the President was asked to write to Tullie House 'as to the future care of the Society's property' there.

Robin Collingwood: Archaeology in the Ascendancy

On W.G. Collingwood's resignation in 1932, his son Robin George Collingwood (1889-1943), the Oxford-based philosopher and Roman historian, was elected President. He was almost bred into the Society: it was said that he 'received his archaeological baptism, carried slung in a shawl on his father's back up the mountainside, to do his first digging in a Roman fort [at Hardknott] at the age of three'.[49] An intense, cerebral man, described by two of his biographers as 'always a rather removed figure, visibly absorbed in his own speculation and scholarship',[50] he seems never to have been held in the same affection by the Society as his father.

In the 1930s, under Robin Collingwood's leadership, the Society's work became increasingly closely focused. Although there was a minor wave of record publication in the mid-1930s and the Parish Register Section maintained a regular flow of transcripts, the focus of activity fell squarely under the heading of archaeology and particularly Robin Collingwood's own specialism, Roman archaeology. From 1929 the Society gave financial support to a programme of excavation on Hadrian's Wall, led by Collingwood's friend, F. Gerald Simpson, director of archaeological research at the University of Durham. The Cumberland Excavation Committee was revived in 1931, its remit continuing to be the study of the Cumberland section of Hadrian's Wall. With Robin Collingwood as Vice-Chairman and Simpson as Director, it was chaired by Mrs Hesketh Hodgson, the first woman to take a leading role in the Society's affairs. Elizabeth Hodgson (née Cookson) (1854-1935) was from an academic family, the daughter of a Cumbrian master of Peterhouse, Cambridge. She and her husband, Thomas Hesketh Hodgson (the Society's President from 1909 to 1915), a civil servant who had inherited the Newby Grange estate near Carlisle, had been members of the Cumberland Excavation Committee almost from its inception in 1894. She was a gifted watercolourist with a talent for close observation, skills which she turned to account in producing the 'most delicate and accurate' archaeological sections and scale drawings, as well as publishing articles on Hadrian's Wall in her own right from the 1890s.[51]

As President, Robin Collingwood was able to steer a significant share of the Society's funds towards this work. By the later 1920s the Society had accumulated sufficient capital to invest money in bonds. When, in 1932, Curwen had succeeded in persuading the income tax authorities that the Society was a charitable body, the Revenue had asked that the Society's balances should be reduced. In consequence, the climate was favourable for Collingwood's desire to fund the excavations. A grant of £100 was made in 1933 with the promise of a further £100 the following year, and further grants (as well as clearing overspends) were made annually up to 1938. In the first few years, the Society's reserves fell sharply until other sources of funding were secured. In 1932, the total balance in all the Society's accounts stood at £768; it had fallen to £626 by 1934, £556 in 1935 and £420 in 1936 but had recovered to £616 in 1937.

Meanwhile, a second arm of the Society had been established to pursue the archaeology of an earlier period. The Committee for Prehistoric Studies was founded in 1932, prompted by a proposal laid before Council earlier that year by Paul V. Kelly and Mary Fair, urging a co-ordinated programme of 'scientific excavation' of prehistoric sites in West Cumberland and Low Furness. The new committee's remit covered the whole of Cumbria and its initial membership, which included Kelly and Fair, covered a wide constituency, including the professional Romanists, Collingwood, Simpson and the young Eric Birley. The committee set to work recording prehistoric sites, aided by a complete set of Six Inch maps of Cumbria received from the Ordnance Survey in 1933. Its first excavation was at King Arthur's Round Table in 1937.

The increasingly archaeological focus led the Society to turn down several initiatives which could have broadened its activities. Two approaches related to the Depression and the soaring levels of unemployment in West Cumberland. In 1934 the Universities Council for Unemployed Camps, which arranged for student volunteers to work with unemployed men on manual work projects, made an approach but Council brushed it aside on the grounds that 'the scheme could not be operated in a satisfactory manner in the Society's area'. The following year Mary Fair asked whether some of the West Cumberland unemployed might be employed by the Society, a suggestion again kicked into touch on the grounds that it would have to wait until the Hadrian's Wall excavations had been completed, 'when experts who could instruct workers would be at liberty to do so'.

More telling, perhaps, in terms of its approach to the study of the past, was the response to an invitation in 1935 from the Royal Historical Society (RHS) to exchange publications. This was refused on the grounds that RHS publications were already received by Tullie House – ignoring the opportunity for the Society's publications to be made available to members of the leading academic historical society in the country. It is striking that, at the same meeting, Council suggested an exchange of publications with the Prehistoric Society. Four years later, another request for a complete set of *Transactions* from one of the foremost historical libraries, that at the Institute of Historical Research at the University of London, was also refused. Led by prominent archaeologists, the Society threw its weight behind the developing discipline of archaeology and was drifting away from academic history, at that date largely closed away in ivory towers.

Robin Collingwood's resignation as President on doctor's orders in 1938 marked the end of an era. He and his father were figures of international standing, who had nevertheless kept a firm hand at the helm of the Society in Cumbria; they would be a hard act to follow. That task fell to Walter Travers McIntire (1870-1944), a former schoolmaster and director of technical education and principal of Tullie House, who played an increasingly active role in the Society after he retired to Milnthorpe in 1924. He was a member of the triumvirate appointed to succeed W.G. Collingwood as Editor of *Transactions* in 1925 – indeed, in the original draft of the Council resolution, McIntire was named 'Editor in Chief' with Robin Collingwood as 'Roman Editor' and T.H.B. Graham as 'Medieval Editor'. In 1932 he took over the role of Hon. Secretary for Antiquarian Correspondence and, when Graham and Collingwood stepped down in 1934, became sole Editor. As President, he also chaired meetings of Council, thus combining the three leading roles in the Society in one person.

The outbreak of war in September 1939 had an immediate impact on the Society's activities. Its planned meeting that month in Carlisle was cancelled; the programme of excursions was effectively suspended. Only a handful of one-day meetings were held across the war years: at Carlisle in September 1940 and in Kendal in August 1941, February 1943 and March 1945. From 1940 *Transactions* was reduced in size and bound only in paper; the work of the Committee for Prehistoric Studies and the Cumberland Excavation Committee ground to a halt. The effects of the war were pervasive: the Society's stock at the printers had to be insured against war damage; Guildhall Library in London sought and obtained replacements for copies of *Transactions* which had been destroyed by enemy action; members of the Society who were prisoners of war were to be excused payment of subscriptions. McIntire's death in post in 1944 meant that that year's *Transactions* was delayed. Weakened by the disruption of the war, the Society's membership had fallen from around 550 in the mid-1930s to 387 by 1945.

The making of the Modern Society (1945 to 2015)

Many aspects of the modern Society had their origins in the years immediately after the Second World War. The wider context of archaeological and 'antiquarian' study was changing. Archaeology expanded as a university discipline, a notable development for Cumbria being the establishment of the Department of Archaeology at the University of Durham in 1956. Meanwhile, the modern sub-discipline of local history was nurtured by the creation of the Department of English Local History at the University of Leicester in 1948 and the burgeoning of local history research classes in the hey-day of university extra-mural activity in the 1960s. In parallel with the expansion of academic study, the number of professionals involved in the study of the past was increasing: what were effectively the new professions of archaeologist and archivist came into existence, as posts proliferated, both in national bodies and in local government (record office archivists, conservation officers, county archaeologists), especially as society at large awoke to the threat to all aspects of heritage from the pace of development. Increasing professionalisation provided an expanding pool of talent on which societies such as the Cumberland and Westmorland could draw but also had the potential effect of relegating voluntary societies to the role of second-class citizens – amateurs in a world where serious study and practical action lay in the hands of professionals.

Post-war revival

The Second World War had left the Society weakened: membership had dropped, archaeological investigation had more or less come to a standstill, and there had been a five-year break in the rhythm of meetings and excursions. But it bounced back quickly: 52 new members were elected when regular meetings resumed in March 1945 and the pre-war pattern of excursions had been revived by the following year. The post-war decade saw two developments which transformed the character of the Society – the establishment of fixed-term presidencies and the setting up of 'regional groups'.

The first major innovation was the move to fixed-term presidencies. Walter McIntire was the last President to serve for more than three years and the last to die in post. All his predecessors had, in practice, been Presidents for life, even though they were technically re-elected annually. Where they had been forced to resign because of ill health (as had been the case with Robin Collingwood, who lived a further five years after stepping down as President), a life tenure had, in effect, been ended prematurely. When Oliver North was nominated for election as President in 1945, J.E. Spence proposed that future Presidents should serve for a limited period of no more than two years. Accordingly, North served a two-year term and was followed by Gerald Simpson, who, however, had to resign after one year because of ill health. When his successor, Kate Hodgson, had completed two years, in 1950, Eric Birley proposed that her first year in office 'should be treated as Mr Simpson's second year' and that she was eligible to serve for a third year. Through his somewhat imaginative interpretation of the rules, the modern three-year term of office was born – Presidents Hodgson (1948-51) and Spence (1951-54) each served for three years but it was not until 1956 that Rule 6 of the Society's constitution was amended to formalise three-year terms. Meanwhile, the office of Chairman of Council, in abeyance since 1920, was revived in 1947, effectively creating a shared leadership, a pairing of responsibility which lasted until 1966. In 1947 past Presidents became life members of Council, enabling the Society to retain their wisdom and expertise. These changes appear to have been instituted to revive and strengthen the Society as it emerged after the difficult war years.

The first post-war Chairman of Council was Eric Birley, who played a pivotal role in the Society's renewal. Eric Barff Birley (1906-1995) was a Romanist whose interest in Hadrian's Wall had been kindled by Robin Collingwood when he was a student at Oxford. He had held a lectureship at Durham University since 1931, becoming the Professor of Romano-British History in 1956.[52] Active in the Society since coming to Durham, he became a key figure on Council, as Chairman of Council from 1947 and Editor of *Transactions* from the following year.

His first concern was to reactivate interest in the Society's work at grassroots level. Establishing a regular programme of winter lectures, the staple fare of many archaeological and historical societies, posed a considerable challenge to a Cumbria-wide society. The 'Lake Counties' form a large region, its centres of population dispersed and fragmented and travel between towns made onerous by Cumbria's mountainous core. In September 1947 Birley raised the question of 'regional activities' and suggested setting up local groups. After soundings were taken, Council appointed two secretaries the following year to take the idea forward: Roy Hudleston for Penrith and Walter Taylor for Carlisle. The inaugural meeting of what became the Carlisle Regional Group was held in September 1949. After a delayed start, the Penrith Group met in September 1951 and the Kendal Group had formed a committee by April 1952. During the process of establishing the initial groups, other towns were also considered as possible centres, including Kirkby Stephen, Workington and Keswick, and soundings were taken to assess the possibility of setting up a group in Furness. Nothing came of these proposals, nor of a later attempt to establish a regional group in Furness in 1985. The formation of the South-West Regional Group in 1957 completed the four-fold structure of affiliated societies which continues today.[53]

The groups rapidly became well established. Carlisle had 76 members within a year of coming into being and had sought a grant from the Society for excavation work at Burgh-by-Sands; some members of the group had acted as volunteers on Kate Hodgson's excavations at Broomrigg in Ainstable. Two years later, in 1952, its membership stood at 160 and the average attendance at winter lectures was in the range 40-50. By 1953 it could claim to be 'firmly established as one of the most active societies in the city' and by the following year its membership had exceeded 200. The trajectories of the other groups were similarly impressive: by 1954 membership of the Penrith Group had reached 94 members and the Group had organised summer outings as well as a winter lecture series, while the younger Kendal Group had risen to 80 members. From the outset, the South-West Group was determined to be an active archaeological body, 'getting out and about as much as possible' during the summer months and only meeting for lectures during the winter. In 1958, when attempts were afoot to update the inventory of ancient monuments in Cumberland, the committee working on this envisaged active help from the

Carlisle, Penrith and South-West groups.

In parallel with the Regional Groups came an attempt to reach out to young people and involve them in the Society's work. Indeed, it was claimed retrospectively that one of the objects of setting up regional groups had been to encourage younger people to engage with the Society. In 1946 Council suggested that local secondary schools might become institutional members of the Society 'with a view to assisting the study of Local History in such schools'. Two years later the effort to engage with schools continued, it being suggested that older pupils could be invited to join excursions and that schools could be supplied with back numbers of *Transactions*. A few schools joined (Brampton Grammar School, Queen Elizabeth Grammar School, Penrith, and Heversham Grammar School in 1948-49) and Birley undertook to arrange for sets of *Transactions* to be given to them. A decade later, the Society introduced the category of Associate Membership for young people under the age of 21 or still *in statu pupillarii* at a university. For a subscription of one guinea, they gained all rights of membership bar the right to vote.

By the early 1950s the regular agenda items at Society's Council meetings included reports from standing committees, under four headings: the three long-established sub-committees (the Cumberland Excavation Committee, the Parish Register Section and the Committee for Prehistoric Studies) and the regional groups. The Cumberland Excavation Committee initially continued to draw heavily on the Society's funds, Council agreeing in 1946 to cover costs of £112 in connection with renewed work on Hadrian's Wall, but from 1948 much of the cost was borne by Durham University.

The Committee for Prehistoric Studies was revived in 1948, under the driving force of two much-loved female leaders of the Society, Kate Hodgson for northern Cumbria and Clare Fell for the southern districts. Both women were almost born into the Society: their parents were leading members, drawn from the leisured classes who dominated the Cumberland and Westmorland in the pre-war years. Katherine Sophia (Kate) Hodgson (1889-1974) was the daughter of Thomas Hesketh Hodgson (President 1909-15) and Elizabeth Hodgson, the Society's pioneering female archaeologist and the first woman to serve on Council. Kate Hodgson studied archaeology in London and carried out numerous excavations on Roman and prehistoric sites across northern Cumberland from the 1930s when she returned to the family home. Clare Isobel Fell (1912-2002) was the daughter of Sir Mathew Fell (Vice-President from 1931), an army medic from a military family from Ulverston. She studied archaeology at Cambridge and worked as an assistant curator in the Museum of Archaeology and Anthropology there from 1947. A well-known prehistorian and a lucid lecturer, she devoted much energy to her beloved Society after returning to Cumbria in 1953. Through her background, she was uniquely placed to draw in both amateurs and professionals, being a professional archaeologist but with strong family and social links in Cumbria.[54]

Across the late 1950s grants continued to be given for other archaeological investigations on a regular basis. In 1958 the Society joined forces with the Dumfries & Galloway Archaeological & Natural History Society to survey and excavate Iron Age and Dark Age sites in the Solway area. A formal agreement was signed with a duration of five years. The Society supported Richard Bellhouse's excavations on Roman sites along the Solway coast, Kate Hodgson's work at Bewcastle and on the stone circles at Broomriggs in Ainstable, excavations at Maryport and at Barnscar and on Romano-British farmsteads. In 1961 Council approved expenditure of £25 to buy a second-hand bus for use on excavations.

Not all initiatives were successful. In 1947 an attempt was made to revive the Society's record publishing activities on a more systematic basis by establishing a 'Records and Publications' committee, modelled on the Parish Register Section. A separate annual subscription of 15s. was to be taken, with a view to publishing one volume each year. £80 had been raised in subscriptions by the following year but this was considered too little to embark on regular publications and the committee seems also to have suffered from weak leadership. Progress had stalled by 1950 but two short publications, a handlist of local newspapers and a study of railway history in Furness, appeared in the Tract Series. A later attempt to form a Committee for Medieval Studies in 1958 also appears to have foundered.

The Society took its role as custodian of knowledge about the region's past seriously and attempted to enforce high standards, even in publications outwith its control. In the early 1950s Council huffed and puffed about errors in local guidebooks. In 1951 it asked the President to make an informal approach to the clerk of Westmorland County Council, urging the county to disown the *Westmorland County Official Guide*; the following year it was exercised by the Coniston guide and suggested that future editions should be vetted by a responsible member of Council, and in 1953 it was worried about numerous inaccuracies in the guide to Millom.

The Society re-defined

The Society's Centenary in 1966 coincided with a period of accelerating change, both in the study of the past and in the character of the Society itself. It is striking that the centrepiece of the Centenary celebrations was an excavation at the Roman fort at Maryport – a fitting culmination to the recent decades during which investigations of Cumbria's Roman archaeology had predominated. The Maryport excavation was to be led by Sir Ian Richmond, professor of archaeology at Oxford and formerly at

Newcastle upon Tyne, who would also succeed Clare Fell as President for the Centenary Year, ensuring that the celebrations would be championed by one of the leading archaeologists of the day. But Richmond's unexpected death in October 1965 threw the plans into disarray. A special meeting of Council decided that Michael Jarrett of Cardiff University, a student of Birley's and at that time a comparatively junior archaeologist, should be asked to lead the excavation, while the Presidency should be offered to Roger Fulford, royal biographer, historian of the Suffragette movement and a president of the Liberal Party, presumably in a bid to ensure that the Society had a socially prominent, public figurehead for its Centenary year (figs. 1.14 and 1.15).[55]

Fig. 1.14. Cover of the centenary programme publication *(image: Cumbria County Council, Carlisle Archive Centre)*

Fig. 1.15. A view of part of the 1966 excavation at Maryport Roman fort. The east wall and an external drain are visible

By the time of its Centenary the Society had regained its vibrancy. Membership had expanded rapidly from the nadir of 387 at the end of the war, recovering quickly to overtop its pre-war levels by the early 1950s, when it stood at around 625. By 1965 the total membership was 685, made up of 612 individuals and 73 libraries. A surge of new members, joining in the years around the Centenary, lifted the total to 796 by 1967. The long list of new members who joined during the centenary year contains 54 names, and suggests that the Society's demographic was changing.[56] It was rapidly moving away from being the socially-select body of the pre-war years, though it remained predominantly drawn from the middle classes, and drew on the increasing numbers of well-educated people retiring to Cumbria. The rise in membership continued, to stand at around 830 by the late 1970s, a level sustained throughout the following decade.

Until 1983 each application for membership had to be signed by a proposer and seconder, a process which became increasingly notional but which nevertheless required new members to have some contact with the Society before joining. Guests were admitted to excursions, which contributed to the success in extending the Society's reach. A key player in encouraging new members was Clare Fell, who rarely missed excursions and other meetings of the Society, where she was a warm and welcoming presence who regularly acted as proposer in support of applications for membership. A stately figure with a twinkle in her eye, she was held in great affection – when she celebrated 50 years of membership in 1987, the Society honoured her with a summer evening dinner party on a launch cruising down Windermere.

As the character of the membership changed, so did the Society's leadership. The increasingly complex array of players involved in Cumbria's past and the growing professionalisation of archaeology and history provided an expanding pool of expertise to be tapped. From the 1950s, Presidents increasingly tended to be drawn from the ranks of professionals and academics. Of the 23 Presidents since 1948, 16 fell squarely into those categories: Presidents Birley, Hudleston, Dickinson, Cramp, Brunskill, Martin, Winchester and Shotter held university posts; Presidents Fell, Charlton, Charlesworth, Hughes, Harbottle, Richard Newman, Breeze and Rachel Newman were archaeological or historic buildings professionals. Most of the 'amateurs' were highly talented scholars who made noteworthy contributions to the study of Cumbria's past: Kate Hodgson the energetic excavator; C.M.L. Bouch the clergyman who pioneered the study of the social and economic history of the county; Jim Cherry the engineer whose archaeological fieldwork opened new horizons on Cumbrian prehistory; and John Todd the lawyer who was a deeply scholarly medievalist. Triennial presidencies have ensured that the Society benefitted from regular injections of new thinking from leading lights in Cumbrian history and archaeology.

As Presidents came and went across the second half of the twentieth century, continuity was provided by the Society's other key officers. Four long-serving Hon. General Secretaries covered between them the bulk of three-quarters of a century, from 1927 to 2002: Gertrude Ainsley served over 30 years, while Herbert Clegg, Joyce Cherry and Richard Hall each held office for a decade or more. Their length of service enabled them to act as keepers of the Society's corporate memory as Presidents' and councillors' terms of office expired. Council cautiously provided the secretaries with some assistance in what was becoming a more demanding role involving increasing correspondence. When Herbert Clegg took on the role in 1959, the Society bought him a second-hand typewriter (as well as paying for some repairs to Miss Ainsley's old one) and in 1962 agreed to install a telephone in his home and to pay the rental costs. Procedures were slowly modernised: abstracts of minutes were circulated to Council members along with the meeting notices from 1954; officers could be repaid out-of-pocket expenses from 1956; an agenda, list of nominations, accounts and a brief report were circulated to members in advance of the AGM from 1961.

Treasurers were almost as long lived: R.E. Porter's 26-year service coincided with Miss Ainsley's time as Secretary, providing a long period of stability either side of the Second World War, and his successor, R.G. Plint, also served for 26 years. The role of treasurer was crucial in enabling the Society to develop the twin activities through which it makes major contributions to modern study of Cumbria's past: publishing and providing financial support through grants to specific projects. Clifford Mayho and Keith Horsfield, the two treasurers who managed the Society's finances for almost three decades from 1984 to 2013, were careful, prudent custodians of its resources. Across their terms of office the Society's reserves grew, enabling it to expand its activities, particularly in the fields of publishing and grant-giving.

Throughout the later twentieth century, meetings and excursions continued to lie at the heart of the Society's activities; indeed, the social aspects of the Society in the 1960s and 1970s increasingly formed the glue binding its members together. The established pattern of excursions was revived in 1946 with meetings around the region and, in many years, a residential visit further afield, particularly after 1958, when Council agreed that there should be one 'home' excursion and one outside Cumbria each year. Attendance boomed: in 1971, 134 people attended the excursion to Hexham and 170 were expected at the second meeting of the season, to be held in the Kendal area.

Under the energetic leadership of two Excursions Secretaries in particular, Joseph ('Fred') Hughes (1962-71) and Margery ('Mally') Mallabar (1974-81), the social aspects of the Society's life developed in new directions. In 1964 Hughes proposed arranging an outing the following May 'to sites of

Fig. 1.16. Several generations attending a May Fell Walk in 1983 *(photograph by courtesy of Angus Winchester)*

Fig. 1.17. The May Fell Walk in 1984 at the summit of Carrock Fell *(photograph by courtesy of Angus Winchester)*

prehistoric interest which were off the beaten track and would involve a certain amount of walking'. The first of what became annual May Fell Walks was held at Moor Divock on Askham Fell in May 1965, attracting over 70 participants and being deemed a great success. By the 1970s the walks, by then led by Clare Fell, had evolved to include sites from a variety of periods. They were refreshingly informal gatherings, involving plenty of fresh air and exercise in Cumbria's ample open spaces, and became inter-generational occasions, attracting large numbers of younger members and their families and friends (figs. 1.16 and 1.17). At the other end of the spectrum of formality, Hughes proposed in 1969 that an annual dinner should be held each December. The dinner at the Langdale Chase Hotel in 1970 initiated an additional fixture in the Society's calendar, which continued until 2008. Informality won out, however, as witnessed by the enduring popularity of the annual 'Summer Evening' at a country house, often one not normally open to the public, instituted in 1987.

Towards the end of the century, publication became an increasingly important aspect of the Society's work. After some delays in the immediate post-war years, *Transactions* continued to appear annually with only occasional slippage. Joint editorships from 1975 to 2006 – where a Kendal-based 'practical' editor, who could work closely with the printer, Titus Wilson's, on a day-to-day basis, was paired with a co-editor who undertook more of the liaison with authors – worked well. The arrangement again provided a valuable measure of continuity, allowing the editors to build up – and the Society to benefit from – a formidable body of expertise in publishing in a period of rapid technological change.[57] That expertise, combined with growing financial resources, enabled the Society to expand its publishing activity from the late 1980s, as described in Chapter 2. The steady flow of titles in five separate series has made the Society the pre-eminent publisher of serious work in Cumbrian archaeology and history, its output embracing excavation reports, scholarly editions of records, book-length studies and shorter (but still substantial) essays in the Tract Series (see Appendix 2). To celebrate its 150th anniversary, the Society embarked on its first major excursion into electronic publishing by digitising the full run of *Transactions* since its outset to make them available online.

Across the twentieth century, the Society financed fieldwork and excavation carried out by individuals and groups. When, from 1974, all areas of archaeological investigation were drawn together into the Fieldwork and Excavation Committee, an increasingly important part of the new committee's role was to consider applications for grant aid. Its successor, the Research Committee (now the Research and Grants Committee), was created in 1987, with a remit to represent both archaeological and historical interests. In general, grants have been of comparatively modest sums to enable specific objectives to be achieved. The Society has regularly funded radiocarbon dating, dendrochronology and other specialist archaeological services, building surveys and publications. It has enabled the Cumbria Industrial History Society to digitise approximately 15,000 images of industrial sites photographed by Michael Davies-Shiel between the 1960s and his death in 2009. Larger grants have also been made, notably a significant commitment to the Cumbria County History Trust from 2010 to enable work to be started on a new Victoria County History of Cumbria.

Reaching out

The Society's public face has changed to reflect the modern world. The revolution in communications and the increasing informality of the Society and its desire to extend its reach, particularly among the younger generation, became a theme from the 1980s. In February 1983 a special meeting of Council was held to consider proposals from a small group appointed to investigate ways of raising the Society's profile and thereby attracting more members. Structures were put in place: a Promotional Sub-Committee was set up and it was agreed that a Press Secretary should be appointed (though there was some delay in finding a suitable person to take this on). Vestiges of social exclusivity were removed: Friday excursions were to be replaced by Sunday visits, to enable as wide attendance as possible, and the membership rules were changed to remove the requirement that applicants had to be nominated by two existing members. It could be said that the transition from cosy club to modern voluntary society had thus been made complete.

A further innovation of lasting significance agreed at the meeting was the production of a twice-yearly newsletter. The idea had been mooted in 1976 by Lord Wilson during his presidency but had not been acted upon. When the first issue of *C. & W. Newsletter* appeared in the autumn of 1983, under the editorship of Angus Winchester, its objective was to be 'an informal digest of archaeological and historical news in Cumbria to help keep our large and scattered membership abreast of both current research and local events in our field of interest'.[58] Initially consisting of a few cyclostyled pages of typing, devoid of pictures, the *Newsletter* was launched amid some suspicion from members of Council, who feared that it might detract from *Transactions*. Expending resources to fund an ephemeral newssheet was also an issue: when, in 1989, the then editor proposed a change in format to increase the attractiveness of the *Newsletter*, this was rejected by Council and, the following year, Council deemed the *Newsletter* to have become too expensive and decided that in future each issue should be limited to five double-sided sheets. However, it rapidly came to be seen as a valued medium, acting as an important part of the glue which held the Society together. It developed, particularly under the vigorous editorship of Margaret Edwards between 1998 and 2009, to become the richly-illustrated colour booklet now circulated three times each year. An important publication in its own right, the *Newsletter* draws together information on all aspects of work on Cumbria's past. It acts as a vehicle to disseminate announcements not only from the different facets of the Society's work but also from a wide range of cognate organisations and other regional societies and regularly carries news of recent finds reported to the Portable Antiquities Scheme, reports on projects undertaken by other bodies and brief reviews of recent publications.[59]

Reaching the wider world continued to preoccupy Council as well. A succession of sub-committees was appointed to attract new members.[60] A school prize scheme was established in 1985, to encourage archaeological or local history projects in secondary schools, and a bursary scheme in memory of Clare Fell in 2003, to nurture nascent interests in archaeology among school and university students. The electronic revolution saw the Society establish a web presence by setting up a website and registering an email address in 1999 (fig. 1.18). One facet of the website's potential which was quickly realised was to create an online index to *Transactions*. Modernisation

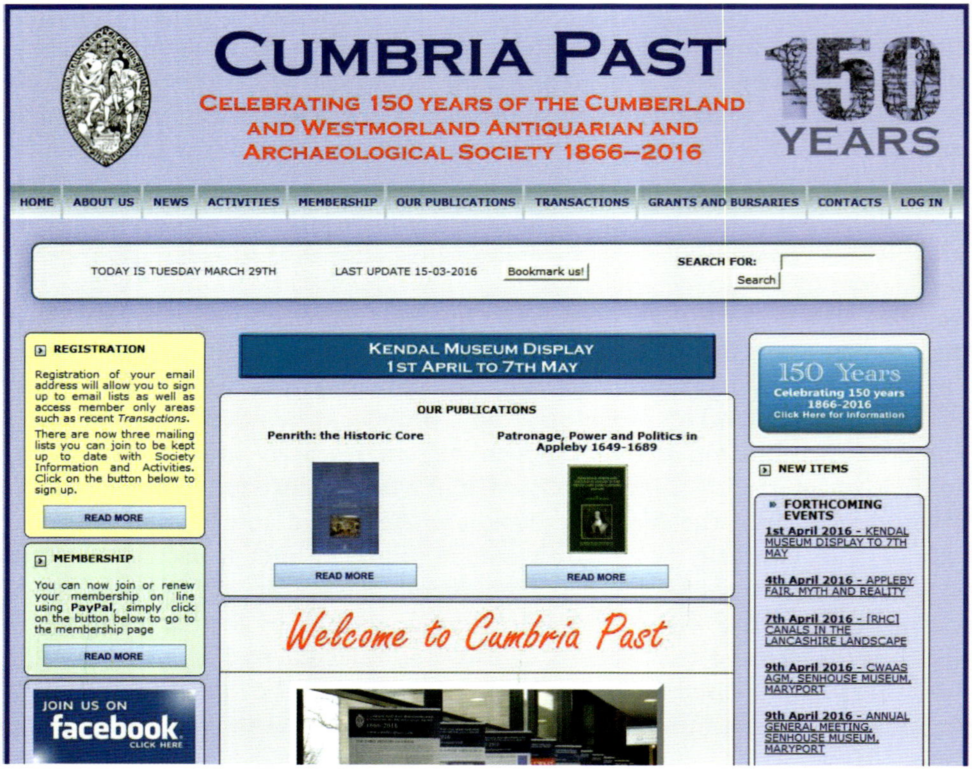

Fig. 1.18. The home page from the website

reached even to the Society's somewhat cumbersome name, which sounded increasingly outdated in a world dominated by sound bites. A change of name had been discussed on several occasions since the 1980s but the Society has been unwilling to part with its venerable label; instead, since 2008, the pithier brand name 'Cumbria Past' has been used alongside the full title for outreach purposes.

One aspect of the Society's relationship with other bodies remained unresolved across several decades. From the beginning, the relationship between the Regional Groups and the parent body had been somewhat uneasy. There was a concern that a majority of members of the committees running the groups should be members of the parent body. It soon became clear that the majority of members of the groups saw them as independent of the Society. By 1954 concern was expressed that the rapid recruitment of members to the groups was not resulting in new members joining the parent body and a sub-committee was set up to consider the relationship between the groups and the parent society. This was the start of a long process of periodic worrying. In one area of common concern between parent body and its increasingly independent offspring -the desire to protect the region's heritage- matters came to a head in 1969. The Kendal Regional Group had protested publicly about the proposed demolition of the classical portico of the gas works meter house in Kendal, much to the anger of Council, which minuted that 'the Group should not protest in the Society's name without prior consultation'. At its next meeting it passed a blanket resolution that all objections to demolition or works affecting listed buildings should come through the secretary of the parent body and not be dealt with by the Regional Groups.

In 1977, when the Kendal Group brought to Council a set of proposed rules, Council suggested that all four groups might consider adopting a common set of rules. When Barbara Harbottle questioned the need for 'Local Groups' in 1979, she was given short shrift: the groups were an integral part of the Society and 'there had been much discussion about their existence in the past'. Yet the confusion surrounding the relationship was apparent when, in the same year, the newly-formed Holme and District Local History Society sought to be affiliated to Cumberland and Westmorland, presumably aware of the relationship between the Kendal Regional Group and the parent body, but was refused and told that the existing regional groups were 'an integral part of the structure of CWAAS'. Nevertheless, in 1994 it was necessary to place a notice in the *Newsletter* pointing out that subscription to the parent body did not grant admission to the regional groups' winter lectures.[61] Reflecting on the role of the groups in the mid-1980s, the President, Rosemary Cramp, noted that they were seen by some of their members as a substitute for the parent body, in that membership was cheaper, the groups' meetings were held conveniently locally, and more active involvement was possible.[62] Although she did not explicitly say so, the groups had to all intent and purposes become independent organisations. They continued to report to Council (not always regularly) and the Society sometimes viewed them as recalcitrant offspring.

A CHANGING CONTEXT: PLURALISM IN THE STUDY OF THE PAST

Despite the increasing diversity of the Society's communal activities and concerns, it remained at heart a community of individuals who shared a passion for Cumbria's past. But the context within which the Society sought to fulfil its purposes of 'investigating, describing and preserving' Cumbrian antiquities changed dramatically in the later twentieth century. Several strands can be identified: first, the development of new sub-disciplines to pursue the study of aspects of the past hitherto ignored; second, and related to this, the proliferation of other voluntary bodies in Cumbria with interests in the region's past; third, the increasing professionalisation of archaeology and conservation.

Since the 1950s an array of new areas of interest has developed, each with a strong following among members of the public, reflected in the formation of specialist voluntary bodies, both nationally and locally. Local history, family history, industrial archaeology, garden history, vernacular architecture – all have spawned separate societies in Cumbria and have impinged on the work of the Cumberland and Westmorland. Through its Parish Register Section, the Society had a long track record of publishing the raw material for family history and, although the Section continued its work, if less intensively from the 1960s, no attempt seems to have been made to capitalise on the blossoming of family history testified to by the formation of the Cumbria Family History Society in 1976. An attempt was made to revive the Parish Register Section by forming a new committee in 1980 but the committee failed to meet and the Section was formally wound up in 1991.

A similar lack of initiative characterised the Society's relationship with the nascent field of local history. Although there were close relations between the Society and the record offices in Carlisle and Kendal from the 1960s and *Transactions* published increasing numbers of local historical studies, the dominance of archaeology tended to mean that local history was left to develop outside the Society. The interest was catered for by courses mounted in Cumbria by the Workers' Educational Association and the extra-mural departments of Liverpool and Newcastle universities from the 1960s and by the increasing numbers of local history societies which sprang up in towns and villages. In 1987, during one of the perennial discussions of how the Society might extend its membership, J.D. Marshall noted the existence of 'many small local history societies across the county with whom the Society had little or no contact'. An attempt was made to rectify this over the following years. On the Society's behalf, Angus Winchester, then of Liverpool University's extra-mural department, established a parish history group at Caldbeck in 1988, which formed the launch pad for a local history conference held at Carlisle in 1991. The Society agreed to take the lead in holding a Local History Forum each year and appointed a group to identify all the local history societies in the county and to foster coordination between them. But the outcome could not have been what the Society anticipated. Although the Society's Research Committee wished the Society to take 'a prominent role in Local History matters', the working group was 'wary of too close an association with the Society'. In the end, a new body, the Cumbria Local History Federation, was born in the autumn of 1992.

If developments in local and family history tended to take place outside the Society, new areas of study relating to tangible remains of material culture were embraced by the Society with more enthusiasm. The study of traditional buildings came on to the agenda in 1955 when the President, C.M.L. Bouch, sought systematic information on 'typical small farms and domestic houses', a subject recently covered in *Transactions* in a pioneering article by Ronald Brunskill on such houses in the Eden valley (see Chapter 5). No separate section or committee of the Society developed out of the nascent field of vernacular architecture but *Transactions* has carried further important studies of traditional buildings. More concrete action followed the growth of interest in industrial heritage, as de-industrialisation began to bite still further (see Chapter 7). In 1964 the possibility of establishing a sub-committee on industrial remains was discussed and a Committee for Industrial Archaeology came into being during the centenary year of 1966, initially under the chairmanship of W.W. Marshall of Seascale. It quickly developed a style and life of its own, under the leadership of J.D. Marshall and Michael Davies-Shiel. The first newsletter of the committee, issued under the title *Lakeland Industrial Archeology* [*sic*] *Newsletter* in 1969, did not go down well with Council. Despite being prefaced by a note stating that 'All opinions in this Newsletter ... are the sole responsibility of M. Davies-Shiel', it was deemed to be 'not in conformity with the Council's views'. As with relations with the regional groups, the nub of the problem was probably the involvement of non-members in activities carried out in the Society's name. In the newsletter, Davies-Shiel had reported that Herbert Clegg, the Society's General Secretary, had stated that members of a sub-section were normally expected to be members of the Society 'but in this new venture there may well be many I.A. folk who are not in CWAAS and this rule might be waived for a time, though not for [members of] the sub-committee itself'. He then went on to suggest that applicants to join the parent body might backdate their nomination forms in order to receive the 1969 volume of *Transactions*, a ruse which may explain the newsletter's cool reception by Council.[63] When the Cumbria Industrial History Society was founded in 1985, concerns were expressed that the new body might bypass the Industrial Archaeology Committee but Council welcomed the proposal to found the new society and made a donation towards it.

A third trend, the increasing dominance of professional staff in the fields of archaeology and conservation, profoundly changed the Society's role in the study and preservation of historic and archaeological monuments. By the 1970s a new direction was needed. The Inspectorate of Ancient Monuments and the Department of the Environment were playing increasingly prominent roles in excavation, which was becoming more sophisticated, particularly as the highly-specialised scientific procedures associated with environmental archaeology became the norm. Local authorities (including, in Cumbria, the Lake District National Park Planning Board) were also taking an increasingly active interest in sites and monuments – Cumberland County Council appointed a county archaeologist in 1973. The authorities' concern extended to the preservation of industrial heritage, so that, by 1976, the Industrial Archaeology Committee could state that 'amateurs were not needed as much as in the past'. In the rapidly changing context, Clare Fell and Dorothy Charlesworth reported to Council in 1973 on the future role of the Society in excavation and fieldwork. They noted that 'The age of small scale amateur excavation has passed as techniques have become more sophisticated' – indeed, excavation had already passed from old county societies such as Cumberland and Westmorland to the universities and to central government. The Society's Excavation Committee (the reincarnation of the Cumberland Excavation Committee in 1958, with new terms of reference to include all periods) was moribund – since its inception, it had only met three times, in 1964-65. What should the role of the Society be? Clare Fell suggested that a fresh start was needed. 'Unless some drastic and effective action is taken now', she concluded, 'the C. & W. will fail to adjust to the requirements of the present day and become an excursion society with little real function'.[64] As a result of their reports, the Excavation and Prehistoric Studies Committees were dissolved in 1974 and replaced by a Fieldwork and Excavation Committee, whose function was to liaise with central and local government and the universities and to receive and advise Council on applications for grants towards archaeological work.

As has been noted, the Society had long played a formal role in conservation, acting locally as the eyes and ears of the Inspectorate of Ancient Monuments and the Ministry of Works and its successors. The system of correspondents continued into the post-war decades but the Society's role came increasingly to overlap with the work of professionals. As post-war modernisation gathered speed, particularly during the 'brave new world' decade of the 1960s, Council meetings were increasingly dominated by concern about threats to archaeological sites and historic buildings in the face of development, particularly the relentless drive to improve roads. The impact of road widening schemes on ancient monuments and historic buildings kept the Society on its toes: in a two-year period in the mid-1960s concerns were expressed about potential damage to the cairn on Dunmail Raise (echoing those expressed as long ago as 1867 – see p.10), the henge at Mayburgh and the Roman milestone at Kirkby Thore, the destruction of sixteenth-century farm buildings at Cark Hall and the impact of street-widening in Carlisle. The decade culminated in a major challenge, when the route of the M6 was driven north through Cumbria: in 1968 Council asked the Regional Groups to keep a watching brief on the line of the new section of motorway. This was the precursor to the setting up of a Field Study Section in 1971, which made site visits to areas affected by development, not only the M6 and upgrading of the A66 but also afforestation in the far north of the county.[65]

The Society's place in protecting the built heritage came to the fore when an attempt was made in 1972 to revive its role in commenting on planning applications affecting listed buildings. In the 1960s the Society had taken action on a case-by-case basis. It protested vigorously in 1964 against the proposed flooding of the Winster valley for a reservoir, but felt it could not intervene to prevent the flooding of the Hodbarrow mines at Millom when its support was sought in 1968. In 1969 the Society coordinated a fundraising appeal for major repairs to Wraysholme Tower and deputed a representative to attend the public enquiry about the proposed demolition of Appleby police station. As seen in the dispute with Kendal Regional Group over action to preserve the gas works portico, the parent body was keen to retain close control. Acting as the representative of the Council for British Archaeology (CBA), the Society received all planning proposals to demolish listed buildings and was also on Cumberland County Council's list of bodies to be informed of wider proposals affecting such buildings. These mechanisms were not always effective, however: in 1966 letters from CBA alerting the Society to proposed demolitions arrived too late for Council to take action and it was agreed that in future such letters should be forwarded immediately to the three correspondents acting for the Society in the Carlisle, Appleby and Kendal areas. By 1972 that system was creaking. Only in Westmorland was effective oversight in place, Michael Bunney, a Kendal architect, scouring the local press for notices of planning applications and notifying the Society of threats. Elsewhere, other players, such as the Civic Trust and local civic societies, were increasingly taking a lead. Council's attempt to find a way forward led to heated discussion: John Borron, who had drawn up a discussion paper on the subject, urged the formation of a small sub-committee; Roy Hudleston argued against, hoping that the Society 'would not become another preservationist society'. A working group was set up, which led to the appointment of Michael Bunney as the Society's correspondent for all matters concerning the demolition or alteration of listed buildings. No long-term solution could be found: Bunney withdrew from active involvement in 1979, to be replaced by a new system of correspondents, acting on the Society's behalf at district council level. After the submission of what was considered to be a hefty expenses claim in 1982, the Society no longer appointed representatives. When the Society's policy on conservation was revisited in 1991, it was felt that the greater prominence of archaeological and conservation interests on planning committees than in the past obviated the need for regular input from the Society.

A similar protracted story of a transfer of responsibility from the Society to local government professionals played out in the Society's other longstanding role, that of identifying and recording archaeological sites. When the Committee for Prehistoric Studies was revived in 1956, the system of local correspondents was renewed and when, two years later, an attempt was made to update the inventory of ancient monuments in Cumberland, the Society took an active lead, envisaging help from members of the Regional Groups in the county – indeed, by 1959 specimen entries had been received from the South-West Group. The danger of duplication of effort emerged in 1964, when opinion was divided on Council as to what the Society's role in updating the inventory should be when it was believed that the Ancient Monuments Commission intended to publish an inventory itself. The record cards and Six-Inch Ordnance Survey maps marked up to locate archaeological sites, which the Society passed on to Cumbria County Council, formed the foundations of the Cumbria's Sites and Monuments Record, the precursor to the modern Historic Environment Record. Convergence of interest between the Society and the local authority resulted in a blurring of lines by the mid-1980s. In 1984 the secretary of the Society's Fieldwork and Excavation Committee, Tom Clare (who was also Cumbria County Council's county archaeologist), asked local correspondents to record archaeological sites in their local areas. When the matter was discussed again at Council in 1986 concern was expressed about confusion over whether the correspondents were working on behalf of the Society or for the County Council. The following year it was agreed that the development of the Sites and Monuments Record meant that the Society's role could now be no more than a monitoring one, as detailed recording would be carried out by the County Council.

The shifting relationship between the Society as a voluntary body and the changing role of local authorities was also visible in the Society's relationship with Tullie House. As well as holding the Society's collections and library, Tullie House had been a regular venue for meetings since the Victorian era.

When, in 1970, Carlisle City Council informed the Society that in future a charge would be made (7s. 6d. per meeting), Council greeted the news with indignation and asked them to reconsider, which they declined to do. Reorganisation in the 1980s resulted in the separation of library and museum, the former being moved to a new building in The Lanes, Carlisle; the latter remaining at Tullie House. Attempts to compile a list of the Society's property at Tullie House proved difficult, as much of it had by then come to be viewed as an integral part of the local collection, indistinguishable from other material. When Carlisle Library moved to The Lanes it declined to accept the Society's books and journals, which remained at Tullie House, posing something of a headache across the 1980s and 1990s. The Society's excavation archives and other material remained in the museum, which continued to receive further deposits from the Society.

By the 1980s, therefore, the Society was far from being the only body concerned with Cumbria's past. The near monopoly of influence the Society had enjoyed in its early days had long passed, as the statutory framework governing the historic environment had become more complex and as voluntary bodies with an interest in the region's past proliferated. In some aspects (notably archaeological fieldwork and historic buildings preservation), the Society engaged with the changing context and remained an active contributor; in others (including much of the growth of local history) it stood aloof. There was some concern about new players entering the Society's realm. Great suspicion initially greeted the growth of metal detectorist groups in the late 1970s, but their genuine interest in their finds and their willingness to act responsibly soon won the Society over. A sense that the Society's territory was being encroached upon greeted the foundation of Search, an independent archaeological society in southern Cumbria. In 1981 Council refused a request for a notice publicising the new group to be read at the Society's AGM (but agreed that a poster might be displayed). Concern was minuted the following year when Search sought funding from the South-West and Kendal Regional Groups for its excavations in Kentmere. Claiming to be affiliated to the Society (though it was pointed out that it was merely an institutional member) it carried out an 'unauthorised excavation' at Levens.

Looking to the future

As the Society entered the new century and began to approach its 150th anniversary, the time was ripe to take stock of its changed and changing character and role. On his election as President in 2005, David Shotter initiated a review of all aspects of the Society – a process that became known as 'Assessment, Reform and Action' (ARA). Noting the changing context within which the Society now operated, he identified a need:

> to clarify the Society's relationships with other bodies – professional organisations, educational institutions, agencies of national and local government, the 'Heritage Industry' and the host of smaller and more localised societies that has sprung up over the last half-century or so. We need, too, to ask serious questions about what our members expect of us as a 'County Society' and how we may better serve their aims and wishes.

The review was completed by the end of 2006 and a final report was presented to the AGM in April 2007, leading to amendments to the constitution in 2008.

As a result of the review, the society's committee structure was modified. Standing Committee, composed of senior officers of the Society, which had been created at the beginning of the millennium to meet in the gaps between meetings of Council and to ease the inherent difficulty of taking decisions in Council meetings which might be attended by up to 40 members, was placed on a permanent footing. The Industrial Archaeology Committee, which had been given a new constitution in 2005, and the Editorial Committee (subsequently renamed the Publications Committee in order to

Fig. 1.19. The Society's Facebook page

reflect its wider remit in managing and promoting the society's full range of publications) continued, as did the Research Committee, renamed the Research and Grants Committee and with a wider brief. A new committee, the Outreach Committee, was established in 2007, its aims being to increase

Fig. 1.20. Regan Housby's contribution to Silloth Primary School's entry for a project on the First World War, grant-aided by the Society (2014)

Fig. 1.21. Rachel Newman leading a study tour at the alum works, Ravenscar, North Yorkshire

the membership of the Society, develop the links between the parent body and the affiliated groups, publicise the contents of *Transactions*, develop the website and create a link with schools. It has led to wider adoption of the brand name 'Cumbria Past' on publicity and on the web, the writing of a 'Welcome' booklet for new members to foster a sense of belonging to the Society, the development of the website and a Facebook page, and a concerted effort to improve the society's links with young people through the creation of an annual grant to schools (figs. 1.19 and 1.20).

The Society's relationship with its regional groups was also clarified. Their independence was formalised when a clear definition of affiliated status was adopted in 2005 and made explicit when two of the groups subsequently changed their names to the Kendal Historical and Archaeological Society and the South West Cumbria History and Archaeology Society in 2012. The character of the four groups has diverged somewhat. The Kendal group, its income boosted by a large membership and, in David Starkey, a high-profile president, has been able to give grants to support history and heritage in the town, and to run a fieldwork group working in association with the Lake District National Park archaeologists in Longsleddale. The South-West group remains active in fieldwork, though its extensive rural area makes it difficult to hold events accessible to all. Conversely, the Carlisle and Penrith groups remain comparatively small and their activities limited to winter lectures and summer outings. In order to support regional groups, the parent body sponsors celebrity lectures for each affiliated society in rotation.

At the heart of any voluntary society stand its members, the modern representatives of those who were urged by James Simpson at the Society's inaugural meeting in 1866, to 'work diligently, labour patiently, and meet often'.[66] In an increasingly professionalised world and as members of a Society which directs much of its collective resources into publishing and grant-making, what is the role of its members? Active fieldwork continues, as new opportunities have been grasped to record and raise awareness of aspects of landscape heritage which hitherto have been ignored by other agencies. In 2007 the Society established three volunteer projects, organised at grassroots level with minimal fuss, to record dated buildings, war memorials and mileposts and direction signs. The pattern of excursions, such a core element of the Society's life for most of his history, has changed. By 2006 the Society's activities programme was in some disarray as a result of resignations from the Activities Committee and – more fundamentally – changing habits and desires of the membership, which was leading to a substantial loss of interest in the established programme of excursions. The ARA review resulted in a temporary revival of the committee, but it soon folded. However, a programme of activities, always intended to be informative but also sociable events, has continued as individual members stepped into the breach to take responsibility for organising specific activities. These have included one-off visits such as visit to the Spadeadam Blue Streak missile site and a study tour to the Whitby area (figs. 1.21 and 1.22), as well as elements of the established programme, including the annual May Fell Walk and the Summer Evening event.

New ventures have included an adventurous pilgrimage to Iceland in W.G. Collingwood's steps in 2012 (fig. 2.9), and a series of autumn 'Urban Walks', complementing the rural May Fell Walks, initiated in the same year (fig. 1.23). The Society also sponsors educational events, notably the biennial Dorothy Charlesworth Lectures on aspects of Roman archaeology, established in 1983, and the joint lectures with the affiliated regional groups. It has increasingly joined with other bodies to offer study opportunities, notably collaborating with the Centre for North-West Regional Studies (now the Regional Heritage Centre) at Lancaster University in a series of day conferences on a regular basis since 2004. Other recent joint ventures include a conference on upland landscapes with the Society for Landscape Studies in 2013.

The Society thus continues to adapt to changing circumstances, as it has done across much of its century-and-a-half of existence. Successive generations have embarked upon new initiatives as they seek to further the aims of a body founded in the very different world of mid-Victorian Britain when 50 or so gentlemen and a handful of ladies met at Penrith in September 1866. James Simpson predicted then that, even after much diligent labour by

Fig. 1.22. A surviving Blue Streak rocket booster section at Spadeadam *(photograph by courtesy of Margaret Edwards)*

Fig. 1.23. Banks Yard, Cockermouth, visited by Society members during the urban walk in 2015 *(photograph by courtesy of Trevor Grahamslaw)*

members of the Society, there would be no lack of subjects 'to engage their interest and secure their attention'. 150 years later, those words remain as true as ever.

NOTES AND REFERENCES

1 Newspaper cutting in Cumbria Archive Service, (hereafter CAS), (Carlisle), DSO/1/1. The following account is largely based on the formal records of the Society, preserved in surviving minute books for 1866-73, CAS (Carlisle), DSO/1/1; 1907-70, DSO/1/4-5, 16-18; 1970-92, DSO/1/102; accounts of proceedings in *Transactions* for the period when minute books are missing (1874-1906), and the *Newsletter*, 1992-2015. Unless otherwise stated, information and quotations are derived from those sources.

2 *Carlisle Journal*, 14 July 1871. I am grateful to Adrian Allan for identifying and locating the source of the cutting pasted into the Society's minute book and for his invaluable labours in drawing up a catalogue of the Society's archives, without which the task of researching this chapter would have been significantly more difficult.

3 For a discussion of these societies, see P. Levine, *The Amateur and the Professional: antiquarians, historians and archaeologists in Victorian England, 1838-1886* (Cambridge, 1986) and J. Beckett, *Writing Local History* (Manchester, 2007), 70-85.

4 For these men, see B.J.N. Edwards, 'Reginald Bainbrigg, Westmorland antiquary', *CW3*, 3 (2003), 119-25; A.J.L. Winchester, 'Bainbrigg, Reginald (1544/5-1612/13)', *ODNB*; *John Denton's History of Cumberland*, ed. A.J.L. Winchester (joint publication: Surtees Society 213/CWAAS, Record Series XX, 2010).

5 For these, see A.J.L. Winchester, 'Machell, Thomas (*bap.* 1647, *d.* 1698)', *ODNB*; D.J.W. Mawson, 'Todd, Hugh (*c.*1657-1728)', *ODNB*; D.J.W. Mawson, 'Dr Hugh Todd's Account of the Diocese of Carlisle', *CW2*, 88 (1988), 207-24; F.G. James, *North Country Bishop: a biography of William Nicolson* (London, 1956); D.W. Hayton, 'Nicolson, William (1655-1727)', *ODNB* (*Oxford Dictionary of National Biography*).

6 W. Hutchinson, *History of the County of Cumberland* (2 vols., 1794-97); S. Jefferson, *The History and Antiquities of Carlisle* (Carlisle, 1838); *The History and Antiquities of Leath Ward* (Carlisle, 1840) and *The History and Antiquities of Allerdale Ward above Derwent* (Carlisle, 1842). For a survey of antiquarian writing on Cumbria, see A.J.L. Winchester, 'Cumberland and Westmorland', 91-106 in C.R.J. Currie and C.P. Lewis (eds.), *English County Histories: a guide* (Stroud, 1994).

7 For these honorary members, see M. Nicholson, 'Simpson, James Young (1811-1870)'; J.D. Pickles, 'Guest, Edwin (1800-1880)'; A. Burns, 'Greenwell, William (1820-1918)'; and W.W. Wroth (rev. C.M. Fraser), 'Bruce, John Collingwood (1805-1892)', all in *ODNB*.

8 J. Simpson, 'The present state of antiquarian research in Westmorland and Cumberland', *CW1*, 1 (1874), 1-18 quotation 18. Simpson's paper, delivered in 1866, was printed as the first paper in *Transactions*; its title differs from that listed on the contents page of the volume which reads 'The need of antiquarian research in Cumberland and Westmorland'.

9 DSO/1/1, minutes of General Meeting, 29 Aug. 1867, minutes 3 and 4.

10 DSO/1/1, minutes of meeting at Penrith, 23 Sept. 1868, minutes 1 and 2.

11 Newspaper cutting, CAS (Carlisle), DSO/1/1.

12 Three meetings were held in each of 1876, 1877 and 1881 but only one in 1883.

13 Summary based on DSO/1/1; reports of Proceedings in *Transactions* and DSO/1/14 (file of excursion leaflets from 1886).

14 *CW1*, 4 (1880), 546.
15 The returns are in Carlisle Library, 2A9. I am grateful to Adrian Allan for this reference.
16 *CW1*, 2 (1876), xix.
17 *CW1*, 9 (1888), 152-56.
18 See editorial in *Newsletter*, 33 (Spring 2000).
19 See G. Macdonald (rev. P.W.M. Freeman), 'Haverfield, Francis John (1860-1919)', *ODNB*.
20 Reports of the initial years of the Cumberland Excavation Committee are in *CW1*, 13 (1895), 453-69; 14 (1897), 413-33; 16 (1900), 80-99.
21 'No. 1 – for the year 1866-7', published in 1870, contained 8 papers and 80 pages. Subsequent papers were numbered 'IX' onwards and pagination was continued. The first full volume included papers read up to Sept. 1873 and appeared in 1874. For further details, see Chapter 2 below, n. 21.
22 *CW1*, 9 (1888), 395; 10 (1889), 282, 284; 15 (1899), 331.
23 Obituary in *CW1*, 8 (1886), 532-35. Portraits of all Presidents can be found alongside their biographies in Appendix 1.
24 See obituaries in *CW1*, 16 (1900), vii-xx and *Carlisle Journal*, 6 Mar. 1900; also E.I. Carlyle (rev. A.J.L. Winchester), 'Ferguson, Richard Saul (1837-1900)', *ODNB*.
25 R.S. Ferguson and C.J. Ferguson, 'Lanercost Priory', *CW1*, 1 (1874), 95-140.
26 R.S. Ferguson, 'The heraldry of Cumberland and Westmorland', *CW1*, 1 (1874), 300-17.
27 J.S. Dearden, 'Collingwood, William Gershom (1854-1932)', *ODNB*. For a fuller account of Collingwood and his role in Cumbria, see M. Townend, *The Vikings and Victorian Lakeland: the Norse medievalism of W.G. Collingwood and his contemporaries* (CWAAS, Extra Series XXXIV, 2009), esp. Chapter 2.
28 For a bibliography of Collingwood's publications, see Townend, *Vikings and Victorian Lakeland*, 279-85.
29 Physical description from Dearden, *ODNB*.
30 For the seal, see Townend, *Vikings and Victorian Lakeland*, 221-22. For identification of the altar, see Margaret Edwards, 'Face to Face', *Newsletter*, 32 (Autumn 1999).
31 DSO/1/4, Council minutes, 7 July and 8-9 Sept. 1910.
32 DSO/1/5, 60.
33 DSO/1/5, 135, 169.
34 DSO/1/5, 176.
35 See obituary in *CW2*, 33 (1933), 312-13.
36 For these men, see their obituaries in *CW2*, 21 (1921), 284; 37 (1937), 229-30 and 41 (1941), 223.
37 For the role of women in the Society and in the study of prehistory in particular, see D. Barrowclough, *Prehistoric Cumbria* (Stroud, 2010), 42-49.
38 DSO/1/4, Council minutes, 11-12 Sept. 1913, resolution 6.
39 *CW2*, 8 (1908), 370-71.
40 Brochure pasted into DSO/1/4; 'Proceedings', *CW2*, 8 (1908), 370-73.
41 DSO/1/14 (brochure); 'Proceedings', *CW2*, 5 (1905), 273-75.
42 The brochure for the Tour of Galloway in 1925 named Porter as 'Hon. Sec. Excursions': DSO/1/14. Porter resigned in Sept. 1945.
43 T. Champion, 'Protecting the monuments: archaeological legislation from the 1882 Act to *PPG 16*', in M. Hunter (ed.), *Preserving the Past: the rise of heritage in modern Britain* (Stroud, 1996), 38-56.
44 DSO/1/5, 115-16.
45 DSO/1/4, Council minutes 26 June 1912, June 1913; 27 Apr. 1916; general meeting minutes, 27 June 1912.

46 For the wider history of the VCH in Cumbria, see J.V. Beckett, 'The Cumberland & Westmorland Antiquarian & Archaeological Society and the Victoria County History', *CW3*, 11 (2011), 207-25.

47 Beckett, 'CWAAS and the VCH', 219.

48 This was probably the Vertical Plan Chest and Map Chest Drawer in the museum store at Tullie House, which contained maps, plans, drawings, watercolours and other papers when it was listed in 1992: information from Adrian Allan (2015).

49 Eric Birley, speaking in 1950, as reported in 'Proceedings', *CW2*, 51 (1951), 189.

50 S. Collini and B. Williams, 'Collingwood, Robin George (1889-1943)', *ODNB*.

51 Obituary in *CW2*, 36 (1936), 237-38. Examples of her drawings adorn the early reports of the Committee, such as her coloured section of the Turf Wall in *CW1*, 14 (1897), 188-89.

52 A.K. Bowman, 'Birley, Eric Barff (1906-1995)', *ODNB*.

53 DSO/1/17, 69. The records of the Regional Groups themselves are currently held in the following repositories – Carlisle: Carlisle Library, Jackson Library 2A9 and CAS (Carlisle), Acc. H 11579; Kendal: CAS (Kendal), WDSO 99; Penrith: CAS (Kendal), WDSO 99/4; South-West: CAS (Carlisle), DSO 1/99.

54 See Barrowclough, *Prehistoric Cumbria*, 44-48; 'Kate Hodgson FSA, 1889-1974, President 1948-51', *Newsletter*, 76 (Summer 2014), 15; J. Cherry, 'In Memoriam: Clare Isobel Fell, M.A., F.S.A.', *CW3*, 2 (2002), 317-19; K.E. Sharpe, 'The Lady of the Lakes, Clare Isobel Fell and the role of local societies for women in archaeology', in P.J. Cherry (ed.), *Studies in Northern Prehistory, Essays in memory of Clare Fell* (CWAAS, Extra Series XXXII, 2007), 1-23.

55 See R. Hart-Davis, 'Fulford, Sir Roger Thomas Baldwin (1902-1983)', *ODNB*.

56 DSO/1/18, list of new members admitted 1966-67. The list is incomplete (it omits the author, who joined as an Associate Member in 1966).

57 As described in Richard Hall, 'W.G. Wiseman: appreciation of an editor', *CW3*, 9 (2009), 1-4.

58 *C. & W. Newsletter*, 1 (Autumn 1983), [1].

59 Since the Newsletter's inception the editors have been: 1-10 Autumn 1983-Spring 1988, Dr Angus Winchester; 11-15 Spring 1989-Autumn 1991, Phillip Dalziel; 16-27 Spring 1992-Autumn 1997, John Marsh; 28-62 Spring 1998-Autumn 2009, Margaret Edwards; 63-71 Spring 2010-Autumn 2012, Professor Mike J. Lea and Kate R. Lea (joint editors); 72- Spring 2013 to date, Dr Jean Turnbull.

60 Including the Promotional Committee (established 1983), Recruitment & Publicity Committee (1998-89) and Outreach Committee (2007 onwards).

61 *Newsletter*, 20 (Spring 1994).

62 DSO/1/102; R.J. Cramp, 'Note on the present and future state of the Society', undated [filed among Council minutes for 1986].

63 *Lakeland Industrial Archeology* [*sic*] *Newsletter*, 1 Jan. 1969. Copy in CAS (Kendal), Search Room.

64 DSO/1/102, file of Council papers and minutes, 1970-4: C.I. Fell, 'Thoughts about Cumberland & Westmorland Excavation Committee', typescript report, 30 Oct. 1973, and 'Miss D. Charlesworth's Report' [undated].

65 DSO/1/18, Minutes of General Meeting, 6 Apr. 1968; DSO/1/102, Council minutes 12 Nov. 1971; programme of Field Study Section, 1972.

66 Simpson, 'The present state of antiquarian research', 1.

Chapter 2
The Society and its Publications

I.D. Caruana and W.G. Wiseman

The first resolution at the inaugural meeting of the Society on 11 September 1866 determined that the Society would investigate, describe and preserve the antiquities of the two counties and give the public 'either in the shape of written papers or printed pamphlets, the results of their explorations and discoveries, thus contributing to our county history'.[1] Papers were read at the inaugural meeting and either read, or taken as read, at subsequent meetings but, despite the intention, nothing was actually published until 1874.

Volume I of the Old Series of *Transactions* appeared in 1874, and its success encouraged the publication of subsequent volumes and also probably contributed to the determination to publish volumes additional to *Transactions*. At the Society's AGM in 1876 a resolution was passed that the Society, and in particular its editor, Chancellor Ferguson, should take steps towards the publication of *Miscellany Accounts of the Diocese of Carlile*, Bishop Nicolson's Visitation and Survey of the Diocese of Carlisle in 1703-04. Some record of the discussion around the resolution survives: 'Mr Jackson: it may be the commencement of a series of similar character. – The Chairman: that is exactly what I have in view'.[2] This book appeared in 1877 as Volume I of the Extra Series (fig. 1.9). It initiated a publications programme which has been one of the most significant achievements of the Society, ensuring that the works of significant regional and national historians and archaeologists relating to Cumbria have been made available to the interested public in handsome, well-printed editions.

Transactions

Titus Wilson

The firm of Titus Wilson (later Titus Wilson & Son) of Kendal has printed almost every volume of *Transactions*. Therefore the history of *Transactions* is inextricably linked with the firm *ab initio*. Titus Wilson was a founder member of the Society,[3] and was elected Honorary Secretary in 1871, but he had clearly been involved in the administrative workings of the Society before his actual appointment.[4] Indeed, a notice regarding the payment of subscriptions, dated 18 August 1870 at Kendal, was issued under the name of T. Wilson, on behalf of the Council, and a notice dated 5 June 1871 regarding the forthcoming AGM was signed 'T. Wilson, Secretary *pro tem.*', but by the meeting held on 12 July 1871 he was listed as 'Hon. Sec.'.[5] In 1898 he was held in such regard that the members presented him with 'a valuable and elegant silver salver', as 'a slight memento of their gratitude to him for the long and valuable services he had rendered to them during thirty-one years'. On 13 July 1911, following his retirement from that office because of 'continued ill-health', he was elected an Honorary Member 'as a mark of appreciation of his services'.[6] When he died in October 1917 he was the last surviving founder member of the Society (fig.2.1).[7]

Titus Wilson had been born at Kendal on 6 August 1834, the eldest son of Titus Wilson, whitesmith, of Market Place, and his wife Mary.[8] Following apprenticeship to a local printer he went for a time to Edinburgh and London, before returning to Kendal and, in about 1860, taking over the long-established printing and publishing business of John Hudson and Cornelius Nicholson at 28 Highgate (fig. 2.2). Throughout the latter part of the nineteenth century he expanded and developed the printing and publishing activities of the firm, specialising in historical and learned books, mainly of local interest.[9] In the 1871 census enumerators' books he was described as a bookseller, stationer and printer, and in 1881 a stationer and printer employing four men and four boys. He was a significant figure in the Borough of Kendal – a town councillor from 1876 to 1907; mayor 1887-88; alderman in 1889; borough JP in 1890 – as well as being chairman of many and varied local organisations and societies, and of course the Hon. General Secretary of the Cumberland and Westmorland for many years (see Chapter 1).

Fig. 2.1. Titus Wilson *(reproduced by courtesy of Kendal Town Council)*

He and his wife Lucy, also a member of the Society, lived at Aynam Lodge, Kendal. Lucy died on 30 January 1905 and after a period of ill health Titus died on 24 October 1917.[10] His obituary in *The Westmorland Gazette* on 3 November 1917 described him as a 'very well-known antiquary, his name in that connection being recognised throughout the country ... [a] man of calm and dignified character who was endowed with a wonderful memory. ...He had artistic tendencies and a wide knowledge; while as an antiquarian and archaeologist, he was pre-eminent ...'. His 'In Memoriam' in *Transactions* records how much the Society was 'indebted to the kindly tact and business capacity which he never tired of spending for the Society's advancement'.[11] Apart from his work as Secretary he contributed papers to *Transactions* in the 1880s on 'Remains at Hugill near Windermere' and 'The Roman road over Whinfell', and in 1890 he undertook some archaeological work on the site of the Roman fort at Watercrook.[12]

After the resignation of Titus as Secretary in 1911, his son, Edward William Wilson, took over the family firm and, having assisted his father's work for the Society for many years, succeeded as Hon. General Secretary.[13] Edward died in 1927 and, at the meeting held on 28 April that year, Miss Gertrude Ainsley 'of Messrs T. Wilson and Son', a bookkeeper and Edward's assistant secretary, was asked to become, 'for the time being, the General and Financial Secretary'.[14] In the event Miss Ainsley remained in that post for 32 years until 1959, when she retired and was elected an Honorary Member. She died in 1975, marking a secretarial link with the firm of Titus Wilson of almost 90 years.[15]

Fig. 2.2. Titus Wilson's shop in Highgate, Kendal at the end of the nineteenth century. From J.F. Curwen, *Kirkbie Kendall* (Titus Wilson, Kendal, 1900), 78. *(image courtesy of Cumbria County Council, Kendal Library)*

Following the death of Edward Wilson, the firm was taken over by Frank Bellingham Pollitt, formerly owner of *The Westmorland Gazette*. He became a member of the Society and, as proprietor of Messrs. Titus Wilson & Son, 'he took an active interest in the printing and publishing' of *Transactions,* 'in the preparation of which for the press his ready co-operation will be missed'.[16] He died in 1935 and ownership passed to his son Charles Jordan Bellingham Pollitt, who made his father's assistant, Fred Wilson, his partner. He 'set to work with tenacity and imagination to turn Titus Wilson into a printing office of distinction' ... 'the flow of work from the universities and learned societies passing through the office today is only a testimony to his success'.[17] Charles, in turn, was a member from 1935 until his death in 1975, and contributed a note on 'New Bank Yard, Kendal' in 1964.[18]

Transactions has been printed by Titus Wilson from the first volume in 1874 until the present time, with the exception of a period from 1991 to 1995 when the firm was taken over by Thomas Reed Printers of Sunderland and the volumes had to be printed by Alan Sutton Publishing Ltd. of Stroud. Reed's went into receivership in 1996 and the name of 'Titus Wilson & Son', together with the goodwill, was purchased by Dixon Printing of Kendal, who also employed a number of the former staff in their premises in Burneside Road, Kendal (fig.2.3). In 1996 *Transactions* was re-united with the name of Titus Wilson & Son and production continues until the present day.

Fig. 2.3. Titus Wilson & Son: composing room *c.*1950. *(Image courtesy of Titus Wilson & Son)*

The Series

At the meeting held at the Athenaeum, Maryport on 7 July 1870, Revd James Simpson announced that the first volume of the Society's *Transactions* would be ready the following week, and the members would have it sent to them. On 18 August 1870, Titus Wilson, in a notice issued to subscribers, announced that the first part of what we now know as the Old Series Volume 1, consisting of 80 pages for the years 1866-67 and edited by Revd James Simpson, was ready for the subscribers, who, according to a handwritten note at the end of the notice, presumably in Wilson's hand, would be sent their own copy.[19] However, it is unclear whether this part of Volume 1 was ever distributed. When in 1873 the second part of Volume 1 was assembled, it was decided to bind the two parts together, and when this two-part volume was printed by Titus Wilson and published in 1874, it became known as Volume 1.[20] From the start the size of the volume was demy octavo (8½ x 5½ inches), was untrimmed and included photographic plates and pull-out diagrams. The original type-face was Book Style, and until 1901 the volume was bound in brown paper covers with black lettering. The print run of the 'Old Series' was usually tightly related to the number of members.

Transactions was, as Geoffrey Martin observed in his excellent retrospective in 2000, 'originally an annual report of the members' activities, concerned mainly but not exclusively with the conduct of their meetings, and naturally including reports of papers read and communicated there'.[21] From the beginning, despite the name of the Society, papers were included which related to Lancashire North of the Sands - Furness Abbey, Hawkshead and Cartmel received particular attention - and, even before the 1974 boundary changes, Sedbergh and Dent were not neglected. In fact *Transactions* has, from the outset, covered the whole of the present-day county of Cumbria.

The second volume did not appear until 1876 but had a print run of 250, and opened with a report on 'Excursions and Proceedings' and a list of members.[22] In total, the 'Old Series' comprised 16 volumes, the final volume being published in 1900. By then '*Transactions* were still a record of business, but that business was increasingly the publication of learning addressed to a wider audience than the members alone'.[23]

Individual volumes of the 'Old Series' were not indexed but at the annual meeting held at Carlisle on 23 July 1885, the Hon. Secretary presented a printed copy of a new index of the first seven volumes of *Transactions* which had been prepared by W.B. Arnison, Esq., and asked for instructions as to the way in which it was to be published. It was resolved that 500 copies be printed, and that each member be supplied with a copy *gratis*.[24] With the new century a *Catalogue–Index* was compiled by Archibald Sparke, Carlisle City Librarian, in 1901, 'supplying entries under authors, titles and subjects of all numerous articles' of the 'Old Series', together with an itinerary of places visited by the Society between 1866 and 1899. However, it was not until 1981 that a composite index of the 'Old Series' was produced by Joyce Cherry, then Hon. Secretary of the Society.

With the election of William Gershom Collingwood as Honorary Editor at the meeting on 20 June 1900 *Transactions* was rationalised, and future issues were designated the 'New Series'. One volume was produced annually from 1901, with the 'unmistakable edge of professionalism'.[25] In 1930 the question of the advisability of beginning another new series of *Transactions* was discussed but it was resolved that the present series should be continued.[26]

The New Series volumes were bound in grey cloth with gold lettering, and the new Society 'seal' or 'badge', designed by Collingwood, was embossed on the front cover, but the pages were still untrimmed. The contents of each volume were expanded to include full papers, *addenda antiquaria* (in 1951 changed to 'Notes'), a general index, a list of members, notes for contributors of articles, 'In Memoriam' notices, a statement of receipts and expenses, an on-going list of publications, and occasional reviews of recent general publications. At a meeting on 21 March 1933 the issue of having the pages of future volumes of *Transactions* trimmed was discussed and agreed. No difference would be made in the height of the volumes but the width would be very slightly reduced.[27] This format remained substantially the same until 1977, when the then editor, Joseph (Fred) Hughes, instigated a change from demy-octavo to crown quarto, primarily because the new format would greatly reduce the increasing number of pull-outs which were required. It also reduced printing costs, therefore saving the Society money. When this took place there was also a change in the type paper, which allowed illustrations to be printed on text paper as opposed to art paper, and the plantain type-face was adopted as it was more appropriate for text paper.[28]

In 2001 a 'Third Series' was commenced and heralded a change of colour – hardbacks were bound in blue cloth with gold lettering, the softbacks in blue covers with red lettering – and a new, simplified Society logo, designed by the Society's then General Editor, J.P.D. (Pat) Ball, graced the front cover and spine. The contents that had come to define the New Series have continued to the present day, although some of the residual items have been dropped, mainly because of pressure of space for papers. 'Proceedings' – details of excursions and a brief summary of the meetings held – were no longer included after 1965, although composite summaries of the excursions were printed in 1977, 1987, 1988, and 1996, but there the practice ended completely. The list of members is no longer included. However, changing interests led to the listing of brief details of archaeological projects in the county from 2004 (with an hiatus in 2014), and from 2010 a list of publications and completed theses on Cumberland and Westmorland has been added.

As interest in the contents of *Transactions* was widening beyond Society members, the print-run of the New Series was increased from 1908 onwards so that spare copies might be sold to non-members.[29] That practice continues to the present day, although the number of extra volumes has been reduced; new members frequently wish to supplement their collections, and the trade in 'back-numbers' is well recognised in the antiquarian bookselling world. The Society has always observed the general principle that the cost of the production of *Transactions* would be borne out of the members' subscriptions, but with increasing printing costs occasional concern has been raised and the question of increasing the subscription has had to be considered from time to time to meet those costs.[30]

Of these issues the question of the size of the volume has been the most debated. The size has often been governed by the number of papers submitted but at other times cost has also dictated the length. In 1929, at a time of a deficit in the General Fund, it was resolved that it be suggested to the editors of *Transactions* that it was desirable to limit the annual volume to about 300 or 350 pages. However, in 1932 the chairman was able to report that the Society was to be considered a charity, and that the difficulties regarding its balances would therefore be reduced. It was accordingly resolved that the ban imposed on the editors limiting the size of *Transactions* be lifted.[31] Despite this freedom granted to the editors, the average size of the volumes, except in times of emergency, has remained at around the 300-page mark.

That sizeable volumes have been published annually was particularly remarkable during the First and Second World Wars. Production of volumes during the Great War (1914-18) had continued without interruption, despite inevitable delays and difficulties, although by 1918 its size had been reduced to 200 pages, and 'owing to the difficulties of binding', the volume was bound in a temporary cover, 'which will be replaced when circumstances permit'. At the AGM in September 1940, the Hon. Editor, W.T. McIntire, explained that 'owing to the necessity for economy in the present state of affairs, the size of volumes of *Transactions* must be reduced', and the volumes were issued in paper covers.[32] The 1944 edition amounted to only 194 pages. 'What is remarkable', wrote Professor Martin in his retrospective in *Transactions* in 2000, 'is that despite the dislocations and distractions of wartime, there were always papers, and paper, available for an annual volume'.[33]

Notwithstanding the fact that, from 1901, each volume has had an index, there have been a number of composite indexes and 'catalogue' indexes of the 'New Series' but, despite the fact that the Society had long maintained a special index fund, these have appeared on a rather intermittent and inconsistent basis. *An Index-Catalogue* (1901-1912) was compiled in 1915 by Daniel Scott; an index for volumes 1913-1925 was compiled by W.G. Collingwood and printed in 1928, and an *Index to the Transactions* (1960-89) was produced by Joyce and James Cherry.[34] In the twenty-first century digitisation has meant that the complete run of *Transactions* has an online index, which can be readily accessed via the Society's website and from 2015 this has been extensively extended by making all the past issues from 1874 fully available and searchable online.[35]

From its inception *Transactions* has been the premier historical and archaeological journal for the publication of papers relating to the area that became the post-1974 county of Cumbria. Its status was further enhanced in 1984 when *Transactions* was registered with the British Library and was assigned an International Standard Series Number (ISSN). Its academic credibility increased again from the 1990s since when all papers have been refereed or peer-reviewed. On occasions *Transactions* has been reviewed in the journal *Archives* and has been well received – in 1995 it was described as 'a handsome and well-produced volume that contains much of interest' – and in 1997 the reviewer commented that it 'maintains the high scholarly standards of earlier volumes'.[36]

The Editors

At the meeting on 11 July 1867 at the Crown Hotel, Penrith, a Printing Committee was appointed consisting of Council Members Revd James Simpson, Robert Ferguson and John Whitwell to facilitate the resolution passed at the inaugural meeting to print, if approved by the Council, the papers read at the meetings. However, by the time that Volume 1 was printed in 1874 the actual editors were listed as Revd Canon Simpson and Richard Saul Ferguson.[37] The subsequent biennial volumes of the Old Series were all edited by Ferguson, although Simpson continued to support the enterprise from behind the scenes. The 'In Memoriam' devoted to him states that, '... his shrewd common sense, great local knowledge, and keen sense of humour made him a genial check upon the eccentricities antiquarians are liable to fall into when they have imbibed a little too much learning. To his kindly supervision and criticism may be ascribed the comparative freedom of these Transactions from such blemishes'.[38] Simpson's influence may be seen lying behind Ferguson's comment in 1876 that 'in the course of his work he had great difficulty in keeping down some current errors; but he hoped by this time contributors had become aware that William the Conqueror was never in Cumberland, and Thomas de Morville of Burgh did not kill Thomas a'Becket'.[39] That the editor's role was growing in significance was apparent in 1882 when the Society adopted revised rules stating that the Editor, although he was always elected to the post, was to become one of the officers of the Society and a member of the Council.[40] Ferguson's tenure, which lasted until his death in 1900, did much to establish the reputation of *Transactions*.

W.G. Collingwood succeeded Ferguson as editor, established the New Series and reorganised *Transactions* as a series of bound annual volumes, the contents brought up to a new standard, both in text and illustration, and the cover decorated with his design (fig. 1.10). He exercised a firm editorial hand, re-writing and improving many of the papers himself, and included numerous articles of his own on a variety of subjects. In 1908 as a result of a dispute between Collingwood and a contributor of a paper to *Transactions*, a special meeting was convened and the following resolution was unanimously passed:

> That in the opinion of the Council, the Editor's discretion – as to what to admit, revise, or omit when editing papers sent in for publication in *Transactions* – must be absolute and his decision final.[41]

Editorial decisions have not subsequently been formally challenged in this way, and Collingwood's contribution to the Society through his editorship of *Transactions* was highlighted in his obituary: 'His lasting monument among ourselves is the thirty-two volumes of *Transactions* that have been either edited by him or produced under his guidance…'.[42]

W.G. Collingwood was sole editor until 1920 when his son, Robin George Collingwood, philosopher and historian, joined him. They continued together until 1925, when W.G.'s illness brought the partnership to an end. R.G. Collingwood was then joined by Thomas Henry Boileau Graham, a barrister, and Walter Travers McIntire, a director of technical education, and that triumvirate continued until 1934, when Graham retired 'on the grounds that his failing health no longer enabled him to do the work in the way in which his high standards required that it should be done'.[43] When Collingwood, who had not been in good health for some time, also retired,[44] McIntire carried on the editorship alone until his death in 1944.[45] The ecclesiastical historian, John Compton Dickinson, then took over the reins until Eric Barff Birley, the archaeologist and historian, replaced him four years later. Birley continued until 1956, together with Canon Charles Murray Lowther Bouch from 1951-56, and they, in turn, were replaced by Christopher Roy Hudleston, a journalist and lecturer in the Department of Palaeography and Diplomatic at Durham University. He was a prodigious author of papers over the years of his involvement with the Society and left a lasting legacy of work, particularly in matters genealogical. Hudleston retired from office after 18 years in 1974, having had the assistance of Brian Blake from 1957-58. In 1975, Alan Harris and Joseph (Fred) Hughes took the reins – Alan retired three years later and John Charlton took his place until 1982. At that point they were succeeded by County Archivist, Bruce Copley Jones, and William George Wiseman. This duo guided *Transactions* through a period of great change, the advent of an Editorial Committee and the arrival of computerisation, and worked as a team until health problems resulted in Bruce's retirement in 2006.[46]

In 2008 Professor Patricia L. Garside was appointed as joint editor with W.G. Wiseman, who retired the following year. Professor Garside soon established a small editorial group which included Professor Michael Mullett and Dr Ruth Hughes, an editorial approach that has been maintained by Professor Ian Whyte when he became Editor in 2013. Not only have these teams maintained the excellent traditions and reputation of *Transactions* but a number of new features have been introduced which have made the journal even more accessible. A contents list is now printed on the back cover, there is an abstract at the start of each article, and a header records the bibliographic information. A new departure has been the commissioning of articles. In 2010 a number of papers on industrial history were commissioned in order to create a volume honouring the work of Mike Davies-Shiel, and in 2011 a group of papers relating to Cumbrian identities, resulting in part from a joint conference with the Centre for North-West Regional Studies at Lancaster University, and held at Ambleside, was published. From 2013 *Transactions* has been published in mid-summer rather than in what had become its traditional slot towards the end of the year.

The oversight of *Transactions* lay initially with the Printing Committee established in 1867. From 1882 there has been a Publications Committee in one form or another.[47] In 1988 a larger Editorial Committee was created, and the publication programme rapidly expanded. The reconstitution of this committee in 1994 meant that the Editor of *Transactions* ceased to be responsible for other publications, and in 1995 Council approved the appointment of a General Editor to oversee the increasing production of those additional volumes. In 2007 the Committee was renamed the Publications Committee which better reflected its new, much wider, remit.

Papers and Contributors

In the early days of the Society, contributors to *Transactions* were mainly clergymen and other gentlemen. They were mostly enthusiastic amateurs with an antiquarian or archaeological bent, although some, such as John Augustus Cory, a practising architect and county surveyor of Cumberland, were able to write with a more professional authority.[48] An analysis of the complete Old Series reveals that clergymen were by far the largest number of contributors but that five authors were women, at least two were medics and one was an Icelander, Eiríkr Magnússon, a graduate of Trinity College, Cambridge, and librarian at that university. The most prolific authors at that time were the editor himself, Richard Saul Ferguson; Henry Swainson Cowper, archaeologist, traveller and writer; Revd W. Slater Calverley, vicar of Aspatria; William Jackson, magistrate and antiquarian; Michael Waistell Taylor MD of Penrith; Revd Thomas Lees, vicar of Wreay; and Revd Henry Whitehead, vicar of Lanercost.[49]

The early papers reflect the classical education and Oxbridge bias of the members, with a particular fascination with Roman activity. Other areas of interest included monumental inscriptions, heraldry and parish registers, local folklore, farming practices and some pioneering papers on industrial history. The request from the Society of Antiquaries of London in 1886 to make recommendations for structures that should be scheduled resulted in the Society suggesting five such sites, three of which were scheduled.[50]

Members of the Society were involved in archaeological investigation from the beginning, and reports were published in *Transactions*. Amongst the most significant were the reports of Francis Haverfield's Cumberland Excavation Committee between 1894 and 1903.[51] In more recent times the creation of the Carlisle Archaeological Unit in July 1977, with a brief to excavate and publish threatened sites in the City and District of Carlisle,[52] and the establishment of the Cumbria and Lancashire Archaeological Unit in 1979 (which became the Lancaster University Archaeological Unit in 1986 and Oxford Archaeology North in 2001), alongside the creation of other commercial units, have resulted in a spate of articles in *Transactions*, reflecting the discoveries based on modern archaeological methodology.

Antiquarianism developed into a more systematic study of the history of the region with the creation of the County Record Offices in 1962 which enabled historians to use sources that had been hard to access previously, and the establishment of Lancaster University in 1964 which helped to train a new generation of historians and to provide an academic structure for the study of Cumbrian and North-West history. Despite the professionalisation of the historian, as Angus Winchester has commented, the 'antiquarian tradition has never died in the pages of *Transactions*' and the hand of the enthusiastic amateur can still be discerned.[53] This is particularly true in the area of industrial history, where, as shown in Chapter 7, *Transactions* has published papers by both amateur enthusiasts and professionals which has 'placed the Society in the forefront nationally'.[54]

The Society was an enlightened and emancipated organisation from the beginning. Women were members virtually from the start and soon contributed papers to *Transactions*. The first female contributor was Miss Mary Powley with a paper entitled, 'Past and Present among the Northern Fells'. This paper related in part to the difference in meaning between 'heath' and 'heaf' with regard to fell sheep. The Revd Simpson took issue with the writer's interpretation and, following a public discussion, his 'counter-view' was printed as an appendix to Miss Powley's paper. In it he wrote that he was sorry to find himself, 'in opposition to a lady, but I must venture to question the accuracy of Miss Powley's theory'.[55] Nothing daunted she wrote again in the next volume, 'The curfew bell in Cumberland and Westmorland', and again in 1880 with 'A plea for the old names',[56] a subject that has once again become fashionable.

Miss Powley was followed by Miss Fanny Bland of Paris in 1881 who communicated a family tree showing 'A link between two Westmorlands' about the Bland family link between our Westmorland and the Westmoreland in Virginia.[57] Mrs Henry Ware [Ellen King Goodwin], daughter of the Bishop of Carlisle, and second wife of Henry Ware, Bishop of Barrow-in-Furness and President of the Society, contributed a number of articles in *Transactions* as well as writing the supplement to the second edition of *The Old Church Plate in the Diocese of Carlisle* in the Extra Series in 1908.[58] Miss Mary Elizabeth Noble of Bampton, who, apart from her work on the parish registers of Bampton, Askham and Shap, published five papers on the Shap and Bampton region between 1903 and 1911.[59] Miss Mary Louisa Armitt produced an in-depth study of freeholders and fullers in Grasmere in 1908 (see Chapter 6).[60] Between the early 1920s and 1950s Mary Cicely Fair of Eskdale, a founder member of the Committee for Prehistoric Studies, was a prodigious author with 36 short papers in *Transactions* on many and varied subjects, mainly relating to the west of the county.[61] Mrs T. Hesketh [Elizabeth] Hodgson, a member of the original Cumberland Excavation Committee in 1894, provided many of the illustrations and drawings for the reports of that committee, as well as contributing a number of papers under her own name on excavations on the Roman Wall, and co-authoring papers together with her husband Thomas Hesketh Hodgson.[62] Their daughter, Katharine (Kate) Sophia Hodgson, went on to become a major stalwart of the Society (President 1948-51) and her first paper, co-authored with her mother, appeared in 1910.[63] She contributed many papers to *Transactions* and her final unpublished excavations appeared in 1975 in a paper jointly authored by G.G.S. Richardson and Clare Isobel Fell.[64] Clare Fell (President 1963-66) was described as the 'guiding light in Cumbrian archaeology for many years' in her obituary in *The Times*.[65] Her first paper in *Transactions* appeared in 1940, followed by many major contributions to our understanding of Cumbrian prehistory and, in particular, the Langdale stone-axe industry.[66]

Over nearly a century and a half, papers printed in *Transactions* have reflected the wide variety of interests of their authors. They have also demonstrated that background is no bar to serious historical study. Professional historians and archaeologists have rubbed shoulders with people whose voices, dedication and enthusiasm shine out from the pages of each volume. They range from Colour Sergeant Noakes, who wrote 'A short narrative of the services of the 55th, or Westmorland Regiment',[67] to James (Jim) Cherry, a chemist in the nuclear industry, his wife and son, who revolutionised our understanding of Cumbrian prehistory, based upon painstaking and meticulous fieldwork, with almost 50 papers over a period of as many years. The contributors' interests have been as varied as their backgrounds, from 'The mountain sheep; their origin and marking', by the Revd Thomas Ellwood,[68] via 'The regional roots of Feminism: a Victorian woman newspaper owner', by Peter

Lucas, a former journalist,[69] through to complex archaeological surveys, and significant contributions to national debates about the meaning of identity. The contributors have not all been local to Cumbria; indeed over recent years papers have been received and published from authors in Canada, United States of America, Australia, Spain, France, and Austria. The digitising of *Transactions* as one of the 150th Anniversary projects and its availability on the Society's website will have the effect of extending the reach of the journal still further. *Transactions* will endure as a mine of information on our heritage and as a monument to the endeavours of all its contributors since 1874.

Books*

Introduction

Chancellor Ferguson's vision of the Society as a publisher, not only of *Transactions* but also of volumes of historical significance, has been a cornerstone of Society activity. The first additional publication followed three years after the first volume of *Transactions* and since then some 155 books have been published. The quality of the work and its sheer quantity, all of it the product of the voluntary efforts of members of the Society, are impressive (fig.2.4).

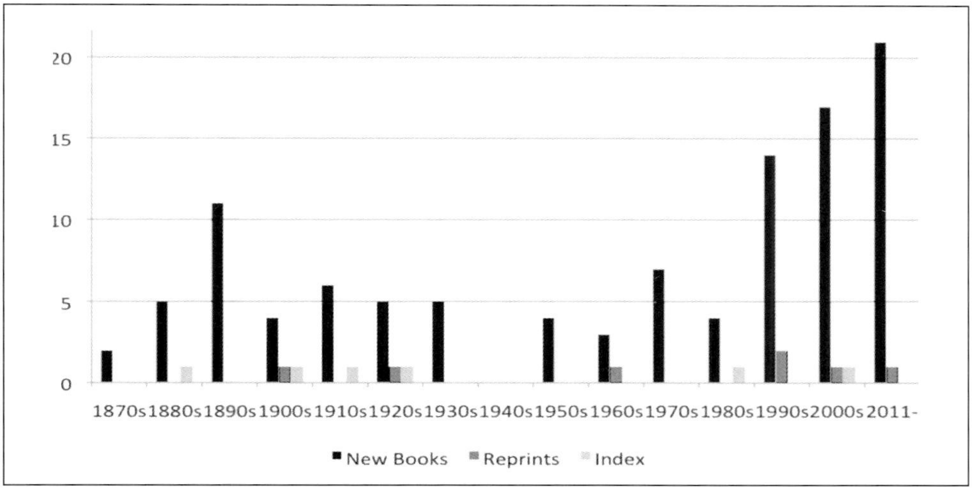

Fig. 2.4. The publication of volumes by decade (excluding Parish Registers)

* See Appendix 2 for full bibliographic entries for all Society publications. For reasons of brevity and ease of reference, series mentioned in this chapter are referred to as follows: ES = Extra Series, RS = Record Series, TS = Tract Series, Res. S = Research Series, CARR = Cumbria Archaeological Research Reports.

With the exception of the 1940s, the Society has published volumes in every decade, with two particular surges of activity, the 1890s and the period since the 1990s. The first volume in this prodigious programme of publication was Chancellor Ferguson's edition of Bishop Nicolson's *Miscellany Accounts of the Diocese of Carlile* (ES I) which appeared in 1877. In order to expedite its publication a liaison group was established which included Canons Prescott and Hodgson as representatives of the Dean and Chapter of Carlisle Cathedral. Progress towards publication was rapid and by December 1876 it was being reported that Thurnams (of Carlisle) had offered to undertake the publication 'at their own risk and expense'.[70] Editorial responsibility for this and all subsequent publications through to 1987 lay with the editors of *Transactions*.

The Society has created a number of series of publications, of which five are still active; the Parish Register series has been discontinued.

> *Extra Series* (from 1877) – the nature of volumes in this series has changed through time. It has always been a catch-all to include titles not covered by the other series. Initially this meant longer documentary records which were not Registers in the Record Series, but gradually came to include analytical works of historical content (and anything which did not fit naturally elsewhere). Recently, some books aimed at a more popular market have been published.
>
> *Tract Series* (from 1882) – this series was designed for shorter publications including documentary or archive publications. In recent years short books of historical content have also been published.[71]
>
> *Record Series* (originally known as the *Chartulary Series*) (from 1897) – initially this series was designed exclusively for ecclesiastical registers, but is now for the publication of primary texts.
>
> *Parish Register Series* (1912-73) – this series published transcriptions of parish registers. The original intention was to publish a volume every year.
>
> *Research Series* (from 1979) – this series publishes reports of substantial archaeological excavations.
>
> *Cumbria Archaeological Research Reports* (from 2009) – this series was created for archaeological reports which are too long for *Transactions* articles, and only require short print-runs.

Each Series was initially recognisable by its bindings. Both the Extra and Record Series were produced in hardback with reddish-brown and green covers respectively, and with volume numbers distinguished by the number of stars printed on the front cover and spine (fig. 2.5). In contrast, most volumes in the Tract Series were published in soft covers in a number of pastel colours but, as with volumes in the Parish Register Series, they were eventually published in grey.

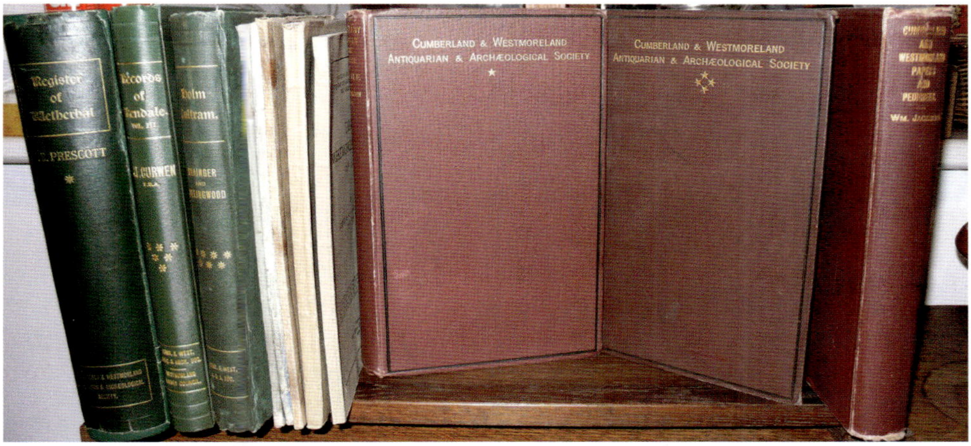

Fig. 2.5. Book covers of early publications: Record Series (green) and Extra Series (reddish-brown) with some early Tracts in between

Fig. 2.6. A variety of books published since 2007

With a few exceptions these colours remained in use until the 1980s. From 1988, with an increasing number of titles being published, many as softbacks, individual covers were re-designed to reflect the book's content and also to look attractive on the shelves of book sellers (fig. 2.6). The first volume to benefit from this new policy was an edited book of letters concerning Levens Hall (RS X) which was printed in both hardback and softback and incorporated on its cover a contemporary view of Levens. Since then it has become normal to publish volumes either as a hardback with a dustjacket or as a softback. The decision as to which binding is used is based on the significance of the book, its length and the likely effect of a higher retail price on expected sales. On occasions stiff covers, a useful alternative to conventional cloth bindings, have been used. Where the Society takes books from the Surtees Society or the British Record Society which still use their traditional format for covers, the practice has been to produce a special dust jacket for the Society's own copies.

In the early years the Society had little money available to finance this programme of publications, so most volumes were sold through subscription. Mrs Ware's 1908 second edition of R.S. Ferguson's book on church plate (ES III) provides evidence of the limited money available. The edition consisted of 250 copies of the new work bound with sheets of the original edition that Thurnams had found in their warehouse. An additional 50 sets of the new material were printed and bound in paper for the benefit of those who already had the first edition. All of this was managed by Thurnams and the work was sold by subscription.[72] As a consequence of this and subsequent experiences the Record Publication Fund was established in 1912 (see Chapter 1).

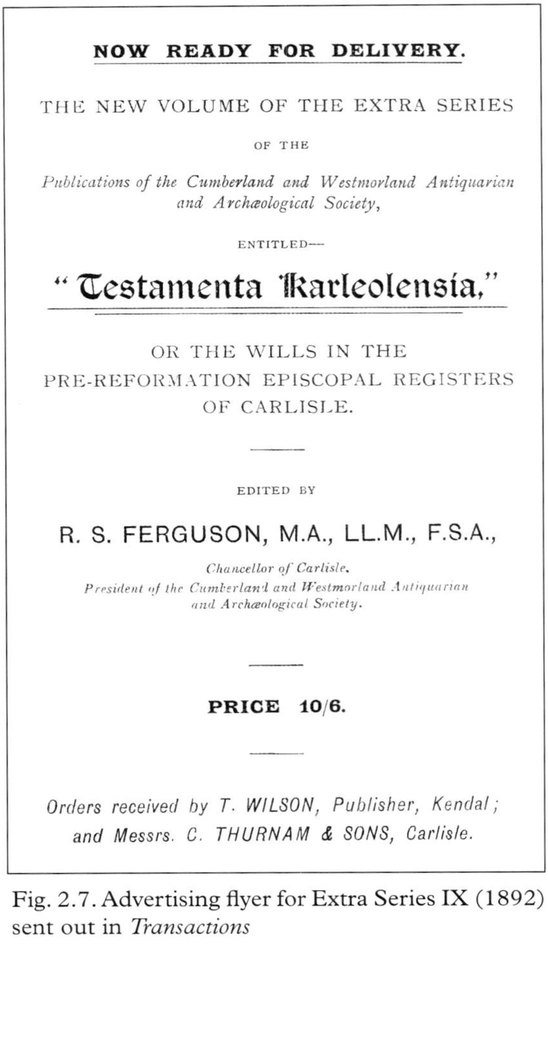
NOW READY FOR DELIVERY.

THE NEW VOLUME OF THE EXTRA SERIES

OF THE

Publications of the Cumberland and Westmorland Antiquarian and Archæological Society,

ENTITLED—

"Testamenta Karleolensia,"

OR THE WILLS IN THE PRE-REFORMATION EPISCOPAL REGISTERS OF CARLISLE.

EDITED BY

R. S. FERGUSON, M.A., LL.M., F.S.A.,

Chancellor of Carlisle,
President of the Cumberland and Westmorland Antiquarian and Archæological Society.

PRICE 10/6.

Orders received by T. WILSON, Publisher, Kendal; and Messrs. C. THURNAM & SONS, Carlisle.

Fig. 2.7. Advertising flyer for Extra Series IX (1892) sent out in *Transactions*

Charles Thurnam printed the first four Extra Series volumes (1877-87). Volumes V (1891) to X (1894) were published by Titus Wilson of Kendal in conjunction with Thurnams (fig. 2.7). However, Thurnams dropped out of the picture with Volume XI (1899).[73] At this time London firms also appear alongside the local publishers: Bernard Quaritch of Piccadilly,[74] George Bell,[75] Elliot Stock,[76] and Bemrose & Sons.[77] These businesses combined bookselling and publishing and their participation gave the Society's books a national outlet.

After the First World War Titus Wilson printed most volumes and the Society acted as its own publisher, although from 1928 the Parish Register section used the Herald Company in Penrith as their printers. As there was no discernible cost-saving this was probably for the convenience of Col. Haswell, who took over as chair of the committee about that time, and who lived in Penrith. As with the volumes of records published in the Record and Extra Series, the publication of parish registers was financed through subscriptions. The Record Publication Fund went on to support not only the Society's publications of records, but also non-Society publications such as *Holker Muniments*,[78] and *Jacobite Risings*.[79] This fund continued up to 1971.[80]

Another method of financing publications was through joint publications with like-minded organisations. The first of these was *The Episcopal Registers of Carlisle* (RS II) which was published jointly with the Canterbury and York Society. This was followed by *The Place-names of Cumberland and Westmorland* in 1915 (ES XIV) which was published in collaboration with the University of Manchester,[81] and, in the same year, *the Register of the Priory of St Bees* (RS III) which was published in association with the Surtees Society. The advantage for the Society of such arrangements was that the Society bought an agreed number of volumes from the partner organisation, and their sale covered the Society's limited financial outlay. Joint publications have remained a part of the publications programme ever since.

With the exception of the volumes of parish registers, the concept of subscription died out during the later 1940s and 1950s, no doubt abetted by the diminishing number of annual subscribers. However, subscriptions were reinstated for the two volumes on Cumberland and Westmorland families and heraldry (ES XXI and ES XXIII) published in 1975 and 1978. Both books were printed in *de luxe* versions, in addition to the normal hardbacks. The Westmorland and Lonsdale volume also carries the imprint of the Lake District Museum Trust as partners in the publication.

With the disappearance of Titus Wilson & Son during the 1990s, the Society had to seek new printers for all its publications. Sutton's, Henry Ling of Dorchester and the Athenaeum Press of Gateshead were all engaged at different times. By 2003 the re-formed Titus Wilson & Son had again become the printer of choice, not only because of the quality of their work, but also because of the help provided by staff in getting books ready for printing. The use of Badger Press in Bowness-on-Windermere for the more recent CARR series was a decision reached after discussion with Titus Wilson, who did not feel comfortable with the short print runs required for the series.

1877-1918

By the end of the First World War, four Series were already in existence. An early priority was the desire to publish the county's documentary record: municipal charters, cartularies and early antiquarians' histories. Alongside such volumes were some concerned with genealogy and the built environment. In 1912 the first transcript of parish registers was published.

Two of the most significant collections of municipal records, those of Carlisle and of Kendal, were amongst the earliest volumes in the Extra Series (ES IV and ES VII). The Record Series began with editions of cartularies from Wetheral and Carlisle (RS I and RS III). The special problems associated with this type of publication are illustrated by the difficulties in producing the Carlisle volume.[82] The enterprise was proposed in 1905 and Part 1 was issued in September 1906. The transcriptions were sent to press periodically but with increasing delays due to the poor health of the editor, W.N. Thompson. Part 2 eventually appeared in 1908. The intention was for the whole register to be completed in two volumes and for there to be an introduction and index. Thompson died in 1911, having transcribed only about one-third of Part 3. The original register was then taken temporarily to the Public Record Office where the editorial work was completed, and an introduction written by T.F. Tout. The final part finally appeared in 1913, jointly published with the Canterbury and York Society. The creation of the Record Publications Fund in 1912 with a minimum annual subscription of 10s. 6d., 'for which subscribers shall receive the volumes issued by the assistance of the Fund, up to the amount of their subscriptions',[83] attracted eight or nine subscribers annually, but as volumes appeared very intermittently, the inaugural subscribers had to wait until 1915 for the next volume, *The Register of the Priory of St Bees* (RS III).

The ten volumes in the Tract Series prior to 1918 focused on publishing the writings of antiquarians. These included *Fleming's Description of Westmorland* (1882) (TS I), *John Denton's Account of Cumberland* (1887) (TS II), and Todd's *City and Diocese of Carlisle* (1891) (TS V). The next two titles, *Hutton's Beetham Repository* (1906) (TS VII) and *Elizabethan Keswick* (1912) (TS VIII), were essentially hefty transcripts of records, more akin to volumes published in the Record Series. In 1907 the Society made a rare foray into the realm of dialect (TS IX): its coverage of Furness in that volume was also an early example of the recognition of the peninsula as part of the territory covered by the Society.

Genealogy was represented by two volumes published in 1891 and 1892 (ES V and ES VI). Important studies of architecture and artefacts in the environment began during the 1890s, with books on manorial halls and early sculptured stones (ES VII and ES IX). These were followed by a volume on castles and fortified towers in 1913 (ES XIII). By 1918 14 volumes had been published in the Extra Series and three in the Record Series.

The idea for publishing parish registers came with the creation of a sub-committee (Canon Bower, H.S. Cowper and W.G. Collingwood) in 1905 to 'consider the means for transcribing and printing Parish Registers in the Diocese of Carlisle'.[84] In April 1906 it was agreed to adopt the Phillimore scheme of register publication (fig. 2.8), which was confined to marriage registers, and Major Ferguson accepted the post of the Society's series editor.[85] The following year it was reported that four registers had been transcribed and 12 more were in hand for publication by Phillimore. Four further volumes had been transcribed for separate publication.[86] Ferguson resigned the following year and was replaced by C.W. Ruston-Harrison who continued as series editor until 1920.[87]

The first two volumes appeared under the Phillimore imprint although it is clear that they were a joint enterprise: 'These volumes are issued under the patronage of the Cumberland and Westmorland Antiquarian and Archaeological Society, who have undertaken to subscribe for 30 copies of each volume – a subsidy which, it is hoped will enable continuous and steady progress to be made with the work'.[88] These two volumes contained six registers in total, all bar one transcribed by members of the Society.[89] There is no indication that the Society advertised its copies

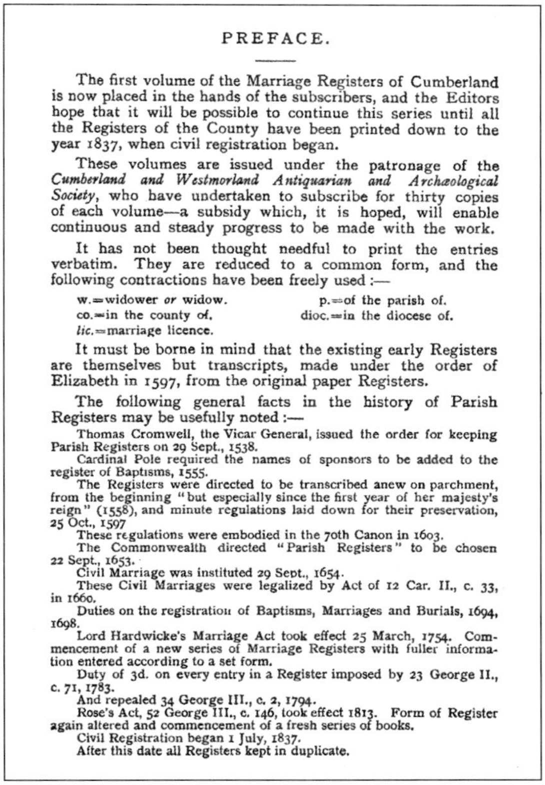
PREFACE.

The first volume of the Marriage Registers of Cumberland is now placed in the hands of the subscribers, and the Editors hope that it will be possible to continue this series until all the Registers of the County have been printed down to the year 1837, when civil registration began.

These volumes are issued under the patronage of the *Cumberland and Westmorland Antiquarian and Archæological Society*, who have undertaken to subscribe for thirty copies of each volume—a subsidy which, it is hoped, will enable continuous and steady progress to be made with the work.

It has not been thought needful to print the entries verbatim. They are reduced to a common form, and the following contractions have been freely used :—

w.=widower *or* widow. p.=of the parish of.
co.=in the county of. dioc.=in the diocese of.
lic.=marriage licence.

It must be borne in mind that the existing early Registers are themselves but transcripts, made under the order of Elizabeth in 1597, from the original paper Registers.

The following general facts in the history of Parish Registers may be usefully noted :—

Thomas Cromwell, the Vicar General, issued the order for keeping Parish Registers on 29 Sept., 1538.

Cardinal Pole required the names of sponsors to be added to the register of Baptisms, 1555.

The Registers were directed to be transcribed anew on parchment, from the beginning "but especially since the first year of her majesty's reign" (1558), and minute regulations laid down for their preservation, 25 Oct., 1597

These regulations were embodied in the 70th Canon in 1603.

The Commonwealth directed "Parish Registers" to be chosen 22 Sept., 1653.

Civil Marriage was instituted 29 Sept., 1654.

These Civil Marriages were legalized by Act of 12 Car. II., c. 33, in 1660.

Duties on the registration of Baptisms, Marriages and Burials, 1694, 1698.

Lord Hardwicke's Marriage Act took effect 25 March, 1754. Commencement of a new series of Marriage Registers with fuller information entered according to a set form.

Duty of 3d. on every entry in a Register imposed by 23 George II., c. 71, 1783.

And repealed 34 George III., c. 2, 1794.

Rose's Act, 52 George III., c. 146, took effect 1813. Form of Register again altered and commencement of a fresh series of books.

Civil Registration began 1 July, 1837.

After this date all Registers kept in duplicate.

Fig. 2.8. Preface to W.P.W. Phillimore and C.W. Ruston-Harrison (eds.), *Cumberland Marriage Registers, Marriages, Vol.1* (London, 1910) covering marriages at Workington and Moresby to 1812 with appendices to 1837

for sale generally and, given how the later productions were marketed, it is likely that their copies were mainly taken up by subscribers. Receipts for both volumes are listed in the General Accounts for 1910-11 and 1912-13.[90]

Only two volumes of Phillimore's Cumberland series, published with support from the Society, ever appeared. In 1911 the Society set up its own Parish Register Section, and began its own Parish Register Series the following year under Ruston-Harrison. At the Spring 1912 meeting of the Society it was agreed that volumes would be published alternately between the two counties, that the transcripts would be based on the Registers themselves with additions from the Bishops' Transcripts, and that only ten additional copies would be printed beyond those committed to by subscribers.[91] The series rapidly became very dependent upon a small number of enthusiasts who often transcribed registers for parishes in areas where they lived. Six parish registers had been transcribed and printed by 1918, four being the work of Henry Brierley who continued to edit volumes through to 1933, concentrating on parishes around Penrith and in the Eden valley. Col. John Francis Haswell prepared even more editions for publication between 1925 and 1945 (see Chapter 1 and Appendix 2).

Financing these volumes was always a battle. With 53 subscribers paying 10s. 6d. *per annum*, printing costs were not covered and the committee appealed for additional subscribers. In fact some volumes appear to have been sponsored by individuals. The cost of the volumes on Milburn appears to have been borne by its editor since it was noted in 1914 that they 'would be issued freely this year to members of the Section as the gift of Mr Henry Brierley'.[92] At the same meeting Canon Rawnsley offered to pay for the printing of the Crosthwaite registers, though these did not start to appear until 1929. To encourage sales the volumes were listed in the List of Publications printed annually at the end of *Transactions*.

The 1890s was the most prolific decade for publishing in this era, almost certainly due to the influence of the Society's editor, Chancellor Ferguson, who authored five and edited two of the 11 volumes published during the decade (fig.2.4). The rate of publishing was not maintained but surprisingly publishing continued during the First World War, perhaps because the Society's authors were well above the age of conscription. Six books were published between 1915 and 1918, three of them being parish register volumes. That the volume which was due to be published in 1916 failed to materialise was perhaps a consequence of war. Expenses increased, with the 1918 parish register volume (Skelton) costing £114, compared with £54 for Barton the previous year.[93] In consequence the retail cost of volumes increased from 10s. 6d. to one guinea.

The authors of many of the early volumes in the various series were almost all drawn from a small number of Society members, many of them being either the founders or distinguished and prolific contributors to *Transactions*:

R.S. Ferguson, Dr M.W. Taylor, W.G. Collingwood, Revd W.S. Calverley, J.F. Curwen and H. Brierley.

1918-1945

The interwar years saw the Society continue to focus its publishing efforts on the printing of documentary sources and parish registers with the Record Series broadening its initial remit of monastic cartularies to encompass other significant collections of documents, some of these being compilations based on material originally collected for the ill-fated Victoria County History for Westmorland (see Chapter 1). During the 1920s it published three volumes of records of Kendal (RS IV, V, VI). These were followed by Curwen's own edition of the *Later Records of North Westmorland* (1932) (RS VIII) which was published in collaboration with Westmorland County Council. Another publication at this time was a compilation of ecclesiastical records associated with Holm Cultram (RS VII). Shorter volumes of records related to individuals such as Sir Daniel Fleming and Edward Wilson were published in the Tract Series (TS XI and XII). Henry Brierley and J.F. Haswell continued to dominate contributions to the Parish Registers Series with the parishes ranging much more widely than previously to include several in Westmorland and others in more distant parts of Cumberland such as Millom and Lamplugh. The extensive registers of Crosthwaite parish were transcribed and a start was made on those of Penrith. Although volumes appeared regularly throughout the interwar years, subscription income of around £45 *per annum* did not always cover the cost of the publications as in the case of both 1932 (Cliburn) and 1925 (Millom). W. Lewthwaite covered the deficit for Millom volume with a donation of £48 16s., a strategy also evident a couple of years earlier when W.E. Nanson subsidised the Brough Registers to the tune of £50.[94] During the 1930s the Society helped by making regular grants out of the General Fund.

At this time the Extra Series included histories of specific places such as Gosforth and Gilsland (ES XV and XVI), as well as the *Index to Nicholson and Burn's History and Antiquities of Westmorland and Cumberland* (1934) (ES XVII) and the pioneering *An Armorial for Cumberland* (1937) (ES XVIII).

During the Second World War publishing ceased except for *Transactions* itself and the Parish Register Series which saw six more volumes, all edited by J.S. Haswell.

1945–1988

It took some time after the end of the Second World War for book publishing to get started again. The Parish Register Series continued with a volume on

Holm Cultram in 1948 but, despite the committee's expansion, the Section was no longer able to maintain an annual publication programme. The project was not helped by the withdrawal of the indefatigable J.F. Haswell. Volumes continued to appear, but sporadically and with widening intervals. Eight volumes appeared between 1948 and 1968. The final transcriber was W.B. Stout, who lived at Seascale and edited registers from Whitehaven (1964) and St Bees (1968).

An attempt was made to revive the Parish Register Section during the 1970s by its secretary Sheila MacPherson, who was also the Kendal archivist. However, despite the completion of the transcription of registers for Grasmere, Morland and Muncaster, these were never published as the annual subscription of one guinea did not cover the projected printing costs. A proposal to raise the subscription to around £5 to £6 did not find favour and in 1990 a decision was taken to terminate the series. This did not reflect unwillingness on the part of the Society to publish registers, however, since henceforward it was agreed that parish registers would be handled in the same way as any other additional publication.[95] The Society had already given a commitment to publish the registers of Burton-in-Kendal which appeared in the Record Series in 2004 (RS XVIII), heavily subsidised. Two problems beset the continuation of Parish Register publications. One was their economic viability; the second concerned the academic standards which the Society set for its publications. There was no shortage of transcripts of registers available, many deposited in record offices, but as the Society required that anything it published be thoroughly checked this demanded more editorial time than was available.

By the end of the Series the distribution of parishes, although reflecting the interests of the transcribers, was broadly county-wide with concentrations in the Eden Valley/Penrith area and on the Solway plain. The west of the county was on the whole poorly served and there are no registers published for Carlisle and its region.[96]

Volumes in the other series began to be published again from 1951. In that year there were pamphlets on the Furness Railway and early newspapers (TS XII and XIV) which absorbed the subscriptions from the unsuccessful Records and Publications committee created in 1947 (see Chapter 1). A further volume of records, this time from the Naworth estate, was published in the Record Series (RS IX) in 1959. Volumes began to be published again in the Extra Series from 1963. The first was an antiquarian text, part of the manuscript collection compiled by Thomas Machell (ES XIX) which covered the Kendal area.

Generally speaking fewer transcriptions of documents were published. The Tract Series moved away from publishing records to an eclectic mix of useful, but small-scale, volumes of historical interest. Some were narrative histories such as *A Short History of the Manor of Witherslack* (1971) (TS XVIII), the forerunner of a number of subsequent histories of places. Others were bibliographical, such as a handlist of newspapers. The publication of graveyard tomb inscriptions in St James, Whitehaven (1963) (TS XVI) and Ulverston (1973) (TS XIX)), a useful parallel to Parish Register publications, did not lead to any further such publications by the Society; graveyard transcripts generally remain as 'grey' literature in church vestries and record offices. This period also saw the publication of the two reference works on families and heraldry already mentioned.

From the 1960s the Society published a range of archaeological books which began with a highly technical study of the building inscriptions from the Wall (ES XX). However, excavation reports did not figure significantly in the additional publications of the Society until 1979 since previously excavation reports had been published in *Transactions* even when they exceeded the page lengths that would now be regarded as acceptable. In 1966, the year of the Society's centenary, an exploration of the Roman fort at Maryport (ES XXII) was published. There appears to have been some difficulties in seeing this volume through to publication because of the novel publishing demands posed by the scale of excavation reports in a new era of archaeological investigation.[97] Consequently the Society initiated a new series designed to better enable the publication of archaeological reports. This is known as the Research Series and the first two volumes, *Romans in North-West England* (1979) (Res S I) and *Prehistoric Habitation Sites on the Limestone Uplands of Eastern Cumbria* (1987) (Res S II), contained respectively the reports on Tim Potter's important series of excavations at Watercrook, Ravenglass and Bowness, and the Cherrys' pioneering fieldwork on the fells around Orton. The latter was published in A4 format which has become the preferred size for archaeological reports since it maximises the possibilities for illustrations.

1988-2015

By 1988 the Society accepted that its publications programme demanded more resources than had previously been available. In that year a larger Editorial Committee was created, and for the first time its members were listed in *Transactions*, and the Society's publications programme rapidly expanded. In 1993 an Honorary Editor of the Research Series (Mike McCarthy) was appointed, and in 1995 this appointment was followed by an Honorary Editor of the Extra Series (P.W. Edwards). The reconstitution of this committee in 1994 meant that the Editor of *Transactions* ceased to be responsible for other publications, and in 1995 Council approved the appointment of a General Editor to oversee the publishing of the additional volumes. The first Honorary General Editor, J.P.D. (Pat) Ball, was appointed in 1997. Since then Dr Jean Turnbull and Professor Colin Richards have successively held that post. In 2007 the Editorial Committee was renamed the Publications Committee which better reflected its new, much wider, remit.

The consequence of this new structure was a surge in publishing activity (fig. 2.4), starting with an important contribution to the developing discipline of industrial history, Wood's publication on the coal industry (ES XXIV). Two other particularly important books have been Henry Summerson's background to the excavations taking place in Carlisle during the 1980s (ES XXV), commissioned by English Heritage, and the very popular *The Vikings and Victorian Lakeland* by Matthew Townend (2009) (ES XXXIV) which brought together both Collingwoods, the Vikings, and the Lake District, all set within a cultural history. Its publication resulted in successful study visit to Iceland in 2012 organised by the Society which followed in the footsteps of W.G. Collingwood who had toured there in 1897 (fig.2.9).[98]

These publications reflect the developing status and profile of the Society's publishing arm with the Society increasingly becoming the publisher of choice for academic books related to Cumbria. Since 1988 the Society has published books jointly not only with English Heritage, but also with the Surtees Society (RS XI, XVI, XXII), the Society of Antiquaries of Newcastle upon Tyne (ES XXXVII), the British Record Society (RS XIX), and the Senhouse Museum Trust (ES XXVII and XXXI). The latter two were initiated and funded by the Senhouse Museum Trust and published for them by the Society with both parties benefitting from the arrangement. Significant for the Society was that the two books were *festschrifts* dedicated to Mike Jarrett, one of the leaders of the Society's 1966 excavations at Maryport, and to Richard Bellhouse, a Vice-President of the Society. Other *festschrifts* for prominent scholars involved with the Society have been *Studies in Northern Prehistory* (2007) (ES XXXIII) in honour of Clare Fell, and *North-West England from the Romans to the Tudors: Essays in Memory of John Macnair Todd* (2014) (ES XLI).

Ecclesiastical history has been particularly well served by the Society in recent years. Dr Lawrence Butler's edition of *The Cumbrian Parishes 1714-1725 from Bishop Gastrell's Notitia* (1998) (RS XII) finished a project begun in 1845.[99] The Bishop (of Chester's) extensive notes included information on all his parishes within his Archdeaconry of Richmond. Chetham Society volumes had covered the Lancashire parishes; the Welsh parishes had been published in 1906 in *Cheshire Sheaf.* Dr Butler later completed the project with a volume on the Yorkshire parishes which were in deaneries in the southern part of Cumbria.[100] In 2011 he supplemented this publication with *The Church Notes of Sir Stephen Glynne for Cumbria (1833-1872)* (ES XXXVI). Since then the Society has published R.B. Wordsworth's edition of *The Cockermouth Congregational Church Book (1651-c.1765)* (2012) (RS

Fig. 2.9. The Collingwood pilgrimage group outside Borg y Myrum church, Iceland. The inset shows Teresa Smith, W.G. Collingwood's granddaughter, pointing out her father, Robin Collingwood, who was one of the models used by W.G.C. for this painting in 1898 of 'Christ blessing the little children', now over the altar. *(photograph courtesy of Mike and Kate Lea)*

XX1), David Weston's history of Rose Castle (ES XL) and Jane Platt's edition of Chancellor Walter Fletcher's Diocesan Book (RS XXII).

The Society's series, like *Transactions*, has also attracted contributions from scholars associated with universities across the country, such as Professor Richard Sharpe's volume on the Normans in Cumbria (TS XXI) and Professor Peter Roebuck's study of the entrepreneurial Parker family (ES XLIII). The

Society has also benefitted from the academic output and editorial skills of Lancaster University staff such as Professors Angus Winchester (ES XXVII, RS XVI and XX), Michael Mullett (TS XXIV and 25), Keith Stringer (ES XXXV and XLI) and an increasing number of postgraduates trained at that institution such as Dr John Todd (RS XI and TS XX), Dr Bill Shannon (TS XXII), Roger Smalley (ES XXXVIII) and Dr Jane Platt (RS XXII). These years also saw titles on a wide variety of subjects including stained glass (ES XXVI), fortified buildings (ES XXIX), clay dabbins (ES XXX), medieval grave slabs (ES XXXII) and the Websters, a Kendal architectural firm (RS XVII). Publication of the first three of these volumes was the culmination of research projects funded in part by the Society, and the last volume was appropriately launched in Kendal Town Hall in a room designed by the Websters.

The Society has also sought to reach new audiences with the reproduction of two eighteenth-century maps, by Thomas Jefferys and by Thomas Donald, first produced in 1770 and 1774. The initiative had come from the editor Paul Hindle, and their popularity has led to both maps being reprinted (RS XIV and XV). Two recent books designed to reach a more general audience, have been a history of Carlisle (ES XXXV), which was sponsored by English Heritage to highlight the results of many years' excavation in the city, and a book on Cumbria's links to the Arctic (ES XXXIX).

The operation of archaeological units in the region during the 1990s provided the Society with new publishing challenges and opportunities. In 1990 and 1991 major publications reported on the Carlisle Archaeology Unit's excavation of part of the Blackfriars monastery and earlier Roman and Anglian remains in its Blackfriars Street excavation (RES S IV) and on the excavation on the waterlogged site at Castle Street (RES S V). For the first time microfiche was included as part of Society publications. These were followed during the 1990s with reports on excavations of the Roman forts at Bewcastle, Old Penrith and Hardknott (RES S VI, VII, IX).

Other volumes in the series owed a great deal to the vision of David Sherlock, Inspector of Ancient Monuments with English Heritage, and to the historian Henry Summerson. It was David Sherlock who commissioned the two multi-disciplinary studies on Brougham Castle and Lanercost Priory (RES S VIII and X). These combined a detailed fabric survey and analysis, with an exhaustive history including a survey of the pictorial records. The format of these books has become a model for all further work on the fabric of monuments.

The Research Series remained dormant between 2000 and 2013 but resumed with the publication of *Draining the Cumbrian Landscape* by Ted and Stella Davis (2013) (RES S XI) which combines a narrative text with a comprehensive gazetteer of tile-making sites on a CD-ROM. This is the first time this publishing device has been used by the Society.

In 2007 the Society embarked upon a new Series, the Cumbria Archaeological Research Reports (CARR). This series was conceived as filling a gap between reports in *Transactions* and full-scale research volumes. In earlier years such reports would have gone into *Transactions*, which is one reason for the low levels of extra publication in the inter-war years. As it was envisaged that these reports would have low sales and limited print runs, digital technology was considered suitable. Badger Press in Bowness-on-Windermere had the relevant expertise and has designed and printed all the volumes. The immediate impetus was the publication of the work of the late Barri Jones on Burgh-by-Sands (CARR 1), under the general editorship of Ben Edwards, but subsequent volumes have been overseen by Marion McClintock. The aim has been to produce an annual volume publishing the result of middle-level excavations which would remain unpublished otherwise.

Conclusion

The Society has served the history and archaeology of Cumbria well over the years and in many ways, but it is likely that the Society's publication programme will prove to be its most lasting legacy. For most of the Society's 150 years, interesting ideas and new research have been made available, not only to members, but to an interested public in Cumbria and beyond. Both *Transactions* and the various series of publications have, in different ways, contributed to placing the county on the historical and archaeological map.

In the early years *Transactions* provided one of the few opportunities for an emerging body of researchers to publish material related to the region. Although the nature of the contributions has altered as the disciplines of history and archaeology have changed, and some early interests such as folklore and genealogy have largely disappeared, the significance of the journal has increased. Some of the Society's major contributions and the developing academic strength of *Transactions* over the years were identified by the contributors whom the President, Professor Geoffrey Martin, invited to contribute to 'A Retrospective' in the 100th volume of the New Series in the year 2000,[101] As Professor David Shotter commented in his overview of the Society's contribution to understanding the Roman period: 'the eighteenth and nineteenth centuries were the period of the antiquarian in the study of Roman Britain, the twentieth has belonged to archaeologists, historians and, increasingly, to applied scientists'.[102] These developments have all been reflected in the pages of *Transactions* and have helped to meet the challenge represented by the increasing number of other journals willing to publish, either in paper format or online, articles about the history and archaeology of our region. *Transactions* may no longer be the only journal for researchers of the history and archaeology of Cumbria to consult, but no serious study of Cumbria can be written without it. It is in this context that the 150th Anniversary project to digitise the entire contents of *Transactions* and to make them available online is so important.

One of the strengths of *Transactions* has been that so many of its editors have occupied that office, either solely or as joint editors, for a considerable number of years. This has ensured a continuity of style and a close working relationship with the printers, Titus Wilson & Son. Throughout its lifetime editors have ensured that a liberal approach has been taken with regard to the inclusion of papers for publication, both in terms of welcoming papers from both amateurs and professionals and also in accommodating to changing enthusiasms and interests. Dr John Marshall in his contribution to 'The Retrospective' noted the 'general innovative tendency [which] has certainly been visible in the Society's publishing history', and its specific contribution to 'the industrial archaeology and history of iron making', where it has been in the forefront nationally.[103]

The Society has developed the series of additional publications which, with 132 volumes of *Transactions*, have made available documents that would otherwise be difficult to access, have engaged with Cumbria's past from prehistory to the twentieth century, and have incorporated in the process almost every sub-discipline in the study of history and archaeology. Those contributing to its success have included archaeologists and historians, academics and students, clerics, medics and members of other professions or none. The authors have drawn on their knowledge, expertise and affection for the history of what is today Cumbria, constantly expanding and challenging our understanding of its past. Throughout its 150-year history, its publication programme has ensured that both the county and the Society have been placed firmly on the map. This volume is the 156th to be published by the Society. It will certainly not be the last.

Notes and References

1 CAS (Carlisle), DSO/1/1; J.F. Curwen, 'Notes on the early history of the society', *CW2*, 33 (1933), 1.

2 *CW1*, 3 (1878), xv-xvi. All references to pages in *Transactions* without an article title are to reports of 'Excursions and Proceedings'.

3 On 15 July 1897, when Titus Wilson was re-elected as Secretary, the President remarked that it was the thirtieth year he had been elected to that office and the following year it was said that he had rendered service for 31 years. However, he is not shown on the list of founder members and he does not actually appear in the lists of members published in *Transactions* until 1904 when he is shown as having joined in 1866. *CW1*, 15 (1899), 107, 333; *CW2*, 4 (1904), 374.

4 Curwen, 'Notes on the early history', 2.

5 DSO/1/1.
6 DSO/1/1; DSO/1/4; *CW1*, 15 (1899), 332-33; *CW2*, 12 (1912), 406.
7 'In Memoriam', *CW2*, 17 (1917), 265-66; J.F. Curwen, *Kirkbie-Kendall* (Kendal, 1900), 76-77.
8 1841 Census.
9 *Titus Wilson Computer Typesetting Guide* (Kendal, n.d.), 3.
10 *Westmorland Gazette*, 27 Oct. 1917. He was buried in Parkside Cemetery, Kendal on 27 Oct. 1917.
11 *CW2*, 17 (1917), 266.
12 *CW1*, 6 (1883), 86-90; *CW1*, 7 (1884), 90-95; *CW2*, 8 (1908), 107, reporting on his finds in 1890.
13 DSO/1/4; *CW2*, xxvii, 242.
14 DSO/1/5.
15 'In Memoriam', *CW2*, 75 (1975), 384.
16 'In Memoriam', *CW2*, 35 (1935), 291.
17 *Westmorland Gazette*, 10 Oct. 1975.
18 *CW2*, 64 (1964), 395.
19 DSO/1/1.
20 Curwen, 'Notes on the early history', 2; DSO/1/1; *CW1*, 3 (1878), xxi. Inside a volume bound as Volume 1, printed by Titus Wilson in 1874, with the Editors shown as 'The Rev. Canon Simpson LL.D. 1866-7 and Richard S. Ferguson M.A. LL.M. 1868-73', the author found a second frontispiece marked 'No. 1 – For the Year 1866-7 printed by T. Wilson in 1870', followed by a contents page listing eight papers (consisting of 80 pages). What appears to have happened is that the first part of volume 1 was the portion announced by Titus Wilson, consisting of 80 pages and that in 1873 these pages were bound with the second part to form what we now know as Volume 1 since, at the meeting on 21 June 1871, 'The Publication of the Transactions was ordered to be gone on with', i.e. the second part of Volume 1. The two parts of Volume 1 were printed by Titus Wilson at 28 Highgate, Kendal and were clearly well received because, at the Council meeting on 11 Dec. 1876, it was resolved that 100 copies of Part I be reprinted, 'the Editor to carefully revise before going to press'.
21 G.H. Martin, 'A Retrospective', *CW2*, 100 (2000), 261.
22 *CW1*, 2 (1876), title page detail.
23 Martin, 'A Retrospective', 261.
24 *CW1*, 8 (1886), 309.
25 Martin, 'A Retrospective', 261.
26 DSO/1/5.
27 DSO/1/5.
28 I am most grateful to Raymond Fielding, former Printing Director at Titus Wilson, for his first-hand knowledge of this change.
29 *CW2*, 9 (1909), 310.
30 See *CW2*, 51 (1951), 205-06; *CW2*, 52 (1952), 194; *CW2*, 58 (1958), 191; *Newsletter*, 17 (Autumn 1992).
31 DSO/1/5.
32 References to paper issues: *CW2*, 19 (1919), 162; 52 (1952), 194ff.; DSO/1/4; *CW2*, 41 (1941), 213; *CW2*, 43 (1943), 234; *CW2*, 43 (1943), 199.
33 Martin, 'A Retrospective', 262.
34 See Appendix 2 for full bibliographic details of these Indexes.
35 Cumbria Past, www.cumbriapast.com. Public access, but with reduced search facilities and no access to the last ten years of *Transactions*, is also available through the Archaeology Data Service, http://archaeologydataservice.ac.uk/archives/view/cumberland/.

36 *Archives*, XXII, 94 (April 1995); XXII, 96 (April 1997).
37 DSO1/1; *CW1*, 1 (1874), frontispiece; *CW2*, 33 (1933), 2.
38 'In Memoriam', *CW1*, 8 (1886), 534.
39 *CW1*, 3 (1878), 16.
40 *CW1*, 6 (1883), 507-08.
41 *CW2*, 9 (1909), 326; *Crockford's Clerical Directory* (1932), 523. A number of letters had passed between W.G. Collingwood, as Editor, and H.B. Greenop, a member of the Society and a clergyman from Workington, and a contributor of a paper for *Transactions*. Greenop had challenged the power of the Editor to omit a certain illustration, which he deemed necessary in an article written by him. This led to the special meeting in 1908 at which Council supported their editor. Greenop's article was not subsequently published in *Transactions*.
42 'In Memoriam', *CW2*, 33 (1933), 308-10.
43 *CW2*, 37 (1937), 230.
44 'In Memoriam', *CW2*, 43 (1943), 211-14.
45 'In Memoriam', *CW2*, 44 (1944), 166-68.
46 'In Memoriam', *CW3*, 14 (2014), 5-7.
47 *CW1*, 6 (1883), 507-08; *CW2*, 2 (1876), 394.
48 C. Roy Hudleston and R.S. Boumphrey, *Cumberland Families and Heraldry* (CWAAS, Extra series XXIII, 1978), 71.
49 Archibald Sparke, *Catalogue-Index to the Transactions 1866-1900* (Kendal, 1901).
50 *CW1*, 9 (1888), 154-56; *CW1*, 10 (1889), 271-74.
51 'In Memoriam', *CW2*, 20 (1920), 255-57.
52 M.R. McCarthy, 'Carlisle Archaeological Unit 1977-79', *CW2*, 80 (1980), 164-65.
53 A.J.L. Winchester, 'The medieval and early-modern period', *CW2*, 100 (2000), 269.
54 J.D. Marshall, 'Industrial history and the modern period', *CW2*, 100 (2000), 271.
55 *CW1*, 2 (1876), 171-86; 354-74, quotation 372. Credited as 'Miss Powley'. Women authors' first names, even initials, were rarely stated in the early editions of *Transactions*.
56 *CW1*, 3 (1878), 127-33; *CW1*, 4 (1880), 19-22, 280-84; *CW1*, 6 (1883), 272-79. Described as the 'Cumberland Poetess', Mary Powley was born in Langwathby, baptised there 4 July 1811, the daughter of John Powley and Mary née Hobson. She wrote a number of valuable papers on Cumberland folklore and dialect, including *Echoes of Old Cumberland* (Carlisle, 1875). A spinster, described in the 1881 Langwathby Census as an 'annuitant from bank shares', living with her cook and a housemaid, she died in 1882 and is buried at Langwathby.
57 *CW1*, 5 (1881), 24-25; Paris address taken from the list of members of that year.
58 'In Memoriam', *CW2*, 11 (1911), xi, 488.
59 'In Memoriam', *CW2*, 25 (1925), 387.
60 'In Memoriam', *CW2*, 12 (1912), 437-38.
61 'In Memoriam', *CW2*, 54 (1954), 307-10.
62 'In Memoriam', *CW2*, 36 (1936), 237-38.
63 Mrs and Miss Hodgson, 'Three relics of the seventeenth and eighteenth centuries', *CW2*, 10 (1910), 85-88.
64 'Unpublished excavations by the late Miss K.S. Hodgson', *CW2*, 75 (1975), 17-28.
65 *The Times*, 3 Oct. 2002.
66 C.I. Fell, 'Bronze Age connections between the Lake District and Ireland', *CW2*, 40 (1940), 118-30; 'In Memoriam', *CW3*, 2 (2002), 317-19.
67 *CW1*, 2 (1876), 100.
68 *CW1*, 15 (1899), 1-8.
69 *CW3*, 2 (2002), 277-300.
70 *CW1*, 3 (1878), xxi.

71 Bruce Jones described the various series in *Newsletter* 35 (Autumn 2000), 3. His description of the Tract Series differs in some respects from that advanced here.
72 *CW2*, 7 (1907), 308-09.
73 Extra Series XI (1899) was published by Titus Wilson alone.
74 Extra Series II (1879) with Thurnam; Tract Series I (1882). Quaritch is the distinguished antiquarian bookseller, still extant.
75 Extra Series I (1877), III and IV, all with Charles Thurnam. George Bell was a well-known publisher.
76 Record Series I (1897), Extra Series IX and X (1893, 1894). Elliot Stock was a publisher.
77 Extra Series V (1891) and VI (1892). Bemrose were publishers evolving from printers in Derby.
78 *CW2*, 51 (1951), 241-43: £41 10s. for printing.
79 *CW2*, 56 (1956), 206. R.C. Jarvis, *The Jacobite Risings of 1715 and 1745: compiled from documents in the possession of Cumberland County Council* (Cumberland County Council, Record Series, 1 1954).
80 £16 17s.6d.: *CW2*, 52 (1952), 245-47: £36 8s. for RS9 and £150 for TS15: *CW2*, 60 (1960), 235-36. In 1966 this account contributed to a reprint of 50 copies of Curwen's *Castles and Towers* (Extra Series XIII), apparently organised by subscription for the Society's centenary. In 1966/67 it financed *The Building of Hadrian's Wall* (Extra Series XX) and, in 1971, *Westmorland Protestation Returns 1641-2* and *A Short History of the Manor of Witherslack to 1850* (Tract Series XVII and XVIII).
81 *CW2*, 15 (1915), 202.
82 Described in an editorial note to part 3 (1913).
83 Rules adopted 7 Sept. 1916, V.3: *CW2*, 17 (1917), vii.
84 Council meeting 14 Sept. 1905: *CW2*, 6 (1906), 325.
85 *CW2*, 7 (1907), 292.
86 *CW2*, *8* (1908), 369.
87 *CW2*, 9 (1909), 320. After 1920 the post was no longer separately designated in the list of committee members.
88 Preface to W.P.W. Phillimore and C.W. Ruston-Harrison (eds.), *Cumberland Parish Registers* Vol. 1 (London, 1910). A similar preface appears in Vol. 2 (1912). 150 copies were printed and the Society took its agreed 30 copies: Accounts for 1910-11, *CW2, 12* (1912), 460; Accounts for 1912-13, *CW2*, 14 (1914), 512.
89 Vol. 1: Workington 1670-1837 (transcribed by Miss Patricia Curwen); Vol. 2: Crosby on Eden 1665-1836 (T.H. Hodgson); Gosforth 1572-1837 (Dr C.A. Parker); Harrington 1652-1837 (Miss Patricia Curwen); Stanwix 1662-1837 (C.W. Ruston-Harrison). Moresby was transcribed by the incumbent, Revd H.J. Allen who was not a member of the Society.
90 *CW2*, 12 (1912), 460: £6 1s. 10d. for volume 1; *CW2*, 14 (1914), 512: £5 19s. for volume 2.
91 *CW2*, 13 (1913), 399-400. Some notice of this had already reached Phillimore when *Cumberland Parish Registers*, volume 2 was published in 1912. The Preface contains an appeal for the value of continuing to publish within a national series. During its lifetime the Series published 22 volumes for Cumberland and 20 for Westmorland.
92 *CW2*, 14 (1914), 482.
93 *CW2*, 20 (1920), 278. At the Spring meeting of 1920, the membership subscription was raised from 10s. 6d to one guinea because of similar rising costs, 240-41.
94 *CW2*, 24 (1924), 400; the reason is given at 377-78: 'assisting the too slender resources of the Section in bringing out this book'.
95 Secretary's Report in *Newsletter*, 13 (Autumn 1990), 2-3.
96 Furness registers have been published by the Lancashire Parish Register Society.

97 Details revealed in Richard Bellhouse's papers at the Senhouse Roman Museum.

98 G. Avery (M. and K. Lea eds.), *The Collingwood Icelandic Pilgrimage 2012* (CWAAS, 2013); See also, *W.G. Collingwood's Letters from Iceland*, M. and K. Lea eds., (R.G. Collingwood Society, Cardiff, 2013), 1-4.

99 F.R. Raines in Chetham Society volumes VIII (1845), XIX (1849), XXI (1850) and XXII (1850).

100 *The Archdeaconry of Richmond in the Eighteenth Century: Bishop Gastrell's Notitia, the Yorkshire parishes 1714-1725* (L.A.S. Butler ed.) (Yorkshire Record Society, vol. 146, 1990).

101 G. Martin *et al.*, 'A Retrospective,' *CW2*, 100 (2000), 261-72.

102 D.C.A. Shotter, 'The Roman period', *CW2*, 100, (2000), 266.

103 Marshall, 'Industrial history and the modern period', 271.

Part 2

The Society's Areas of Interest

Chapter 3
Archaeology

David J. Breeze, Antony Dickson and Rachel Newman

The Society was founded at a time when the name of such bodies was changing from 'Antiquarian' to 'Archaeological', and the Cumberland and Westmorland Antiquarian and Archaeological Society is unusual in having both names in its title. As seen in Chapter 1 the Revd James Simpson, who gave the first paper at the inaugural meeting in 1866, used the word antiquarian rather than archaeology in his title, 'The present state of antiquarian research in Westmorland and Cumberland'.[1] It is of interest that his paper was given a different title in the contents page for the first volume of *Transactions* in 1874, 'The need of antiquarian research in Cumberland and Westmorland', thereby providing a rationale for the nascent Society. The article as it appeared in *Transactions* ranged widely in the interpretation of 'antiquarian', embracing documents and customs as well as more traditional archaeological remains; in fact, Simpson's approach was unsurprisingly more 'antiquarian' than 'archaeological'. Just to complicate matters further, the running heading of the paper is 'Archaeology in Westmorland and Cumberland'.

Such ambivalence is in many ways not surprising. Amongst the other 42 articles in the volume are reports on 'recently opened Tumuli' and 'Roman remains recently found in Carlisle' which are firmly archaeological, as well as articles of antiquarian and architectural interest on largely upstanding buildings such as Carlisle Cathedral, Lanercost Priory, Yanwath Hall, Brougham Castle and Kendal Castle, all structures which have subsequently attracted the attention of the Society, as well as some heraldry and genealogy and recognisably 'historical' articles. The volume also set the tone for the future by including contributing authors from outside the county, such as Canon Greenwell and Dr Bruce.

Over the following 150 years the Society has demonstrated a strong commitment to archaeology and its activities have proceeded along well-established lines. There have been four main strands: the recording of discoveries including the recording of archaeological sites through excavations in advance of threats, such as quarrying or graveyard extensions; the undertaking of surveys of specific areas and types of monuments,[2] sometimes linked with the wider issues of the protection of ancient monuments; the provision of grants; and the publication of findings in a variety of forms. Through these activities the Society has been at the heart of archaeological research within the county for the last 150 years, often leading the agenda, and always supporting the endeavours of generations of archaeologists and scholars.

PREHISTORY

KEY DEVELOPMENTS AND CONTRIBUTIONS

Despite James Simpson's inaugural address in 1866 referencing prehistoric monuments, and William Greenwell's subsequent paper on 'Recently opened tumuli in Westmorland and Cumberland',[3] the Society's interest in prehistory was slower to develop than research on the visible remains of the Romans or the castles and abbeys of the Middle Ages. Yet, these counties have a considerable number of very conspicuous prehistoric monuments, mainly in the form of stone circles, and several of these were surveyed and published in some of the earliest volumes, with attempts made to compare them (fig. 3.1).[4] Possibly as a consequence of the Society of Antiquaries' request to receive recommendations for monuments that might be scheduled (see Chapter 1), Mayburgh Henge and King Arthur's Round Table attracted early attention with good plans published.[5] Charles Dymond led this interest in stone circles. Lesser features, in the form of cup-marked stones, also featured in *Transactions*, as did, at a later date, caves.[6] Another kind of contribution was the study of the prehistory of a specific area such as Geltsdale.[7]

It was the Collingwoods, father and son, who began a more systematic survey of the prehistory of the county. In the 1920s W.G. Collingwood offered two major contributions with his inventories of the ancient monuments of Cumberland, Westmorland and Lancashire North of the Sands.[8] Running to 133 pages, the survey was parish based and the monuments were arranged by type and period. These formed the raw material for his son's 1933 'introduction' to the prehistory of the area.[9] R.G. Collingwood also offered a brief summary of current understanding of British prehistory, followed by his own interpretation of the material in the county, supported by maps, and leading on to conclusions and finally proposals for further research. He emphasised the need for more cataloguing, mapping of the known remains, and the drawing of conclusions. He encouraged fieldwork and surveys, including excavation where appropriate, although he also offered cautious words about the disadvantages of examining prehistoric upland sites. Not surprisingly as an editor, he emphasised the need to publish. Although there

Fig. 3.1 Castlerigg stone circle, one of the iconic monuments of the county, drawn by Thomas Allom (from Thomas Rose, *Westmorland, Cumberland, Durham and Northumberland Illustrated*, London, 1832-35)

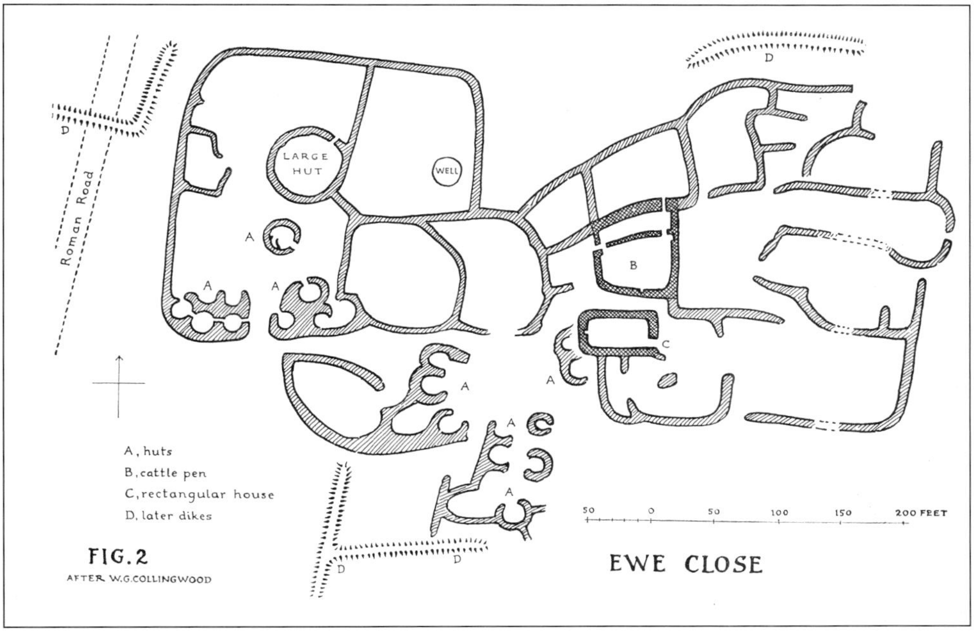

Fig. 3.2. Plan of Ewe Close settlement in R.G. Collingwood, 'Prehistoric settlements near Crosby Ravensworth', *CW2*, 33 (1933), 205, fig. 2

was a gap of some 50 years, Collingwood's surveys later formed the basis for the modern Historic Environment Record maintained by Cumbria County Council and became the baseline for all archaeological research there.

The Collingwoods did not just prepare surveys; they also undertook excavations. W.G. opened a new chapter in the study of rural settlement with the 'exploration of the Romano-British Settlement at Ewe Close, Crosby Ravensworth', financed by the Society's newly-formed Research Fund.[10] His reports included plans, photographs and descriptions of the finds, but no discussion in the style expected today.

His son Robin had cut his archaeological teeth examining the Roman fort at Ambleside where he excavated from 1913 to 1920 (fig. 1.13). Two decades later he also turned his attention to rural settlements, analysing his father's notebooks, reviewing the evidence for Ewe Close and adjacent sites and, most importantly, considering the social organisation indicated by the

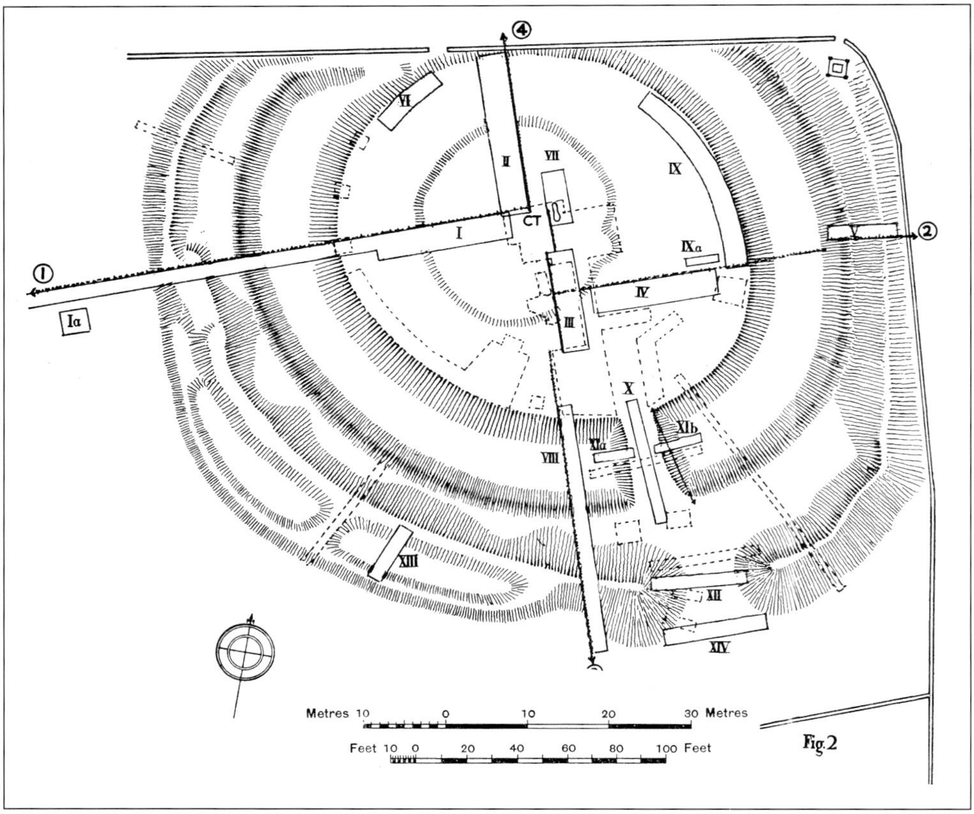

Fig. 3.3. Plan of King Arthur's Round Table by R. G. Collingwood in G. Bersu, 'King Arthur's Round Table. Final Report, including the excavations of 1939...', *CW2*, 40 (1940), fig. 2 opposite 206

evidence (fig. 3.2). He suggested the existence of 'a small tribe or sept having one chief village of some 15 to 20 families, one smaller village of eight or ten families, and half-a-dozen isolated farms'.[11] For the clutch of settlements he proposed a population of between 150 and 200 people, earning their living through a mixed economy. He hazarded a date in the late Bronze Age for the start of the settlements with their life continuing through the Roman period, as indicated by pottery of the second and third centuries. Collingwood presented a coherent view of these Iron Age/Roman upland settlements which was to survive for decades. In fact, it was not until 1956 that members of the Society began to study such sites again.[12]

In 1937 R.G. turned his attention to one of the major ancient monuments of the county, King Arthur's Round Table, a little to the south of Penrith. He completed the first season of excavation but was too unwell to continue. Gerhard Bersu, a refugee from Nazi Germany and one of the foremost archaeologists of his day, took over for the second season (fig. 3.3).[13]

Collingwood had chosen to examine King Arthur's Round Table following the investigation of the henge at Avebury and the discovery of Woodhenge. He believed that he would find evidence for a timber circle within the Round Table, and did indeed find such a feature. Bersu's approach to excavation, however, was rather different. He examined the geology of the site and

Fig. 3.4. The site of the Langdale axe factory *(photograph courtesy of Aaron Watson, per Richard Bradley)*

concluded that Collingwood's postholes lay beneath natural geological strata; he interpreted them as animal burrows. As Richard Bradley has put it, 'Bersu's work at King Arthur's Round Table was a triumph of technique over content; Collingwood's a triumph of mind over matter'.[14] Grace Simpson later wrote on the problems of interpretation at this site, offering a personal reminiscence of visiting Bersu's excavation.[15]

W.G. Collingwood's papers led to the establishment of the Committee for Prehistoric Studies, which began to list discoveries in 1935. The same period witnessed a significant discovery: 'a flint chipping floor' on Walney Island, the first evidence for Mesolithic activity in the county.[16] Exactly a decade later there was another important fillip to early prehistoric studies: a paper by Brian Bunch and Clare Fell on the stone-axe factory at Great Langdale, discovered 30 years before (fig. 3.4). This heralded the start of many years of work at the site, and also encouraged the search for other such remains in the county, as well as consideration of the distribution of the axes.[17] Flint scatters were recognised at about this time by Mary Fair in the sand hills to the north of Ravenglass, and in 1960 these became the subject of Jim Cherry's long-running research project along that stretch of coast, which involved the introduction of pollen analysis.[18] The reports on the investigation of these early sites formed the main prehistoric contributions to *Transactions* until the end of the twentieth century. Concurrent with the fieldwork and excavation reports was a developing interest in museum collections, illustrated by a number of articles in *Transactions* on Bronze Age metalwork and pottery.[19]

Clare Fell continued to work on the Great Langdale stone-axe factory and encouraged the involvement of professional archaeologists, often from further afield, as well as the application of new techniques such as petrological analysis.[20] Her original idea that the particular band of rock which yielded the axes should be explored further proved to be fruitful. Additional work clarified that extraction activities included quarrying in association with nearby sites for working the axes, while her suggestion of a relationship between procurement and summer grazing still remains in favour.[21]

Clare Fell was also a strong supporter of others who were seeking to understand the archaeology of the county.[22] Her support was warmly acknowledged by Bob Bewley, whose work in Cumbria in the 1980s on the Solway Plain for his PhD still forms the basis for our understanding of the prehistoric settlement in that area.[23] As part of his survey, Bewley undertook excavations at significant sites, including the Neolithic settlement at Plasketlands, which yielded evidence of what is still the only dated settlement of this period in Cumbria, a Bronze Age settlement at Ewanrigg by Maryport, and various Iron Age/Romano-British settlements (fig. 3.5).[24] Bewley acknowledged how interest in the prehistoric settlements often seemed to relate to the Romans rather than to understanding the settlements for their own sake. His approach concentrated on the individual site, letting the excavated material speak for itself with only a relatively basic interpretation offered.[25] However, these sites produced little by way of material culture and are difficult to date.

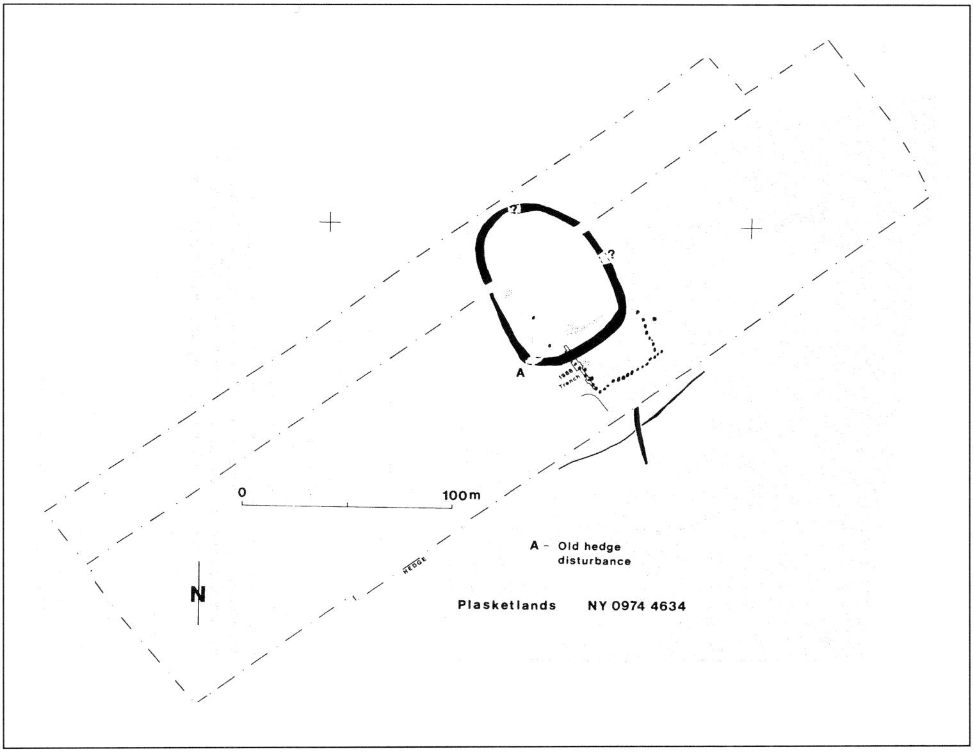

Fig. 3.5. Plan of Plasketlands enclosure in R. Bewley, 'Survey and excavation at a crop mark enclosure, Plasketlands, Cumbria', *CW2*, 9 (1993), 3, fig. 2

Earlier research concentrated on discrete monuments or types of monuments. More recently, there has been a move away from that focus to the study of landscapes, building on the seminal work instigated by the Lake District National Park Authority.[26] Winifred Pennington's work in the area started in the 1940s and she pioneered the use of pollen analysis as a tool for understanding vegetation and landscapes. Her 1970 review of 'Vegetation history in the north-west of England' noted that it 'was inevitable that a region so ecologically attractive as the country which lies between the Morecambe and Solway sands, between the Pennines and the Irish Sea, should arouse the curiosity of the historical ecologist'.[27] Although she herself did not publish through the Society, she drew on its publications, and many of her successors have contributed papers to *Transactions*.[28] In her 1970 review she dated the start of agriculture in the county to about 3000 BC, following slightly earlier traces of 'human interference with primary vegetation' on the west Cumberland coast in the Mesolithic period.[29] She argued that the Bronze Age saw a decline in the upland oak forest around 1000 BC, with cereal cultivation penetrating the uplands during the Roman period as well as becoming more extensive in the lowlands. She concluded it was clear that by the time the Romans arrived the North West had largely been cleared of its woodland.[30]

Nick Higham has sought to place the later rural sites in their wider landscape setting through examining the remaining visible dykes in the uplands of northern Cumbria.[31] He noted the proximity of many of these dykes to indigenous settlements, including some of the Roman period, and concluded that the purpose of the dykes was to separate areas of winter grazing and summer pasture; and that the lack of fences round the fields of this period would have made such banks necessary. More recently the work of Andrew Hoaen and Helen Loney in the northern fells, supported by the Society amongst others, is a good example of this approach. Although they have concentrated on cairns and cairnfields, primarily dating to the Bronze Age, they have come to appreciate that these small monuments are part of a much longer relationship between the local people and their environment, for example on Sizergh Fell to the south.[32] They have also argued that woodland remained longer in these valleys than on the more intensively-farmed ground around the Lakeland hills and in the broader river valleys. Other work on the cairns on Sizergh Fell by Mark Edmonds and Helen Evans has revealed longevity of use.[33] There and elsewhere in the county such monuments, carefully placed in the landscape, continued in use from the Neolithic period into the Bronze Age, although apparently with different burial practices.

Parallel to this reappraisal of monuments in their landscapes, have been the re-consideration of earlier reports and a re-examination of artefacts from earlier excavations lodged in the country's museums. The former includes Richard Bradley's analysis of the work undertaken in the 1930s at King Arthur's Round Table by Collingwood and Bersu. In the latter category falls Terence Manby's re-analysis of the Neolithic pottery recovered from Ehenside Tarn in 1871.[34] The recent advances in our knowledge of this period coupled with the interest of 'outsiders' has led to the production of a number of significant overviews.[35]

Cumbrian Prehistory Overview

No evidence survives in Cumbria for early Palaeolithic activity, primarily because of subsequent glaciation, and much of the evidence for the Late Palaeolithic/Early Mesolithic period is now submerged under the Irish Sea.

However, there is evidence for Late Upper Palaeolithic occupation from cave sites on the Furness and Cartmel peninsulas and also on the southern side of Morecambe Bay. There is some confusion as to the stratigraphic integrity of some of the sites, but finds of diagnostic flint tools point to a possible late Upper Palaeolithic and an early Mesolithic presence. Much of this work was undertaken by and/or reported on by Chris Salisbury in articles in *Transactions* in 1992 and 1997.[36] More recent work has been undertaken on the Furness peninsula cave sites by Doug Stables and the Morecambe Bay Archaeological Society, supported by the Society in the form of funding for radiocarbon dating.[37]

For the Late Mesolithic period, most sites are defined by microliths, which are part of a narrow blade, geometric lithic industry, usually dated to about 6500-4000 BC. Jim and Peter Cherry did much to identify Mesolithic sites in the areas stretching from Levens in the south to St Bees in west Cumbria, and also on the limestone uplands around Shap and Orton.[38] It was their collection of Mesolithic material on the west coast that prompted the excavations at Monk Moors and Williamson's Moss by Clive Bonsall under the auspices of *The Eskmeals Project* (fig. 3.6).[39] The earliest date for the sites comes from Monks Moor, at 6000-5350 cal BC. Peter Cherry continues to work on the lithic collections recovered by his family, making interesting contributions on the role of raw materials.[40] His work, in conjunction with the further results from recent excavations, emphasises the importance of raw materials in understanding social interactions between Cumbria, Scotland and the North East of England, probably just before Cumbrian stone axes appeared in the archaeological record.

For the Early Neolithic period, there is evidence from the lithic record that locations favoured in the Late Mesolithic still retained significance. There is a distinct possibility that a Late Mesolithic lithic technology continued into the very early part of the Neolithic period, although scientific dating for this is yet to be established. Dating for the period is problematic and Plasketlands stands out as a rare example where good dating has been obtained. The results from developer-funded archaeology are now beginning to add to an understanding of chronological developments. Interestingly, much of this is from sites on the Solway Plain, where there are also large numbers of axe finds, often associated with former wetlands. Ehenside Tarn also has a significant Early Neolithic character, especially the pair of wooden 'tridents' found there, which on current dating evidence appear to be Early Neolithic. It is also at this time that the axe-production sites in the Langdale/Scafell area took off. A few large enclosures, such as that surviving as cropmarks adjacent to Long Meg and her Daughters, could have been involved in the movement of axes out of the region. Also associated with the Early Neolithic period are long mounds and cairns. None has been the subject of modern excavation,

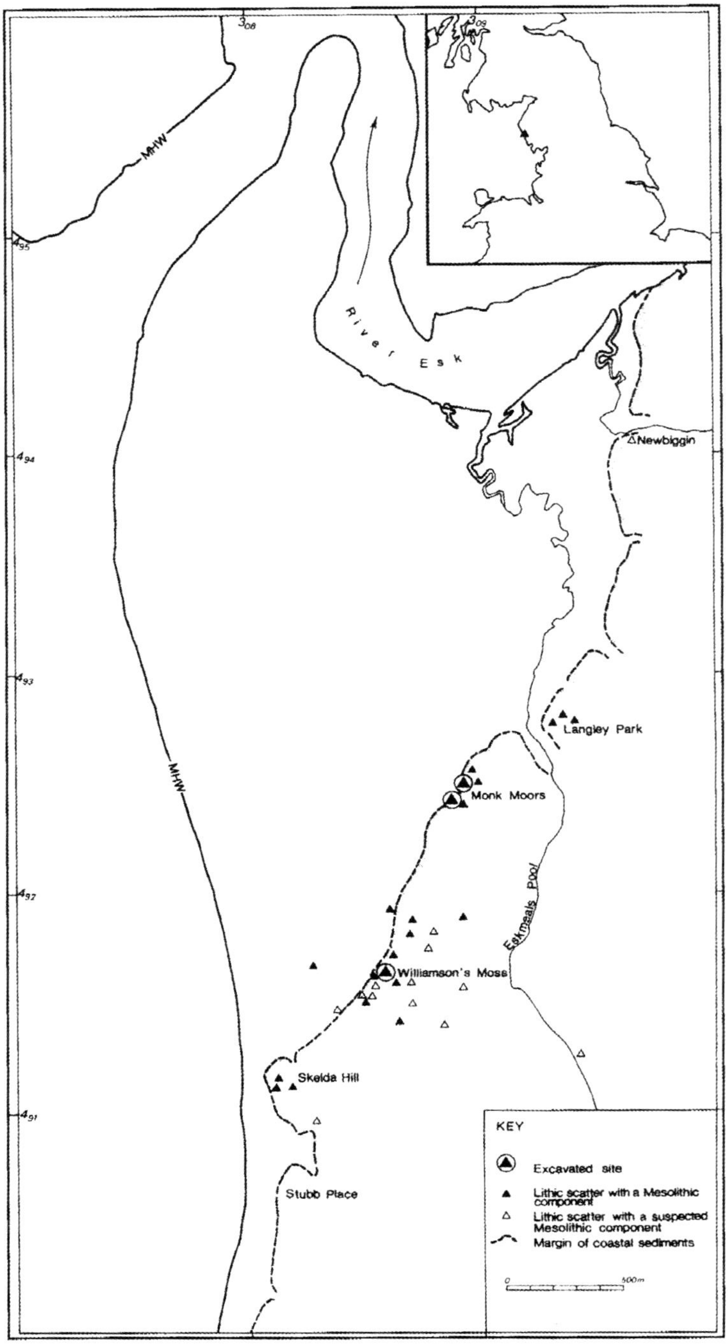

Fig. 3.6. Distribution of Mesolithic Sites in the Eskmeals area, C. Bonsall, 'Human-environment interactions' in P.J. Cherry (ed.), *Studies in Northern Prehistory* (CWAAS, Extra Series XXXIII, 2007), 28, fig. 2.2

and the interpretation of some are dubious, for example at Trainford long barrow in the Eden Valley. Nevertheless, the results of early antiquarian excavations, such as those by Canon Greenwell at Raiset Pike, established a link between mortuary structures and the material culture of these sites with burial mounds in East Yorkshire, where he was also a prolific excavator.[41] This link between the east and west of Northern England, and beyond, is also represented by the movement of Yorkshire till flint inwards to the region from the very Late Mesolithic period, particularly in the Shap/Orton area and the Eden Valley, and the movement of Cumbrian stone axes in the opposite direction. Finds of Early Neolithic pottery are quite rare, but reports by Terry Manby of diagnostic early Neolithic wares from Ehenside Tarn, and a scatter of sites from other areas, indicate its presence.[42]

Rock art, a phenomenon largely of the Bronze Age, although difficult to date closely, is fairly commonplace in Cumbria. Within the central fells it is found on rock faces and on huge earthfast boulders such as Copt Howe in the Langdale valley; it could have acted as a marker for routeways along valleys and could have been related to events at axe-production sites. Beyond the central fells, it is more commonly found on smaller, moveable boulders and is referred to as portable rock art. Examples of portable rock art are found along the Eden Valley and include, amongst others, decorated stones at Long Meg, Little Meg, Glassonby, Redhills and Honey Pot Farm (Figs. 3.7 and 3.8). The motifs on Long Meg suggest a long currency of use stretching back into the Neolithic period.

The axe-production sites in the central fells were still important in the Late Neolithic period. It is also likely that most of the major monuments, such as the large stone circles, the henges in the Eden Valley and on the west coast, and the complexes focused on the Shap stone avenue and Long Meg, were formalised in the Late Neolithic (fig. 3.9). In addition to the earlier antiquarian surveys and plans, more recent work has been carried out at Mayburgh Henge and King Arthur's Round Table and Long Meg.[43]

Stone circles and monument complexes are of interest, as they tend to be situated at river confluences and adjacent to rivers in major valley systems, particularly the Eden. Finds of Cumbrian axes at some sites suggest that they were also involved in the movement of axes along major route-ways into Yorkshire, the North East, Scotland and South West. Lithic scatters with Late Neolithic/Early Bronze Age technological affinities have been recorded from the west coast and in the Shap/Orton area, and more recently in the Eden Valley at the confluence of the Eden and Eamont. Those at the latter site and at Shap/Orton contain significant quantities of till flint, which is most probably derived from east Yorkshire and strengthens the connections between Cumbria and the eastern side of the country. Finds of Middle/Late Neolithic pottery, such as Peterborough Ware and Grooved ware, particularly

Fig. 3.7. Little Meg *(photograph: Dorothy Charlesworth)*

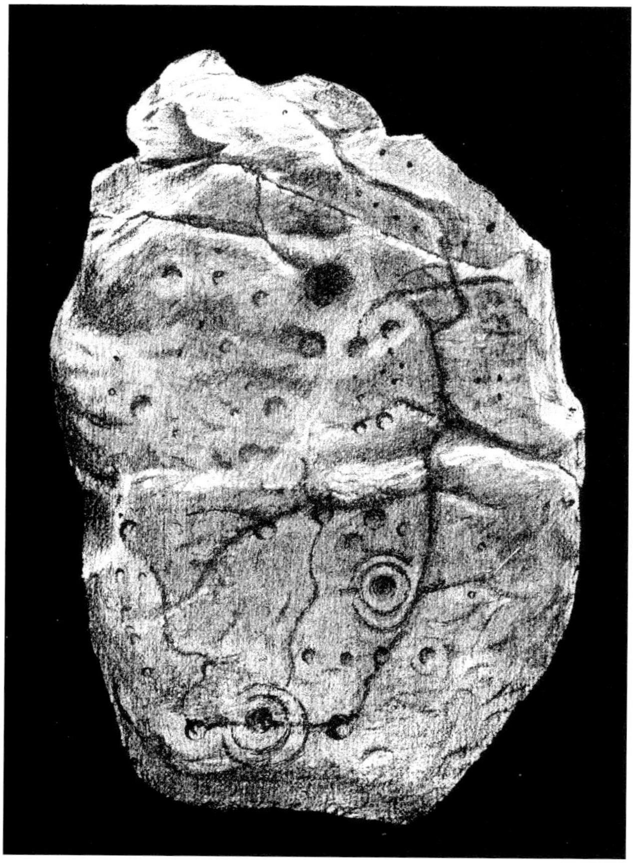

Fig. 3.8. Cup and ring marks on a stone at Redhills in M.W. Taylor, 'On a cup-marked stone found at Redhills, near Penrith', *CW1*, 6 (1883), opposite 113

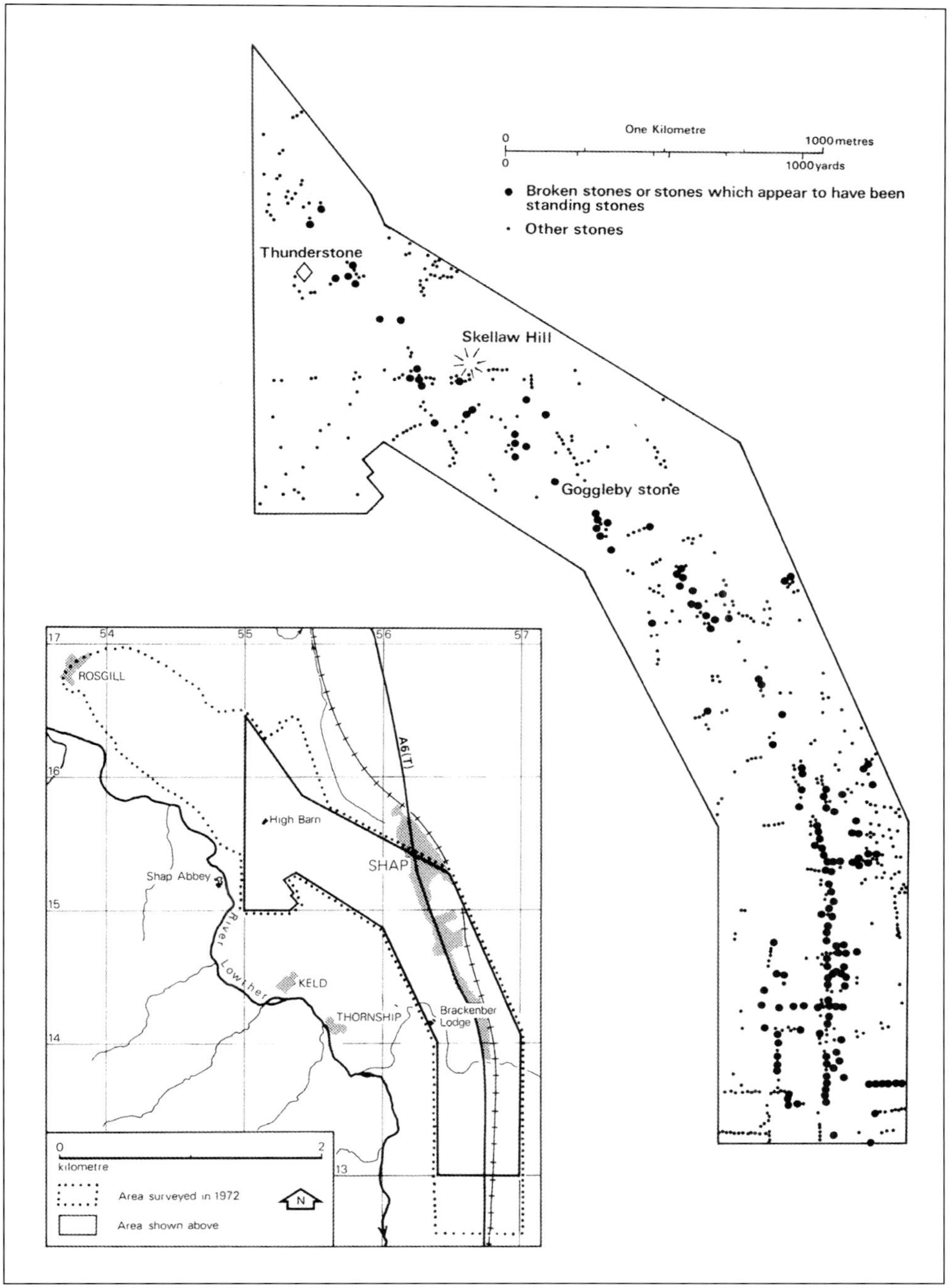

Fig. 3.9. Plan of Shap stone avenue and complex in T. Clare, 'Recent work on Shap Avenue', *CW2*, 78 (1978), 7, fig. 1

at Shap and Orton, have also been recorded.[44]

The extended use of some sites from the Late Neolithic period into the Early Bronze Age is exemplified by a site at Oddendale, Shap, which began life as a timber circle in the Late Neolithic period and developed over the centuries into a ring cairn and associated features in the Early Bronze Age (fig. 3.10).[45] Recent excavations near Carlisle are also providing evidence of an extended sequence of activity on the site from the Late Mesolithic through to the Late Bronze Age.[46]

Other sites which could have Late Neolithic/Early Bronze Age developments include the Lacra stone circles on the west coast. Beaker pottery is recorded from a variety of locations in the region, along with Bucket

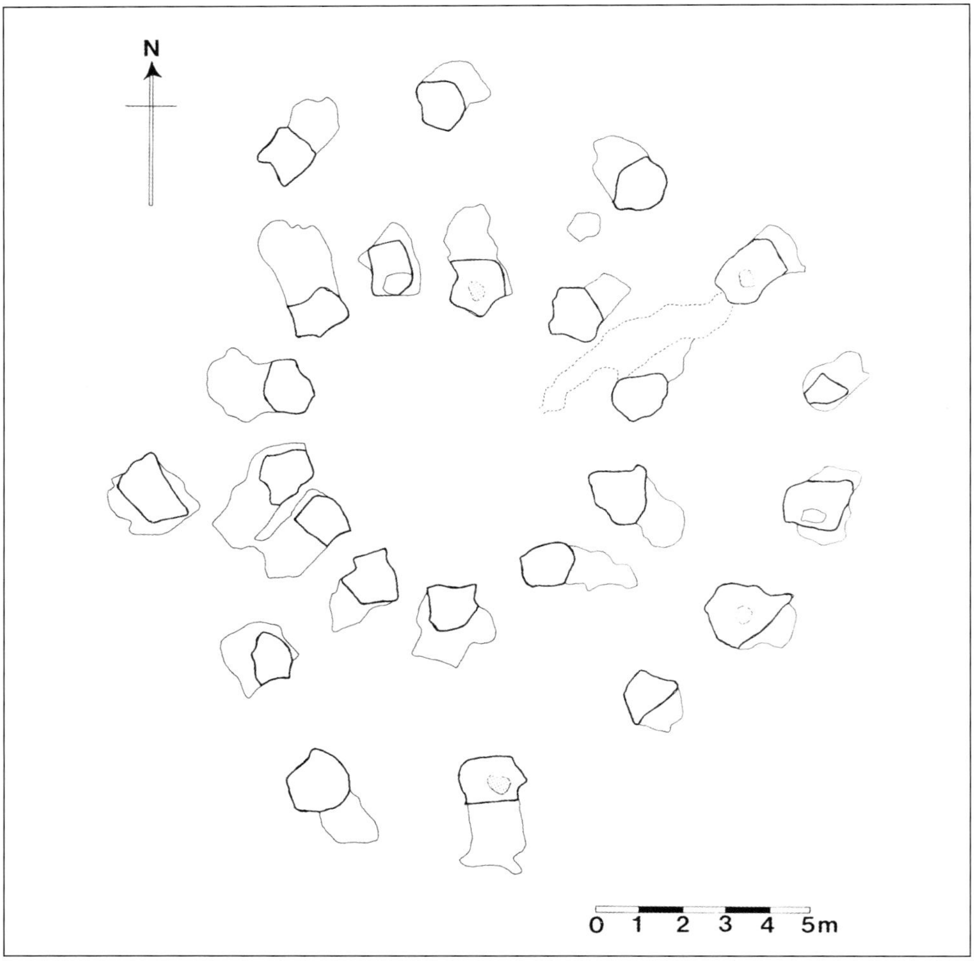

Fig. 3.10. Plan of Oddendale cairn in P. Turnbull, and D. Walsh, 'A prehistoric ritual sequence at Oddendale, near Shap', *CW2*, 97 (1997), 17, fig. 3

Urns, Cordoned Urns and Food Vessels. Very few are known from modern excavated contexts, although burials associated with Beaker pottery have been recorded at Levens and Sizergh in south Cumbria, and stray finds have been recovered during field-walking surveys.[47] Collared Urns from potential cremation cemeteries are also known, but sites such as that at the former Garlands Hospital, Carlisle were excavated in the late nineteenth century and very little information about them survives. The more recent excavation of a cremation cemetery at Ewanrigg provides much-needed detail on such monuments.[48] Beyond this, Bronze Age burials are known from a variety of contexts including stone circles, various types of cairns, barrows and natural features. Strong connections between material culture and natural places, such as clints and grykes in limestone areas and water courses, also become more prominent in the Early Bronze Age.[49] The Cherry family has recorded lithic scatters with Bronze Age technological affinities from the west coast, suggesting occupation since the Early Bronze period at least in some areas. Perforated axe hammers also have a distribution centred in southern Cumbria, with a potential source recorded at Coniston. The majority of the most significant reports on the archaeology of the Mesolithic, Neolithic and Bronze Age in the county have been published by the Society.

Farming began in the centuries before 3000 BC with, at first, the lighter soils being tilled, the trees being felled and the soil broken by stone axes. These are one indicator of settlement and, together with burials, demonstrate the spread of people across the county. There were clearly wider communications in that Langdale stone axes were distributed across England and Scotland and over the sea to the Isle of Man and Ireland. The appreciation that Cumbria has been farmed for over 5000 years is important. The Romans arrived over half-way through this period. By that time, a pattern had been established which is clear through the analysis of the environmental evidence discussed above. There was certainly cereal cultivation but, owing to the heavier rainfall along the west coast and exacerbated by the Lakeland hills, pasture was more important than, for example, in the lands to the east of the Pennines. This remains true today, and creates difficulties with obtaining a good general aerial survey coverage of the county. Although aerial survey has been a major impetus to the discovery of settlements of late prehistory, because of the nature of land cover in Cumbria its deployment has been mainly restricted to the Solway Plain and the Eden Valley.[50] This at least complements the earlier work in the eastern uplands of the county. However, in view of the few excavated examples, the dating of most settlements cannot be determined within the Iron Age and the Roman period. What is clear is that the sites identified by Bewley fit within the broad nature of Iron Age/Romano-British settlements of northern England.[51] Only further excavation will be able to offer more precise dates.

Finally, the rich archaeological database relating to the county merits continuing study. In the light of the well-known find at Lindow Moss in Cheshire two papers in *Transactions* have reconsidered the significance of two of Cumbria's bog bodies, one discovered at Seascale Moss in 1834 and the other at Scaleby Moss in 1845.[52] The former was a naked adult male placed in the bog with a stick, characteristics shared with known sacrificial victims of the late Iron Age or early Roman period; the circumstances and date of the Scaleby burial are not clear.

The Romans

Under the influence of Chancellor Ferguson, the Society in its early years developed a keen interest in the archaeological remains of the Roman period with Ferguson publishing what he termed 'an attempt at a survey of Roman Cumberland' in several parts. He started by concentrating on the documentary evidence and the Roman roads to provide a framework for his study and then moved on to surveying sites and recording artefacts.[53] Other members recorded the Roman remains, including Walls Castle, the Roman bath-house at Ravenglass, one of the rare buildings of this period in Britain still standing to first-floor level (fig. 3.11). This was followed by excavation in 1881.[54]

Fig. 3.11. Walls Castle, the popular name for the Roman bath-house at Ravenglass, has been of interest to the Society since its earliest days. It has recently been provided with new interpretation panels and was revisited by the Society in its anniversary year, 2016. *(Photograph: Chris Healey, Minerva Heritage)*

Ferguson encouraged others to study the Roman remains in the county. Foremost among these was Joseph Robinson, a bank manager in Maryport.[55] He excavated first at the Roman fort at Beckfoot in 1879, and then the civil settlement at Maryport in the following two years, before turning his attention to the towers along the coast. He examined one on Christmas Day 1880 and published a number of reports, including one with Ferguson on the tower on Risehow, still the most southerly in the sequence (fig. 3.12).[56] In 1886, however, Robinson left Maryport under a cloud and his archaeological career came to an end.[57] His was to be the last serious work on the Roman remains along the Cumberland coast for 50 years.

Since the 1880s members of the Society and others have continued to investigate Roman archaeology and to publish their results in *Transactions* and other Society publications. It is of particular importance that *Transactions* remains a journal of record, by listing on an annual basis recent work in the county. The many contributions of David Shotter, who reported on Roman coin finds for over 40 years from 1972, stand out in this respect, and have steadily improved our knowledge of Roman activity in the region. He has regularly updated and republished the findings as catalogues with valuable syntheses.[58] More recently, as with the study of prehistoric Cumbria, archaeologists from outside the area have become increasingly significant in the investigation of Roman Cumbria. Much has been published in other journals but *Transactions* has always carried articles on the period and in recent years the Society has expanded into the publication of volumes on urban excavations as well as publishing some of the most important books about the Romans in the North West. In recent publications, the Society has moved on again to discuss changing attitudes and perceptions to the Roman legacy over the centuries. William Shannon's *Murus ille famosus* challenged decades, if not centuries, of misunderstanding about the depiction of Hadrian's Wall during the Middle Ages; he emphasised the continuity of the record, and offered a possible identification of Hadrian's Wall in his reading of *murus pehtis* or *pictis*

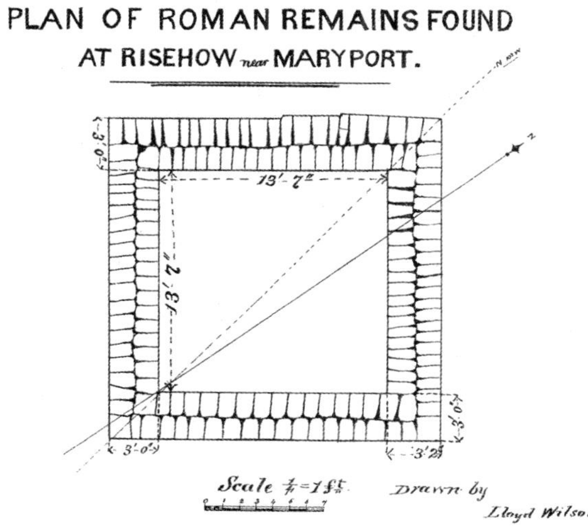

Fig. 3.12. Plan of Risehow Tower in R.S. Ferguson, 'An attempt at a survey of Roman Cumberland and Westmorland, continued, Part V', *CW1*, 5 (1881), opposite 124

on a late Anglo-Saxon map. More recent work on the Wall has been analysed by David Breeze in a review of archaeological thought about the frontier.[59]

Hadrian's Wall

Robinson's departure from the North West coincided with work of an altogether different nature. John Collingwood Bruce of Newcastle had been the leading figure on Hadrian's Wall for nearly 40 years. He had led the first Pilgrimage along the frontier in 1849 at the time when some people in Newcastle were sceptical about his descriptions of Hadrian's Wall after he had inspected the remains the previous summer.[60] Some 20 people, together with local participants, spent the week from 25 June to 3 July 1849 visiting the Wall from Wallsend to Bowness, travelling by a variety of horse-drawn transport, with the event commemorated in the local newspapers – and in a poem! The event marked the start of Bruce's remarkable career. He published his first book on Hadrian's Wall, *The Roman Wall*, two years later, and thereafter was 'King of the Wall' for the rest of his life. (fig. 3.13).[61]

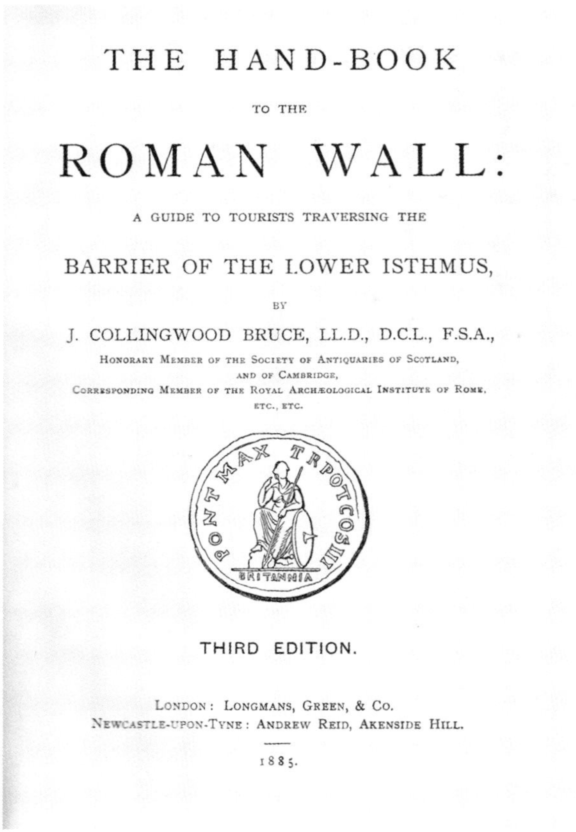
THE HAND-BOOK

TO THE

ROMAN WALL:

A GUIDE TO TOURISTS TRAVERSING THE

BARRIER OF THE LOWER ISTHMUS,

BY

J. COLLINGWOOD BRUCE, LL.D., D.C.L., F.S.A.,

Honorary Member of the Society of Antiquaries of Scotland, and of Cambridge, Corresponding Member of the Royal Archæological Institute of Rome, etc., etc.

THIRD EDITION.

London: Longmans, Green, & Co.
Newcastle-upon-Tyne: Andrew Reid, Akenside Hill.

1885.

Fig. 3.13. The title page of the third edition of the *Handbook to the Roman Wall* by J. Collingwood Bruce published the year before the 1886 Pilgrimage of Hadrian's Wall. The first edition of *The Roman Wall* was published in 1851 and was followed by two further editions in 1853 and 1867 and three shorter versions which became the *Handbooks to the Roman Wall* in 1863, 1884 and 1885

For some years he was pressed to lead another Pilgrimage and finally, in 1886, this was held, organised by both the Society of Antiquaries of Newcastle upon Tyne and the Cumberland and Westmorland Antiquarian and Archaeological Society (fig. 3.14). In preparation for the event, a committee was appointed and prepared for the Pilgrimage by undertaking some excavations on the line of the Wall.[62] They found time for only two excavations, at MC 48 (Poltross Burn) and in Carlisle, where they sought the location of the Roman bridge. Even so, they exceeded their budget of £50. There was certainly much more of the archaeological remains to see in 1886, and the Society helped the Pilgrims by marking out some of the less visible elements, for example, at Stanwix, Willowholme and Etterby (fig. 3.15). This Pilgrimage was also notable for its first foreign participant. Its importance was two-fold: this was the first excavation campaign organised by the Society as opposed to investigations by individual members, and it was also the first collaborative event with their fellow archaeological society.

While the Society's appetite for Hadrian's Wall had been whetted, it was a series of coincidences which led to further and more detailed work. One such event was the death of John Collingwood Bruce in 1892, honorary member of the Society and for long the doyen of Roman frontier studies in Britain. But, as George Neilson emphasised, Bruce had long been holding back the presentation of new ideas.[63] As the hold of Bruce declined, the new ideas started to flow. One of the first in the field was Francis Haverfield who was to become the leading scholar of Roman Britain. A few years before Haverfield

Fig. 3.14. Pilgrims at Lanercost in 1886 *(copyright: Great North Museum and Society of Antiquaries of Newcastle upon Tyne)*

Fig. 3.15. One of the markers erected in Stanwix to mark the line of Hadrian's Wall for the Pilgrims in 1886 *(photograph courtesy of Ian Caruana)*

had started studying and reporting upon the inscriptions of Roman Britain. In 1892 he published a review of the epigraphic evidence relating to Hadrian's Wall and, with his interest fired, he turned to archaeology to try to answer some of the basic questions about the relationships between the various elements of the frontier.[64] He approached the Society and it established an Excavation Committee which continued to provide financial support for the ten-year campaign. Members of the Society were also eager participants in the venture. Haverfield started work in 1894 by examining the Vallum. In his second season he discovered the existence of a Turf Wall, which complicated his task, but he remained close to his original intentions throughout, though also taking time to examine roads and the relationships between the Vallum and the forts on the Wall.[65] It is fair to say that the work was not as successful as it might have been, partly because archaeological excavation was in its infancy as a discipline, and Haverfield himself had no previous experience as an archaeological director. The best commentaries on his work were by one of his female collaborators, Mrs Elizabeth Hodgson, who wrote several parallel reports in 1897 and 1899, always signing herself as 'Mrs. Hodgson'.[66] One most important contribution to the future study of the Wall, however, was Haverfield's inquisitorial approach.

Haverfield operated along much of the length of the Wall at the same time as J.P. Gibson was examining individual structures, to be joined by F.G. Simpson in 1907. In 1909 they tried to find the Roman crossing of the Poltross Burn but, failing in that purpose, they decided to examine the adjacent milecastle, the subject of the work undertaken by the Society in 1886.[67] The site was then completely excavated and the subsequent report became a classic. They now turned their attention to the problem of the relative dates of the Turf and Stone Walls in Cumberland, working in the sector around Birdoswald, where the two elements follow different trajectories. They were able to prove that thereabouts the Turf Wall was rebuilt in stone during the reign of Hadrian. Gibson died in 1912, however, and it was not until 1927 that Simpson returned to Cumberland. In the next year he was joined by I.A. Richmond and together they created a formidable team which investigated many of the problems of the Turf Wall over the following 20 years.[68] Amongst these problems was the pattern of structures along the Turf Wall, the sequence of building, and the fort at Birdoswald and its history (fig. 3.16). The structural history of this last site was extended to the whole of the Wall line. Most of the work of Simpson and Richmond was concentrated on the eastern five miles of the Turf Wall and, although they excavated one tower in 1937, it was the exigencies of war which led to the more significant work – the almost complete excavation of the milefortlet at Cardurnock in 1943 and 1944. Perhaps inspired by this, Simpson returned to the area and located two further fortlets and towers on the coast.[69] By 1950 Richmond confidently asserted that they had solved all the major problems of the Wall.[70] Richmond along with R.G. Collingwood tended to be the interpreters of the work for a wider audience, with the latter providing much of the underpinning philosophy. Collingwood also aided Wall studies by producing a schedule of sites, numbering all the milecastles and turrets from Wallsend to Bowness-on-Solway.[71]

The Pilgrimages continued throughout this period, although the ten-year pattern had been broken by the First World War. A Pilgrimage was hastily organised in 1920 and the paucity of numbers was balanced by the hearty discussions. The pattern was again broken by the Second World War, but in 1949 a Centenary Pilgrimage was held and the ninth year of the decade has been followed since then for successive Pilgrimages. Eric Birley organised the first Congress of Roman Frontier Studies in Newcastle to coincide with the Centenary Pilgrimage and that conference has continued ever since on a three-year cycle.[72] The early Pilgrimages were reported upon after the event in newspapers and archaeological journals, including *Transactions*. Such reports continued to be produced until 1959. An innovation in 1930 by R.G. Collingwood was the production of a handbook for the Pilgrims. External events led to the failure to publish a handbook in 1959, but the compensation was Eric Birley's *Research on Hadrian's Wall*, published two years later. The

Fig. 3.16. The excavation of Birdoswald in 1929 which was grant-aided by the Society. In the foreground, from left to right are, John Charlton, Eric Birley, a student, F.G. Simpson, a student, Kurt Stade, Shimon Applebaum and R.G. Collingwood (Charlton, Birley and Collingwood all served as Presidents of the Society). To the left is Thomas Hepple, the foreman, while the workmen are in the background. The photograph was taken by I.A. Richmond

handbooks continued to be produced up to 1989, but in preparing for the 1999 Pilgrimage the organising committee, containing members of the two societies, decided on a new approach involving a more detailed review of research over the past decade, and this was indeed followed ten years later.[73]

Knowledge of the Roman military installations along the Cumberland coast remained extremely patchy, but the hour brought forth the man: Richard Bellhouse, an agricultural engineer. It is to the Society's credit that they provided the financial support for his investigations which lasted for 35 years from 1954 to 1989 and led to the discovery and examination of ten fortlets and ten towers, although he sought the location of at least ten others in vain.[74] Single-handedly, Bellhouse transformed our knowledge of this element of the Hadrianic frontier in Britain (fig. 3.17).

Fig. 3.17. Richard Bellhouse in D.J. Breeze, 'Richard Bellhouse 1916-2012', *CW3*, 13 (2013), 1-3

The 1960s saw the start of a long period of review of the history of Hadrian's Wall, and by implication the history of the whole of northern Britain and beyond.[75] The main result was to loosen the straitjacket of relating every change at each fort, fortlet and tower to the beginning or end of a Wall period, so allowing sites to have different histories.

Outpost and Hinterland Forts

Hadrian's Wall took up much of the energy of the Roman archaeologists of the Society and the county in general, but its foreland and hinterland were not forgotten. Netherby lies underneath the ancestral home of the Graham family, but Bewcastle is more accessible, archeologically if not geographically. Richmond was there in the 1930s, John Gillam examined the bath-house in the 1950s and Paul Austen worked in the north-west corner in the 1980s. Bewcastle is particularly unusual in its hexagonal shape, presumably responding to the ground on which it sits.[76] The wider significance of the fort is its probable name, *Fanum Cocidii*, the shrine of the god Cocidius, and in its probable abandonment with the other outpost forts early in the fourth century, leaving Hadrian's Wall as the most northerly line of military installations.

On many of the forts in the hinterland of the Wall, work has been relatively small scale. These include Low Borrowbridge, Brough-under-Stainmore, Kirkby Thore, Brougham, Old Penrith, Old Carlisle, Blennerhasset, Caermote and Papcastle.[77] Two problems affect our interpretations of these sites: the fact that many excavations were undertaken a long time ago, before excavation techniques were sharpened; and the small amount of dating material which they have yielded. On the other hand, some forts have seen extensive excavations over the last 100 years.

The Society's early interest in Ravenglass has already been noted. Ferguson and others soon turned their attention inland to Hardknott, with members of the Society supervising the clearance of the fort walls, its main internal buildings and its bath-house between 1889 and 1892, and producing a report which included a list of the artefacts recovered.[78] These were early days for such excavations and the excavators were unable to ascertain the function of the buildings, which today we recognise as the headquarters building, commander's house, granaries and bath-house. Dorothy Charlesworth returned to Hardknott in the 1960s to examine the buildings prior to consolidation by the Ministry of Works.[79] The samian ware recovered there suggests that occupation was largely confined to the Hadrianic period.

Ambleside lay at the eastern end of the road across the southern Lakeland hills from Ravenglass. R.G. Collingwood was at work there before the First World War, his excavations revealing evidence for two forts (fig. 1.13).[80] By this time, the purpose of the internal buildings was clearer. Ambleside continued in occupation into the late fourth century and is particularly notable for producing a tombstone of an ex-centurion and a clerk 'killed in the fort by the enemy'.[81] As at Hardknott, the gates and principal buildings of the fort have been laid out for public display.

Tim Potter's work at Ravenglass focused on the fort rather than the bath-house which had been the subject of the Society's previous attention. A ditch was claimed to surround a fortlet which was in turn interpreted as part of the system of milefortlets and towers found much further north beyond St Bees Head. It was succeeded by a fort, probably built late in Hadrian's reign and occupied into the late fourth century. Ravenglass has produced remarkable evidence for continuity of occupation. A lead sealing of *cohors I Aelia Classica* and a diploma issued to a soldier of that unit in 158 were found at the site, while the *Notitia Dignitatum* records the unit at Tunnocelum; if it is accepted that the regiment did not move, this is one of the longest known occupations of a fort by any unit in the Roman Empire.[82]

Potter also excavated at Watercrook.[83] The turf-and-timber fort appears to have been built at the end of the first century with the defences rebuilt in stone under Hadrian and again later in the century, probably after the abandonment of the Antonine Wall about 160. Occupation continued into the fourth century, but possibly not to the end. Outside the fort, two areas have been examined, producing evidence for extramural buildings, one with occupation ending about 220.

Roman camps attracted early attention. Ferguson reported on Crackenthorpe, but it was the surveys of Ian Richmond which were of fundamental importance to the wider study of marching camps.[84] Crackenthorpe and Reycross were identified as representing the invasion of north-west England by the Roman army (fig. 3.18).

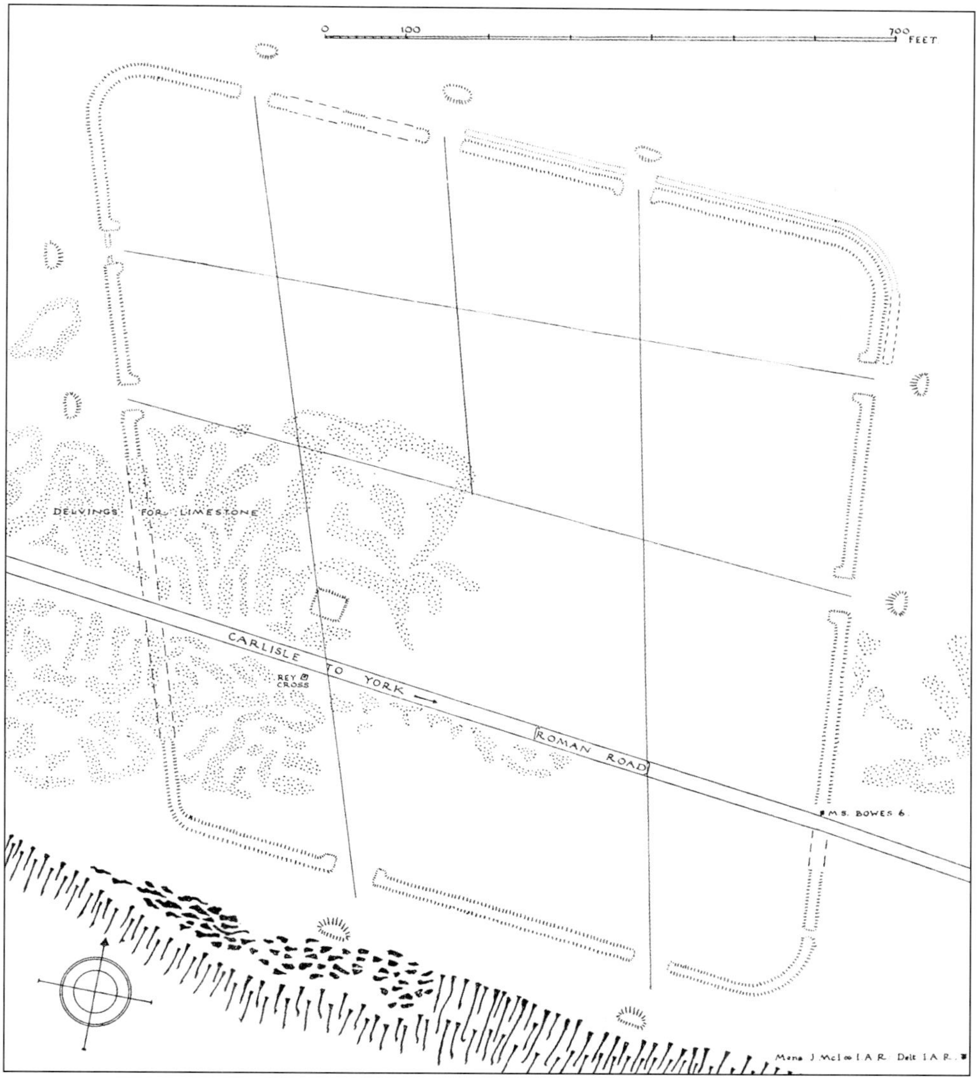

Fig. 3.18. Plan of Reycross camp in I.A. Richmond and J. McIntyre, 'The Roman camps at Reycross and Crackenthorpe', *CW2*, 34 (1934), opposite 50, fig. 1

At the other end of the scale there are fortlets and towers though the former are rare except along the coast. R.G. Collingwood examined Barrock Fell in 1931, finding late fourth-century pottery.[85] This is the same date as the material found at Maiden Castle on the Stainmore Pass where there also appears to have been a civil settlement.[86] Also on the Stainmore Pass are several towers. Richmond sought to make these into part of a long-distance signalling chain linking York with Carlisle, though subsequent excavation has demonstrated some of the difficulties with this hypothesis. The tower at Bowes Moor, excavated in 1990, produced only fourth-century material, including pottery dating to the last third of the century; investigations at other towers failed to reveal any dating evidence.[87] On the whole, archaeologists have not supported Richmond's interpretation.

Industrial activity, probably mostly associated with the army, has been recorded at a number of places, with the predominant evidence being for the production of tiles and pottery. Kilns have been recorded at Scalesceugh south of Carlisle worked by legionaries, at Muncaster near Ravenglass, and at Brampton, all mainly of early second-century date.[88] Mining was an activity supervised by the army. At Brough-under-Stainmore many lead sealings have been found, stamped with the names of army units and used to seal official packages. Four are stamped *METAL*, which points to the commodity being transported. It is likely that the metal was lead, mined in the vicinity of Whitley Castle.[89] There has, however, been no archaeological investigation to confirm such activity.

Soldiers retire and they die. At Beckfoot, a cremation cemetery lies beside the sea and is regularly damaged by erosion. Several funeral pyres have been recorded, one yielding weapons, as well as pottery vessels containing cremated bones. This cemetery was in use from the second to the fourth century and shares some similarities with that sample excavated outside the fort at Low Borrowbridge in the Tebay Gorge.[90] At Brougham, a cemetery was examined in advance of road-widening. This contained cremations dating to the third century and some inhumations which were probably fourth century. Some bodies were cremated on couches, others, including women, with horses.[91]

Civilians

The visible military remains were the main impetus to research on the Romans in the county, but civilian sites did not go unnoticed. An early paper considered 'the influence of the Roman occupation upon the distribution of population' with the discussion ranging widely over place-names and the influence of Christianity, rather than the recognition of genuinely Romano-British rural settlements.[92] The paucity of finds on rural settlements has continued to plague their study, even after the introduction of radiocarbon dates, as suitable material for dating is often not available. Hence, it is usually not easy to distinguish between pre-Roman and Roman-period settlements.

The extramural settlements outside the Roman forts are, however, a different matter. In 1880/81 Joseph Robinson examined some buildings north of the fort at Maryport, now the subject of re-excavation. Recently Maryport was also the subject of an extensive geophysical survey by TimeScape (fig. 3.19). This revealed not only the fort and civil settlement, with their roads and ditches, but nearby rural settlements. A similar pattern was recorded by Barri Jones at Old Carlisle. Such roads, however, cannot generally be traced other than a few metres beyond the civil settlements and so the wider

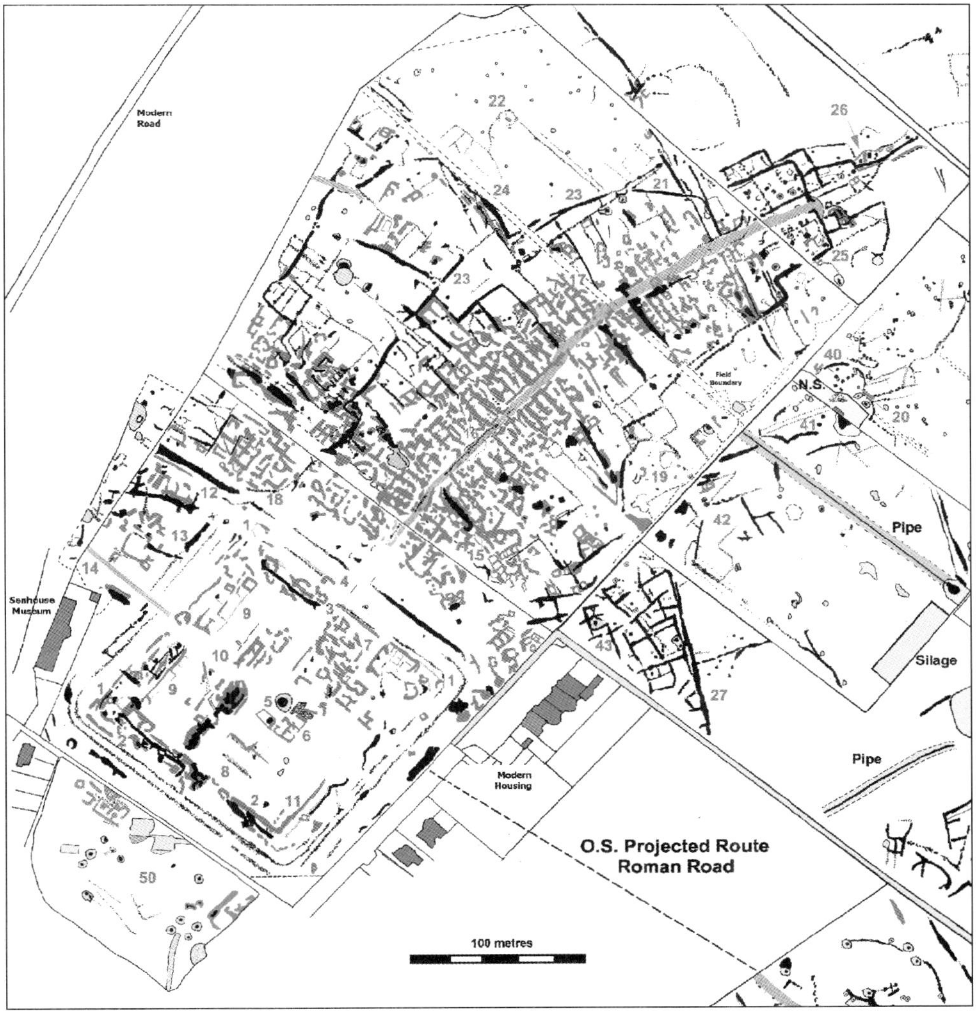

Fig. 3.19. Maryport geophysical plan by TimeScape *(reproduced by kind permission of J. Alan Biggins)*

relationships remain undiscovered. TimeScape have worked at other sites, including Birdoswald and Castlesteads on the Wall, and have produced geophysical surveys which demonstrate extensive extramural settlements, some larger in area than the forts at their core. It is not known, however, whether all the buildings were occupied at the same time nor who and how many people lived in them.

Carlisle

For many years the great invisible site in the county was Carlisle. This was because there was little by way of redevelopment in the historic core until the 1970s. Chance discoveries were reported in *Transactions*; these were all of a civilian nature and the fort remained elusive. In 1978 Dorothy Charlesworth published a paper in the *Archaeological Journal* bringing together what little was known about the Roman remains of Carlisle.[93] The same year, she started her own excavation at Annetwell Street, which led to the confirmation of the site of the fort and led on to further excavations by herself, Ian Caruana and John Zant, both then of the Carlisle Archaeological Unit (fig. 3.20).[94]

Fig. 3.20. Photograph of Carlisle excavation in the early 1980s. The photograph shows the southern ends of buildings in the interior of the fort in the foreground with the intervallum road behind and an oven and small structures in the intervallum area beyond. Early 2nd century AD *(photograph courtesy of Ian Caruana)*

Dendrochronological examination of timbers indicated that the trees were felled in the winter of 72/73, confirming the dates assigned to the earliest samian pottery from the site by J.P. Bushe-Fox.[95] The foundation- and end-dates of subsequent forts on the site were also clarified by dendrochronology. The first fort lasted some 30 years, but in that time was refurbished twice. Its successor lasted a similar period of time, but again was amended. A period of abandonment from the 140s to the 160s coincided with the occupation of the Antonine Wall. Military activity continued until the early fifth century.[96] It was not just the precision dating provided by dendrochronology that was significant, but the environmental material cast an interesting light on life in the fort: 'some features seem to have accumulated human cess and/or animal waste on a fairly casual basis, along with moss, frequently used for personal cleaning'. In other words, soldiers did not make it to the latrine on time, or just chose to defecate elsewhere. It would appear that 'large numbers of flies and other insects [that were] breeding in what appears to have been puddles of rotting waste in some parts of the site, could have been significant vectors in the spread of disease ... the two commonest, the house fly ... and the stable fly ... can spread salmonella, typhoid, diarrhoea, and possibly even poliomyelitis'.[97] This is a considerable challenge to our view of Roman cleanliness as represented by the Housesteads latrine.

Carlisle also provided the first – and so far only – writing tablets from the county.[98] One appears to refer to the *ala Sebosiana*; another lists the consumption of barley and wheat and is therefore a valuable contribution to the discussion of Roman army rations; a third lists the soldiers who had lost their lances (*Tab. Luguval.* 1, 16 and 44). A writing tablet found at Vindolanda refers to the centurion in charge of the region at *Luguvalium* (*Tab. Vindol.* II 250).

Unlike other areas of the county, archaeology in a dense urban environment such as Carlisle has always been more difficult for the unfunded amateur and since the 1970s it has fallen to the professional units responding to commercial pressures and with access to modern techniques and funding. Perhaps not surprisingly the results have often appeared not in *Transactions* but elsewhere.

Recent Developments – Current Understanding

Much of the work described above was carried out by members of the Society and published in *Transactions* (with offprints, especially of Hadrian's Wall, being made widely available) or in the Society's other publications. It has been joined by other publications on Roman sites. These, however, have been piecemeal and sporadic. There have been three major campaigns, all supported by the Society: Francis Haverfield on Hadrian's Wall from 1894 to 1903;

Gerald Simpson and Ian Richmond, also on Hadrian's Wall, after 1927; and the long campaign of Richard Bellhouse, mainly on the Cumberland coast. Reports on the tracing of Roman roads, and on the survey and excavation of Roman camps and forts, have all been published through the Society. It is doubtful if there is a Roman fort in the county which has not been the subject of a review article by R.G. Collingwood or Eric Birley.

As a result of all this work our knowledge of Roman activity in the area has been expanded and our understanding of its significance transformed. The Society's contributions have underpinned many of the more general publications on that period and have influenced work on key sites which have emerged in recent years by scholars operating outside the region and the Society. Placing to one side any earlier Roman military intervention, the collapse of the Brigantian client state in 68/69 was the occasion for a campaign which reached Carlisle where a fort was established using timbers felled in the winter of 72/73. Other forts were constructed at that time or soon afterwards, but the Roman armies swept onwards to victory at Mons Graupius, somewhere in modern Scotland, in 83. Subsequent withdrawal from the more northerly conquests and the consolidation of the frontier on the Tyne-Solway isthmus in 102-105 led to more forts being built in Cumbria. The situation was reinforced by the construction of Hadrian's Wall in the 120s.[99]

A great contribution of the Society to Romano-British studies has been the elucidation of the building history of that frontier. One long-held view was that the forts lying to the south of Hadrian's Wall on the Stanegate were abandoned when the Wall was built. The excavations at Carlisle helped to disprove that; Vindolanda and Corbridge as well as Carlisle were rebuilt or refurbished about the time that the Wall was occupied, with some evidence from Nether Denton hinting at the same situation.[100] The occupation of Lowland Scotland and the Antonine Wall for about 20 years from 142 brought about a reduction in the number of forts in Cumbria, but withdrawal south led to the reoccupation of most of these forts in the 160s.[101] Most of them were still occupied about 400 according to the *Notitia Dignitatum*, a list of the senior officials of the Roman Empire, though in many cases a different unit occupied the fort.

So much for military deployment, but it is necessary to scratch beneath the surface to seek the reasons for this pattern of forts. The traditional approach has been to see army units as supporting those troops based on Hadrian's Wall in the face of hostile pressure from the northern tribes, pressure which certainly existed in the second and fourth centuries.[102] A different explanation was offered by Brian Dobson in 1970.[103] He argued that the concentration of forts in northern England in the years following the abandonment of the Antonine Wall in the 160s was nothing to do with ensuring the security of the northern frontier but all to do with finding locations for the regiments in the large army of Britain. This was rejected by Paul Bidwell and Nick Hodgson, who preferred to see the issue as one of internal security coupled with a need to have troops available to deal with attackers on the northern frontier.[104] In particular, they directed attention to the concentration of forts in Cumbria, so repeating the traditional view for their presence but adding a further consideration – a concern with internal insecurity.

A different slant was offered by Nick Higham. He acknowledged the possibility that the army needed to hold down a considerable and potentially hostile population but he also suggested that forts were located in relation to supplies of grain, that is, close to good farmland,[105] although in fact there is little evidence for cereal cultivation in Cumbria at this time. He emphasised that the two aspects are not mutually exclusive: people lived where there was good farmland and for both reasons this was a good place to locate Roman forts. Higham's argument receives some support from the Theodosian Code, dating to 369, in which it is stated that the Praetorian Prefect 'shall order supplies of subsistence allowances to be brought to the forts by the provincials nearest to the borders'.

In 1974 John Mann drew attention to the implications of the appearance in the *Notitia Dignitatum* of new-style military units in many of the northern forts. Mann argued that the forts were abandoned in the peaceful conditions of the later third century but reoccupied in the face of new threats in the form of the Picts and Scots from about 300 onwards, when 'their distribution, mainly on the two main routes north to the Wall from York, shows that they were intended as mobile reinforcements for the forces *per lineam valli*, not as a means of holding in subjection the area south of Hadrian's Wall'.[106] The suggestion that troops were withdrawn from northern Britain in the later third century has been challenged by Sheppard Frere and by Paul Bidwell and Nick Hodgson who argued, on the basis of their interpretation of the archaeological evidence, that these forts were not abandoned.[107] My own review of the evidence left me agnostic as the archaeological evidence did not appear to be sufficiently strong to point in either direction.[108] However, new units certainly arrived to occupy forts in northern England, new military installations were built and others were reoccupied, such as the fortlet at Barrock Fell and the fort at Burrow Walls both, it would appear, in the late fourth century.[109] The army of Britain was strengthened by the addition of new units in the fourth century and by a field army at the end of the century, though where that was based is not known. So far as we can understand, the Roman army was in a healthy state on the abandonment of Britain by the Roman Empire in 409.

A further consideration is the relationship between the military and the civilians in Cumbria, an issue even more intractable than the reasons for the military deployment. This is because of the lack of cultural material on rural sites. Whatever the form of contact, it did not lead to significant quantities of Roman material finding its way to the local farmsteads. There are ways in which this might be explained such as the Roman form of taxation or the manner in which the Roman army acted as the upper level of society so preventing the growth of a 'normal' settlement hierarchy.[110] Yet the lack of such material is interesting given the manner in which extramural settlements outside Roman forts appear to have related to the surrounding countryside. The earlier aerial photographs of Barri Jones which showed roads leading from the civil settlement outside the fort at Old Carlisle into the countryside suggested a close relationship. Subsequent geophysical surveys at forts in the county have reinforced that impression. A typical Romano-British-style rural settlement lies on the far side of the ridge occupied by the fort at Maryport, apparently linked to the Roman road pattern.[111] The fundamental problem, however, is the paucity of Roman artefacts on rural sites and until there is more information it is doubtful if we can proceed much further with this aspect of the Roman period in the county.

Faced with this lacuna in the archaeological record, Barri Jones offered a different approach, comparing the morphology of settlements north and south of the Solway to determine if it was possible to recognise the impact of Rome.[112] He noted that 70 per cent of the sites south of the Solway are of the 'elliptical univallate variety', the sub-rectangular sites account for only 18 per cent of the total, and only just over one per cent are bivallate. Nearly seven per cent of the sites were associated with some form of sub-rectangular field system or equivalent. North of the Solway the norm remains the elliptical univallate enclosure, with bivallate or multi-vallate sites accounting for 19.5 per cent of the total and sub-rectangular sites rare with only 3.6 per cent of the total, and with field systems very unusual. He also emphasised the greater density of sites south of the Solway. He concluded that settlement density was thinner north of the Solway; that sites were more heavily defended; that they were largely elliptical in shape, and lacked field systems, and that the existence of more sub-rectangular sites coupled with field systems south of the Solway argued for their Roman date. He put down the differences to the existence of Hadrian's Wall, which allowed the growth of a prosperous and stable agricultural economy.

Jones elaborated his argument, but some points may be made about his core evidence. First is that the conclusions are based on a relatively small evidential base. Second is that the main type of site both north and south of the Solway is the elliptical univallate enclosure, with 70 per cent of the sites to the south of this type and 77 per cent to the north. Finally, the argument that sub-rectangular sites have to be Romano-British in date, an argument based simply on their shape, has been rejected; Jobey pointed out that these sites are found primarily on the Northumberland plain, whereas the elliptical sites are mainly found on the rounded hill-tops.[113] Further aerial survey and excavation should improve the database and allow further discussion to take place. In the meantime, little progress on this issue has been made in the last 30 years.

Post-Roman

Early Medieval

The period after the end of Roman governance, and before the development of a recognisably medieval landscape of small towns and villages, is difficult to characterise, because of a lack of type sites, material culture and documentary sources. It was a time of great change politically, as the seemingly monolithic Roman Empire fragmented, to be replaced by smaller polities, before, in the tenth century, the nation states of England and Scotland started to be constructed. It was, however, a time when literature indicates that 'culture' blossomed, particularly in the sixth to ninth centuries. First the British kingdom of Rheged grew in dominance and flourished, especially under its renowned king, Urien,[114] then, as Rheged declined, the Anglian kingdom of Northumbria rose to prominence at the beginning of the seventh century, for much of that century dominating the Anglo-Saxon kingdoms of the Heptarchy. It also produced the great historian, the Venerable Bede.[115] In the mid-ninth century, however, it in turn fragmented under pressure from Viking incursions, particularly that of the 'Great Heathen Host' in 866.[116] For the next 200 years, the political situation remained confused, until William II (Rufus) took Carlisle in 1092, claiming it as the north-western outpost of England.[117]

The Society has had an important role in developing an understanding of the chronology of this difficult period, with the publication of several seminal articles, including those on Gospatric's Charter by Revd F.W. Ragg in 1905, and those on the historical development of the region by D.P. Kirby in 1962 and P.A. Wilson in 1966.[118] In strictly archaeological terms, little detail is known even today about Cumbria in these centuries. The two main strands of evidence are place-names, and the hugely significant corpus of stone sculpture that exists in Cumbria, particularly along the west coast, and in the Eden and Lune valleys.[119] The Society does not seem to have been particularly interested in place-names themselves, although contributors did consider significant church dedications, indicating the likelihood of early medieval foundations.[120] *Transactions*, especially from the 1880s to the 1930s, did, however, play a crucial part in publishing descriptions and, on occasions, illustrations of early stone sculpture (fig. 3.21). It was these descriptions, particularly regular articles by W.G. Collingwood between 1903 and 1926, but also the work of the Revd Calverley, that formed much of the basis of the definitive work on these pieces: the second volume of the *British Academy Corpus of Anglo-Saxon Stone Sculpture*.[121]

Fig. 3.21. Illustration from W.G. Collingwood, 'The Giant's Thumb' [Penrith], *CW2*, 20 (1920), opposite 53

Excavation of sites from the period is very rare, but the examination of the drain at the early Christian site at Dacre was published by F. Hudleston in 1932.[122] Whilst the full results of excavations there in the 1980s will be published elsewhere, *Transactions* has proved valuable as a means of placing interim statements in the public domain, both for Dacre and for several others excavated by the professional archaeological units that were founded in the later 1970s.[123]

Until very recently, physical evidence for a Viking presence in the region was largely limited to distinctive styles and iconography of the stone sculpture, isolated objects, and the contents of antiquarian reports. Again, *Transactions* was the medium by which many of these finds, particularly the antiquarian reports, were placed in the public domain.[124] The most valuable are undoubtedly the three articles published over a period of 30 years by J.D. Cowen, who produced a collated record of all the material other than sculpture that had been reported in Cumbria.[125] *Transactions* has also published the results of a limited modern re-excavation of the site of a Viking burial near Aspatria, first excavated in 1789, which has added valuable new details.[126] This work also spurred the re-evaluation of a stone found in 1789, as a result of which this was reinterpreted as belonging to the early medieval period.[127]

Cumbria does contain a monument of some mystery, but of importance, in the form of the Thingmount, or Law Ting, as it was called in the nineteenth century, in Little Langdale (fig. 4.1). This was described by Henry Swainson Cowper in 1891, providing context to such sites as meeting places of the Vikings, where laws were agreed. The article is of importance, however, in that it not only describes the mound in detail, but also provides a surveyed plan of the site, one of the earliest examples of landscape survey in Cumbria.[128]

The Medieval and Post-Medieval Periods

The level of interest shown in *Transactions* for the archaeology of the centuries after the Norman Conquest is notably lower than that for both the prehistoric and the Roman periods. To be fair, there are many articles concerning medieval and post-medieval sites, particularly from the early years of the Society, but these tend to be descriptions of standing buildings, integrated with historical accounts of the families that occupied them (see Chapter 5). These did not concentrate only on the great buildings of the area like castles and monasteries;[129] many discussed parish churches and gentry buildings, and a few some lesser buildings. In this vein, Taylor's *The Old Manorial Halls of Westmorland and Cumberland* was an early exemplar.[130] The extent of the Society's work is yet another example of the forward thinking of the first contributors to *Transactions*, and why these volumes are such a valuable resource. Indeed, Taylor's work, and that of other contributors, was built upon 100 years later, by Denis Perriam and John Robinson in their illustrated gazetteer.[131] There were also articles that described and catalogued church plate, medieval gravestones and other architectural fragments, misericords, and even masons' marks.[132]

One of the earliest accounts of an excavation is of a medieval site, Calder Abbey, but this is the exception that proves the rule.[133] It is not an account of a scientific excavation but, as its title honestly relates, of 'explorations', which cleared the overburden to reveal specific architectural features. In this, they differed from a modern archaeological approach, which would have recorded the subtleties of the overburden, as well as the architectural features! The Calder Abbey 'explorations' were followed by much more extensive works at Furness Abbey, an early foray into what was then Lancashire (see Chapter 1), undertaken in the 1890s by Sir William St John Hope, then Assistant Secretary of the Society of Antiquaries of London, who had at that time a reputation for the study and excavation of medieval monasteries (fig. 3.22).[134] This article demonstrated St John Hope's laudable commitment to publishing significant work locally, rather than in a national journal, such as *Archaeologia*, to which he had easy access. The work is, however, recorded in the context of an account of the chronological development of various elements of the abbey, rather than as a formal excavation report. It nevertheless has formed the

Fig. 3.22. Furness Abbey: west side of transepts looking east, *CW1*, 16 (1900), 241

basis for all the modern work at the Abbey.[135] Both sites were subsequently re-assessed, Calder by Mary Fair in 1953 and Furness by John Dickinson in 1967, as well as more recently.[136] In 1906, excavations were undertaken at Holm Cultram Abbey, after a doorway was found during alterations to the church. The excavations in front of this doorway revealed an expanse of tiled floor, and detailed plans were made of this, including the patterns on the tiles. However, nowhere is the position of the doorway in relation to the church shown on plan! In those days, it was considered appropriate to locate the work by the written word alone.[137] Other early excavations included establishing the plan of the priory church at Conishead.[138]

Clearance work was also undertaken adjacent to the church at Ravenstonedale in 1928 and 1929.[139] This site of a Gilbertine priory is unusual in Cumbria, since most of the religious houses belonged to the major orders, and the results obtained – a mixture of decorated grave slabs and a suite of buildings – led the excavators to suggest that they had found a late medieval manor house. The site was subject to consolidation and re-evaluation in the 1980s, which established that the earliest structures were likely to form part of a conventional cloister but that the building was later adapted to something approaching a manor house.[140] The clearance work in the 1920s had removed much valuable information without adequate recording however, so much of the proposed sequence is speculation. This approach was common at the turn of the nineteenth century, as can be seen from the report on the well-chapel at Church Brow, Gosforth, examined under the leadership of W.G. Collingwood.[141]

Early reports in *Transactions* were not limited to descriptions and clearance of religious sites, however, as contributors also undertook fieldwork to record notable earthworks. Two such are the reports on the Bishop's, or Baron's Dyke, which crosses Hadrian's Wall at Bleatarn, east of Carlisle, and on the boundary at Rydal, the latter arising from disputed ownership.[142] These articles, while short, included measured profiles of the earthworks, as well as a description, strikingly modern concepts for such early work. Other investigators noted the presence of lynchets and other evidence of cultivation, without necessarily being able to interpret the remains.[143]

The beginning of the twentieth century saw the start of regular contributions to *Transactions* by T.H.B. Graham about townships and parishes within the medieval Barony of Gilsland in north-eastern Cumbria. Whilst his approach was more historical than based on classical fieldwork, he used early mapping to draw a picture of the development of the area, and particularly concentrated on teasing out the townfields of each settlement. These maps provide a vital tool for any landscape archaeologist. Graham published on average at least one article every year from 1907 until his death in 1937, and encouraged a raft of others to compile accounts of parish and township townfields throughout Cumbria.[144]

The ancient bridges of the region were another early interest of contributors to *Transactions*. These included packhorse bridges, brought together in an important article by W.G. Collingwood, in which he not only described the structures, but published a photograph of each as well.[145] In addition, specific ancient bridges were described and photographed, such as Bow Bridge close to Furness Abbey (fig. 3.23), and that at Lanercost, examined by R.G. Collingwood because of a claim that it was Roman in origin, a claim which he dismissed.[146] Fords and ancient roads were also scrutinised, and, on occasions the work of various scholars came together This happened with Paul Kelly's study of an ancient route in Furness and with the work of Melville and Hobbs, who subsequently described a bridge on the route.[147] Historical references to the fording of the Solway were also published.[148]

Occasionally, considerable ingenuity was displayed by the early members of the Society. For instance, historical research alerted Revd Gordon to the fact that the present parish church of Addingham was not in its original position, a point raised during the Society's excursion to the area in 1912. Hutchinson had noted in 1794 that the church had once stood at the north-western extremity of the parish, close to the River Eden, but had been washed away by the river, leaving only a small part of the churchyard remaining.[149] Revd

Fig. 3.23. View of Bow Bridge in P.V. Kelly, 'A bridge of monastic date and other finds at Furness Abbey', *CW2*, 26 (1926), 262

Gordon followed up the initial discussion at the 1912 excursion with his own research, studying documentary sources and undertaking a site inspection, which convinced him that evidence of the church would remain in the Eden. The fortuitous circumstances of the hot summer of 1913 resulted in the river being exceptionally low, so Gordon seized his opportunity and marshalled a 'body of men' in rowing boats with grappling hooks to scan the river bed to retrieve anything of potential interest and to log where the stones had come from. By this means, he retrieved several stones of significance, which had survived their immersion remarkably well, including two demonstrating the early medieval origins of the site, as well as a further medieval tombstone.[150]

Other excavations tended to be eclectic. H. Swainson Cowper excavated some rectangular structures between Great and Little Langdale, and in the process produced rare 'ethnographical' evidence, including a photograph, of the 'wigwams' used by bark peelers in Furness (fig. 3.24).[151] An article on the caves of 'Isis Parlis', in the river cliffs on the opposite bank of the Eden to the church of Ninekirks, combined historical and folkloric information with a description of the caves, as they survived in 1913, as well as quoting an extract from the *Penrith Observer* of June 1913, which described the excavation of the largest cave.[152] Whilst rare, occasionally articles appeared that examined assemblages of artefacts, such as that describing, and publishing a photograph of, sherds of medieval pottery. The author noted, however, that this material had been identified (having been dug up apparently by rabbits!) in the course of work to find prehistoric sites, but he laudably felt that other information found in the course of this 'quest' should be placed on record.[153]

Reports on these sites were also influential in the development of modern archaeological publication. Thomas Hay was particularly assiduous during the Second World War in recording his observations. These included pitsteads and small limekilns, lynchets, and a description of a so-called goose bield in Ennerdale. This unusual feature would almost certainly puzzle the modern archaeologist, and needed oral history to provide an interpretation – as a fox trap! [154] Sadly, whilst there are photographs of many of these features, mapping to illustrate their whereabouts is wanting. This changed somewhat in 1945, when Hay published a brief article on a clearly extensive landscape survey in Buttermere, where he recorded a number of features, which he mapped.[155] Early members of the Society also showed an interest in industrial archaeology with their articles again demonstrating remarkable forward thinking, including the chemical analysis of slags as early as 1912 (see Chapter 7).[156]

From the 1950s onwards, excavation became a more prominent aspect of research into medieval and post-medieval Cumbria. There was also a notable growth in the reporting of finds associated with such sites, rather than merely describing the features uncovered. This change in outlook seems to have

Fig. 3.24. Bark peelers' hut in H.S. Cowper, 'A contrast in architecture', *CW2*, 1 (1901), opposite 142

owed much to Robert Hogg, Keeper of Archaeology and Geology (1949-66), and later Curator of Tullie House Museum and Art Gallery (1966-75), who was very active in Carlisle and its surrounding area from the early 1950s. His publications started with reporting accessions to the museum, such as a fine medieval jug, which included detailed descriptions. He also took opportunities to excavate, either as a matter of rescuing information in advance of development or in a research context, and during that decade he was involved with excavations on the fortified manor house at Burgh-by-Sands and on several sites in Carlisle.[157] The first such excavation in 1950 was that at the Burgh site, which was matched by an article providing the history of the Barony of Burgh, to give a context to the excavation.[158] Although only a relatively small element of the site was sampled, it nevertheless provided not only an idea of the phasing and overall plan of the site, but also of its relationship to the reconstruction of Hadrian's Wall in stone, astride which it was built. The evolution of Hogg's reports can be seen in the lack of reference to any of the finds from this work, in contrast to his reporting of medieval material excavated in Carlisle in 1953. Whilst the majority of the features excavated there were Roman, and the main thrust of the report was on this material, it nevertheless also contained a seminal analysis and report on medieval pottery from the city, including detailed drawings, as well as a report on some firing experiments. This was followed between 1954 to 1956 by excavations at Tullie House itself, where again the excavation was concentrated on Roman features, but a detailed report on the medieval pottery was also produced.[159] These pottery reports have ever since formed the basis of an understanding of medieval pottery, not just in Carlisle, but in Cumbria as a whole. Hogg's work marks the beginning of archaeological excavations and reports that are recognisably 'modern' in format and content although, until the end of the 1970s, such material in *Transactions* is quite sparse, with sites such as that at Millhouse in the Lune Valley being the exception. This medieval house site was surveyed within its landscape, the house was then excavated, and the results published with detailed catalogues of the finds.[160]

The year 1979 heralded a further sea change, not just because after that date each volume of *Transactions* regularly contained several excavation reports, largely as a result of the creation of professional archaeological units in the region, but also because of the establishment of the Society's Research Series, which was designed to bring larger archaeological reports into the public domain. Whilst, like much of the archaeological content of *Transactions*, the series has a bias towards Roman sites (perhaps the consequence of the power that Romanists have wielded in the Society), nevertheless, excavations of several significant medieval sites have also been published over the last 35 years, including early medieval and medieval sites in Blackfriars Street (the site of the Dominican Friary) and Castle Street, Carlisle, as well as building surveys and excavations at Brougham Castle and Lanercost Priory.[161] The latter two sites have also been supplemented by articles in *Transactions*, with small-scale work at Lanercost reported on in 1998 and excavations at Brougham Castle in 1992 and again in 2001.[162] The creation of the Cumbria Archaeological Research Reports (CARR) series has enabled surveys of a number of significant medieval sites to be published since 2011, to the great benefit of the county's medieval history. Finally, the Extra Series has made occasional forays into the realms of archaeology such as the important volume drawing together archaeological and historical sources to produce an overview of the development of Carlisle.[163]

The dissemination of the results of excavations and other fieldwork in the Society's publications can broadly be divided into three groups: work on the greater monuments, such as castles and monasteries, together with 'gentry' houses; urban excavations; and sites in a rural context, including industrial sites (see Chapters 5 and 7). Excavation work on the greater monuments has tended to be small in scale, and targeted towards managing specific issues of conservation. This has included work at Egremont Castle, Clifton Hall, near Penrith, the Fratry and Carlisle Cathedral, Piel Castle near Barrow-in-Furness, the environs of Cartmel Priory, Crookdake Hall, Wigton, and Down Hall, Aikton.[164] Recent volumes in the Society's CARR series document work on the cloisters at Holm Cultram Abbey, and the excavations undertaken in the late 1960s at Aldingham Motte on the Furness Peninsula.[165]

Reports of urban excavations have tended to concentrate on Carlisle, particularly small-scale work on the walls, and findings related to medieval and post-medieval stratigraphy above the better-preserved Roman levels in the city centre.[166] The CARR series has also included a volume describing two sites at opposite ends of the historic city. That detailing the medieval and post-medieval sequences in the northern defences of the city at Rickergate was one of the first major reports on medieval Carlisle to be produced.[167] Some individually important sites have also been reported on in *Transactions*, such as the excavations at St Nicholas' Hospital, immediately beyond the medieval city, and the building survey and excavations of the Carnaud Metal Box site, again immediately outside the historic city.[168] Other towns have fared less well, although excavations within Egremont's town centre, Appleby, Ulverston and Kendal, as well as on the Old Fort at Whitehaven, have been published. The latter was the main defensive point for the harbour, probably constructed in the earlier part of the eighteenth century.[169] In 2012 the Society published a report on the medieval and post-medieval sequence of occupation of adjoining burgage plots in Cockermouth.[170] Of the smaller towns, Penrith has perhaps seen the most work published, but, of course, like any urban area, this can only represent a small proportion of what may survive. The results of excavations on the site of the modern market, immediately to the north of the parish church, were published in 2000, and more recent work in advance of two redevelopments has also been published.[171] The regeneration of brownfield sites in urban areas has also created an opportunity for a range of industries to be examined (see Chapter 7).

In a rural context, an early example of modern excavation in difficult conditions was published in 1979. This reported on the excavation of a shieling site in Bewcastle, by the then Field Study section of the Society (see Chapter 1), in advance of forestry planting. This provided important details for a type of site ubiquitous in many upland areas, but little studied. Another such site was excavated in the Howgills in the 1990s. Both demonstrated the difficulties of excavating sites with little in the way of a material cultural assemblage to tease the fullest interpretation from the limited evidence. In 1979, *Transactions* published a note on the survey of deserted farmsteads in Miterdale and, in the next few years, survey work on shielings and peat-storage huts in Eskdale was also reported on (see Chapter 6).[172]

The importance of combining historical research with archaeological fieldwork was demonstrated in Buttermere, where a study of a vaccary at Gatesgarth Farm was followed serendipitously by limited excavations, producing evidence for a longhouse.[173] Another successful investigation combined excavation work on the bank of the River Derwent in upper

Borrowdale, which was subject to rapid erosion, with analysis of a sample of peat taken some five years before by staff of the University of Oxford. Together, these provided evidence for large-scale woodland clearance dated by radiocarbon assay to the thirteenth to fifteenth centuries, a time of change to both the climate and the landscape, the latter wrought by the development of large monastic holdings in the uplands.[174]

The legacy of monasteries on the wider landscape has been examined in the last 20 years, albeit in quite small-scale, detailed work. Excavations in advance of repairs to the sea defences at Skinburness revealed an earlier element, underlying a post-medieval rebuild, that had been reinforced on the seaward side with substantial timbers held in place by stakes. Whilst this early work was not dated precisely, there are documentary references to a grange of Holm Cultram Abbey at Skinburness, which in turn developed into a small town that was destroyed by the sea at the beginning of the fourteenth century. Tradition has it that the first sea defence was constructed shortly after, and there are documents from the sixteenth century referring to such defences.[175] In a similar vein, a fishery on the River Eden is believed to have been part of an early grant to Wetheral Priory, although the opportunity to examine the existing salmon coops, following the great flood of 2005, demonstrated that the surviving structures belonged to post-medieval management of the Corby Castle estate, with artificial islands being constructed in the seventeenth or eighteenth century, and the coops themselves being constructed in the later eighteenth or nineteenth century.[176]

Wider rural landscapes have been examined, often in advance of large-scale development, such as opencast mining to the east of Whitehaven. There, in the Keekle Coalfield, four post-medieval farmsteads were recorded prior to demolition, and their footprints were then excavated, together with a sample of the surrounding landscape.[177] The area on the western side of Stainmore was also examined in advance of improvements to the A66. Unsurprisingly, this work focused on earlier routeways, examining hollow-ways by both survey and excavation, as well as recording the farmhouse at Craco prior to demolition, and subsequently excavating its footprint. In addition, a section was cut through a probable deer park boundary at Augill Bridge.[178] Earlier, smaller-scale work in advance of improvements to the A66 at Brough revealed evidence of possible medieval, and certain post-medieval, buildings on the edge of Church Brough, as well as a possible earlier line of the main road.[179] A totally unexpected discovery in the course of infrastructure development was that of a medieval dugout boat, found in the peat of a former tarn during the creation of a British Gas pipeline through Shap. This remarkable vessel was later proved to have been made from a tree felled in the thirteenth century.[180] Much of Cumbria's industrial past also still lies in open countryside but work on these sites has tended to have been directly associated with their management, frequently limiting the extent of the research possible.

More recently, developments on the edges of settlements have tended to be associated with residential expansion, particularly around Carlisle, where such work at Rickerby House and Cumwhinton has produced information on medieval and post-medieval occupation on the periphery of settlements behind the street frontages. Both produced evidence for corn-drying kilns and Cumwhinton also yielded important evidence for a local pottery industry.[181] Evidence for medieval pottery kilns is remarkably sparse in Cumbria, though their existence is strongly implied by the presence of wasters, as at Cumwhinton. Plotting the incidence of pottery in gardens in Arnside and Silverdale has done much to establish the focus of potting in these settlements.[182] Similarly, though on a smaller-scale, sites have been found at St Bees where John Todd recorded both the mill leat and a corn-drying kiln on the edge of the village, both associated with the priory.[183] Brian Roberts has also published surveys of several medieval earthworks, including Maulds Meaburn and near Crosby Ravensworth.[184] A more unusual piece of work involved small-scale excavations on the footprint of the medieval parish church at Farlam, which was demolished in 1859-60, a new church being built by Anthony Salvin on a nearby site. This work located the medieval building, which survived only as rubble foundations, and allowed its dimensions and layout to be compared with the sketch in the Lanercost Cartulary and nineteenth-century watercolours, the latter apparently painted shortly before the church was demolished.[185]

Conclusion

Cumbria has been fortunate in the calibre of the archaeologists who have worked there, and the area has seen much work that was pioneering. Perhaps the most significant fieldworker was R.G Collingwood. He did not just excavate but as a philosopher he brought to archaeology his own particular outlook. He argued in favour of survey before excavation and, once a site was chosen for such examination, the formulation of questions about it. Today's archaeologists would support the same principles, though perhaps with wider questions than those posed by Collingwood, but that is the result of more knowledge of the possibilities. He is also notable in believing that material culture was not the only, or even always a secure, way of dating sites. Long before the advent of radiocarbon dating, he stands out as an advocate of logic, famously noting that:

> the negative side of this evidence [for Ewe Close] must be handled with care ... there is reason to believe that they [the pre- and post-Roman Britons of the district] had very little of such nature

> [material culture] to leave clues to the archaeologist. If a village like this had a long life before, during and after the Roman period, it is probable that excavation would yield, as at Ewe Close it did, finds of Roman date and no others.[186]

It took more than 50 years for archaeologists to develop techniques that vindicated this view, with the result that the 'missing' so-called 'Dark Ages' are now being revealed through scientific dating on many sites which have produced only a Roman material culture.

The basic aspects of survey and excavation have been supplemented by a range of scientific techniques. Aerial survey started nearly 100 years ago but much of the county is not conducive to such photography owing to the nature of the terrain and the quantity of pasture rather than arable land. The Solway Plain forms a notable exception. Recent developments using Lidar data (a recording method which can see through vegetation to provide a map of the landscape below) and drones will do much to redress the balance. The Roman remains of the county in particular have been subject to geophysical survey, most notably by Alan Biggins and David Taylor of TimeScape; but again, this is a technique that does not always work well in Cumbria. However, their surveys around Roman forts have produced remarkable results which have revolutionised our understanding of the associated civil settlements.[187] The other major development has been the growth of metal-detector use, which has created an ever-expanding corpus of finds. These have latterly been recorded by the Portable Antiquities Scheme, overseen by the British Museum, which began soon after the 1996 Treasure Act came into force. It is of little surprise that the late 1990s saw several articles in *Transactions* featuring the results of metal detection although, as the website for the Scheme was developed and reporting routines became more established, this subsided.[188]

What we might today call landscape archaeology, the attempt to place sites in their environment, is not new. Yet again, Cumbria saw pioneering work in this field with the development of palynology (pollen analysis), through the work of Winifred Pennington, one of the scholars who helped to create the discipline of palaeoecology, or the study of biological remains, such as bone, shell, plants, insects and microfossils from archaeological sites, with a view to reconstructing elements of living conditions in the past. She was born in Barrow in 1915 and some of her early work was in Cumbria. Unfortunately this was before radiocarbon dates were regularly applied to pollen cores but her work is still used as a basis for the modern understanding of the area's environment, supplemented by radiocarbon dates that are largely supporting, although refining, the conclusions she drew 50 years ago.[189]

In the county, as in most others, the development of archaeological understanding has been strongly influenced by the specific interests of individuals, perhaps most notably exemplified by the Collingwood and Cherry families. Bob Bewley has pointed to the resulting haphazard nature of our knowledge of the archaeology of the county.[190] The world of developer-funded archaeology, only 30 or so years old, is changing the pattern of our knowledge through its indiscriminate approach, in that the new evidence does not relate to the interests of individuals but rather to the economic development of the county. This, however, produces its own biases, as development pressures are largely in lowland contexts, particularly surrounding existing urban centres. This bias is now being reflected in the pages of *Transactions*, as developer-funded work is coming to publication.

In order to predict accurately where there might be archaeological remains, so critical for the development process, a list of all known archaeological sites and material is fundamental. This is why all counties compiled (and maintain, as far as funding will allow) an Historic Environment Record. These were formerly known as Sites and Monuments Records, and have been created over the last 35-40 or so years. Cumbria saw the beginnings of such a list 50 years ahead of its time, unsurprisingly through the forethought of the Collingwoods (see pages 96, 98). In the 1920s, W.G. published lists of the ancient monuments, firstly of Cumberland, and then Westmorland and Lancashire North of the Sands.[191] This was followed by R.G. who, soon after his father's death, produced a seminal article on the prehistory of Cumberland, Westmorland, and Lancashire North of the Sands, which not only summarised the understanding of this long period , but made suggestions about a policy of research, anticipating the development of regional research frameworks by 70 years![192]

Interpretations will inevitably change as new information becomes available and new techniques of survey and excavation, and also scientific study, are developed. The continuity represented by *Transactions* and other Society publications allows these to be tracked, either at a macro-level, as in the changing interpretations of the Roman frontier, or at an individual site level. One example of the latter is the site at Aldingham motte, on the Furness Peninsula, which the Society visited several times. In 1877 James Simpson had subscribed to Thomas West's view that the mound was Roman. Others had thought that it might be funerary, a view which had been advanced by Colonel Bradyll on the basis of his earlier excavations but only reported in 1887 by Chancellor Ferguson, a theory which he summarily dismissed. Another opinion, advanced by W.B. Kendall, was that it was the principal landing place of the Anglians in Furness, a view subscribed to by Chancellor Ferguson in 1887. Yet others had thought it was a Viking 'thingmound', although Collingwood specifically distanced himself from this in 1905. Paul Kelly's paper, read during the excursion in 1923, rehearsed these 'many and divergent' interpretations made by Society luminaries, but felt that the most convincing explanation was that it was a Norman motte, the argument advanced by John F. Curwen in his book of 1913. Excavations were finally undertaken there in the late 1960s, which demonstrated that it was indeed Norman, and finally in 2015 the Society published the definitive report on this interesting site.[193]

What are the challenges for the Society in promoting archaeology in the county today? Cuts to county council funding make it difficult to maintain an adequate advisory service and Historic Environment Record and, while advances in so many scientific disciplines related to archaeology mean that we can learn more, almost with each passing excavation, most certainly with each year, the increases in the costs of archaeological work are commensurately greater. Consequently, the Society finds itself unable to make grants in relation to the cost of a whole project, as it once did, but it can still usefully focus on a particular aspect, for example radiocarbon dating. However, the growth of community archaeology will, perhaps, allow the Society to play a more active part in future research. Perhaps the Society's most significant contribution has been, and will remain, the opportunity for researchers to publish their results through one or other of the Society's publications.

The study of the archaeology in the present-day county suffers from a serious disadvantage: there is no department of archaeology either at the University of Cumbria or at Lancaster University. The result is that research in the county tends to be peripheral to the interests of more distant university staff and the creation of any long-term research project becomes more difficult, although Bob Bewley has shown what is possible through his PhD thesis.[194]

Perhaps it is appropriate to leave the last word to *Transactions*. Its contents demonstrate that even the most important discoveries can be made by chance and this provides encouragement that more will be found. *Transactions* has also reflected a steady move towards greater professionalism, the embracing of a wider social spectrum in archaeological research, and the continuing important role of local archaeologists, both amateur and professional, alongside the contribution of archaeologists based outside the county. But perhaps more than anything, the reading of *Transactions* and the Society's other publications demonstrates an avid interest in the archaeology and history of the county through many generations.

Acknowledgements

We are grateful to Ian Caruana for reading and commenting on an early version of parts of this paper.

NOTES AND REFERENCES

1 J. Simpson, 'The present state of antiquarian research in Westmorland and Cumberland', *CW1*, 1 (1874), 1-18.

2 As well as surveys in *Transactions*, members also contributed to the Archaeological Survey of Britain: R.S. Ferguson, 'An archaeological survey of Cumberland and Westmorland', *Archaeologia*, 53 (1893), 485-531; H.S. Cowper, 'An archaeological survey ... of Lancashire North-of-the-Sands', *Archaeologia*, 53 (1893), 531-38.

3 W. Greenwell, 'Recently opened tumuli in Cumberland and Westmorland', *CW1*, (1874), 19-26.

4 M.W. Taylor, 'On the vestiges of Celtic occupation near Ullswater, and on the discovery of buried stone circles by Eamont Side', *CW1*, 1 (1874), 154-68; C.W. Dymond, 'Gunnerkeld stone circle', *CW1*, 4 (1880), 537-40.

5 C.W. Dymond, 'Mayburgh and King Arthur's Round Table', *CW1*, 11 (1891), 187-219.

6 M.W. Taylor, 'On a cup-marked stone found at Redhills, near Penrith', *CW1*, 6 (1883), 110-18; W.G. Atkinson, 'Report on the exploration of Bonfire Scar Cave and Dobson Cave near Scales in Furness', *CW2*, 27 (1927), 110-16.

7 G.R. Hall, 'On ancient remains, chiefly prehistoric, in Geltsdale, Cumberland', *CW1*, 6 (1883), 456-80.

8 W.G. Collingwood, 'An inventory of the ancient monuments of Cumberland', *CW2*, 23 (1923), 206-76; 'An inventory of the ancient monuments of Westmorland and Lancashire North-of-the-Sands', *CW2*, 26 (1926), 1-62.

9 R.G. Collingwood, 'An introduction to the prehistory of Cumberland, Westmorland and Lancashire north of the Sands', *CW2*, 33 (1933), 163-200.

10 W.G. Collingwood, 'Report on an exploration of the Romano-British settlement at Ewe Close, Crosby Ravensworth', *CW2*, 8 (1908), 355-68.

11 R.G. Collingwood, 'Prehistoric settlements near Crosby Ravensworth', *CW2*, 33 (1933), 201-26; quotation 224.

12 B. Blake, 'Excavations of Native (Iron Age) sites in Cumberland, 1956-58', *CW2*, 59 (1959), 1-14.

13 G. Bersu, 'King Arthur's Round Table. Final Report, including the excavations of 1939', *CW2*, 40 (1940), 169-206.

14 R. Bradley, 'The philosopher and the field archaeologist: Collingwood, Bersu and the excavation of King Arthur's Round Table', *Proceedings of the Prehistoric Society*, 60 (1994), 27-34; quotation 32.

15 G. Simpson, 'Collingwood's latest archaeology misinterpreted by Bersu and Richmond', *Collingwood Studies* 5 (1998), 109-19, republished in A.R. Birley, 'Grace Simpson on R.G. Collingwood as an archaeologist', *Arbeia Journal*, 10 (2015), 35-41. She described how Bersu showed her and her father how Collingwood made a post-hole by pushing 'the top of his trowel in soft gravel, and the small stone slipped under his pressure, until there was a small hollow'. Simpson stated that 'one does not make a post-hole, one finds one', but any 'dirt archaeologist' will recognise Bersu's demonstration and testify to its veracity. This is not to suggest that Collingwood created his post-holes this way, but rather to argue that rather a greater appreciation of the possibilities of interpretation by the more skilled excavator.

16 M. Cross, 'A prehistoric settlement on Walney Island', *CW2*, 39 (1939), 262-82; her reports continued until *CW2*, 50 (1950), 15-19 and her work was continued by F. Barnes, 'Pottery from prehistoric sites, North End, Walney Island', *CW2*, 55 (1955), 1-16.

17 B. Bunch and C. Fell, 'A stone axe factory at Pike O'Stickle, Great Langdale, Westmorland', *Proceedings of the Prehistoric Society*, 15 (1949), 1-20. Clare Fell also published 'A stone-axe factory site, Pike O'Stickle, Great Langdale, Westmorland',

CW2, 48 (1948), 214-15; 'The Great Langdale axe factory', *CW2*, 50 (1950), 1-13. This double publication neatly reflects an issue. Naturally, those supportive of research within a county would wish to publish their work locally and thereby support their society; at the same time, publication in a national journal brings the local work to the attention of a wider community. For further investigations see R.G. Plint, 'Stone axe factory sites in the Cumbrian fells', *CW2*, 62 (1962), 1-26; T.G. Manby, 'The distribution of rough-out, "Cumbrian" and related stone axes of Lake District origin in northern England', *CW2*, 65 (1965), 1-37.

18 J. Cherry, 'Eskmeals sand-dunes occupation sites', *CW2*, 63 (1963), 31-52 is the first report.

19 M.C. Fair, 'Bronze Age swords and daggers of Cumberland, Westmorland and Lancashire North-of-the-Sands', *CW2*, 45 (1945), 34-38. There was also a push to publish material in museums and other collections, cf. K.S. Hodgson, 'Three unpublished collections of Bronze Age pottery: Netherhall, Garlands and Aglionby', *CW2*, 55 (1955), 1-17, T.H. McK. Clough, 'Bronze Age metalwork from Cumbria', *CW2*, 69 (1969), 1-39.

20 P. Claris and J. Quartermaine, 'The Neolithic quarries and axe factory sites at Great Langdale and Scafell Pike: a new field survey', *Proceedings of the Prehistoric Society*, 55 (1989), 1-25; R. Bradley and M.R. Edmonds, *Interpreting the Axe Trade: production and exchange in Neolithic Britain* (Cambridge, 1993).

21 R. Bradley and M. Edmonds, 'Fieldwork at Great Langdale, Cumbria, 1985-1987', *Antiquaries Journal*, 68 (1988), 181-208. For a review of work on the stone axes, T. Clare, 'The view from Friar Cott: ethnographic analogies and the phenomenology of the Lake District axe production sites', in P.J. Cherry (ed.), *Studies in Northern Prehistory: essays in memory of Clare Fell* (CWAAS, Extra Series XXXIII, 2007), 153-72.

22 K.E. Sharpe, 'The Lady of the Lakes: Clare Isobel Fell and the role of local societies for women in archaeology', in Cherry (ed.), *Studies in Northern Prehistory*, 1-23; D. Barrowclough, *Prehistoric Cumbria* (Stroud, 2010), 42-49.

23 R.H. Bewley, 'Clare, Cambridge and the Solway Plain', in Cherry (ed.), *Studies in Northern Prehistory*, 183-88.

24 R.H. Bewley, 'Survey and excavations at a crop-marked enclosure, Plasketlands, Cumbria', *CW2*, 93 (1993), 1-18; R.H. Bewley *et al.*, 'Excavation of a Bronze Age cemetery at Ewanrigg, Maryport, Cumbria', *Proceedings of the Prehistoric Society*, 58 (1992), 325-54; R.H. Bewley, *Prehistoric and Romano-British Settlement in the Solway Plain Cumbria* (Oxbow Monograph 36, Oxford, 1994).

25 Members of the Carlisle Regional Group, 1982, 'Fieldwalking on the Solway Plain', *CW2*, 85 (1985), 250-62; R.H. Bewley, *Prehistoric and Romano-British Settlement.*

26 J. Quartermaine and R.H. Leech, *Cairns, Fields and Cultivation: archaeological landscapes of the Lake District* (Lancaster Imprints 19, 2012).

27 W. Pennington, 'Vegetational history in the north-west of England: a regional synthesis', in D. Walker and R.G. West (eds.), *Studies in the Vegetational History of the British Isles* (Cambridge, 1970), 41-79; quotation 41.

28 Her references stretched back to R.D. Darbishire, 'Notes on discoveries in Ehenside Tarn, Cumberland', *Archaeologia*, 44 (1873), 273-92. For later discussion see D. Walker, 'The dates of human impacts on the environment at Ehenside Tarn, Cumbria', *CW3*, 1 (2001), 1-20; T.G. Manby, 'Ehenside Tarn and the Neolithic pottery of north-western England', in Cherry (ed.), *Studies in Northern Prehistory*, 61-98.

29 Pennington, 'Vegetational history', 67; fig. 17. cf. W. Pennington, 'The effect of Neolithic man on the environment in north-west England: the use of absolute pollen diagrams', in J. G. Evans, S. Limbrey and H. Cleere (eds.), *The Effect of Man on the Landscape: the Highland Zone* (London, 1975), 74-86 where she dates the elm decline, and therefore the beginning of agriculture, to about 3100 BC.

30 J. Turner, 'Post Neolithic disturbance of British vegetation', in Walker and West (eds.), *Studies in the Vegetational History*, 97-116. For an overview of settlements of all periods see R. Hogg, 'Factors which have affected the spread of early settlement in the Lake Counties', *CW2*, 72 (1972), 1-35; and for discussion of coastal change see T. Clare, 'The distribution of some archaeological sites in relation to features of Holocene coastal change', *CW2*, 100 (2000), 1-23. For a consideration of environmental change see C. Wells, 'Environmental changes in Roman north-west England: a synoptic overview of events north of the Ribble', *CW3*, 3 (2003), 67-84.

31 N.J. Higham, 'Early field survival in north Cumbria', in H.C. Bowen and P.J. Fowler (eds.), *Early Land Allotment in the British Isles: a survey of recent work* (BAR BS 48, Oxford, 1978), 119-25. cf. T. Clare, 'Two prehistoric boundary types previously unrecorded in Cumbria', *CW3*, 2 (2002), 21-27.

32 A.W. Hoaen and H.L. Loney, 'Cairnfields', in Cherry (ed.), *Studies in Northern Prehistory*, 189-210.

33 M. Edmonds and H. Evans, 'Made and found: cairns and natural mounds on Sizergh Fell', in Cherry (ed.), *Studies in Northern Prehistory*, 115-40.

34 Bradley, 'King Arthur's Round Table'; Manby, 'Ehenside Tarn'.

35 A. Watson and R. Bradley, 'On the edge of England: Cumbria as a Neolithic region', 65-77 and T. Clare, 'No-man's land revisited: some patterns in the Neolithic of Cumbria', 78-91, both in K. Brophy and G. Barclay (eds.), *Defining a Regional Neolithic* (Oxford, 2009).

36 C. Salisbury, 'The Pleiscocene exploitation of Cumbria: a review of the evidence', *CW2*, 92 (1992), 1-6; 'The Prehistoric occupation of Blenkett Wood near Allithwaite', *CW2*, 97 (1997), 1-10.

37 Quartermaine and Leech, *Cairns, Fields and Cultivation.*

38 Reports on all the south and west Cumbria sites were published as a series of papers in *Transactions* from 1960-2000. The sites on and around the limestone uplands were recorded in J. Cherry and P.J. Cherry, *Prehistoric Habitation Sites on the Limestone Uplands of Eastern Cumbria* (CWAAS, Research Series II, 1987).

39 C. Bonsall, 'Human-environment interactions during the Late Mesolithic of the Cumbria coastal plain: the evidence from Eskmeals', in Cherry (ed.), *Studies in Northern Prehistory*, 26-43.

40 A.J. Dickson and P.L. Cherry, *The Cumbrian Mesolithic: an appraisal of the lithic evidence* (CBA North-West Monograph, forthcoming).

41 W. Greenwell, *British Barrows* (Oxford, 1877), 510-13.

42 Manby, 'Ehenside Tarn'; Cherry and Cherry, *Prehistoric Habitation, passim.*

43 P. Topping, 'The Penrith henges: a survey by the Royal Commission on the Historical Monuments of England', *Proceedings of the Prehistoric Society*, 58 (1992), 249-64; G. Soffe and T. Clare, 'New evidence of ritual monuments at Long Meg and her Daughters', *Antiquity*, 62 (1988), 552-57; T. Clare, 'A magical thing: the layout of the Long Meg enclosures', *CW3*, 9 (2009), 21-27.

44 Cherry and Cherry, *Prehistoric Habitation*, Appendix 1, 73-76; Manby, 'Ehenside Tarn'.

45 P. Turnbull and D. Walsh, 'A prehistoric ritual sequence at Oddendale, near Shap', *CW2*, 87 (1987), 11-43.

46 F. Brown, A. Dickson, R.Gregory and J. Zant, *From an ancient Eden to a new frontier: an archaeological journey along the Carlisle Northern Development Route* (in preparation); http://cndr.oxfordarchaeology.com/background accessed 4 April 2016.

47 For example T.G. Manby, 'Pottery from the eastern limestone uplands of Cumbria', in Cherry and Cherry, *Prehistoric Habitation*, 73-76.

48 R.H. Bewley *et al.*, 'Excavation of a Bronze Age cemetery at Ewanrigg, Maryport, Cumbria', *Proceedings of the Prehistoric Society*, 58 (1992), 325-54.

49 Barrowclough, *Prehistoric Cumbria*, chapter 6 for more detail on Bronze Age burials and H. Evans, *Neolithic and Bronze Age Landscapes of Cumbria* (BAR BS 463, Oxford, 2008), chapter 8.

50 N.J. Higham and G.D.B. Jones, 'Frontiers, forts and farmers: Cumbrian aerial survey 1974-5', *Archaeological Journal*, 132 (1975), 16-53.

51 Bewley, *Prehistoric and Romano British Settlement in the Solway Plain*.

52 R.C. Turner, 'Another Cumbrian bog body, found in Seascale Moss in 1834', *CW2*, 89 (1989), 21-23; 'A Cumbrian bog body from Scaleby', *CW2*, 88 (1988), 1-7.

53 R.S. Ferguson, 'An attempt at a survey of Roman Cumberland and Westmorland with remarks on Agricola's line of march, and on the importance of the camp at Old Carlisle, and on the 10th Iter of Antoninus', *CW1*, 3 (1878), 64-94; 4 (1880), 15-18, 318-28; 5 (1881), 124-31.

54 Revd Canon Knowles and W. Jackson, 'Walls Castle, Ravenglass', *CW1*, 3 (1878), 23-26; W. Jackson, 'An account of some excavations made at Walls Castle in 1881', *CW1*, 6 (1883), 216-24.

55 R.L. Bellhouse, *Joseph Robinson of Maryport* (Otley, n.d. [1992]); S. Harbottle, 'Joseph Robinson – a biographical note', in R.J.A. Wilson and I.D. Caruana (eds.), *Romans on the Solway, essays in honour of Richard Bellhouse* (CWAAS, Extra Series XXXI, 2004), 206-23.

56 J. Robinson, 'Roman camp near Beckfoot (Mowbray)', *CW1*, 5 (1881), 136-48; 'Notes on the excavations near the Roman camp, Maryport, during the year 1880', *CW1*, 5 (1881), 237-57; 'Roman remains near Wolsty Castle', *CW1*, 5 (1881), 258-60; R.S. Ferguson with letters from Mr. Joseph Robinson, of Maryport (1881), 'An attempt at a survey of Roman Cumberland and Westmorland, continued, Part V. Risehow, near Flimby. The Parish of Bowness-on-Solway. Also some recent Roman finds', *CW1*, 5 (1881), 124-31.

57 Harbottle, 'Joseph Robinson', 216-20.

58 The most recent being D. Shotter, *Roman Coins from North-West England: the third supplement* (Centre for North-West Regional Studies, Resource Paper, no. 5, Lancaster, 2011)

59 W.D. Shannon, *Murus ille Famosus (that famous wall): depictions and descriptions of Hadrian's Wall before Camden* (CWAAS, Tract Series XXII, 2007); D.J. Breeze, *Hadrian's Wall: a history of archaeological thought* (CWAAS, Extra Series XLII, 2014).

60 For a brief history of the Pilgrimages with bibliography see B.J.N. Edwards and D.J. Breeze, *The Twelfth Pilgrimage of Hadrian's Wall, 1999* (Kendal, 2000). See also R.O. Heslop, 'The Roman Wall Pilgrimage of June, 1906', *J. British Archaeological Association*, n.s. 12 (1906), 269-81. For a more detailed account up to the 1959 Pilgrimage see E. Birley, *Research on Hadrian's Wall* (Kendal, 1961), 25-47. G. Bruce, *The Life and Letters of John Collingwood Bruce* (Edinburgh and London, 1905), 110-23.

61 J.C. Bruce, *The Roman Wall* (London and Newcastle upon Tyne, 1851).

62 'Excavations on the line of the Roman Wall. Report of the Committee appointed April 20, 1886, laid before the Society at Kendal, September 8th, 1886', *CW1*, 9 (1888), 162-77.

63 G. Neilson, Obituary notice of J.P. Gibson, FSA 'A Vice-President of the Society', *AA3*, 8 (1912), 37-45.

64 F. Haverfield, 'Epigraphic evidence as the date of Hadrian's Wall', *Proceedings of the Society of Antiquaries of London*, 14 (1892), 44-55.

65 F. Haverfield, 'Report of the Cumberland Excavation Committee 1894', *CW1*, 13 (1895), 453-69 was the first report. They continued in *Transactions* until F. Haverfield, 'Report of the Cumberland Excavation Committee for 1904', *CW2*, 4 (1904), 239-49. For discussion of Haverfield's work see: P.W.M. Freeman, *The Best Training-Ground for Archaeologists: Francis Haverfield and the invention of Romano-British archaeology* (Oxford, 2007) and Breeze, *Hadrian's Wall: a history of archaeological thought*.

66 Mrs Hodgson, 'Comparative view of dimensions of the Vallum in Cumberland', *CW1*, 14 (1897), 244-51; 'Notes on the excavations on the line of the Roman Wall in Cumberland, in 1894 and 1895', *CW1*, 14 (1897), 390-407; 'Comparative view of the dimensions of the Vallum in Northumberland', *CW1*, 14 (1897), 408-12; 'Notes on the excavations on the line of the Roman Wall in Cumberland, in 1896 and 1897', *CW1*, 15 (1899), 201-10; 'Notes on the excavations of the line of the Roman Wall in Cumberland, in 1898', *CW1*, 15 (1899), 365-76.

67 J.P. Gibson and F.G. Simpson, 'The milecastle on the Wall of Hadrian at the Poltross Burn', *CW2*, 11 (1911), 390-461.

68 I.A. Richmond, 'Excavations on Hadrian's Wall in the Gilsland-Birdoswald-Pike Hill sector, 1928', *CW2*, 29 (1929), 303-15 was the first report of their collaboration and they continued in *Transactions* on an annual basis until F.G. Simpson, I.A. Richmond and K. St.Joseph, 'The Vallum at High House Milecastle, 50, TW', *CW2*, 36 (1936), 158-70.

69 F.G. Simpson and K.S. Hodgson, 'The coastal mile-fortlet at Cardurnock', *CW2*, 47 (1947), 78-127. For features outside the fortlet revealed by aerial survey see G.D.B. Jones and D.J. Woolliscroft, *Hadrian's Wall from the Air* (Stroud, 2001), 125.

70 I.A. Richmond, 'Hadrian's Wall, 1939-1949', *J. Roman Studies*, 40 (1950), 43-57. For discussion of this statement and its implications see Breeze, *Hadrian's Wall: a history of archaeological thought.*

71 R.G. Collingwood, 'A system of numerical references to the part of Hadrian's Wall and the structures along its line', *CW2*, 30 (1930), 109-15.

72 A.R. Birley, 'Fifty years of Roman frontier studies', in P. Freeman, J. Bennett, Z.T. Fiema and B. Hoffmann, *Limes XVIII, Proceedings of the XVIIIth International Congress of Roman Frontier Studies held in Amman, Jordan (September 2000)* (BAR IS 1084, Oxford, 2001), 1-11.

73 P. Bidwell (ed.), *Hadrian's Wall 1989-1999* (Kendal, 1999); N. Hodgson (compiler), *Hadrian's Wall 1999-2009* (Kendal, 2009).

74 R.L. Bellhouse, 'A newly-discovered Roman road from Drumburgh to Kirkbride', *CW2*, 52 (1952), 41-45 was the first report and they continued in *Transactions*, almost on an annual basis, until 1992. R.L. Bellhouse, *Roman Site on the Cumberland Coast: a new schedule of coastal sites* (CWAAS, Research Series III, 1989) was a review of his work. For the significance of Bellhouse's work see D.J. Breeze 'Roman military sites on the Cumbrian coast', in Wilson and Caruana (eds.), *Romans on the Solway*, 66-94, and the bibliography of his publications in the same volume.

75 The process is described in Breeze, *Hadrian's Wall: a history of archaeological thought*, 91-100.

76 I.A. Richmond, 'The Roman fort at Bewcastle', *CW2*, 38 (1938), 195-237; J.P. Gillam, I.M. Jobey and D.A. Welsby, *The Roman Bath-House at Bewcastle, Cumbria* (CWAAS, Research Series VII, 1993); P.S. Austen, *Bewcastle and Old Penrith: a Roman outpost fort and a frontier vicus* (CWAAS, Research Series VI, 1991).

77 All the military sites of the county are discussed in P. Bidwell and N. Hodgson, *The Roman Army in Northern England* (Arbeia Society, 2009).

78 R.S. Ferguson, C.W. Dymond and W.S. Calverley, 'The Roman fort on Hardknott known as Hardknott Castle', *CW1*, 12 (1893), 375-438.

79 D. Charlesworth, 'The granaries at Hardknott Castle', *CW2*, 63 (1963), 148-52; P. Bidwell, M. Snape and A. Croom, *Hardknott Roman Fort, Cumbria* (CWAAS, Research Series IX, 1999); Bidwell and Hodgson, *Roman Army*, 115-18.

80 F. Haverfield and R.G. Collingwood, 'Report on the exploration of the Roman fort at Ambleside', 1913, *CW2*, 14 (1914), 433-65; R.G. Collingwood, 'The exploration of the Roman fort at Ambleside; report on the third year's work (1915)', *CW2*, 16 (1916), 57-

90; 'Explorations in the Roman fort at Ambleside (fourth year, 1920)', *CW2*, 21 (1921), 1-42; Bidwell and Hodgson, *Roman Army*, 112-15.

81 *Roman Inscriptions of Britain (RIB) 3218,* http://romaninscriptionsofbritain.org/person/3218 accessed 31 Jan. 2016.

82 T.W. Potter, *Romans in North-West England: excavations at the Roman forts of Ravenglass, Watercrook and Bowness on Solway* (CWAAS, Research Series I, 1979), 1-138; P. Holder, 'Roman place-names on the Cumbrian coast', in Wilson and Caruana (eds.), *Romans on the Solway*, 52-65.

83 Potter, *Romans in North-West England,* 139-320; Bidwell and Hodgson, *Roman* Army, 121-23.

84 R.S. Ferguson, 'The Roman camp on Kreiginthorpe (Crackenthorpe) common, near Kirkbythore', *CW1*, 11 (1891), 312-13; I. A. Richmond and J. McIntyre, 'The Roman camps at Reycross and Crackenthorpe', *CW2*, 34 (1934), 50-61.

85 R.G. Collingwood, 'A Roman fortlet on Barrock Fell, Low Hesket', *CW2*, 31 (1931), 111-18; Bidwell and Hodgson, *Roman* Army, 70-71.

86 H. Welfare, 'Maiden Castle fortlet, Stainmore', in B. Vyner, R. Annis and H. Welfare (eds.), *Stainmore, the archaeology of a North Pennine pass* (London, 2001), 96-98.

87 For a review of the evidence and doubts see, D.J. Woolliscroft, *Roman Military Signalling* (Stroud, 2001), 97-102.

88 V. Swan, 'Builders, suppliers and supplies in the Tyne-Solway region and beyond', in P. Bidwell (ed.), *Understanding Hadrian's Wall* (Arbeia Society, 2008), 65-72; D. Welsby, 'Pottery production at Muncaster, Eskdale in the 2nd century AD', *Britannia*, 16 (1985), 127-40.

89 I.A. Richmond, 'Roman leaden sealings from Brough-under-Stainmore', *CW2*, 36 (1936), 104-25.

90 N. Hair and C. Howard-Davis, 'Excavation of the Roman cemetery in 1991 and 1992', in J. Lambert, 'The Roman cemetery at Low Borrowbridge, near Tebay', in J. Lambert (ed.), *Transect Through Time: the archaeological landscape of the Shell North Western Ethylene Pipeline* (Lancaster Imprints 1, Lancaster, 1995), 96-125.

91 H.E.M. Cool, *The Roman Cemetery at Brougham, Cumbria, Excavations 1966-67* (Britannia Monograph Series 21, London, 2004).

92 H.S. Cowper, 'The influence of the Roman occupation upon the distribution of population in Cumberland and Westmorland', *CW1*, 16 (1900), 16-40.

93 D. Charlesworth, 'Roman Carlisle', *Archaeological J.*, 135 (1978), 115-37.

94 D. Charlesworth, 'The south gate of a Flavian fort at Carlisle', in W.S. Hanson and L.J.F. Keppie, *Roman Frontier Studies 1979* (BAR IS 71, Oxford, 1980), 201-20; I.D. Caruana, 'Carlisle: excavation of a section of the annexe ditch of the first Flavian fort, 1990', *Britannia*, 23 (1992), 45-109; I.D. Caruana, *The Roman forts at Carlisle Excavations at Annetwell Street, 1973-84* (London, forthcoming); J. Zant, *The Carlisle Millennium Project: excavations in Carlisle 1998-2001, Volume 1: Stratigraphy* (Lancaster Imprints 14, Lancaster, 2009).

95 J.P. Bushe-Fox, 'The use of samian ware in dating the early Roman occupation of the north of Britain', *Archaeologia*, 64 (1913), 299.

96 Zant, *Carlisle Millennium* Project, 413-67.

97 C. Howard-Davis, *The Carlisle Millennium Project: excavations in Carlisle 1998-2001, Volume 2: Finds* (Lancaster Imprints 15, Lancaster, 2009), 527.

98 R.S.O. Tomlin, 'Roman manuscripts from Carlisle: the ink-writing tablets', *Britannia*, 29 (1998), 31-84.

99 The successful phases of military deployment are traced in D.J. Breeze, 'The Roman army in Cumbria', *CW2*, 88 (1988), 9-22.

100 D.J. Breeze, *J. Collingwood Bruce's Handbook to the Roman Wall* (Newcastle, 2006), 76, 453.

101 Breeze, 'Roman army', 15; Bidwell and Hodgson, *The Roman* Army, 21-22.
102 Breeze, *J. Collingwood Bruce*, 22-34.
103 B. Dobson, 'Roman Durham', *Trans. Architect. & Archaeol. Soc. of Durham and Northumberland*, 2 (1970), 34.
104 Bidwell and Hodgson, *Roman* Army, 43-44.
105 N.J. Higham, 'Continuity studies in the first millennium AD in north Cumbria', *Northern History*, 14 (1978), 3-4.
106 J. Mann, 'The northern frontier after AD 369', *Glasgow Archaeological Journal*, 3 (1974), 34-42.
107 S.S. Frere, *Britannia: a history of Roman Britain* (Routledge: London, 3rd ed. 1987), 173-75; Bidwell and Hodgson, *Roman* Army, 26.
108 D.J. Breeze, 'The Roman military occupation of northern England', *CW3*, 11 (2011), 113-136.
109 R.G. Collingwood, 'A Roman fortlet on Barrock Fell, near Low Hesket', *CW2*, 31 (1931), 111-18; Bidwell and Hodgson, *Roman* Army, 70-71; R.L. Bellhouse, 'The Roman fort at Burrow Walls, near Workington', *CW2*, 55 (1955), 30-45; Breeze, *J. Collingwood Bruce*, 409-10.
110 D.J. Breeze, 'The impact of the Roman army on the native peoples of north Britain', in H. Vetters and M. Kandler, *Akten des 14. Internationalen Limeskongresses 1986 in Carnuntum* (Vienna, 1990), 93; N.J. Higham, *The Northern Counties to AD 1000* (London, 1986), 24-31.
111 J.A. Biggins and D.J.A. Taylor, 'The Roman fort and *vicus* at Maryport: geophysical survey, 2000-2004', in Wilson and Caruana (eds.), *Romans on the Solway*, 102-33.
112 G.D.B. Jones, 'Either side of Solway: towards a minimalist view of Romano-British agricultural settlement in the North-West', in J.C. Chapman and H.C. Mytum (eds.), *Settlement in North Britain 1000 BC – AD 1000: papers presented to George Jobey Newcastle upon Tyne December 1982* (BAR BS 118, Oxford, 1983), 185-204; cf. G.D.B. Jones, 'The future of aerial photography in the North', in N.J. Higham (ed.), *The Changing Past: some recent work in the archaeology of Northern England* (Manchester, 1979), 85-86.
113 G. Jobey, 'Homesteads and settlements of the frontier area', in C. Thomas (ed.), *Rural Settlement in Roman Britain* (London, 1966), 4-6.
114 Urien's name and repute survive in the poems of Taliesin. Hed is reported in the *Historia Brittonum* to have been killed at the siege of Bamburgh in the late 6th century; D.P. Kirby, 'Strathclyde and Cumbria: a survey of historical development to 1092', *CW2*, 62 (1962), 77-94. Kirby's name is misspelt in the contents list of this issue.
115 D. Rollason, *Northumbria, 500-1100: creation and destruction of a kingdom* (Cambridge, 2003).
116 E. Roesdahl, *The Vikings* (London, 1991), 234-37.
117 M. Swanton (trans. and ed.), *The Anglo-Saxon Chronicles* (London, 2000).
118 Revd F.W. Ragg, 'Gospatrik's charter', *CW2*, 5 (1905), 71-84; Kirby, 'Strathclyde and Cumbria'; P.A. Wilson, 'On the use of the terms "Strathclyde" and "Cumbria"', *CW2*, 66 (1966), 57-92.
119 M. Gelling, *Signposts to the Past* (London, 1978); R.N. Bailey and R.J. Cramp, *The British Academy Corpus of Anglo-Saxon Stone Sculpture; 2: Cumberland, Westmorland and Lancashire North-of-the-Sands* (Oxford, 1988).
120 For instance, Revd T. Lees, 'St Ninian's church, Brougham', *CW1*, 4 (1880), 420-24.
121 For instance, W.S. Calverley (edited by W.G. Collingwood), *Notes on the Early Sculptured Crosses, Shrines and Monuments in the Present Diocese of Carlisle* (CWAAS, Extra Series XI, 1899); Bailey and Cramp, *Corpus*.
122 F. Hudleston, 'The recent find in Dacre churchyard', *CW2*, 32 (1932), 75-77.
123 R.H. Leech and R. Newman, 'Excavations at Dacre: an interim report', *CW2*, 85 (1985), 87-93; M.R. McCarthy, 'Carlisle Archaeological Unit 1977-79', *CW2*, 80 (1980), 164-65.

124 R.S. Ferguson [the President], 'Various finds in Ormside churchyard', *CW1*, 15 (1899), 377-80; W.G. Collingwood, 'The Ormside cup', *CW1*, 15 (1899), 381-87; H. Gaythorpe, 'The Rampside sword', *CW2*, 10 (1910), 298-306; C. Hodgson, 'An account of some antiquities found in a cairn, near Hesket-in-the-Forest, in Cumberland, in a letter from Mr Christopher Hodgson to the Revd John Hodgson, Secretary', *AA1*, 2 (1832), 106-09; H. Rooke, 'Druidical and other British remains in Cumberland', *Archaeologia*, 10 (1792), 105-13.

125 J.D. Cowen, 'A catalogue of objects of the Viking period in the Tullie House Museum, Carlisle', *CW2*, 34 (1934), 166-87; J.D. Cowen, 'Viking burials in Cumbria', *CW2*, 48 (1948), 73-76; J.D. Cowen, 'Viking burials in Cumbria: a supplement', *CW2*, 67 (1967), 31-34.

126 Rooke, 'Druidical and other British Remains'; P. Abramson, 'A re-examination of a Viking age burial at Beacon Hill, Aspatria', *CW2*, 100 (2000), 79-88.

127 D. Petts, 'Beacon Hill, Aspatria: an early Christian carved stone rehabilitated', *CW3*, 2 (2002), 103-09.

128 H.S. Cowper, 'Law Ting at Fell Foot, Little Langdale, Westmorland', *CW1*, 11 (1891), 1-5.

129 J.F. Curwen, *The Castles and Fortified Towers of Cumberland, Westmorland and Lancashire North of the Sands together with a brief Historical Account of Border Warfare* (CWAAS, Extra Series XIII, 1913).

130 M.W. Taylor, *The Old Manorial Halls of Westmorland and Cumberland* (CWAAS, Extra Series VIII, 1892).

131 D.R. Perriam and J. Robinson, *The Medieval Fortified Buildings of Cumbria: an illustrated study guide and gazetteer* (CWAAS, Extra Series XXIX, 1998).

132 For instance, R.S. Ferguson, *The Old Church Plate in the Diocese of Carlisle* (CWAAS, Extra Series III, 1882; 2nd. edn., 1908); Revd Canon Bower, 'Grave slabs of the Diocese of Carlisle. Part I', *CW2*, 7 (1907), 165-84. Parts 2 and 3 can be found in *CW2*, 9 (1909), 1-23, and *CW2*, 12 (1912), 86-98; R.S. Ferguson, 'Masons' marks from Furness and Calder Abbey', *CW1*, 6 (1883), 357.

133 A.G. Loftie, 'Explorations at Calder Abbey', *CW1*, 6 (1883), 368-72.

134 W.H. St. John Hope, 'The Abbey of St Mary in Furness, Lancashire', *CW1*, 16 (1900), 221-302.

135 See for example, S. Harrison, J. Wood, and R.M. Newman, *Furness Abbey* (English Heritage: London, 1999).

136 M.C. Fair, 'Calder Abbey', *CW2*, 53 (1953), 81-97; J.C. Dickinson, 'Furness Abbey – an archaeological reconsideration', *CW2*, 67 (1967), 51-80. Detailed recording of the fabric was undertaken during the 1980s, though full publication is awaited; excavations have been undertaken in advance of underpinning the Presbytery: J. Bradley and S. Rowland, 'A reconsideration of the Presbytery at Furness Abbey' (in prep).

137 Mrs T.H. Hodgson, 'Excavations at Holm Cultram', *CW2*, 7 (1907), 262-68.

138 P.V. Kelly, 'Excavations at Conishead Priory', *CW2*, 29 (1929), 149-68.

139 E.P. Frankland, 'Explorations in Ravenstonedale', *CW2*, 29 (1929), 278-92; 'Explorations in Ravenstonedale (II)', *CW2*, 30 (1930), 144-48.

140 P. Turnbull and D. Walsh, 'Monastic remains at Ravenstonedale', *CW2*, 92 (1992), 67-76.

141 W.G. Collingwood, 'Report on excavations at the Holy Well, Gosforth', *CW2*, 2 (1902), 77-83.

142 T.H. Hodgson, 'The Bishop's or Baron's Dyke, Crosby-on-Eden', *CW1*, 14 (1897), 144-46; W.G. Collingwood, 'The medieval fence at Rydal and other earthworks', *CW2*, 30 (1930), 1-12.

143 J.R. Mason and H. Valentine, 'The British village site at Lanthwaite Green and other earthworks in west Cumberland', *CW2*, 24 (1924), 117-22.

144 See for instance, *CW2*, 27, where there are articles by three other authors on townfields, and Graham himself contributed four articles, although on this occasion, all were historical in content.

145 W.G. Collingwood, 'Packhorse-bridges', *CW2*, 28 (1928), 120-28.

146 P.V. Kelly, 'A bridge of monastic date and other finds at Furness Abbey', *CW2*, 26 (1926), 262-69; R.G. Collingwood, 'The so-called Roman bridge at Lanercost, in five notes', *CW2*, 30 (1930), 122-24.

147 P.V. Kelly, 'A bridge of monastic date and other finds at Furness Abbey', *CW2*, 26 (1926), 262-69; 'A medieval road in Furness', *CW2*, 27 (1927), 198-204; J. Melville and J.L. Hobbs, '"Souterhous Brigge" – a medieval bridge in Furness', *CW2*, 45 (1945), 129-33.

148 For instance, Revd C.E. Last, 'The old road at Caldbeck', *CW2*, 44 (1944), 142-45; W.T. McIntire, 'The fords of the Solway', *CW2*, 39 (1939), 152-70.

149 W. Hutchinson, *The History of the County of Cumberland and Some Places Adjacent* (Carlisle, 1794).

150 Revd C.J. Gordon, 'A submerged church in the River Eden', *CW2*, 14 (1914), 328-36.

151 C.A. Parker, 'The so-called "Danish Camp" at Gosforth', *CW2*, 4 (1904), 195-200; H.S. Cowper, 'A contrast in architecture', *CW2*, 1 (1901), 129-43.

152 Revd A. Heelis, 'The caves known as "Isis Parlis"', *CW2*, 14 (1914), 337-42.

153 H. Valentine, 'Ancient pottery in Whinfell parish', *CW2*, 35 (1935), 37-41. The article went on to note the site of a bloomery and an 'earthen enclosure' close to Loweswater.

154 T. Hay, 'Ancient landmarks', *CW2*, 41 (1941), 174-80; 'Lynchets and a settlement', *CW2*, 40 (1940), 131-5; 'The goose bield', *CW2*, 43 (1943), 28-30. The issue of the so-called goose-bields was taken up again by P. Fleming, 'Stone fox traps, borrans and goose bields', *CW2*, 98 (1998), 269-76 who explained the difference between fox traps, (designed to trap foxes using a goose as bait), and actual goose-bields (designed to protect geese from foxes). See also, G. Brooks, 'A Pennine fox trap', *CW3*, 13 (2013), 260-61.

155 T. Hay, 'Buttermere settlements', *CW2*, 45 (1945), 116-21.

156 J.W. Jackson, 'On the discovery of a bloomery at Lindale Church, near Grange-over-Sands', *CW2*, 14 (1914), 256-61.

157 R. Hogg, 'Further accessions to the Carlisle Museum, III: a green-glazed jug from Carlisle', *CW2*, 53 (1953), 207-08; R. Hogg, 'Excavation of the fortified manor-house at Burgh-By-Sands', *CW2*, 54 (1955), 105-18; R. Hogg, 'Excavations in Carlisle, 1953', *CW2*, 55 (1956), 59-107.

158 R.L. Storey, 'The manor of Burgh-by-Sands', *CW2*, 54 (1955), 119-30.

159 E.M. Jope and H.W.M. Hodges, 'The medieval pottery from Castle Street', in R. Hogg, 'Excavations in Carlisle, 1953', *CW2*, 55 (1955), 79-107; M.G. Jarrett and B.J.N. Edwards, 'Report on the medieval pottery', in R. Hogg, 'Excavations at Tullie House, Carlisle', *CW2*, 64 (1964), 41-57.

160 R.A.C. Lowndes, 'A medieval site at Millhouse in the Lune Valley', *CW2*, 67 (1967), 35-50.

161 M.R. McCarthy, *A Roman, Anglian and Medieval Site at Blackfriars Street, Carlisle* (CWAAS, Research Series IV, 1990); M.R. McCarthy, *The Roman Waterlogged Remains and Later Features at Castle Street, Carlisle* (CWAAS, Research Series V, 1991); H. Summerson, M. Trueman and S. Harrison, *Brougham Castle, Cumbria* (CWAAS, Research Series VIII, 1998); H. Summerson and S. Harrison, *Lanercost Priory, Cumbria* (CWAAS, Research Series X, 2000).

162 A.M. Whitworth, 'Lanercost Priory excavations in 1994', *CW2*, 98 (1998), 133-43; J.H. Williams, 'Excavations at Brougham Castle, 1987', *CW2*, 92 (1992), 105-21; J. Zant, 'An excavation at Brougham Castle', *CW3*, 1 (2001), 31-37.

163 M. Brennand and K.J. Stringer (eds.), *From Romans to Railways: the making of Carlisle* (CWAAS, Extra Series XXXV, 2011).

164 P. Turnbull and D. Walsh, 'Recent work at Egremont Castle', *CW2*, 94 (1994), 77-89; G. Fairclough, 'Clifton Hall, Cumbria: excavations 1977-79', *CW2*, 80 (1980), 45-68; M.R. McCarthy, 'Excavations at Carlisle Cathedral', *CW2*, 87 (1987), 270-71; G.D. Keevil, 'Carlisle Cathedral: Fratry watching brief, 1988', *CW2*, 91 (1991), 289-92; G.D. Keevil, 'Excavations at Carlisle Cathedral in 1985', *CW3*, 8 (2008), 37-61; R. Newman, 'Excavations and survey at Piel Castle, near Barrow-in-Furness, Cumbria', *CW2*, 87 (1987), 101-16; R.M. Newman, 'Further structural analysis at Piel Castle, 1987-94', *CW2*, 96 (1996), 121-37; P.R. Wilson and T. Clare, 'Farmery Field, Cartmel', *CW2*, 90 (1990), 195-98; 'C. Wild and C. Howard-Davis, 'Excavations at Priory gardens, Cartmel', *CW2*, 100 (2000), 161-80; I.D. Caruana, E.R.T. Allnutt and A. James, 'Excavations at Crookdake Hall near Wigton', *CW2*, 86 (1986), 267-71; G.G.S. Richardson, 'Down Hall, Cumberland', *CW2*, 72 (1972), 328-29; J. Bennett, A. Herne, and A. Whitworth, '"The Castles", Downhall, Aikton', *CW2*, 87 (1987), 67-82.

165 J. Walker and M. Graham, *St Mary's Abbey, Holme Cultram, Abbeytown, Cumbria* (CWAAS, CARR 4, 2013); D.W. Elsworth and T. Mace (eds.), *Aldingham Motte, Cumbria, and its environs in the Medieval Period* (CWAAS, CARR 5, 2015).

166 M.R. McCarthy, 'Excavations on the city defences, Carlisle', *CW2*, 80 (1980), 69-78; P. Flynn and M.R. McCarthy, 'Excavations and a ground-based radar survey at Long Lane, Carlisle, 1990', *CW2*, 91 (1991), 31-48.

167 J. Zant, I. Miller, C. Howard-Davis and Q. Mould, 'The defences of medieval Carlisle: excavations at Rickergate, 1998-9', in R.M. Newman (ed.), *Carlisle: excavations at Rickergate, 1998-9 and 53-55 Botchergate, 2001* (CWAAS, CARR 2, 2011), 5-69.

168 D. Drury, 'Archaeological work at the Carnaud Metal Box site, James Street, Carlisle', *CW2*, 98 (1998), 233-48; T. Burke and J. Cotton, 'Building survey at the Carnaud Metal Box site, James Street, Carlisle, *CW3*, 1 (2001), 165-74; C. Howard-Davis and M. Leah, 'Excavations at St Nicholas Yard, Carlisle, 1996-7', *CW2*, 99 (1999), 89-115.

169 R. Newman, 'Excavations in Egremont town centre, 1983', *CW2*, 88 (1988), 201-05; S. Whitehead and D.W. Elsworth, 'Medieval remains on Boroughgate, Appleby', *CW3*, 8 (2008), 246-49; C.M. Brooks, M. McCarthy, and M.D. Railton, 'Medieval ceramics from Shaw's Wiend, Appleby-in-Westmorland, Cumbria', *CW3*, 13 (2013), 73-88; S. Whitehead and D.W. Elsworth, 'A medieval road in Ulverston', *CW3*, 8 (2008), 250-54; S. Whitehead, D. Williams, and T. Mace, 'Excavation of medieval burgage plots to the rear of 130-136 Stricklandgate, Kendal', *CW3*, 13 (2013), 89-115; D.W. Elsworth, S. Whitehead, and J. Dawson, 'Results of an archaeological watching brief to the rear of 3 Castle Street, Kendal, and a consideration of the development of Wildman Street', *CW3*, 11 (2011), 239-47; J. Taylor and C. Richardson, 'Excavations at the Old Fort, Whitehaven, Cumbria: a summary', *CW2*, 79 (1979), 121-24.

170 R. Leech and R.A. Gregory, *Cockermouth, Cumbria: archaeological investigation of three burgage plots in Main Street* (CWAAS, CARR 3, 2012).

171 R.M. Newman, N.J. Hair, C.L.E. Howard-Davis, C. Brooks and A. White, 'Excavations at Penrith Market, 1990', *CW2*, 100 (2000), 105-30; J. Zant, *Penrith: the historic core* (CWAAS, CARR 6, 2015).

172 G.G.S. Richardson, 'King's Stables – an early shieling on Black Lyne Common, Bewcastle', *CW2*, 79 (1979), 19-27; N. Hair and R. Newman, 'Excavation of medieval settlement remains at Crosedale in Howgill', *CW2*, 99 (1999), 141-58; A.J.L. Winchester, 'Deserted farmstead sites at Miterdale Head, Eskdale', *CW2*, 79 (1979), 150-55; A.J.L. Winchester, 'Peat storage huts in Eskdale', *CW2*, 84 (1984), 103-15; A.J.L. Winchester, 'Shielings in Upper Eskdale', *CW2*, 84 (1984), 267-68.

173 A.J.L. Winchester, 'Demesne livestock farming in the Lake District: the vaccary at Gatesgarth in the later thirteenth century', *CW3*, 3 (2003), 109-18; M. Railton, 'Archaeological investigation of the remains of a medieval vaccary at Gatesgarth Farm, Buttermere', *CW3*, 9 (2009), 57-67.

174 C. Wild, C. Wells, D. Anderson, J. Boardman, and A. Parker, 'Evidence of medieval clearance in the Seathwaite Valley, Cumbria', *CW3*, 1 (2001), 53-68.
175 F. Grainger (W.G. Collingwood, ed.), *The Register and Records of Holm Cultram* (CWAAS, Record Series VII, 1929); M. Fletcher and I. Miller, 'Recent archaeological work on the Holm Cultam Sea Dyke, Skinburness, Cumbria', *CW2*, 97 (1997), 203-15.
176 M. Railton and G. Davies, 'Archaeological evaluation of the salmon coops at Corby Castle, Cumbria', *CW3*, 7 (2007), 95-106.
177 R.M. Newman, J.A. Quartermaine and P. Tostevin, 'Survey and excavations in the Keekle coalfield, 1987-90: a study of four post-medieval Cumbrian farmhouses', *CW2*, 97 (1997), 173-201.
178 D. Drury, with N. Hair, C. Howard-Davis, and M. Krupa, 'Stainmore, Cumbria: archaeological investigation on the A66 Stainmore to Banks Gate Road Improvement Scheme', *CW2*, 98 (1998), 119-22.
179 M.J. Jones, 'Archaeological work at Brough under Stainmore II: the medieval and later settlement (fieldwork and excavations)', *CW2*, 89 (1989), 141-80.
180 J. Cherry and J. Cherry, 'Dugout boat from Wasdale Beck, Cumbria, 1984', *CW3*, 5 (2005), 103-14.
181 A.P. Masser, 'The medieval village of Rickerby: excavations at Rickerby House, 2001-2', *CW3*, 6 (2006), 61-76; M. Railton, J. Bradley, I. Miller, M. Stoakley, D. Jackson, D. O'Meara and A. Hall, 'Peter Gate, Cumwhinton: archaeological investigation of a medieval rural site', *CW3*, 14 (2014), 63-102.
182 A. White, 'Pottery making at Arnside and Silverdale', *CW2*, 100 (2000), 285-91.
183 J.M. Todd, 'Civil engineering, *c.*1250: the St Bees mill leat', *CW2*, 85 (1985), 123-29; J.M. Todd, 'Kiln at 21 Abbey Vale, St Bees, Cumbria', *CW2*, 87 (1987), 266-68.
184 B.K. Roberts, 'Field survey of Maulds Meaburn, Westmorland', *CW2*, 96 (1996), 45-50; B.K. Roberts, 'Earthworks near Crosby Lodge, Westmorland', *CW3*, 1 (2001), 39-43.
185 I.D. Caruana, 'Excavations on the medieval church of St Thomas, Farlam', *CW2*, 92 (1992), 124-34.
186 Collingwood, 'Prehistoric settlements near Crosby Ravensworth', 203-04.
187 Biggins and Taylor, 'The Roman fort and *vicus* at Maryport', 102-33; A.J. Biggins and D.J.A. Taylor, 'The Roman fort at Castleheads, Cumbria: a geophysical survey of the *vicus*, *CW3*, 7 (2007), 15-30.
188 See, for instance, J. Marsh, 'A probable medieval coin hoard from near Natland, Kendal', *CW2*, 97 (1997), 254; A. White, 'A Bronze Age axe from Levens', *CW2*, 98 (1998), 297; C. Richardson, 'A catalogue of recent acquisitions to Tullie House Museum and reported finds from the Cumbrian area 1990-1996', *CW2*, 99 (1999), 1-51.
189 See, for instance, D. Hodgkinson, E. Huckerby, R. Middleton, and C.E. Wells, *The Lowland Wetlands of Cumbria* (Lancaster Imprints 8, Lancaster, 2000); Quartermaine and Leech, *Cairns, Fields, and Cultivation.*
190 R. Bewley, 'Clare, Cambridge and the Solway Plain', in Cherry (ed.), *Studies in Northern Prehistory*, 183-88.
191 Collingwood, 'Inventory', *CW2*, 23 (1923); *CW2*, 26 (1926), In 8 & 9 above.
192 Collingwood, 'Prehistory of Cumberland …'; M. Brennand (ed.), *The Archaeology of North-West England: an archaeological research framework for the North-West Region. Volume 1: Resource Assessment*, Archaeology North-West 8 (Manchester, 2006); M. Brennand (ed.), *Research and Archaeology in North-West England: an archaeological research framework for the North-West Region. Volume 2: Research Agenda and Strategy*, Archaeology North-West 9 (Manchester, 2007).
193 'Excursions and proceedings', *CW1*, 3 (1878), xxix-xxxi; Chancellor Ferguson, 'Two moated mounds, Liddell and Aldingham', *CW1*, 9 (1888), 409-11; 'Excursions and proceedings', *CW2*, 6 (1906), 321; P.V. Kelly, 'Aldingham motte and grange', *CW2*, 24 (1924), 271-77; 'Excursions and proceedings', *CW2*, 38 (1938), 304-05; Curwen, *The Castles and Fortified Towers*, 34, 271; Elsworth and Mace, *Aldingham Motte*, fn. 165 above.
194 Bewley, *Prehistoric and Romano-British Settlement*, fn. 24 above.

Chapter 4
Folklore, Customs and Traditions

Alan G. Crosby

The learned societies founded in the middle decades of the nineteenth century with the aim of studying the history, antiquities and archaeology of particular localities were born into an uncertain world. The well-established approaches of the antiquarians – people who might be portrayed as dilettante students of topics which were simply those of personal interest – were being challenged by the greater rigour of the emergent academic discipline of history. In northern England the nascent University of Manchester, growing from Owen's College (founded in 1851) and eventually chartered as a university in 1880, and the older University of Durham (founded in 1832 and chartered five years later) both promoted the more systematic and organised study of history, albeit a history heavily focused on the constitutional, legal and political dimensions. What, in such a context, was the role and place of societies such as the Cumberland and Westmorland, which in their early decades were almost exclusively the preserve of the comfortably off and abundantly leisured classes rather than that of professional academic historians?

This was a widespread problem, which is apparent in the experience of organisations such as the Manchester-based Chetham Society, with its obscurely-phrased 'mission statement' of publishing 'the remains historical and literary associated with the palatine counties of Lancashire and Cheshire'. In that case, the first 40 years from its foundation in 1843 saw a growing divergence between the aims of, on the one hand, those who might be seen as 'well-meaning amateurs' and, on the other, the academic historians at the fast-growing university. The Chester Archaeological Society, founded in 1849, likewise saw, after its rebirth in the 1880s, an emerging difference of style and substance, between the prosperous gentlemen who brought interesting objects to meetings and who valued the society as much for its dinners and excursions as for its pursuit of archaeology as a discipline, and those who regarded methodological rigour and systematic research and investigation of the city's past as the main purpose of the organisation.[1] The Cumberland and Westmorland, founded in 1866, was no different. In the mid-nineteenth century the boundaries between disciplines were blurred, while the disciplines themselves were still crystallising, and there was an inherent tension between a perspective which regarded archaeology and history as leisure pursuits and one which sought a more 'scientific' and academic approach to both.

Should such organisations include as part of their remit the study of the vernacular, and the unstructured and largely undocumented dimensions to life in the past? Or should they focus more strictly on an overtly academic approach to history, looking at themes of national relevance from a local or regional perspective? If the latter, the potential membership might be severely restricted, and the opportunities for the society to attain a wider appeal would be substantially reduced. If the former prevailed, however, the society potentially risked being regarded as lightweight, amateur or of marginal value.

This dichotomy was highlighted by the initial prevalence, and the eventual disappearance, of what can loosely be termed 'folklore', a popular theme in the early decades of the society and one which occupied a substantial place in *Transactions* volumes, but which was waning in significance by the Edwardian period and later vanished altogether. In the middle to late nineteenth century the amateur study of folklore was regarded as worthy of close attention. For the Cumberland and Westmorland its relevance to local and regional history had an extra dimension, since folklore in its widest sense was seen as a key to the expression and elucidation of 'Cumbrian-ness', the historically important and highly distinctive character of the region and its people, and helped to demonstrate how the particularities of the past had shaped the unique character of the present. In common with most county antiquarian societies in the mid-nineteenth century, the Society concerned itself with the traditions, folklore and customs of its area, but interest in such matters was not only stronger than in some other parts of the country, but was also directed in no small measure by a consciousness that, for example, the characteristic dialect and speech of the area were living embodiments of a Norse heritage which could also be traced in other aspects of vernacular culture. Its folklore, traditions and customs demonstrated a special identity which was considered worthy of research.

In 1811 the first work published on the subject appeared. The *Sketch of Cumberland Manners and Customs: partly in the provincial dialect, in prose and verse, with a glossary* was a quirky and frequently mocking account, notably dismissive of substantial parts of the population: 'The subterraneous inhabitants of Alstone Moor seeing nothing but bleak mountains above ground, nor any thing besides rocks and ores in the bowels of the earth, have but few ideas, which are confined, and their manners rude. They work hard about four days in the week, and drink and play the other three'.[2] It covered courtship and marriage customs, hirings and fairs, wakes, seasonal feasts and celebrations, sports and diet. In the 1850s, before the establishment of the Society and thus *faute de mieux*, the local and folk historian A.C. Gibson had published his more substantial article on 'Ancient customs and superstitions of Cumberland' in *Transactions of the Historic Society of Lancashire and*

Cheshire.[3] The arrival of the Cumberland and Westmorland a decade later gave a welcome local means of presenting and publishing such work.

The definition of 'folklore' was, of course, imprecise and shifting. The term was first coined in 1846 by William Thoms, essentially to describe what he called the 'lore of the people'.[4] Charles Phythian-Adams has recently summarised it as a 'body of pre-scientific ... beliefs through which humanity seeks to explain (and, when need arises, to exploit) its place in relation to forces of nature and the supernatural'.[5] In 1890 the editorial in the first issue of *Folklore,* the journal of the Folklore Society, claimed, rather ambitiously, that 'Folk-lore has now been extended to include the whole vast background of popular thought, feeling and usage, out of which and in contrast to which have developed all the individual products of human activity'.[6] For many nineteenth-century contributors who read papers to meetings of the Society, the definition of folklore was possibly even more extensive for they used the term to include, almost as the heart of the matter, the recording and study of vernacular traditions and lifestyles which were 'time-honoured', rooted in the soil, topography and social structure of the locality, and – an important point – which were then fast dying out or being forgotten. In this their perception was perhaps closer to that of people such as Artur Hazelius (1833-1901), the eminent Swedish folklorist and scholar who spent many years studying the vernacular material culture of Scandinavia and in 1891 opened the celebrated open-air museum at Skansen in Stockholm.[7] Hazelius perceived an inter-relationship between dialect, belief and artefact in the historical setting of a pre-industrial and pre-consumer age. The amateur folklorists of Victorian Cumbria, though highly unlikely to know of his work, would have been entirely in sympathy with that view.

Consequently, they saw no demarcation between the study of folklore and that of other dimensions to local and regional history. The 1894 obituary for the recently–deceased Vice-President, Canon Thomas Lees (born in 1829), noted:

> He was an able ecclesiastical antiquary, his knowledge of the arrangement, ritual, and custom of the church being wide, varied, and accurate. Always a voracious reader, and endowed with a tenacious memory, he accumulated vast stores of information on all sorts of subjects connected with history, dialect, folk-lore, and genealogy, which he was ever ready to communicate to his friends and brother antiquaries.

The use of the word 'antiquary' in a non-pejorative sense, and the interlinking of folklore with other themes largely disregarded by academic historians of the period, capture the spirit of the later-Victorian world. The obituary noted another common characteristic: 'his dislike of writing, combined with his rare modesty, restricted his contributions to literature'.[8]

Folklore was also seen as rooted in place and physical space, not least because, almost by definition, it could not be fixed in time. The only certainty about its chronology was that it was coming to an end in the mid-nineteenth century with the advent of the railway age. In the introduction to her paper 'Past and present among the Northern Fells', read at the Appleby meeting in July 1875, Miss Powley of Langwathby observed that these traditions were 'a record of primitive customs, and fast-fading local peculiarities, dear to the sons of the soil, but perhaps of little public interest'. She went on to suggest that 'every member of this Society is interested, to an extent proportioned by his property, whether as owner or occupier, in the wastes which stretch, skyward, as it seems, often for many a mile, ridge over ridge, beyond the inhabited and inclosed portions of the parish to which they belong'. Those areas, beyond the reach of the modern age, were, she suggested, the places where traditions might be discovered and recorded.[9]

The clear danger that such traditions might be lost, and the importance of the mission to record them, was powerfully expressed by the Revd H.J. Bulkeley in his 'Some east Cumberland superstitions', published in 1886. He argued that although

> material relics of the past, such as old stones and old documents, have to be preserved with a kind of religious care, or they run a great risk of being destroyed ... there is another class of memorials of past and passing life, which are much more shifting and evanescent than any stone or document, which must change or disappear as time goes on, and of which almost the only possible record is by pen and ink. In this age of railways, newspapers, and primary education, superstition, however deep-rooted and sometimes beautiful, is bound to die, even though it die hard.

Inherent in this perspective was the view that 'superstition' (for which we may read 'traditional belief') was likely to be intellectually suspect, because of its irrationality and illogicality, and was destined to die because rationality and progress would sweep it away but, although it came from the common folk and was therefore socially inferior, it might have its naïve charm and even beauty, and a certain historical interest.

Indeed, as the impact of the modern age was felt even in the furthest recesses of the remotest dales, the perceived genuine and authentic quality of the past could be sharply contrasted with the cheap and tawdry commercialism and superficiality of the present. The prolific writer Henry Swainson Cowper argued that only by researching the true traditions and lifestyles of previous generations, and of those contemporaries who, albeit precariously, retained the old ways, could a real insight into the past be obtained.[11] Writing about 'obsolete and semi-obsolete' domestic appliances, he proposed that nothing could be

> more indispensable for the true understanding of the home life of a rural district, than a familiarity with the surroundings and appliances of the people, before everything was reduced to a cut and dried uniformity by the introduction of steam traffic, and machinery in general ... A chat with a Cumberland village patriarch about old times, will soon put the uninitiated into a mist about details for the simple reason that allusions will almost surely be made to contrivances which, though bright in the patriarch's memory, are now to be seen only in the most retired dalesmen's homes, if indeed they have survived at all.

This might, he considered, represent progress, for 'some of these appliances ... like the brank and the stang, which are not domestic, but punitive, have given way before the relaxation of the communal judicial codes, which has followed as a natural re-action the barbarous ideas of less enlightened ages'. But for Cowper, as for so many others, the guilty party could readily be identified: 'the majority [of traditional appliances] have disappeared before the influence of railway traffic, which has brought within reach of all classes cheap and serviceable, if often badly constructed and always inartistic, appliances of a domestic and other character'.[12]

By the end of the nineteenth century a certain unease is often apparent in the preambles to articles on folklore, for the authors (most of whom had read their papers to meetings of the Society) were clearly aware that there might be mockery or lofty academic condescension towards their choice of such 'lightweight' topics. In 1896 Swainson Cowper apologised at the outset for the fact that 'it may possibly be somewhat out of place to bring before the notice of a practical body such as the Cumberland and Westmorland Antiquarian and Archaeological Society, subjects so eminently unpractical and fanciful as those mentioned in the title of this paper'. But he pointed out in justification that

> there is not, within the district worked by this Society, anything in the shape of a Folklore Society, and I venture to think that some of the curious customs and superstitions ... are, indeed, worthy of some sort of notice at our hands, for all of them, even those foolish ghost stories of more modern date, embody rather the traditional survivals of a past age, than the feelings of the present day.

Touching upon a key aspect of postulated regional identity – the ethnic make-up of the area – he claimed that the local people were not notably superstitious, because to be superstitious was 'rather racial' and that Celtic counties, rather than Scandinavian or Anglo-Saxon ones, displayed much more of this type of belief.[13]

The potential for amused mockery or academic disdain can be amply demonstrated. At the beginning of the twentieth century, for example, Mrs Hodgson of Newby Grange contributed a paper which was whimsically titled 'On some surviving fairies', with contents which were no less archly whimsical:

> The shyness of the British fairy in modern times has given rise to a widespread belief that the whole genus must be regarded as extinct. No doubt the great increase of the three R's, which are the natural enemies of fairies, has driven them to take refuge in the least accessible neighbourhoods; but occasional specimens are still to be obtained. The injudicious collector who hunts, so to say, with horn and hounds, will draw every cover blank ... We have, however, found two or three living examples which I now exhibit, only withholding the precise habitat, as in the case of some rare ferns, which botanists are quite justified in protecting from the dangers of too fierce a light of publicity.

The substance, such as it was, of the brief article comprised the recounting of three folk tales from unnamed places, and references to a few rhymes and children's tales from Caldbeck.[14]

This was an extreme case, but simple recitation of examples of folk tales and beliefs was a mainstay of the folklore writers. Bulkeley's account of East Cumberland customs included descriptions of charming or curing toothache by hammering a rusty nail into a tree; pace-egging rhymes;[15] and superstitions relating to yew trees. There is extensive coverage of popular belief in malicious fairies, with an example from Elliotstownholm on the banks of the White Lyne near Lanercost where 'they used to ride little horses, and their feet, jingling in their silver stirrups, have been heard by people still living. They smoked, too, and their little pipes were sometimes picked up'. Moving on to boggles, Bulkeley observed that they were 'sometimes not very amiable. They are very common. But the belief, even in boggles, has much waned, and there are not a few who laugh at them, and try to account for them'. Examples given included a woman in white at Asketon Park, and a Bewcastle boggle which rode behind the rector, looked at him from a gallery, 'and with a scream disappeared'.[16]

Many of the articles loosely about folklore can best be described as flimsy. There is no analysis or attempt to interpret the evidence, and the substance is very limited. All too often, furthermore, the articles are completely lacking in any context or comparison with other parts of Britain or even of the region.

They are no more than ragbags of miscellaneous information gathered because of its quaintness and may well have been conceived as such. Even the great W.G. Collingwood erred in this regard in his 1906 paper entitled 'Late and magic runes in Cumberland'. He began by quoting a letter of 1685 from Carlisle, which referred to a book of spells and magical receipts allegedly taken very recently 'from the Pocket of one of our Moss-troopers; wherein, among many other conjuring feats, was prescribed a certain Remedy for an Ague, by applying a few barbarous characters to the Body of the Party distemper'd'. The article then quoted a number of references from Scandinavian sources to the use of runes for magic, referred to a couple of examples of runic writing in Cumbria (the 1816 discovery of a runic ring at Kingmoor and the runes at Dearham and Carlisle Cathedral), and concluded, in a serious anti-climax, that no magic runes have been found in Cumbria.[17]

A more systematic and coherent approach was adopted in 1901 by Canon Thornley in his paper on children's games from Kirkoswald. He emphasised that everything in the paper was the result of talking to the children and getting first-hand information and examples, a methodology later adopted by Peter and Iona Opie, the most prominent experts on children's games and literature. Thornley sought to demonstrate that the games and amusements were an integral part of the annual calendar of the community, determined by the season and the weather, that they were (to use a term which he would not have employed) very clearly gendered, and that in some instances historical antecedents and provenance could be postulated. He noted the sharp differences between girls' games (with much use of skipping, rounds and hoops) and the 'more boisterous and mischievous employment' of boys, with their conkers, marbles and hopscotch. An important feature was his recognition that games were constantly evolving, and could reflect historical events or could readily adapt to contemporary circumstances. For example, the contrasting cries in a boys' game ('We are fighting for the Pope' or, 'We are for the English Queen') originated in the sixteenth century, whereas the contemporary Kirkoswald version of 'Eena meena mina mo', sung in girls' games, had incorporated the modern age ('Penny on the water / Tuppence on the sea / Thrippence on the railway / Out goes she').[18]

Of major importance, and closely associated with other strands of scholarly investigation which led to a strong emphasis on dialect and language, were the early enquiries into the highly-distinctive speech patterns of the Lake Counties. The late-eighteenth century opening-up of the district to visitors from outside and, before long, their permanent settlement in the area, prompted research on local dialect in a form which was significantly different from that in most other parts of England. Whereas in areas such as Lancashire and the South-West it was primarily local people, literate but not of high social status, who sought to capture and preserve their speech and dialect in 'grassroots' vernacular literature, in the Lake Counties much of the early investigation was undertaken either by outsiders, or by those from the elite ranks of local society. Their work was informed by a fascination with the Celtic and Norse legacy, and by a precocious awareness, greatly encouraged by Wordsworth's idealistic view of the purity of the Scandinavian forms, that the dialect of Cumberland and Westmorland preserved, in a living form, terminology which could readily be equated with the contemporary speech of Norway and Iceland.

In the early 1870s Revd Thomas Ellwood, rector of Torver, discovered the fascination of Lake District dialect and speech patterns, began to collect the vocabulary, and attempted to interpret and analyse it etymologically. The earliest published material on this general theme goes back to the beginning of the nineteenth century with, for example, de Quincey's essay on the Danish origins of Cumbrian dialect which, though inaccurate, identified an important research topic. However, in papers read at Furness Abbey in August 1877 and Whitehaven four months later Ellwood set out his observations on the numerals used for sheepscoring in the Lake Counties, a subject beloved of rural writers, dialect specialists and romantics ever since. Ellwood – in contrast to many contemporary folklorists (or vernacularists) – emphasised the comparative, for he had been in communication with many others working in the same field, among them Dr Trumbull of Hartford, Connecticut, who claimed that 'there were numerals in use at present, or [which] had formerly been in use, among the North American Indians of Maine, of Rhode Island, and Massachusetts, almost identical in sound and bearing the same peculiarities and alliteration and rhythm with those found in the north of England'. This potentially extraordinary avenue of linguistic exploration was soon dropped, but Ellwood pointed out the Latin roots of some of the counting numerals (such as 'dick' = *dec-* for ten) and, more importantly, the common Celtic heritage in the Isle of Man, Wales and various parts of the Lake District including Wasdale Head and Coniston (recording similar words, such as 'pimp', 'pip', 'mimph', 'pep' and 'pepsy', for five). In his second paper he eclectically widened the geographical scope by including not only Teesdale, Knaresborough, Brittany, and Cornwall, but also Epping Forest and Cincinnati among his examples.[19]

Ten years later, Ellwood published a more challenging paper entitled 'Notes upon some of the older word forms to be found in comparing the language of Lakeland with the language of Iceland'. He explained that in 1869-72 Dr Kitchin, later dean of Winchester and then Durham, had lived at Brantwood 'and while there, he had in hand, as delegate of the Clarendon Press, Oxford, the proofs of Cleasby and Vugfusson's Icelandic Dictionary', which was then passing through the press. 'Knowing that I was a Cumbrian, he kindly asked me to look at those proofs and see whether I could suggest any affinities to our Cumberland, Westmorland, and Furness dialect. I was able to point out a number of words which were identical, or nearly so in Icelandic and the dialect of Cumberland and this portion of Lakeland'. Ellwood, fired with enthusiasm, began collecting dialect words and thus far had spent 17 or 18 years on this and had unearthed words and customs 'among our dalesmen of which not any note had been taken before ... I have inquired incessantly amongst the dalesmen, and wandered into most of the nooks and corners of Cumberland and Lakeland'. In a significant interpretation he argued that whereas philologists had hitherto interpreted the Norse period as one of plunder, careful study suggested 'the peaceful disposition of those who first settled here and left their language' because 'the great bulk of the words are field names and farm names, the terms applied to husbandry operations, and names applied to sheep and cattle, or used in their care and management, words applied in butter making, cheese making, knitting, and all domestic duties and concerns of every day life'. He also noted that these words do not survive only as nouns, but also in secondary and consequent forms, and also as verbs, suggesting 'their continued currency as representative of habits, customs, superstitions, and modes of life'.

Anticipating the approach adopted in Bill Rollinson's celebrated television programme a century later in which farmers from Wasdale and Mosedalr in Norway were brought together and found much that was mutually intelligible,[20] Ellwood decided that the best way of making comparison 'was to get a Lakelander to talk to an Icelander'. He found one in the person of Eiríkr Magnússon, university librarian at Cambridge (many years later described as Ellwood's 'long-distance and long-suffering collaborator').[21] They went through some 600 Norse words drawn from the dialect of the Lake Counties and showed that many of them were still used in identical form and meaning by Icelandic farmers and shepherds: examples included fell, dale, knab, knott, rake, ground, gimmer and brandreth.[22]

The fascination with the Norse period and its impact upon Cumbrian culture and society became a powerful force in the Society's work in the later nineteenth century, inspired in no small measure by the work of Ellwood and his collaborators. In 1891 an excursion went to Little Langdale and there at Fell Foot the members inspected the 'thing' mount, where Swainson Cowper read a paper which discussed the legislative systems of early Scandinavian nations and the open-air assembly places including Tynwald on the Isle of Man and the mound at whose foot they were standing (fig. 4.1).[23]

Two years later the indefatigable Ellwood and his colleague Eiríkr Magnússon published a lengthy article on the Icelandic 'Landnama Book', with sections in Icelandic (fortunately with translation) and a very wide-ranging discussion of dialect, folklore, place-names and traditional customs in the two areas.[24] Topics included the parallel use of terms and words (such as *eldhouse*/*eldhús* meaning 'firehouse'); the use of names which include Thor such as Thursby or Thurstonwater; stone circles and their possible reuse in Norse times as meeting places; the name Sowerby and its use in Cumbria; 'by' names, as shown by Anderson in his rhyme on the Thursby witch ("There's Harraby an Tarraby/An Wigganby beseyde/There's Oughterby

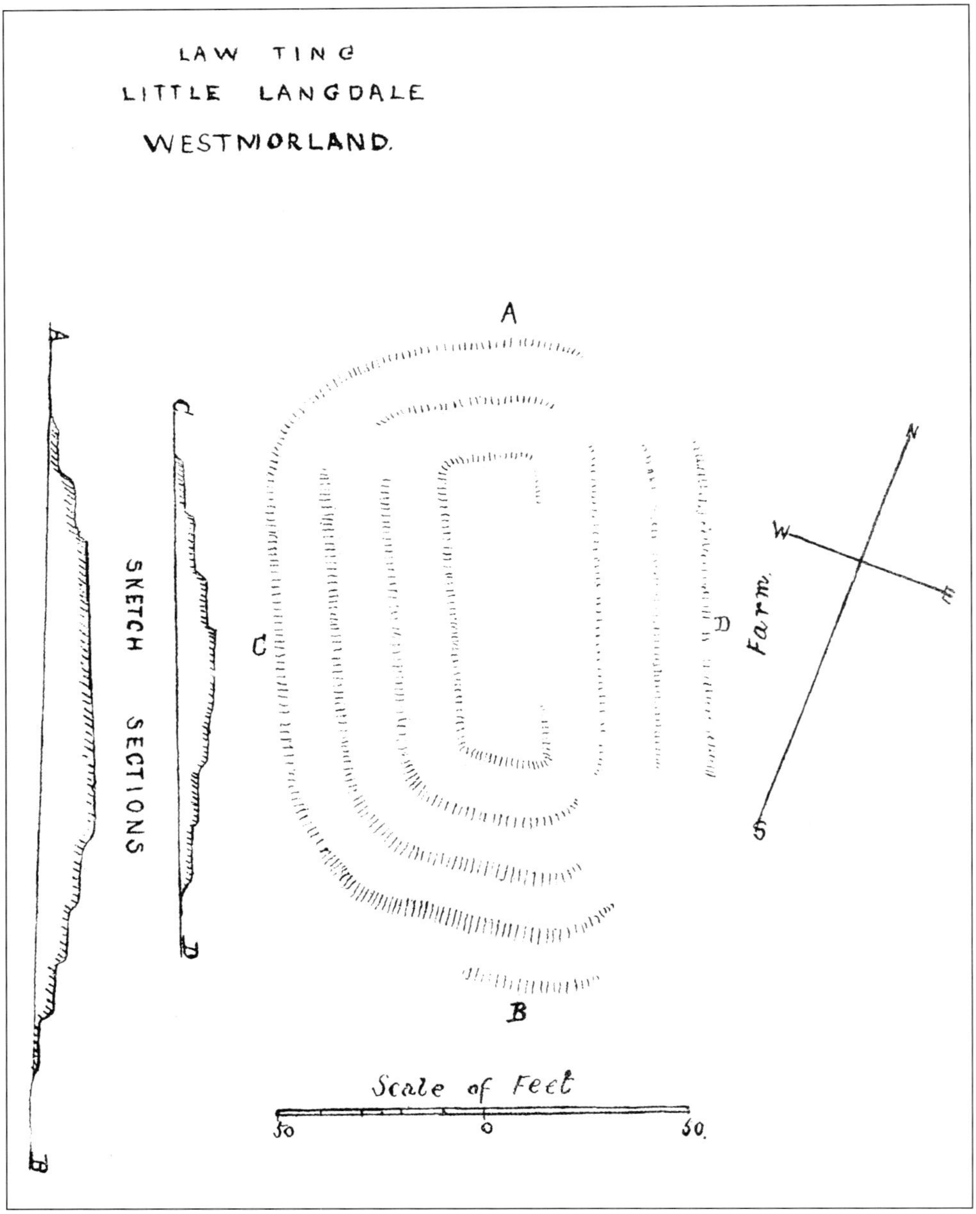

Fig. 4.1. H.S. Cowper, 'Law Ting at Fell Foot, Little Langdale', *CW1*, 11 (1891), opposite 2

an Souterby/An "Bys" baith far an weyde"]; ash and rowan trees and their folkloric significance; and the remarkable correspondence of place-names (including Swindale, scales, *kaldáor* or 'cold' names, garths, holm). The conclusion of the article is most emphatic about the importance of all of this: 'Our place-names have the most close and striking affinities and at times also identities with the place-names of Iceland ... Scandinavian mythology enters very largely into our folklore and superstitions'. Ellwood later widened his scope to consider other dimensions to the Scandinavian contribution. In 1899 came his work on Herdwick sheep, in which he discounted the legend that they descended from 40 beasts which swam ashore from a Norwegian shipwreck, but argued that nonetheless they were of Norse origin.[25] 'My own inference', he wrote, 'would be that those sheep came with those early settlers who have left behind them so many of the vocables, so much of the folk-speech, and so many of the customs of the Norse'.

Some contributors were concerned with the legends that had gathered round particular places, or were associated with landmarks and objects. Thus, in 1883 R.S. Ferguson gave a paper about the turf maze on Rockcliffe Marsh, first asking whether or not it was of Celtic origin and then claiming that local herdsmen and shepherds traditionally cut 'labyrinthine figures' in the marsh turf, known as 'Walls of Troy' (fig. 4.2). Examples were quoted, including that cut by 16-year old Christopher Graham in 1815 at 'Willie of the Boats', the old ford over the Esk at Metal Bridge, and another, 150 yards away, which Ferguson investigated on the ground. Unsatisfactorily, though, he concluded that the idea was brought by 'foreign sailors', and even proposed (apparently with no evidence at all) that the vessel in question was specifically the *Sainte Genevieve* of Dunkirk, which ran brandy into the creeks of the Solway.[26] Two decades later, in contrast, Henry Penfold was coldly analytical and far more conscious of historical verification in his review of the legends associated with the Capon Tree at Brampton, declaring it to be 'a necessary though an unpleasant task to unshroud this venerable oak and to clear away the fairy tales – of judges under its branches regaling themselves on capon and wine, of the popularly supposed idea that this tree was the place where thousands of border raiders were executed, of tales of Capon Tree boggles; these and many others just as mythical will disappear under the plain light of history'(fig. 4.3). He argued that the name derived from the Anglo-Saxon *cepan*, 'to meet, go about, seek, keep, catch' and that it was a meeting place on the road at the edge of the parish. An aged local resident recalled that it was a rendezvous point for ruffians bound for fairs and markets, and Penfold proposed that the association with executions originated in the hanging there of six Carlisle Jacobites after the collapse of the 1745 rising, quoting contemporary documentary sources to corroborate the theory.[27]

Fig. 4.2. 'Labyrinth on Rockcliffe Marsh', *CW1*, 7 (1884), opposite 69

Fig. 4.3. 'The Capon tree as it was in 1833', *CW2*, 5 (1905), opposite 129

As late as 1924 W.G. Collingwood wrote, possibly light-heartedly, on the entry for Ravenglass in Camden's *Britannia*, which stated that 'They talke much of King Eveling that heere had his court and roiall palace'. Collingwood suggested that 'folklore was not then supposed to be worth the attention of a scholar', thus implying, perhaps optimistically, that in the mid-1920s it was worthy, and then confessed that 'many of us have wished to hear what it was they told him about King Eveling, and who King Eveling can possibly have been, in history or in romance'. He observed that John Denton's manuscript history of Cumberland refers to 'Lyons Garde' at Ravenglass and therefore proposed that this is a corruption of Lyonesse, that 'Eveling' is likewise a corruption of 'Avalon', and that the legend survived in the area because of the longevity of British settlement. 'And so', he says ironically, 'Ravenglass used to be fairyland!'[28]

The interest in these traditions was part of a much wider academic and scholarly concern for the vernacular culture of the region, as exemplified by the early moves towards preservation of certain key buildings (see Chapter 5) and, more widely, the sense that landscape preservation would retain for posterity key elements of the distinctive character of the Lake District. This helps to explain the early interest in the distinctive material culture of the Lake Counties, with a series of articles which considered the types of artefacts to be found in farmhouses and smaller manor houses, and in some cases the dwellings of those lower down the social scale: thus, there were contributions on, *inter alia*, knitting-sheaths or knitting-sticks in 1881 and again in 1917; iron candlesticks (1893); toast-dogs and frying pans (1895); a contrivance for producing fire (1907); and luking-tongs (1911). The artefacts and implements from yeoman houses could be seen in the context of the much-debated and much-criticised concept of the 'statesmen' (a point sometimes made explicitly) and was integral to the emergence of a Lake District identity which might be presented to the visitor and the external investigator.

The investigation of the material vernacular culture of the past was not simply because objects and artefacts were tangible and collectable, or because they were integral to the developing iconography of Cumbrian-ness, but also because they were of central importance at meetings of the Society. Members brought along examples – sometimes numerous examples – and displayed them, so that the items could be handed round and discussed. A published paper of some sort usually followed, ideally with drawings or sketches to illustrate the distinctive features of the objects in question. Thus, at a meeting in 1881 the president, R.S. Ferguson, brought along and displayed 28 examples of knitting sticks or knitting sheaths, mainly collected from the Wigton area (fig. 4.4). These were stuck into the girdle or apron string, on the knitter's right hand side, in order to support three or four knitting needles during knitting. They were, Ferguson noted, 'objects whose use has just ceased, or only lingers in out-of-the-way places'. During the discussion the theorising was characteristically untrammelled by mundane realities. Revd Mayhew observed that 'the dagger type' reminded him of knives and daggers depicted on Mithraic stones found in the vicinity of the Roman Wall and it was agreed that 'in all probability the type originated thus; and thus their Eastern aspect was accounted for'. Others seemed 'Italian' in appearance and were explicable because of Roman influence, while those with a 'northern look' were clearly of Viking origin.[29]

A much more scientific approach was displayed by H. Swainson Cowper in his meticulous classification of candlesticks and lights in 1893. The subject was considered to be of historical interest because 'betwixt gas and electric light, the wax candle and tallow dip bid fair to be permanently snuffed out in the struggle for existance [*sic*]'. Cowper, cross-referencing with the description of the manufacture of home-made dips or lights given by Gilbert White in *The Natural History of Selborne*, categorised the Cumbrian artefacts into six groups: rush holders having no socket for a dip; candle and rush holders combined, with wooden stands; tripedal candle and rush holders; pendant candle and rush holders; tall standard candle and rush holders to place on ground; and spiral candleholders. Each was illustrated with local examples from his own very extensive collection, including drawings on the plate pages (fig. 4.5). The research behind the presentation and paper was clearly very thorough, with no idle speculation but instead a serious attempt to identify provenance and including a very detailed account of the effectiveness of each type of light.[30]

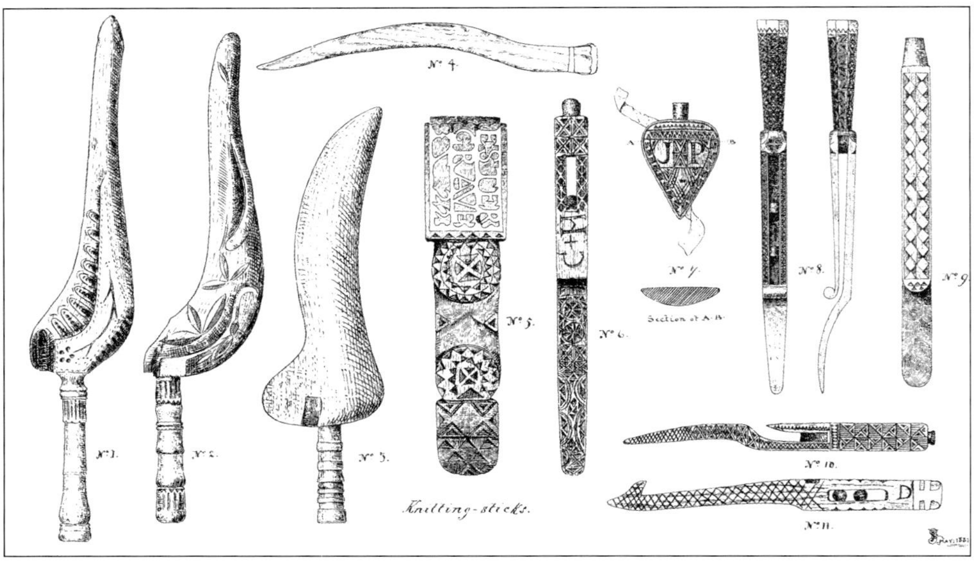

Fig. 4.4. R.S. Ferguson, 'Knitting-sticks', *CW1*, 6 (1883), opposite 92

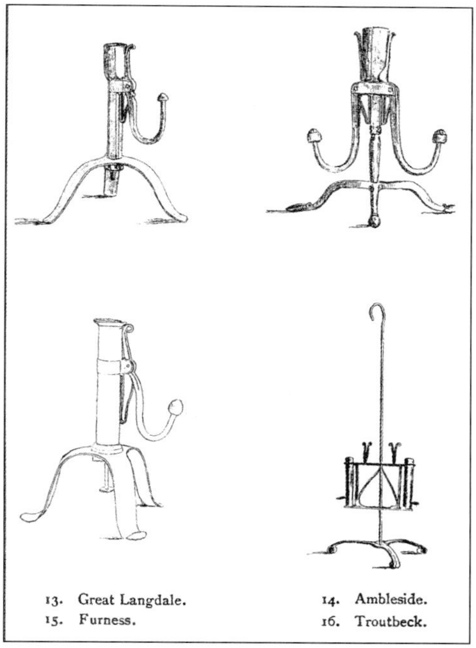

Fig. 4.5. Plate IV from H.S. Cowper, 'The domestic candlestick of iron in Cumberland, Westmorland and Furness', *CW1,* 12 (1893), opposite 117

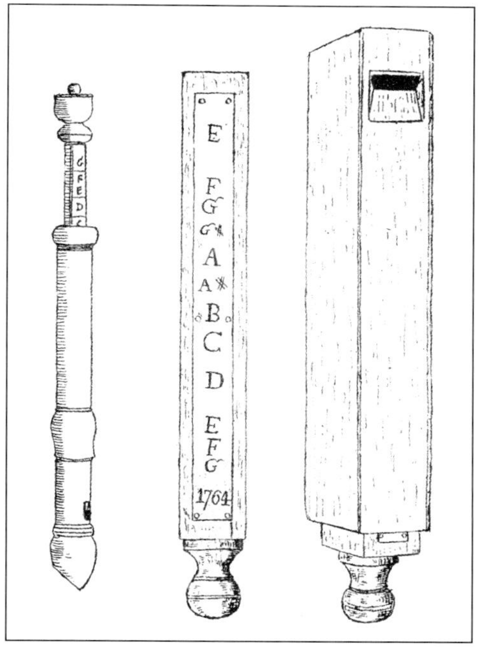

Fig. 4.6. 'Pitchpipes from Hawkshead and Cartmell Fell (*sic*)', from H.S. Cowper, 'On some obsolete and semi-obsolete appliances', *CW1,* 13 (1895), opposite 100

Cowper followed up this article by a more diffuse account of 'obsolete contrivances in Lakeland', ranging from spindles and whorls, via handmills and querns, cooking spits and fire dogs, more candlesticks, pewter plates, pitchpipes, dairy appliances, farming equipment, chests and purses, and items for the destruction of game and vermin, to travelling accessories (fig. 4.6).[31] His view that the dating of these objects was often well-nigh impossible is exemplified by the comment that a whorl from Wythburn had incised decoration which could be 'of late Bronze or early Iron Age [or] simply the rude decoration of comparatively modern date, the scratchings perhaps of a farm lad, who fashioned the whorl for a sweetheart or sister, two or three centuries ago. Such ornament is just as much what we should expect from a Cumberland youth, whose only tool would be his pocket knife, as from the art craftsman of a semi-savage tribe of the so-called Bronze Age'. This romantic style of expression is demonstrated by other contributors, perhaps most notably William Little in his 1904 talk entitled 'The evolution of the bottle, illustrated from a Westmorland dust-bin'. The speaker brought along a collection of bottles of which four had 'local antiquarian interest' because they had come from Townend in Troutbeck, home of the Browne family: 'emptied by a bygone generation of Brownes, they had lain in a dusty heap time out of mind, until the present head of this old "statesman" family kindly placed some of them at the writer's disposal. From the crust still adhering to the inner surface their latest contents must have been red wine – probably Burgundy'.[32]

The bringing of artefacts to meetings was typical of the antiquarian approach of many nineteenth-century learned societies, where gentlemen (and, much less frequently, ladies) enjoyed a social discourse with the discussion of objects as its centrepiece. They were the essential visual aids in a world where even magic lantern slides were a novelty, and they gave members 'hands-on' participation in a way which was rediscovered by museums a century and more later. The papers which accompanied them were often informal, even chatty, and were also often very short. Some, when they appeared in print, amount to no more than three or four pages. But the speculation that resulted was often academically unsound, and the practice steadily dwindled in the early twentieth century, to be superseded by the reading of longer and more overtly scholarly papers and falling victim to the view that folklore was increasingly regarded as outside the scope of serious academic discussion. In 1911 Mary Louisa Armitt gave a short paper on 'luking-tongs', used for plucking weeds from corn, in which she discussed her documentary research on the unpublished Rydal Hall account books, as well as fieldwork in Furness where James Wood of Sunbrick produced a pair and another man, now middle-aged, 'said he had used them until about 26 years of age' but lamented that 'farming was all changed now'. That statement serves as an epitaph for the folklorists of the Society, whose driving force was indeed the fact that the world 'was all changed now'.[33]

By the mid-1920s folklore was deeply unfashionable as a subject, and to be associated with it was embarrassing for anybody with serious academic intentions. It was bracketed with the word 'antiquarian' as a badge of the well-meaning but harmless dilettante amateur. As noted earlier, even in the 1890s there was some unease about the inclusion of talks and papers on folkloric subjects, and after the First World War few dared to reveal themselves as being interested in such topics. Between the wars scientific archaeology, document-based history and specialist sub-disciplines in, for example, etymology, place-names, and pre-Conquest sculpture, began to emerge, giving an academic rigour to subjects that had once been the preserve of country vicars and leisured county ladies. Nevertheless, the themes themselves did not go away, and some remained of major interest even though the approach began to change fundamentally. A link between the old and new styles is evident in the work of T.E. Casson, who in 1937 and 1944 published two papers about the awkward transition period between mythical history and documented history. The first concerned the fourteenth-century Cumbrian romance 'Horne Childe', set on Stainmore. Casson argued that the poem possibly resulted from medieval folk memories of two events – the battle in 954 at which Eric Bloodaxe was killed, and the alleged meeting between William the Conqueror and Malcolm Canmore at the partition cross on Stainmore summit in 1072.[34] In the second he traced the development of the legends around the Brigantian queen Cartimandua, moving from the only historical evidence – the terse comments in Tacitus – via Welsh folklore, late-medieval literary compilations, to the sixteenth-century Scottish chronicles of Hector Boethiu. Casson finished with an amusing echo of the style of the Victorian folklorist: 'Whether, however, the grave of the ill-omened Cartimandua lies in the Cumberland hills, we do not know. It may be that by some black and wind-swept tarn beneath the crags the indignant spirit of the lady rises and wails to the ambient desolation'.[35]

While Casson was musing on the dark legends that had gathered around the Pennine edge of the county a new interest in the vernacular was apparent, though now it was strictly academic. This was not of course folklore in the earlier sense, but it reflected a heightened awareness of traditional ways of life and customary patterns of social and agricultural activity in the Lake Counties. Hitherto, for example, such vernacular architecture had scarcely been mentioned in *Transactions* but in 1943 Thomas Hay published a very brief note on what he called 'goose bields', the small stone enclosures with overhanging sides which, baited with a goose, were used for trapping foxes in the Lake District.[36] Very modest in its ambition, this article was part of a growing awareness of vernacular buildings and structures which can be seen in the context of the rapid inter-war expansion of National Trust involvement in the region, via its extensive land acquisitions and the emphasis on the protection of traditional architecture encouraged by people such as Beatrix Potter. A far more ambitious and weighty successor was Angus Winchester's 1984 article on the peat storage huts of Eskdale, which discussed the field survey on which the article is based, analysing the structures in terms of construction, geographical context and purpose, supported by oral evidence of use as late as the 1930s, comparisons with elsewhere, and an inventory of examples. In its focus on a poorly-documented but important vernacular tradition it recalled the spirit of the more progressive and systematic Victorian investigators, though it is radically different in its objectives and methodology.[37] The same applies to the work on Cumberland bee shelters and bee boles published by Penny Walker and Eva Crane in 1991 (fig. 4.7), and on similar structures in Furness and Cartmel by Eric Green in 1997, while the difference between stone fox traps (fig. 4.8) and 'goose bields' was pointed out by Peter Fleming in 1998.[38]

Likewise, the revisiting of ancient legends was shown to have a place in an academically-demanding world. In 1952 Canon C.E. Last addressed the vexed question of Bega, perhaps the most famous 'legendary' Cumbria saint. In the 1920s W.G. Collingwood had argued that she was one of many mythical

Fig. 4.7. Eight bee boles at Abbey Farm, St Bees, 1973 (the straw skep is new), *CW2*, 91 (1991), 238

saints, the name being a corruption and misidentification of the Anglo-Saxon *halgan beage* or 'holy bracelet' (translated into dog Latin as *sancta beaga*). Canon Last convincingly rejected this proposition, and assembled a body of evidence about the identity of the saint and of the legends which had accumulated around her shadowy existence.[39] Almost 30 years later John Todd, a renowned scholar of medieval Cumbria, tackled the same subject, looking at place-name and personal-name evidence for her cult, the recorded miracles, and the spurious legend of the bracelet. With relish he set down a miracle which, by its rather racy nature, would not have suited Victorian clerical antiquarians:[40]

Fig. 4.8. 'The fox trap at Hookriggs', *CW2*, 98 (1998), 274 (*photograph: Peter Fleming*)

> There was a man of Galloway – whence the bogey-men of the north of England so often came – who was warned by his mother not to commit theft, rapine, or violence on the land of St Bega. And he jeered 'why, what can that little old woman do to me?' and then 'moving his hand to the more private parts of his buttocks, he said with a blasphemous mouth, "here, here, she will shoot me"'. So he came to St Bega's land, and stole a horse, and rode off on it. But he was observed and some lads of the village gave chase with their bows. And as the thief lay along his horse's neck, to present a smaller target, one of the lads drew a bow at a venture ... and you can guess the rest.

Todd concluded that Bega was a real historical figure, but that 'we must search for [her] not in the glorious years of the Northumbrian kingdom, but the dark years of its fall. But our search may well be disappointed'. As Janet Martin observed in 2001, 'historical legends are widespread and tenacious. Every part of the country has stories of underground passages between monasteries and nunneries, of houses built of old ships' timbers, of illustrious persons living and dying in seclusion. Those strands of fantasy often, and understandably, embroider the story of a man or woman who for some reason or another attracted curiosity, perhaps because they did not fit into a familiar pattern'. These wise words were the preamble to her highly effective hatchet job on the legend of the 'Finsthwaite Princess', in which she forensically examined a piling up of fantasy and falsehood, and especially the absurd recent stories which first appeared in print in the 1960s-1980s. She demonstrated the manifest impossibility of the claim that Clementina Johannes Sobiesky Douglass, who was buried in 1771 at Finsthwaite, could have been the daughter of Bonnie Prince Charlie and hence the princess of the legend.[41]

How should we judge the contribution of folklore in the work of the Society? Later writers have often drawn upon the substantial corpus of material on folklore-related subjects which has appeared in *Transactions* over the decades. In 1974, for example, Bill Rollinson published his best-selling popular work, *Life and Tradition in the Lake District*, which echoed many of the themes which had been of interest to the folklorist antiquarians a century before – vernacular material culture, traditional patterns of social and economic activity, and the central role of dialect in fostering regional identity.[42] The book's bibliography references 20 articles from the Old and New Series, indicating that some, at least, still had relevance and value. Furthermore, the mid- to late-nineteenth century interest in the traditions, customs and dialect of the Lake Counties is now a subject of historical research in its own right, as exemplified by Peter Lucas's article on the 'dialect boom' in Victorian Furness, published in 2005, and D.S. Roberts's 1999 analysis of de Quincey's paper on the Danish origins of Lake District speech.[43] For scholars in the twenty-first century the articles of 150 years ago provide some of the raw material which helps us to understand the emergence of a locally-based historical culture in the English regions and counties, a key element in the broadening of the popular appeal of history itself as subject of study. These articles are, therefore, now serving an entirely different purpose – we use them to gain insights into the late Victorian intellectual mind and social attitudes.

As academic disciplines history and archaeology evolved rapidly during the second half of the nineteenth century and, as we have seen, by the time of the First World War the first signs of a rejection of the 'antiquarian' approach were becoming apparent. This was a trend which affected all those societies which, like the Cumberland and Westmorland, had started out as purely amateur organisations in which like-minded people came together to listen to, and debate, subjects of common interest. During this first period of the Society's existence it was, as noted above, perfectly permissible for members to bring along bits of intriguing ironware to meetings, to show them to fellow-members and to discuss their provenance and purpose. Likewise, it was quite acceptable for short papers on folklore to be presented (as, occasionally, were papers on natural history and geological subjects). The authors of papers did not have to include references or demonstrate strict adherence to the rules of scholarship, and it was considered quite legitimate to speculate and hypothesise in a way which might now be frowned upon.

As academic rigour was imposed, discussion of folklore, traditions and customs became increasingly marginalised – these topics were no longer taken seriously, and they appeared to lack proper academic credentials. Therefore from the early 1920s consideration of them diminished rapidly. In the later-twentieth century there was a revival of interest, as awareness of the history of conservation, heritage and the perceptions of Lake District and Cumbrian identity gave a new relevance to the Victorian and Edwardian articles, and their authors who had introduced some of these topics. In the twenty-first century the theme of language, landscape and regional identity has become central to writers such as Robert Macfarlane, while the lost world of obsolete appliances depicted and explained by Swainson Cowper in his *Transactions* articles has provided the Cumbrian-based artists Richard Skelton and Autumn Richardson with opportunities to meditate on 'the customary persecution and exploitation of animal life in Cumbria, offering alternate historic, mythic and folkloric contexts for these artefacts which imply different attitudes towards the natural world' in their 2014 exhibition at Abbot Hall Art Gallery.[44] Today, in the context of Lake District studies, the articles published over the years in *Transactions* have an honourable place – and in some cases an important one.

Notes and References

1 A.G. Crosby, *'A Society with No Equal': the Chetham Society 1843-1993* (Chetham Society 3rd ser. vol. 37, 1993), 36-40; A.G. Crosby, *The Chester Archaeological Society: the first one hundred and fifty years 1849-1999* (Chester Archaeological Society, 1999).

2 *Sketch of Cumberland Manners and Customs: partly in the provincial dialect, in prose and verse, with a glossary* (Carlisle, 1811), 38.

3 A. Craig Gibson, 'Ancient customs and superstitions of Cumberland', *Transactions of the Historic Society of Lancashire and Cheshire*, 10 (1856), 96-110.

4 W.J. Thoms, 'Folk-lore', *The Athenaeum*, 22 and 29 Aug. 1846.

5 C. Phythian-Adams, 'Folklore, customs, and civic ritual', in D. Hey (ed.), *The Oxford Companion to Family and Local History* (Oxford, 2008), 167.

6 *Folklore,* 1.1 (1890), 1.

7 http://www.skansen.se/en/kategori/english; Herman Hofberg (ed.), *Svenskt biografiskt handlexikon* (1906), 467-68 available at http://runeberg.org/sbh/a0467.html. Accessed 2 Dec. 2015.

8 Obituary for Canon Lees, *CW1,* 13 (1895), 3.

9 Miss Powley, 'Past and present among the Northern Fells', *CW1,* 2 (1876), 171-86.

10 Revd H.R. Bulkeley, 'Some East Cumberland superstitions', *CW1,* 8 (1886), 225-32.

11 Henry Swainson Cowper (1865-1941) was a Middlesex-born, Harrow-educated resident of Hawkshead. His colourful life included pioneering archaeological investigations in the Tarhuna area of Libya, journeying overland from the Mediterranean to Bombay (written up and published as *Through Turkish Arabia* in 1894) and writing a treatise on the history of weapons and gunpowder (1906). His archaeological enthusiasms were primarily responsible for his growing fascination with the cultural artefacts of Cumbria, his adopted home.

12 H.S. Cowper, 'On some obsolete and semi-obsolete appliances', *CW1,* 13 (1895), 86-102.

13 H.S. Cowper, 'Hawkshead folk-lore – charms, superstition, witchcraft, and traditional customs', *CW1,* 14 (1897), 371-89.

14 Mrs Hodgson, 'On some surviving fairies', *CW2,* 1 (1901), 116-18. Her scepticism is evident in her comment on the popular belief in 'fairy butter' that the real nature of the commodity was explained in Canon Atkinson, *Forty Years in Moorland Parish* (London, 1891). It was a fast-growing, yellow, edible fungus. In the early volumes of *Transactions* there are very few contributions by women, and most of those which were published relate to folklore, suggesting not only that the CWAAS was a male-dominated society in its earlier decades, but perhaps also that whimsical folklore was, at least at that time, regarded as 'suitable' for women (unlike the possibly more robust pursuit of archaeology)!

15 Pace-egging: a traditional folk play performed at Easter.

16 Bulkeley, 'Some East Cumberland superstitions'.

17 W.G. Collingwood, 'Late and magic runes in Cumberland', *CW2,* 6 (1906), 305-12.

18 Canon Thornley, 'Children's games as played at Kirkoswald', *CW2,* 1 (1901), 268-79.

19 T. Ellwood, 'Numerals formerly used for sheepscoring in the Lake Country, No.1', *CW1,* 3 (1878), 381-84; 'Numerals formerly used for sheepscoring in the Lake Country, No.2', *CW1,* 3 (1878), 385-97.

20 *A Tale of Two Dales* (Border TV/Norwegian Broadcasting Company, 1988).

21 A. Wawn, in foreword to T. Ellwood, *Lakeland and Iceland comprising The Landnama Book of Iceland as it illustrates the Dialect, Folk Lore & Antiquities of Cumberland, Westmorland and North Lancashire and A Glossary of Words in the Dialect of Cumberland, Westmorland and North Lancashire which seem allied to or identical with the Icelandic or Norse* (first published 1894 and 1895, combined facsimile edition Llanerch Publishers, 1995), unpag. [iv].

22 T. Ellwood, 'Notes upon some of the older word forms to be found in comparing the language of Lakeland with the language of Iceland', *CW1,* 9 (1888), 383-92.
23 H.S. Cowper, 'Law Ting at Fell Foot, Little Langdale', *CW1,* 11 (1891), 1-6.
24 T. Ellwood with Eiríkr Magnússon, 'The Landnama Book of Iceland, as it illustrates the dialect, place names, folklore, and antiquities of Cumberland, Westmorland, and North Lancashire', *CW1,* 13 (1895), 283-311.
25 T. Ellwood, 'The mountain sheep: their origin and marking', *CW1,* 15 (1899), 1-8.
26 R.S. Ferguson, 'A labyrinth on Rockcliffe Marsh', *CW1,* 7 (1884), 69-73.
27 H. Penfold, 'The Capon Tree, Brampton, and its memories', *CW2,* 5 (1905), 129-42.
28 W.G. Collingwood, 'Who was King Eveling of Ravenglass?', *CW2,* 24 (1924), 256-69.
29 R.S. Ferguson, 'Knitting-sheaths or knitting-sticks', *CW1,* 6 (1883), 91-93.
30 H.S. Cowper, 'The domestic candlestick of iron in Cumberland, Westmorland and Furness', *CW1,* 12 (1893), 105-27.
31 Cowper, 'On some obsolete and semi-obsolete appliances'.
32 W. Little, 'The evolution of the bottle, illustrated from a Westmorland dust-bin', *CW2,* 4 (1904), 213-16.
33 M.L. Armitt, 'The luking-tongs: their meaning and use', *CW2,* 11 (1911), 199-201.
34 T.E. Casson, 'Horn Childe and the Battle on Stainmore', *CW2,* 37 (1937), 30-39.
35 T.E. Casson, 'Cartimandua, in history, legend and romance', *CW2,* 44 (1944), 68-80.
36 T. Hay, 'The goose bield', *CW2,* 43 (1943), 28-30.
37 A.J.L. Winchester, 'Peat storage huts in Eskdale', *CW2,* 84 (1984), 103-16.
38 P. Walker and E. Crane, 'Bee shelters and bee boles in Cumbria', *CW2,* 91 (1991), 237-62; E. Green, 'Bee boles and related structures in Furness and Cartmel', *CW2,* 97 (1997), 231-38; P. Fleming, 'Stone fox traps, borrans and goose bields', *CW2,* 98 (1998), 269-76.
39 C.E. Last, 'St Bega and her bracelet', *CW2,* 52 (1952), 55-66.
40 J.M. Todd, 'St Bega: cult, fact and legend', *CW2,* 80 (1980), 25-36.
41 J.D. Martin, 'The Finsthwaite Princess: the making of a myth', *CW3,* 1 (2001), 155-64.
42 W. Rollinson, *Life and Tradition in the Lake District* (London, 1974).
43 P. Lucas, 'The dialect boom in Victorian Furness', *CW3,* 5 (2005), 199-216; D.S. Roberts, 'Thomas de Quincey's "Danish origin of the Lake Country dialect"', *CW2,* 99 (1999), 257-66.
44 R. Macfarlane, *Landmarks* (London, 2015); R. Skelton and A. Richardson, *Memorious Earth: a longitudinal study* (Kendal, 2015).

Chapter 5
Traditional Buildings

Fiona Wooler and Michael Winstanley

The study of what are usually called vernacular or traditional buildings, particularly rural houses, has been a central concern of the Society ever since it was founded.[1] Ronald Brunskill, one of the leading authorities in this field, had a lifelong interest in Cumbria having first become aware of the varied housing designs when visiting his grandparents as a child. He later served as President of the Society between 1990 and 1993, so it is appropriate to begin with his succinct definition of this area of study:

> The building types … are primarily domestic and rural and vernacular rather than polite in character. In other words they are the products of local craftsmen meeting simple fundamental requirements according to traditional plans and procedures and with the aid of local building materials and constructional methods.[2]

Such buildings reflect the building materials available in specific parts of the region, but also the varied and changing social structure and the history of border conflict. More generally, however, they were influenced by the region's climate and by fluctuations in agricultural prosperity and specialisation (see Chapter 6). In many cases it is the physical fabric which provides evidence for the original and subsequent use of structures and internal spaces. Documentary sources can supplement archaeological and survey evidence and aid in interpretation, particularly in the process of construction and the uses of such buildings, but they are often scanty or completely non-existent for specific properties. The early survey work of the Society is of particular value here since contributors to *Transactions* published plans, photographs and descriptions of the properties as they were over a century ago.

Brunskill has contrasted these 'traditional' properties with 'polite' buildings, the '… products of professional designers fulfilling the more elaborate needs of a formal way of life with the aid of internationally accepted rules and procedures, advanced constructional techniques, and materials chosen for aesthetic effect rather than local availability.'[3] The Society's interest in this latter area is also discussed below.

Large Houses

The Society's initial fascination was with what Brunskill later broadly described as 'large houses' or 'dwellings of people who were of local importance' as opposed to 'the great houses' belonging to people of 'national importance' on the one hand and the farmers' and cottagers' 'small houses' on the other. This was a broad classification which he refined but retained in his later works.[4]

The first edition of *Transactions* contained several reports on standing buildings such as castles and churches but particularly 'halls', notably Yanwath Hall and Blencowe Hall, both near Penrith, and Wharton Hall near Appleby. The Society often visited such houses on excursions and Dr Michael Waistell Taylor noted in his introduction to the paper connected with the visit to Yanwath in 1867 that 'There is no part of Cumberland or of Westmorland so rich in examples of old manorial halls as the district around Penrith', where almost every village had its old 'hall'. These, he suggested, had once been the residence of manorial lords, although at the time many were tenanted 'by the principal farmer of the place'. He described Yanwath Hall as a good example of a fourteenth-century North of England fortified manor house and his tour of the property outlined its architectural features.[5] He described the plan

Fig. 5.1. 'Yanwath Hall' by John Thompson 1895 *(reproduced by permission of Cumbria County Council, Carlisle Library)*

form, original uses of the structures and the dating of the various phases, including the earliest – the pele tower – which he suggested may have been constructed in the early fourteenth century and which he considered to be an example of 'the border towers of the same epoch, built for defence and as a place of refuge for men and cattle from the incursions of Scottish marauders' (figs. 5.1 and 5.2).[6]

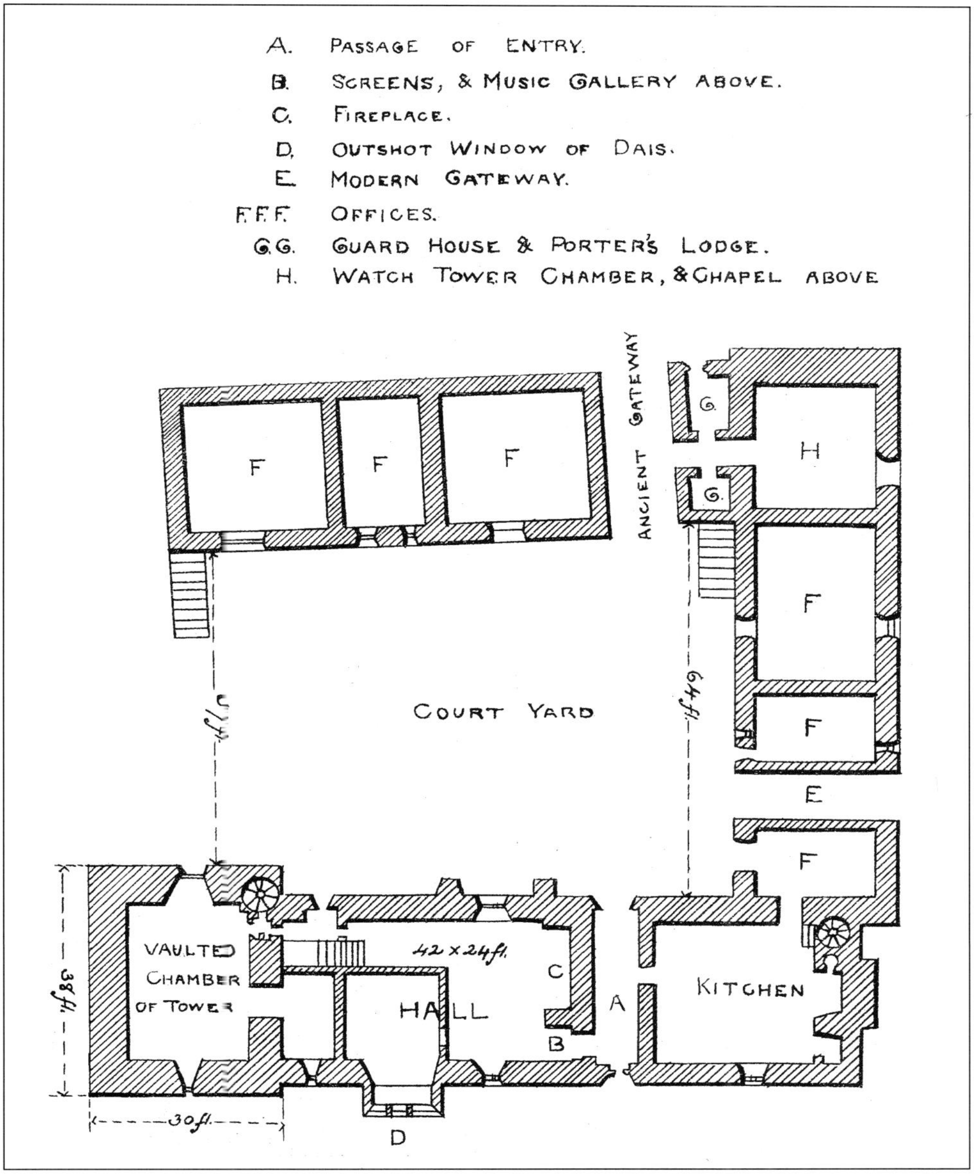

Fig. 5.2. Ground plan of Yanwath Hall, *CW1*, 1 (1874), opposite 50

Taylor was responsible for further articles on halls in *Transactions* between 1876 and 1893,[7] but his most significant publication was *The Old Manorial Halls of Westmorland and Cumberland* in 1892 which brought together the fruits of his research over the previous quarter of a century. This remains a valuable source of information on their development and their physical structure as it was observed in the late nineteenth century. In his preface Taylor, who was a Vice-President of the Society, noted that his intention was to preserve in permanent form descriptions of the existing condition of 'the Pele Towers, Old Manorial Halls, and Domestic Structures of which so many remarkable specimens still survive in the two counties of Westmorland and Cumberland'. Within this his primary purpose was to trace the historical development of styles which occurred at different historical periods in the construction of old manor houses and in the domestic life and customs associated with them 'from the beginning of the fourteenth century to the Restoration'. But he did so by describing each property in turn since, he argued, many of them exhibited evidence of several phases of development.[8]

A final thematic chapter in his book discussed the 'legends and inscriptions over doorways' since 'the entrance, or gateway, or doorway has ever been the part of a building which has received the largest share of architectural skill and decoration'.[9] Taylor also described the carved stone inscriptions in these houses including the earliest example he had identified: an external mural tablet over the gateway at Brougham Castle near Penrith, where an inscription, 'Thys made roger', commemorates the erection of a range by Roger de Clifford at the end of the thirteenth century. Some of the more informative inscriptions and date stones were from the sixteenth and seventeenth centuries such as at Crakeplace Hall in the parish of Dean: '1612 Christopher Crakeplace built the same when he was servant to Baron Altham'.[10] Such relatively elaborate inscriptions on domestic buildings seemingly fell out of usage by the end of the seventeenth century and Taylor tentatively suggested that a reason for this was the downfall of the Stuarts, when 'a national feeling of discomfiture crept in towards usages which pertained to that dynasty and to former times'. From then on, Taylor observed, 'parading the pretensions of heraldic prerogatives fell away with the decline of the practice of that art, and the architectural style of domestic buildings assumed a new model'. Taylor identified the eighteenth century as a dramatic period of change in terms of the construction of new forms of buildings and the adaptation of older structures with a move from domestic buildings with low mullioned windows, drip moulds, and recessed lintels, to the Italian style of frontage, with a general lack of entrances adorned with the display of heraldic shields, tablets or lines of lettering.[11] Sadly Taylor did not live to see the fruits of his work published. A moving preface to his book included his obituary, reporting that he had died on 24 November 1892 'while the final sheets of the index were passing through the press'.

Interest in 'halls' continued into the twentieth century with H.S. Cowper, Charles J. Ferguson, J.H. Martindale and even W.G. Collingwood all contributing articles to *Transactions*, often with plans, drawn, in the case of Cowper's description of Coniston Hall, by John Bell, a local land agent,

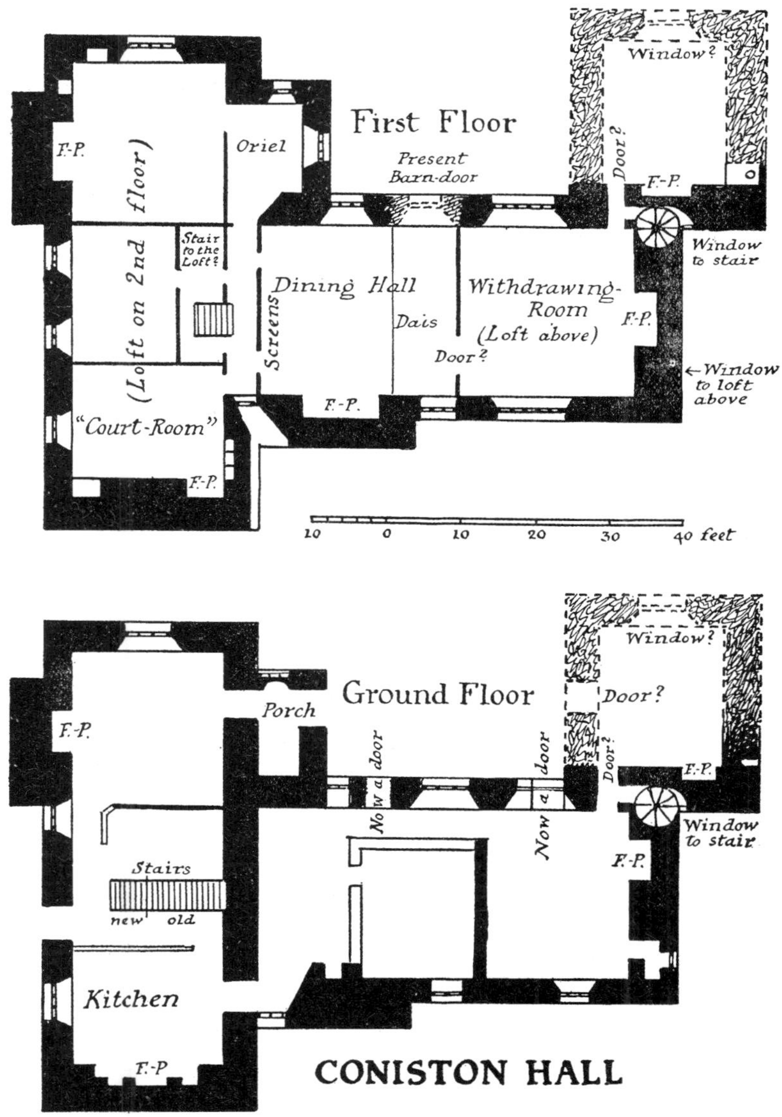

Fig. 5.3. Plans of Coniston Hall, *CW2*, 10 (1910), 358, elaborated by Collingwood from original drawings by local land agent, John Bell for H.S. Cowper's earlier article, *CW1*, 9 (1888), opposite 357

whose plan was revised and extended for Collingwood's later study (fig. 5.3).[12] Several of the properties were, or seem to have originated as, defensive structures dating from the Middle Ages, providing a constant reminder of the county's troubled and war-ravaged history.[13] 'Medieval fortified buildings' attracted particular interest. They found their chronicler in John F. Curwen, an active member of the Society from 1887 who published extensively in *Transactions* over a period of more than 30 years, especially on a variety of domestic, religious and fortified buildings. Like his fellow contributors, his articles were often connected with Society excursions to the sites and included plans and photographs of houses, such as Catterlen Hall which the Society visited in September 1906 (fig. 5.4).[14] The cumulative results of his research, *Castles and Fortified Towers of Cumberland, Westmorland and Lancashire North of the Sands,* including a gazetteer of known sites, was published by the Society in 1913.[15]

A comprehensive catalogue of the architectural details of similar houses constructed before 1715 was published in the Westmorland volume of the *Royal Commission on the Historical Monuments of England* (RCHME) in 1936.[16] Yanwath was the subject of a challenging, revisionist analysis by W. Douglas Simpson in 1944 who referred to the probable extent of a 'tower-house province' stretching across Scotland and the four northern counties.[17] Pele towers and semi-fortified houses continued to be attractive venues for Society's excursions, with Catterlen and Yanwath again visited in 1947 and 1951 respectively.[18]

Fig. 5.4. Catterlen Hall, *CW2*, 7 (1907), opposite 115

In July 1955 Ronald Brunskill led excursions to Kirkby Thore, Ormside and Gaythorn halls and his accompanying paper, read at the sites, illustrated 'the improvements in spatial standards during the three centuries [14th- 16th]' in terms of size and convenience.[19] Two years later *Transactions* published his pioneering classification template for 'large houses' based on extensive research undertaken for his MA at Manchester University.[20] He was primarily concerned with establishing the development phases and typologies of these 'large houses' in general. He identified seven, two of which were fortified, while three shaded into what might be called 'polite' architecture:

1) Pele towers, isolated multi-storey structures erected during the fourteenth century, containing within four walls the entire living accommodation. He identified only one true pele tower in the Eden Valley (Catterlen Hall), but recognised the form was more important elsewhere;
2) Semi-fortified houses of which Yanwath Hall was seen as the best recorded example. The fifteenth-century plan consisted of three units, a single storey hall, a three-storey fortified tower, and at the other end a single storey kitchen or service unit;
3) Houses with multi-storey porches, of which Hornby Hall near Penrith was a good example, consisting of one long rectangular block of two storeys, containing the hall in the centre, the parlour at one end and the kitchen at the other, with the house being entered by a three-storey porch;
4) Non-fortified houses with no clear provision for security;
5) Anglo-Baroque houses, which were influenced by Dutch ideas, of which Mansion House at Eamont Bridge (dated 1686) was an example;
6) Palladian houses, where nearly all examples were symmetrical and constructed as single blocks without projections, such as The Nunnery near Armathwaite (erected *c.*1715);
7) Regency and Revival houses, which included The Grange at Temple Sowerby which has a date on a rainwater head of 1817.

By the 1980s John Robinson (County Architect), Tom Clare (County Archaeologist) and Denis Perriam (Listed Building Inspector) recognised the need for a new gazetteer incorporating both the 157 fortified sites identified by Curwen and the more recent surveys conducted for a variety of academic and planning purposes. The total number of known sites had by then reached 228, with 192 defensive sites in the old county of Cumberland alone, of which 120 were standing structures. In 1998 the Society published *The Medieval Fortified Buildings of Cumbria,* an illustrated gazetteer and research guide which Matthew Hyde described as 'invaluable for its plans and references and for its considerably broader scope than the title would imply'.[21] This gazetteer contained over 500 case-studies, some extant, some only identified through stray references in documents or even local anecdotal evidence.[22] In some cases, such as at Longcleughside, Liddel, the site was included simply because of its presence on small-scale historic maps, in this case a map of 1590, but with no physical evidence still standing. Many of these buildings clearly functioned as residences and, as the preface noted, the most difficult problem was deducing whether a building was 'fortified' or not. Each historic county was subdivided into districts and civil parishes with each property represented by a number on a map to provide information on distribution.

This publication brought to the fore the survival of bastle houses.[23] These were defensive dwellings, generally of two storeys with an external stair or ladder providing access to living quarters at first-floor level, and space at ground-floor level for animals to be brought in for safety during periods of instability in the border region. These were, and still are, particularly evident in the Alston area where the tradition continued long after the Union of the Crowns in 1603, with houses in this defensive style being erected even into the eighteenth century. Based on her recent study of Scarrow Hill, however, Catherine Bancroft has argued that this was not the case in the Naworth area since new non-fortified buildings were being constructed by the early seventeenth century.[24]

Small houses

By the 1950s attention was increasingly turning to farmhouses or 'small houses'. Brunskill's first article had been entitled 'The development of the small house in the Eden Valley from 1650 to 1840' in which he defined the 'small house' as the dwelling of the 'statesman' or yeoman farmer, in contrast to the 'great houses' of the landed gentry, or the large houses of the lesser gentry or more substantial tenant, or indeed the 'cottages' of the landless labourers. He chose 1650 because he regarded it as marking the emergence of types of 'domestic architecture' not exclusively concerned with defence, and 1840 as the point just before rail transport brought about the submergence of local styles in a national style.[25]

Brunskill aimed to record all examples of surviving 'traditional domestic architecture' in the Eden Valley which dated from this period. Of the 993 examples of traditional buildings he classified 748 as 'small houses'. He supplemented his surveying with documentary research to check and amplify the results, so providing a wealth of references particularly from topographical writers of the late eighteenth and early nineteenth century including James Clark's *Survey of the Lakes* (1787) and John Hodgson's account of Westmorland in *The Beauties of England* series (1814). Brunskill provided informative descriptions and floor plans but he also supplied elevation drawings of examples of the various types of dwellings (fig. 5.5), and from these he constructed a detailed classification scheme with five distinct classes of small houses which emerged gradually over this period:

1) Statesman plan (three versions) which appears to have represented the convergence of two courses of development, the subdivision of an early 'long house' and the enlargement of early two-unit dwellings;
2) Double-fronted houses with no outshut which differed from the Statesman plan by the positioning of the front door central to the main elevation, thereby changing the internal floor plan;
3) Double-fronted houses with outshut, where the staircase was provided in a single-storey rear extension (outshut);
4) Double-fronted houses, two rooms in depth (now referred to as the double pile), an improvement of the extension to the rear of a single-pile house by effectively increasing the walls of the outshut to full height and moving the ridge to the centre of the plan;
5) Regency and Revival influence houses, limited to a small number of properties, for example, a property on Bongate in Appleby, dated to 1800, which was embellished with crenellated parapets, a projecting bay, quatrefoil panels, and four-centred arched doorway with fretted glazing bars. Such houses were rare before 1840.

In conclusion, Brunskill noted that 'Each class had its period of popularity but was succeeded by the next, which in its turn was succeeded by yet another class. In no case was there a sudden change from the use of one type of plan to the use of another; in every instance there was a substantial overlap'.[26] Precise dating of individual properties, however, was, and is often difficult. In a short letter two years later Mary Fair cautioned about uncritical reliance on date stones because

> some of the present occupants invent what they do not know, for handing out to enquirers who visit them! One gentleman, having bought one of the ancient homesteads mentioned in the Humberstone survey of 1578, wanted to have that date carved upon his front-door lintel.[27]

Interestingly, at no stage in his early articles did Brunskill use the word 'vernacular' but this featured in the title of his later work in 1974 – *Vernacular Architecture of the Lake Counties*. This brought together, with various elaborations, his phasing of both small and large houses, complemented by sections on cottages, farm buildings, 'industrial vernacular', and 'urban vernacular'.[28] He also included useful chapters on materials, construction techniques and architectural details such as windows and doorways, and internal features, all intended to empower the 'enthusiastic amateur' to embark on systematic recording of examples in the field.[29] Although this book was not published by the Society, Brunskill acknowledged the contributions made by its members, and the classification scheme he employed was clearly derived from the original research in the 1950s. In 1991 Susan Denyer

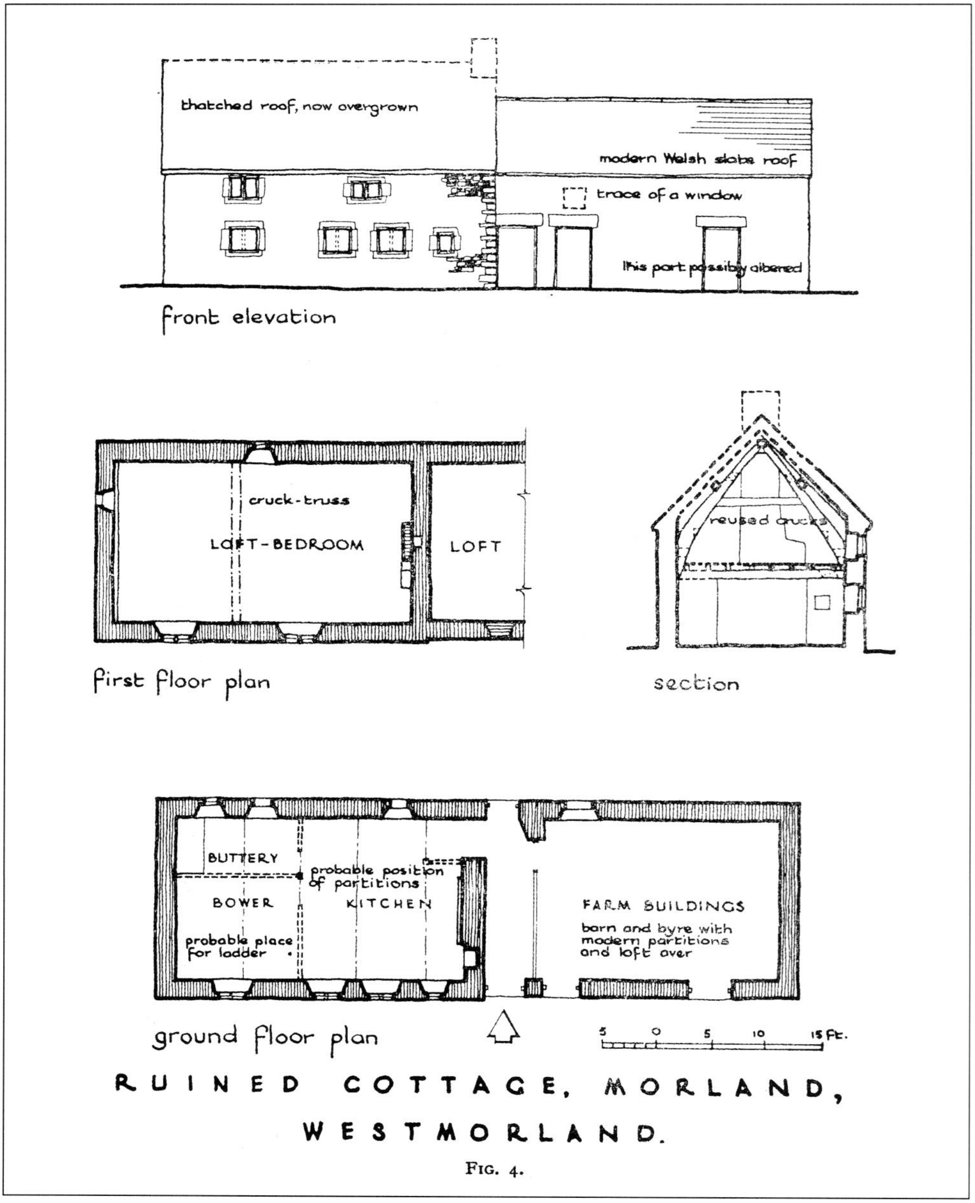

Fig. 5.5. R.W. Brunskill's plans and elevations of a ruined cottage at Morland, Westmorland, an example of what he called 'Statesman (b)' in which the service room was replaced by farm buildings, *CW2*, 53 (1953), opposite 169

published her *Traditional Buildings and Life in the Lake District* in which she acknowledged the help of Brunskill, as well as other Society members such as Angus Winchester, and particularly Janet Martin who carried out the 'extensive archive research for all the farms'.[30] When Brunskill's volume was updated and enhanced in 2002, he, too, reverted to his earlier terminology. *Traditional Buildings of Cumbria* included an expanded section relating to farm buildings, and a new chapter on churches and chapels.[31]

At the same time as Brunskill was undertaking his survey of the Eden Valley, W.M. Williams was studying the farmhouses of south-west Cumbria, as part of his broader sociological study of the Gosforth area. [32] Most were constructed between 1700 and 1900, with only a few dating to before 1700. He particularly noted the absence of pele towers, possibly indicating the lack of need for defence given the area's geographical location in relation to the border with Scotland.[33] Nearly all of the later farmhouses were constructed of the local red sandstone, or 'freestone', obtained from nearby quarries. It was rare for two houses to be exactly the same since they varied in size, age and ground plan, but he distinguished two predominant types. His 'oblong house', characterised by a lateral arrangement of rooms, one-room deep, was not dissimilar to Brunskill's 'Statesman plan' although with subtle differences. Examples included Row Farm and Broom Farm, both of which could not be dated, and Andrew Ground, constructed in the early eighteenth century. His 'square' house was similar to Brunskill's double-fronted residences, and was a more recent form constructed during the mid-eighteenth century, 'when the increased prosperity of the yeoman resulted in the demolition of many of the existing thatched farmhouses'. Another period of intensive building of the 'square' house in the area occurred in the years 1780-1800 when date stones suggest that at least a third of the farmhouses were constructed. He also described an example of a 'square' farmhouse, or what would now be termed a 'double pile', at Thornbank erected in 1795.[34] Williams concluded by suggesting, that although there were similarities between south-west Cumberland and the Eden Valley, the house-forms he had identified had developed differently, and he called for more studies of other parts of the region, particularly the coastal plain.[35]

Clay Dabbins/Daubins

Williams also drew attention to a 'clay daubin', ie. a thatched building, some walls of which were constructed by applying mud to a wattle framework. At the time of the survey some evidence of this method of construction could still be seen, with the interior walls of Andrew Ground described as 'excellent examples of this work'. Low Bridge Petton, Gosforth, a farmhouse of the 'oblong' type, which had the date and initials 'RAF 1697' on one of the main walls of the dwelling house was also constructed using clay. A thatched clay house survived at Hall Senna until 1882, when it was demolished to make way for the stone building which now occupies the site. Williams sought to explain the presence of clay buildings in an area where red sandstone was clearly available as being due to the materials being less expensive to use than stone. He also suggested that clay may have been a common (if not the predominant) method of construction during the seventeenth century, but that over time it had been replaced by local stone, with roofing material also changing from thatch to slate, and the ground plan from 'oblong' to 'square'; this suggested a similar chronology and progression to that noted by Brunskill in the Eden Valley.

Clay daubins had been observed by various visitors to Cumberland in the eighteenth century. William Stukeley on his visit to Netherby in 1725 commented that, apart from a few castellated, fortified houses in the district, 'the houses of the cottagers, they are mean beyond imagination; made of mud, and thatched with turf, without windows, only one story [*sic*], the people almost naked' (fig. 5.6).[36] William Hutchinson in his *History of Cumberland* (1794) referred to some of the 'old houses' in the county, for example those at Holm Cultram, as 'poor clay huts'. In Great Orton he noted more substantial buildings:

> These clay houses are generally made up in a day or two for, when a person wants a house, a barn etc. built, he acquaints his neighbours, who all appear at the time appointed; some lay on clay; some tread it, whilst others are preparing straw to mix it with. By this means, building comes low and expeditious – and indeed it must be owned, that they have brought the art of clay building to perfection. They generally ground with stone [foundations] about a yard high and a house thus built will stand (it is said) 150 or 200 years.[37]

The first detailed study of this form of building appeared in the same edition of *Transactions* as Brunskill's article on the small house. This arose out of the activities of the Society's Regional Groups, which encouraged individuals to present papers on their research but without necessarily intending to produce a published piece of work. During one of these meetings C.M.L. Bouch discussed the topic of clay houses, or clay daubins, and this led to a correspondence with Brunskill and a suggestion from Kate Hodgson that Lamonby Farm at Burgh-by-Sands would provide a suitable case study. Bouch and Hodgson's resulting article provided historical background to the type of building and included C.G. Bulman's architectural description and archaeological assessment of the original structure, and of the additions subsequently made, including the adjoining agricultural building. Lamonby Farm was larger than the cottagers' houses described by Stukeley and had been constructed on stone 'sleeper-walls', as described by Hutchinson, with a roof supported by crucks. It was noted that it was most likely a counterpart in clay of Brunskill's stone-built 'Statesman plan' of late seventeenth to early eighteenth century date, although there were no architectural features to aid in dating. Bulman concluded that it was 'an almost perfect example of those traditional methods of building which persisted unchanged for many hundreds of years, but are now obsolete. Its real interest lies in its structure, built by unskilled local labour, with such materials as were ready to hand'.[38]

The Society's main contribution to the study of these houses, now generally referred to as 'clay dabbins' however, and the essential starting point for anyone interested in them, is the work of Nina Jennings. Building on the work of Brunskill, who had identified approximately 105 clay houses (many of which have disappeared since his initial foray into the subject),[39] and Ray Harrison,[40] and drawing on the expertise of many local individuals and Society members, Jennings sought to undertake a comprehensive survey of standing examples in her area. Between 1993 and 2011 she published several articles in *Transactions*.[41] In her book of 2003, *Clay Dabbins: vernacular buildings of the Solway Plain*, also published by the Society, she described over 150 surviving farmhouses, cottages and farm buildings and attempted to trace their development both in form and in construction methods.[42] Rather than being a simple gazetteer of each property, she used themed chapters to convey the archaeological and documentary evidence for these fascinating buildings, including the historical development of clay structures, the social history associated with them and their construction techniques. The Society also provided financial assistance for the scientific (tree-ring) dating of some of the houses which enabled the origins of some of the properties to be pushed back some 300 years.[43] For example, re-used cruck timbers of the Royal Oak Cottage, Moorhouse were dendro-dated to the late-fourteenth or early-fifteenth century, although a precise felling date from the tree(s) could not be obtained. This evidence indicates that cruck construction buildings of five to six metres overall width, and almost certainly with clay walls, were being erected on the Plain from at least the fourteenth century. As Jennings concluded, 'these buildings are a national treasure; they are an irreplaceable historical record, in some ways unique ... they shed a remarkable light on the inventiveness and competence of ordinary people' (fig. 5.6).[44]

Documentary insights: farms and farmsteads

Studies of clay dabbins, farmhouses and fortified dwellings initially relied heavily on the fieldwork evidence of standing structures, something which was central to the original archaeological purposes of the Society. Documentary evidence to shed light on a specific building's construction or domestic and farming uses has been much less abundant.

Fig. 5.6. Upperby Village, Carlisle by Thomas Bushby, early twentieth century, showing clay dabbins *(reproduced by permission of Cumbria County Council, Carlisle Library)*

From the late 1970s, however, the Society has published a series of important articles by Blake Tyson highlighting the potential significance of estate and family records as sources of information. In his case study of Skelsmergh he used a document from 1602 to construct the location and likely form of 19 buildings of varying sizes containing 61 'paire [s] of trees', identifying the location of several of them, including some farmsteads now lost, and surveying a rare (unlisted) survival at Coppack Howe (fig. 5.7). He concluded by speculating on the wider implications of his case-study for regional and national studies including the extent of such buildings, their size and the large number of trusses that would have been required for their construction.[45]

Tyson also used documentary evidence to shed light on the construction, organisation, cost, plan form, and on the motivations for, and the process of, construction of domestic and ancillary buildings in various parts of the county.[46] The estate accounts of Sir Daniel Fleming of Rydal Hall, for example, provided details about farmsteads and farm buildings on the estate as they were built in the late seventeenth century (see Chapter 6), a case-study which could be used to underpin field work and to compare similar sites and buildings in the region. This source also described the social aspects of their erection. Writing on 28 June 1670, Fleming recorded:

> This day was raised ye Corne Barne at Rydall, they began about 9 in ye morneing, at 12 all ye Bearers had a Dinner, about 5 in ye

> afternoon, they had a great cheese cake, 4s. in ale (besides [that] which was sent and two Pale full of our owne) & 5 pounds of tobacco (viz. I gave 1 pound to ye wrights, 1 pound to ye wallers and 2 pounds to ye other Bearers & my wife gave 1 pound amongst ye women) which comes to 4s. 2d., in all 8s. 2d.[47]

The accounts also listed the trades involved at the time, such as 'wallers', 'wrights' and carpenters (many of whom were named), the materials used,

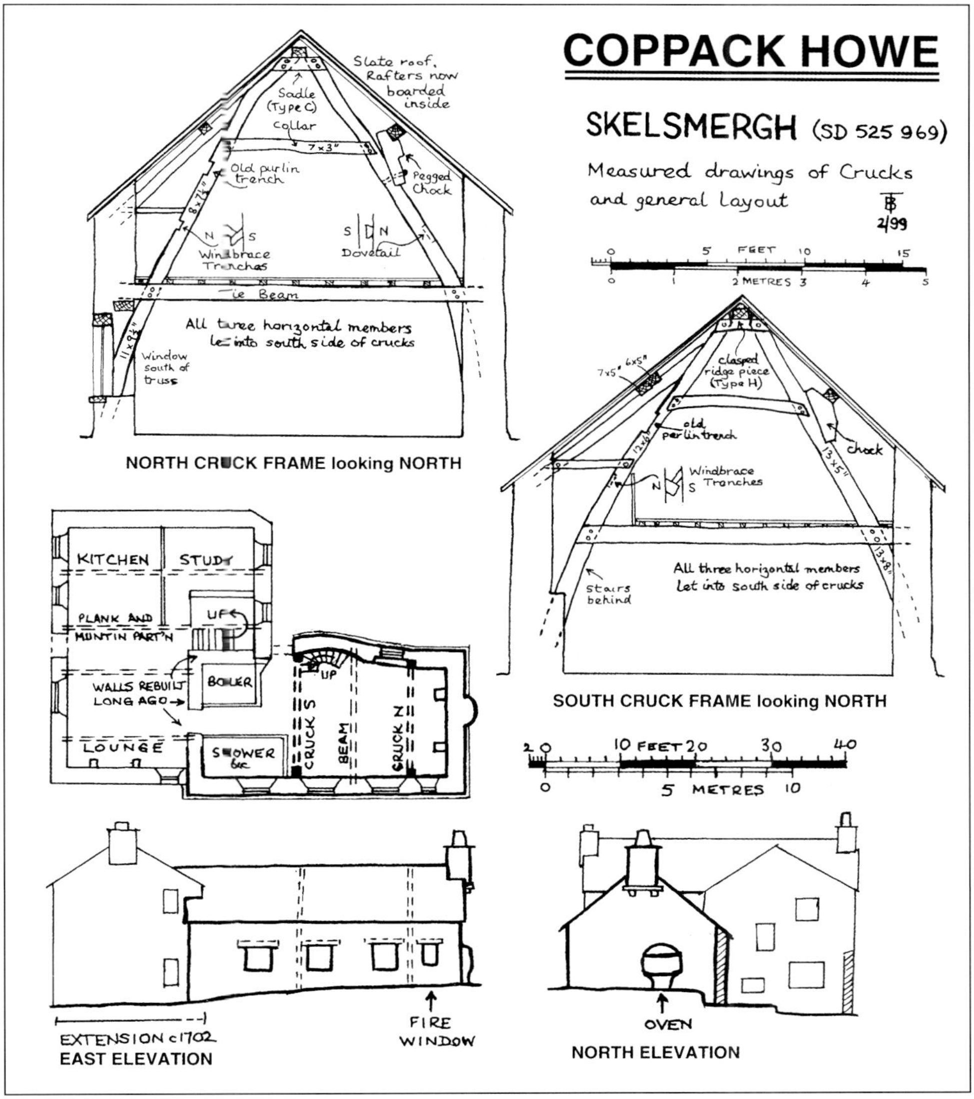

Fig. 5.7. Plans and elevations, Coppack (Coppice) Howe, Skelsmergh, 2000 by Blake Tyson, *CW2*, 100 (2000), 193

and the cost and number of days devoted to specific tasks. As in Skelsmergh Tyson combined his documentary research with survey work but occasionally also reproduced some original plans for agricultural buildings, such as at Lane Barn, Troutbeck, where a plan dated 28 December 1730 clearly illustrated the intended uses of the internal spaces within the structure. This plan annotated the threshing floor at one end, with barn doors in one wall with opposing 'Back Door', which would have served as a winnowing door to provide a through draught for the winnowing process. The building had five 'double bouses' (stalls) on either side of a 'greap' (manure passage) leading from a door placed centrally in the gable, with a stable located between two of the stalls and the threshing floor, accessed through its own doorway in the long axis (fig. 5.8).[48]

Although not shown on this plan, there would have been a loft above all of these internal spaces; this combination of uses within one structure was common in traditional farm buildings in Cumbria. An early eighteenth-century plan in the Browne family records of Townend, Troutbeck, also provided detailed information on the contractors, with one document recording:

> The said persons Walers doe hereby promise to Build a New Barn at Lane in Troutbeck according to the demensions within. That is to say 12 yards long within & 6 yards wide within and 4 yards betwixt ye Loft floor and ye Crook Bauke [part of the roof structure] and to slait, pave, Ly the threshing floor and everything of Waler business about the said barn…Benjamin Browne must pay in Consideration thirteen pounds, the said Work to be Covered before ye 15th of June next.[49]

Peter Messenger's analysis of the farmstead at Lowther in the eighteenth century is also a valuable study, combining surveying with rich documentation to show how the buildings were adapted to meet the changing demands of agriculture.[50]

From Traditional to Polite

It is clear that the study of traditional housing and associated farm buildings has been well represented in the Society's activities throughout its history, providing scope for excursions, sponsorship of publications and a platform for individuals to publish their research. However, as Matthew Hyde noted, 'There is not always a heavy line in Cumbria between the polite and the vernacular'.[51] Houses were adapted or rebuilt incorporating both old and new. In 1978 Tyson used letters sent to George Browne of Townend to document the modernisation of one farm house, 'formerly of traditional vernacular style'

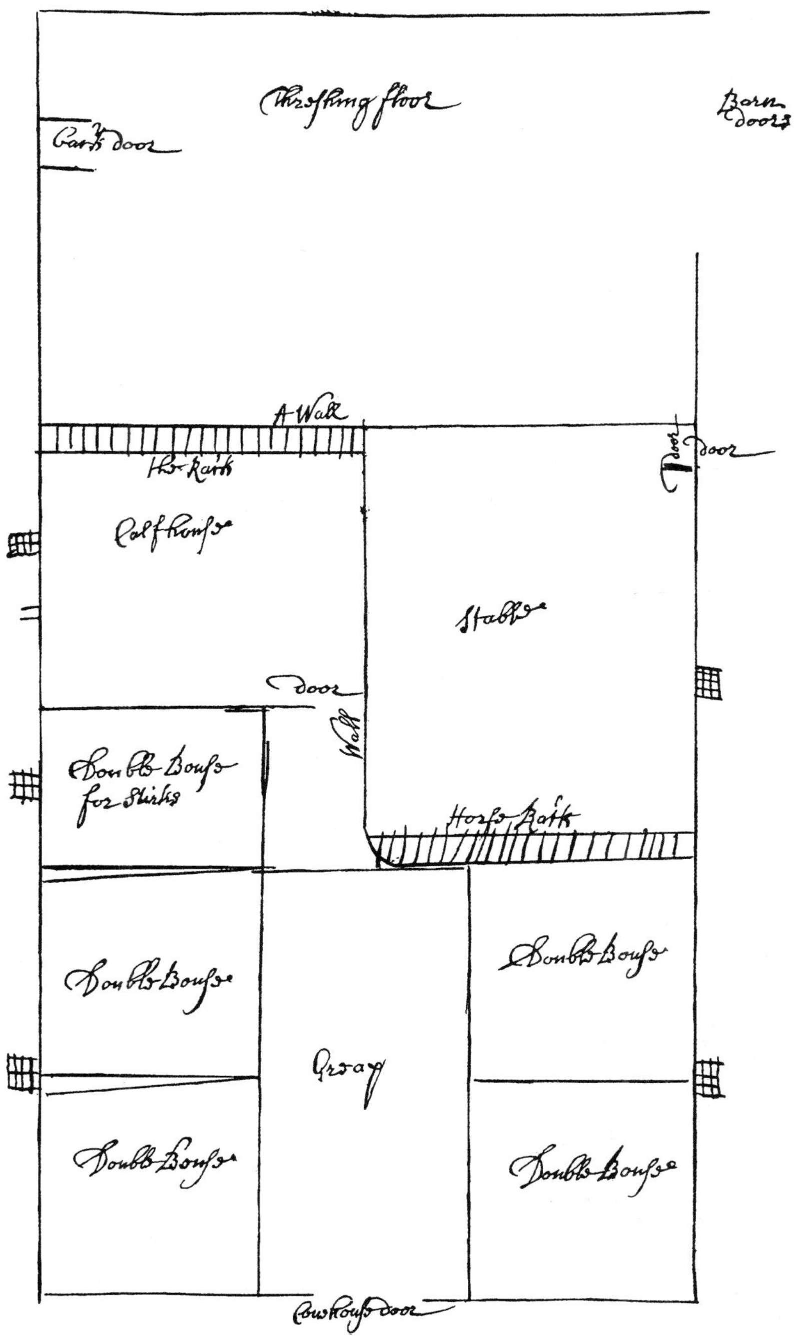

Fig. 5.8. Lane Barn, Troutbeck. Original plan from the wallers' contract dated 28 December 1730, *CW2*, 82 (1982), 153

and to reconstruct the family circumstances which engendered the process. This provided a vivid example of how a Cumbrian migrant to London not only invested in his family's traditional property in the Lake District in the eighteenth century but imported 'polite' ideas into the region, even going so far as to engage the services of Thomas Heaton, who was employed by Thomas English as an architect on Belle Isle.[52] Tyson's study of Cumbrian builders also refused to draw a distinction between 'architects and other builders, or between tutored and vernacular architecture' on the grounds that 'most builders earned their living by undertaking any available construction work irrespective of its social status or intended function'.[53]

The Society's interest in what might broadly be called 'polite' architecture has been less significant. This was certainly a view noted by Timothy Cockerill in his article on the social history of Duddon Hall which appeared in *Transactions* in 2002. This was not a criticism aimed at the Society, but at the study of Cumbrian buildings as a whole which, he argued, had tended to concentrate on 'ancient castles, old manorial halls and historic farmhouses, [while] scant attention has been paid to the lesser country houses of the late eighteenth and early nineteenth centuries', a period when country house building in Cumbria was gathering momentum.[54] Nevertheless there have been several studies of examples of polite architecture, usually site-specific and often relying primarily on family and estate records rather than fieldwork. M.H. Port's articles, complete with contemporary illustrations, on the various stages of development at Lowther Hall and Castle near Penrith, where the Lowthers entertained in 'more than baronial splendour' were published in the early 1980s.[55] Tyson's work on the Red House and the White House, both in Appleby, and Jeremy Godwin's studies of Rickerby and Rickerby House near Carlisle,[56] dealt both with the houses and their commissioning.[57] In 1993 Janet Martin vividly described the building of Wasdale Hall by Stansfeld Rawson, a wealthy Yorkshire banker, in the early nineteenth century, much of it apparently to his own design.[58] Ice-houses, features of many country house estates from the mid-eighteenth century and often architect-designed, have also been explored in a series of innovative articles by Rob David.[59]

The work of named architects has received little attention, although not just from the Society.[60] Currently this relative neglect is being partly corrected with a flurry of interest in later villa architecture, particularly in the Arts and Crafts style, but this has not been reflected in the Society's publications. An exception is Jamie Lund, who has discussed the origins and construction of Wray Castle, an incongruous Gothic Revival castle with two mock ruins in the grounds erected for James Dawson in the early nineteenth century. He cited Beatrix Potter's diaries as evidence for the source of the stone which was brought across the lake and dragged up the hill by a kind of tramway. This article was based on a more extensive unpublished National Trust survey of the estate during 1998 and 1999.[61]

The only publication by the Society, or indeed by any publisher, dedicated to a professional architect based in the county has been Angus Taylor's book, *The Websters of Kendal: a north-western architectural dynasty*, edited by Janet Martin, which looked in detail at the family's prolific output, predominantly evident in south Cumbria.[62] The Websters, father and son, designed in Georgian and occasionally Gothic style with the latter responsible for some significant country houses in the style of the Jacobean Revival, such as Underley Hall near Kirkby Lonsdale (1825-28) and Whelprigg at Barbon (1834). More recently, Janet Martin and Blake Tyson have separately added further details about the family and Tyson has looked at the instigation and development of one particular project.[63]

Conclusion

Nationally the study of what is generally referred to as 'vernacular architecture' developed rapidly from the middle of the twentieth century, epitomised by the formation of the Vernacular Architecture Group in 1952 which brought together an informal study group of architects, archaeologists, historians and museum curators with widely scattered and diverse interests.[64] As Brunskill later noted, since then 'The rapid growth in the numbers and authority of the Group showed that there was a wide general interest in the subject and a largely untapped enthusiasm for the study of surviving buildings of a changing rural economy'.[65] But as we have seen, the Society's own interest in the distinctiveness of the region's traditional buildings, particularly 'halls' and 'fortified buildings' can be traced back to its origins, catering for its members' interests in both archaeology and antiquarianism. In 1955 C.M.L. Bouch had specifically urged the Society to collect 'systematic information on 'typical small farms and domestic houses' (see Chapter 1) and although no separate committee was formed to promote this, as was the case in industrial archaeology the following decade, members of the Society have continued to undertake important work, both independently and for other scholars, and to publish their results. With the recent creation of the Cumbria Vernacular Buildings Group (CVBG) in 2013,[66] which includes many members of the CWAAS, it is to be hoped that further investigations will be undertaken and that the results of some of these could be published by the Society. There is considerable scope for additional work since the only detailed sub-regional studies published so far have been in the Eden valley, Solway Plain and the area around Gosforth. In this context it is noteworthy that, as part of its anniversary year in 2016, the Society is holding a joint conference with CVBG focusing on natural resources available to Cumbrian builders in the past, an area of study relatively neglected but of growing interest in the context of sustainability.

There is scope, too, for exploiting more extensively the survey work undertaken in recent years by professional surveyors, inspectors and historic building consultants as part of the planning process or for organisations like the National Trust. Many of their reports exist only as 'grey literature' but the potential value of these for enhancing our knowledge of traditional buildings can be appreciated by sampling from the large number now freely available on the Archaeology Data Service website.[67] Many of the sites described in these reports have since been developed so that these surveys are often the only documentary and visual evidence of earlier buildings used for their original purposes. Although such professionals have substantially supplemented the survey work, local unpaid experts, many of them Society members, still have a very valuable role as Hyde's extensive credits show.[68]

The Society has undoubtedly been important in opening up and developing this field of study. The challenges in the future will be to build on this record in what is an increasingly diverse and active field and to capitalise on the public interest which clearly exists, not just in the longstanding interest in traditional buildings but hopefully also in the examples of polite architecture which succeeded them.

Notes and References

1 For discussions of industrial structures see Chapter 7.

2 R.W. Brunskill, *Traditional Buildings of Cumbria: the county of the Lakes* (London, 2002), 16. This is a revised edition of his *Vernacular Architecture of the Lake Counties* (London, 1974).

3 Brunskill, *Traditional Buildings*, 16.

4 R.W. Brunskill, 'The development of the large house in the Eden Valley, 1350-1840', *CW2*, 57 (1957), 72-96.

5 M.W. Taylor, 'Yanwath Hall, Westmorland', *CW1*, 1 (1874), 48-59. Taylor made use of the description and plans in J.H. Parker, *Some Account of Domestic Architecture in England from Edward I to Richard II* (Oxford, 1853), 216-19.

6 Taylor, 'Yanwath', 48.

7 'An account of Sockbridge Hall, and of Askham Hall, Westmorland', *CW1*, 2 (1876), 31-45; 'On some of the manorial halls of Westmorland', *CW1*, 2 (1876), 242-64; 'On some manorial halls in Westmorland', *CW1*, 4 (1880), 387-406; 'Middleton Hall', *CW1*, 7 (1884), 96-102; 'Some manorial halls in the Barony of Greystoke', *CW1*, 11 (1891), 73-97; 'Manorial halls in Westmorland', *CW1*, 12 (1893), 15-41; 'Some manorial halls in the Vale of Derwent, ' *CW1*, 12 (1893), 147-66.

8 M.W. Taylor, *The Old Manorial Halls of Westmorland and Cumberland* (CWAAS, Extra Series VIII, 1892), vii-viii.

9 Taylor, *Manorial Halls*, chapter 15, 353.

10 Taylor, *Manorial Halls*, 362.

11 Taylor, *Manorial Halls*, 367.

12 For example, H.S. Cowper, 'Coniston Hall', *CW1*, 9 (1888), 439-47; 'Hawkshead Hall', *CW1*, 11 (1891), 7-49; J.H. Martindale, 'The Old Hall, Cockermouth', *CW2*, 11 (1911), 159-62; 'Hewthwaite Hall', *CW2*, 11 (1911), 163-66; 'Newbiggin Hall, Westmorland', *CW2*, 22 (1922), 158-61; W.G. Collingwood, 'Coniston Hall', *CW2*, 10 (1910), 354-68.

The descriptions of Coniston Hall formed the basis of the entry on Church Coniston in W. Farrer and J. Brownbill (eds.), *A History of the County of Lancaster, vol. 8* (London, 1914), 366-67.

13 D.R. Perriam, 'Recent trends in the study of fortified buildings in Cumbria' in P. Clark and J. Ivy (eds.), *Making Sense of Buildings* (Council for British Archaeology Regional Group Three, 1985), 35.

14 J.F. Curwen, 'Catterlen Hall', *CW2*, 7 (1907), 111-19. Brunskill recalled the impression which 'the romantically weathered tower of Catterlen Hall' had on him a child in the preface to *Traditional Buildings*, 11.

15 J.F. Curwen, *Castle and Fortified Towers of Cumberland, Westmorland and Lancashire North of the Sands, together with a Brief Historical Account of Border Warfare* (CWAAS, Extra Series XIII, 2013).

16 RCHME, *An Inventory of the Historical Monuments in Westmorland* (London, 1936).

17 W.D. Simpson, 'Yanwath Hall', *CW2*, 44 (1944), 55-67,

18 'Proceedings', *CW2*, 47 (1947), 229; 'Proceedings', *CW2*, 51 (1951), 205.

19 R.W. Brunskill, 'Three medieval manor-houses of North Westmorland', *CW2*, 56 (1956), 73-86, quotation 73.

20 Brunskill, 'The large house in the Eden Valley', *passim*; 'Traditional domestic architecture in the Eden Valley', unpublished MA thesis, Manchester University, 1952.

21 D.R. Perriam and J. Robinson, *The Medieval Fortified Buildings of Cumbria: an illustrated gazetteer and research guide* (CWAAS, Extra Series XXIX, 1998); M. Hyde and N. Pevsner, *The Buildings of England: Cumbria* (New Haven and London, 2010), 82.

22 Robinson and Perriam adopted the policy that even if there was only anecdotal evidence for a fortified site in the county, it would be included 'just in case' (pers. comm. Denis Perriam).

23 See also H.G. Ramm, R.W. McDowall and E. Mercer, *Shielings and Bastles* (RCHME, 1970).

24 C. Bancroft, 'Scarrow Hill in the seventeenth century: a reconsideration of vernacular architecture *c.*1600 near Naworth, Cumbria', *CW3*, 10 (2010), 137-46. It is possible to speculate that the late examples in the Alston area may have related more to topography than defence, but more research would be needed to demonstrate this.

25 R.W. Brunskill, 'The development of the small house in the Eden Valley from 1650 to 1840', *CW2*, 53 (1953), 160-89. See chapter 6 for further discussion of the background and significance of this period.

26 Brunskill, 'Small house', 189.

27 M.C. Fair, 'The dating of houses: a caution', *CW2*, 55 (1955), 330. This letter was published posthumously. On their extent and interpretation see E. Garnett, *The Dated Buildings of South Lonsdale* (Lancaster, 2nd ed. 2007).

28 Brunskill, *Vernacular Architecture of the Lake Counties.*

29 See also his *Illustrated Handbook of Vernacular Architecture* (London, 1971, 4th ed. 2000).

30 S. Denyer, *Traditional Buildings and Life in the Lake District* (London, 1991), 9.

31 Brunskill, *Traditional Buildings of Cumbria.*

32 W.M. Williams, 'The farmhouses of south-west Cumberland: a preliminary survey', *CW2*, 54 (1954), 248-64; *The Sociology of an English Village: Gosforth* (London, 1956).

33 Williams, 'farmhouses', 260.

34 Williams, 'farmhouses', 252.

35 Williams, 'farmhouses', 261-62.

36 W. Stukeley, *Itinerarium Curiosum; or, an account of the antiquities, and remarkable curiosities in nature or art, observed in travels through Great Britain, Vol. 2* (1776), 58.

37 W. Hutchinson, *The History of the County of Cumberland …, Vol. 2* (Carlisle, 1794), 515, citing Housman's notes.

38 K.S. Hodgson, C.M.L. Bouch and C.G. Bulman, 'Lamonby Farm: a clay house at Burgh-by-Sands', *CW2*, 53 (1953), 149-59.

39 R.W. Brunskill, 'The clay houses of Cumberland', *Transactions of the Ancient Monuments Society*, n.s. 10 (1962), 57-80; 'Traditional domestic architecture of the Solway Plain', unpublished PhD thesis, Manchester University, 1963.

40 J.R. Harrison, 'Some clay dabbins in Cumberland: their construction and form Part I', *Transactions of the Ancient Monuments Society*, 33 (1989); 'Part 2', 35 (1991).

41 For example, N. Jennings, 'The buildings of Moorhouse, Burgh by Sands', *CW2*, 93 (1993), 237-68; 'Two remarkable Cumbrian clay dabbins', *CW2*, 97 (1997), 257-59.

42 N. Jennings, *Clay Dabbins: vernacular buildings of the Solway Plain* (CWAAS, Extra Series XXX, 2003), 56.

43 For additional dating evidence see N. Jennings and P. Messenger, 'Tree-ring dating of buildings on the Solway Plain', *CW3*, 11 (2011), 247.

44 Jennings, *Clay Dabbins*, 186.

45 B. Tyson, 'Twenty cruck buildings at Skelsmergh, Kendal, *c.*1600', *CW2*, 100 (2000), 181-206.

46 For example, B. Tyson, 'Building work at Sockbridge Hall, its farmyard and neighbourhood, 1660-1710', *CW2*, 83 (1983), 107-24; 'Newlaithes Hall, Carlisle: the evolution and extinction of a Cumbrian courtyard farm', *CW2*, 90 (1990), 235-52.

47 B. Tyson, 'Rydal Hall farmyard: the development of a Westmorland farmstead before 1700', *CW2*, 80 (1980), 113-30, quotation 116. See also his description of a slightly earlier barn, 'Low Park Barn, Rydal: the reconstruction of a farm building in Westmorland in the seventeenth century', *CW2*, 79 (1979), 85-98.

48 B. Tyson, 'Some traditional buildings in the Troutbeck Valley: a documentary study', *CW2*, 82 (1982), 151-76, quotation 153. Tyson also produced detailed survey drawings of the current building.

49 Tyson, 'Troutbeck Valley', 154.

50 P. Messenger, 'Lowther farmstead plans: a preliminary survey', *CW2*, 75 (1975), 327-51.

51 Hyde, *Cumbria*, 38.

52 B. Tyson, 'The Cragg, Troutbeck and the Otley family: a building project and its social setting in 18th-century Westmorland', *CW2*, 78 (1978), 105-20.

53 B. Tyson, 'Some Cumbrian builders, 1670-1780', *CW2*, 96 (1996), 161-86, quotation 161.

54 T. Cockerill, 'Duddon Hall and its owners 1784-1860', *CW3*, 2 (2002), 253.

55 M.H. Port, 'Lowther Hall and Castle', *CW2*, 81 (1981), 122-36; 'Lowther Hall and Castle illustrated', *CW2*, 84 (1984), 191-204.

56 J. Godwin, 'Rickerby: an estate and its owners – Part 1', *CW2*, 92 (1992), 229-50; J. Godwin, 'Rickerby: an estate and its owners. Part II – George Head and after', *CW2*, 97 (1997), 217-30. See the same author's 'Tempest Tower, Little Orton, and its builder James Sibson', *CW2*, 87 (1987), 279-82. These all focus on the owners rather the house and its construction.

57 B. Tyson, 'Two Appleby houses in the 18th century: a documentary study', *CW2*, 85 (1985), 193-218.

58 J.D. Martin, 'Wasdale Hall', *CW2*, 93 (1993), 269-82.

59 R.G. David, 'The ice-houses of Cumbria', *CW2*, 81 (1981), 137-55; 'An ice-house experiment', *CW2*, 82 (1982), 191-93; 'A date for the Levens Hall ice-house', *CW3*, 13 (2013), 261-64.

60 Hyde, *Cumbria*, 84 comments specifically on the lack of material on twentieth-century Cumbria in particular, which he thought 'symptomatic of conservative, conservationist Cumbria'.

61 J. Lund, 'A history of the Wray Castle Estate, Claife', *CW3*, 2 (2002), 231-52.

62 A. Taylor (J.D. Martin ed.), *The Websters of Kendal: a north-western architectural dynasty* (CWAAS, Record Series XVII, 2004). The book was specifically acknowledged by Hyde, *Cumbria*, 55, 82.

63 B. Tyson, 'Francis Webster and the Kirkland tan-yards at Kendal, with a contribution towards his ancestry', *CW3*, 8 (2008), 85-104; 'One branch of the Webster family', *CW2*, 8, (2008), 256-58; J.D. Martin, 'Some new light on the Websters of Kendal', *CW3*, 7 (2007), 113-20.

64 http://www.vag.org.uk/ accessed 31 Dec. 2015.

65 Brunskill, *Vernacular Architecture: an illustrated handbook* (4th edition), 15.

66 http://www.cvbg.co.uk/ accessed 17 Jan. 2016.

67 http://archaeologydataservice.ac.uk/archives/view/greylit/ accessed 15 Jan. 2016. For example, North Pennines Archaeology Ltd, 'Report on Chapel House Farm, Casterton', 2004.

68 Hyde, *Cumbria*, xviii.

Chapter 6
Landscapes of Farming: Agrarian History

Ian Whyte and Michael Winstanley

Cumbria's agriculture had been surveyed in the late eighteenth century, and the writings of Wordsworth and others subsequently created an interest in the lifestyle, values and identities of the Lakeland yeoman or 'statesman',[1] but research concerned with agricultural or rural history *per se* only really emerged from the late nineteenth century. As in other aspects of Cumbrian history, early pioneers operated independently of the emerging university discipline of history and lacked easy access to caches of sources, unless they had the luxury of being able to explore those becoming available in the Public Record Office in London. Consequently, their approach often resembled a form of 'documentary archaeology', unearthing and discussing sources held in private hands, some of which they transcribed in full and which are still of value today. But a small number of gifted local scholars became aware of the growing literature on agrarian history and undertook some in-depth studies. These not only opened up themes which have persisted until the present day, but also enabled researchers both to appreciate the potential distinctiveness of the Cumbrian experience within the national context and to contribute to debates about that national experience.

Innovative though some of these early contributions were, interest in Cumbrian agrarian history has been primarily a post-Second World War phenomenon. This has been fuelled by a variety of factors. Firstly, there was the increasing significance of social and economic history and historical geography, followed by a burgeoning interest in landscape history in the generations following the publication of W.G. Hoskins, *The Making of the English Landscape*.[2] In 1953 the British Agricultural History Society and its journal *Agricultural History Review* were founded. Unusually amongst academic societies, it attracted, and continues to attract, non-university practitioners. It has helped to formulate research agendas which have dominated academic publications ever since. New academic journals reflecting specialisms within the subject have since emerged. The Society of Landscape Studies and its journal *Landscape History* were founded in 1979 and *Rural History* in 1990. Secondly, and linked to this, was the expansion of university education, particularly part-time and extra-mural studies, which created a new breed of university- and college-trained contributors. Research into rural aspects of Cumbria was promoted locally by extramural lecturers like William Rollinson and Angus Winchester, both initially working for the University of Liverpool. Winchester later joined Lancaster University in 1990 where he developed the regional studies which John Marshall had earlier pioneered in the History Department. All three were active researchers of various aspects of Cumbria's rural history. For many years the Centre for North-West Regional Studies also ran a diploma course in local history and a postgraduate diploma and MA in Lake District Studies taught by a variety of specialists. Not surprisingly, since the 1960s, contributors engaged in the study of agrarian history and rural geography within the universities, particularly from Lancaster, have featured more prominently in the pages of *Transactions*, although Society members and other researchers continue to publish significant contributions. The post-war years also witnessed the increasing availability of source material as county record offices provided easier access to estate papers, land tax, enclosure awards, tithe surveys, maps and farm records. All of this has expanded the scope for exploring the distinctive aspects of the local rural economy and landscape.

Common land

The important and enduring role of common land in the county, and specifically the roles of the manor and community in managing that resource, have long been of interest to local researchers. In 1883 Frederic Seebohm's pioneering study of the open-field system of early nineteenth-century Hitchin in Hertfordshire inspired others to consider the landscape both as an artefact which required explanation and as a research resource to explore its development.[3] Although initial studies focused on the open arable fields of lowland England, in 1893 Thomas Hesketh Hodgson produced a valuable study of Great Orton, using a terrier to illustrate 'typical features of the common field system' in order to recreate the earlier landscape of Halltown, near Rockcliffe.[4] The most important early contribution to this topic, however, came in 1908 when T.H.B. Graham of Edmond Castle linked his work on 'The common fields of Hayton' to Seebohm's research.[5] He recognised that such fields were difficult to study, not only because physical evidence for most of them had been obliterated by later enclosures but because sources for their study were 'especially difficult to access, namely, from muniments of title which rarely see the light of day'. Using property deeds and his 'estate plan' he successfully identified the location and subsequent fate of common fields in Hayton. He apologised for what he described as a 'slight and incomplete sketch', but his findings nevertheless continue to be acknowledged by recent scholars of open fields (fig. 6.1).[6] He followed this up with a discussion of the uses to which such fields were put and attempted to identify open or town fields elsewhere in Cumberland.[7] A number of short local studies appeared in 1929,[8] and in 1934 a note by Mary C. Fair illustrated the surviving town field of Drigg, 'Drigg Holme', and how it was still being used by three farmers for growing oats and potatoes (fig. 6.2).[9]

There was no further attempt to estimate the extent of open fields across the region until Gordon Elliott took up the challenge in his Liverpool MA thesis, which explored changes in land use and field systems in Cumberland. In two key articles Elliott expanded on Graham's work, challenging the recognised national view, reiterated by the agricultural historians C.S. and C.S.L. Orwin, that open fields had never been common in Cumberland.[10] Deploying court rolls, estate surveys, surveys of church lands, evidence of shared strips into the nineteenth century and field names, he concluded that they could be found in 220 of the 228 townships in the sixteenth century. Overall they covered about one seventh of the total land surface but were less important in the mountains, mosslands and in the border zone where conflicts

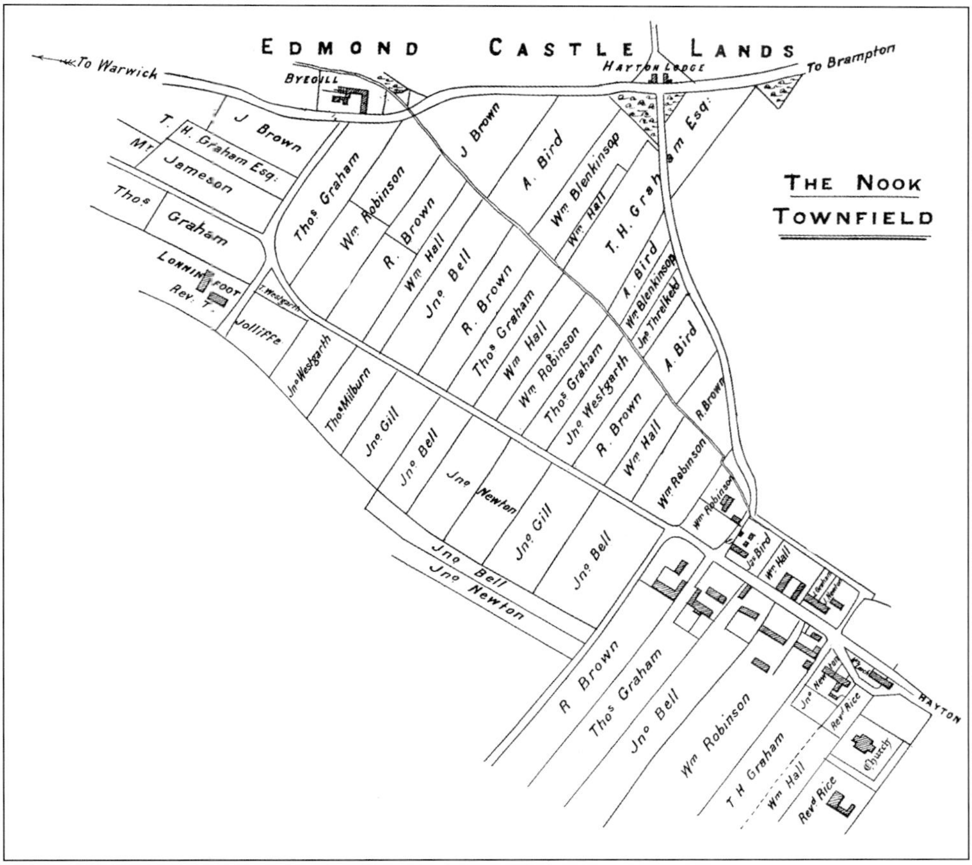

Fig. 6.1. Town fields, Hayton as drawn by T.H.B. Graham, *CW2*, 8 (1908), facing 344

Fig. 6.2. Farmers harvesting potatoes on Drigg townfield, 1934, photographed by Mary C. Fair, from *CW2*, 34 (1934), 41-42

undermined any settled patterns of agriculture. Open fields, however, were not symptomatic of extensive arable specialisation; pastoralism was the mainstay of agriculture and crop rotations were designed to provide maximum grazing over a period of years and in winter months from the stubble. He identified three types: nucleated settlements with open fields, which were the most common; small hamlets and open fields; and the Cistercians' unique open fields at Holm Cultram. He also recognised the importance of sub-regional variations across the county:

> In this respect the county must be viewed not as a uniform whole but as a complex of varying pattern closely related to the physical conditions within the county and reflecting contrasting development histories. The only unifying feature was the persistence of the open fields throughout the 16th century, which is in marked contrast to other counties in Highland Britain, for example, Cornwall and Lancashire, which is a problem which deserves more thorough investigation.[11]

Graham's and Elliott's view that open fields were once common in the Cumbrian lowlands but that they had been relatively small by the standards of Midland England has now been widely accepted.[12] Their demise by means of individual small-scale private enclosure agreements, however, remained largely unrecorded and unnoticed.[13] By the time of Parliamentary enclosure only a few stubborn remnants remained. Elliott's study of the enclosure in Aspatria identified two distinct phases which were probably evident elsewhere. In *c.*1743 the tenants of Aspatria had petitioned the lord of the manor to enclose their open fields and the petition and permission had been granted. The common wastes, however, were not enclosed until 1825 because of the poor quality of the land.[14] The meticulous fieldwork of Roberts has shown how careful observation can reveal much about the landscape history of these more improved areas. He has highlighted the frequency of villages with planned layouts, based on greens and rows, in many parts of Cumbria, such as the Eden valley. Deploying a range of sources from place-names and excavation to the detailed study of landscape remains and earthworks, he has demonstrated the complexity of village morphology and the probable medieval origin of many settlements (fig. 6.3). As he concluded, 'within the palimpsest of the landscape is a record of the cultural achievements by many generations of Cumbrian farmers'.[15]

Despite an interest in lowland open fields, it has been the upland commons and the pastoral economy of the region which have received most attention and, again, raised issues which have received little or no attention in national mainstream literature. Management of the uplands featured in *Transactions* as early as 1876 in Miss Powley's pioneering articles, 'Past and present among the Northern Fells'. She drew attention to the importance of 'Shepherds' Guides' designed for the 'better distinction and separation' of sheep on the fells, 'and for the prevention of disputes' among the 400 men of diverse social backgrounds who enjoyed 'common of pasture' on the eastern fells (fig. 6.4).[16] Central to the management of the fells and commons was the role of the manor. Genealogical studies of the manor had been an integral part of the antiquarian tradition for centuries and were to remain so into the twentieth century. As early as the 1880s, however, it is clear that contributors to *Transactions* recognised the value of manor court records and 'paines' (orders) for extending our understanding of aspects of farming and common land use: grazing rights; encroachment; hedging; rights of way; water supply; estover (wood and timber); turbary (peat digging); the burning of ling and bracken cutting (fig. 6.5).[17]

Despite the variety of cases dealt with by manor courts, Dilley's case study of the Leconfield estate demonstrates that grazing issues became particularly pronounced from the late seventeenth century.[18] More recently, the systems devised in the last two centuries to manage commons after the demise of manorial controls have also been explored with major research projects undertaken on the changing use and management of common land that have contextualised the agrarian history of Cumbria in a wider British and

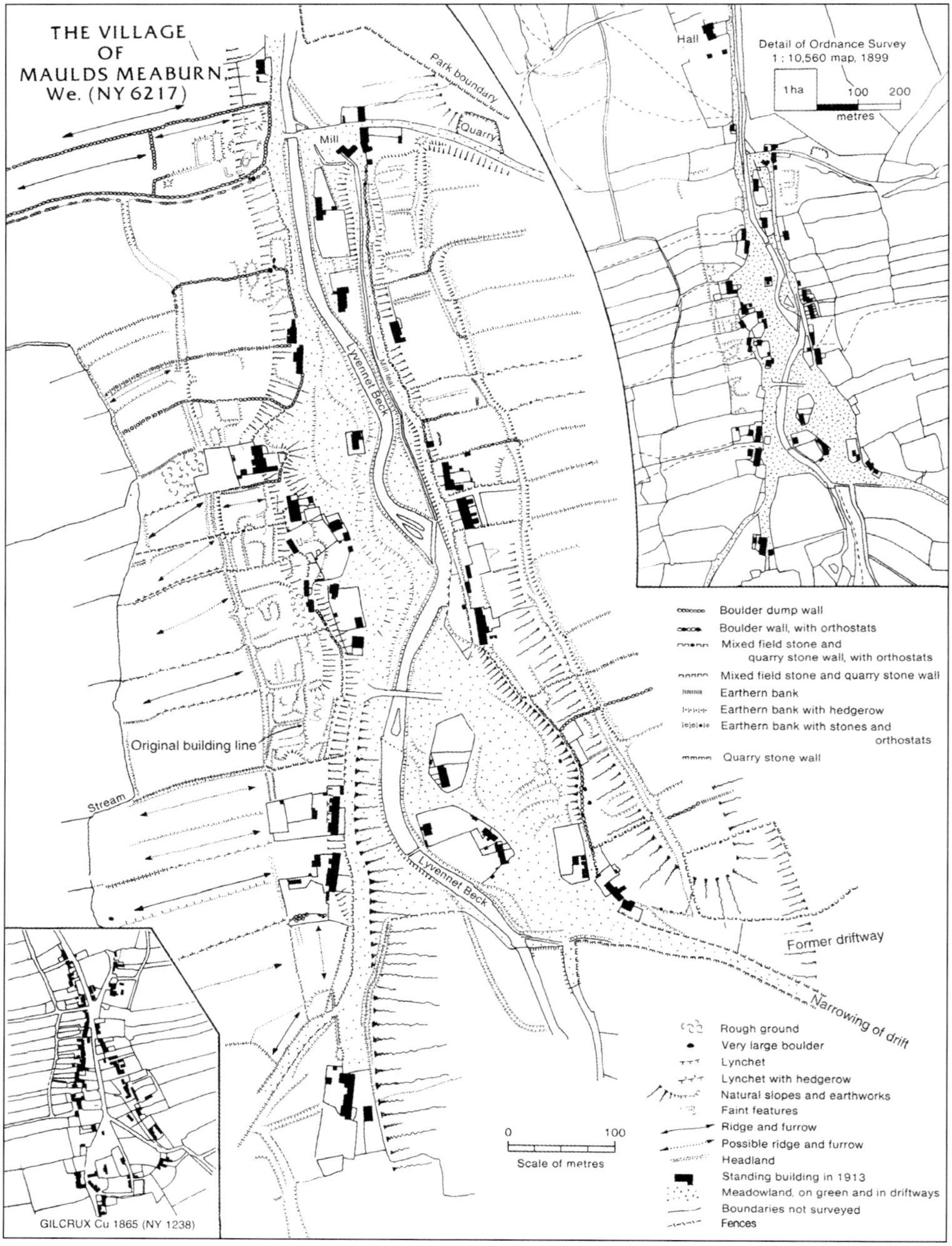

Fig. 6.3. Maulds Meaburn landscape survey, as drawn by B.K. Roberts, *CW2*, 96 (1996), 46-47

European context.[19] This expansion of interest has been spurred on by the process of government registration of commons in 1965, emerging debates about the future of the commons, and the creation of new commoners' associations.

PARISH OF KIRKLAND,
CUMBERLAND.

No. 1.—THOMAS HUTCHINSON, *Kirkland.*—Horn burn, I H on the near horn; face burn, V; near ear forked; tar mark, V on the near, and I H on the far side.

2.—RICHARD ATKINSON, *Kirkland.*—Horn burn, T A and a figure on the near horn; tar mark, T A on the near side, and a stroke across the far buttock.

3.—JOSEPH SALKELD, Esq., *Ranbeck.*—Horn burn, a figure; near ear cut off; tar mark, a pop on the near shoulder, and a swipe from the near hook to the cameral. Field sheep, tar mark S on the near side.

Fig. 6.4. Sheep markings reproduced from an original Shepherd's Guide, *CW1*, 2 (1876), 174

Detailed studies of the uplands have been developed by researchers with local knowledge of the pastoral side of farming and of the importance of boundaries for livestock rearing.[20] The work of Angus Winchester on medieval demesne livestock farming and vaccaries, particularly his wide-ranging *Harvest of the Hills*, typifies such approaches.[21] Winchester's research has successfully fused the sometimes thin documentary record with an historical geographer's eye for landscape to create a nuanced analysis of the ways in which landscape moulded, and was moulded by, farming activities. The mysteries surrounding the remains of early small enclosures and buildings, circular or rectilinear, in remote upland valleys also continue to exert a fascination.[22] The physical remains of shieling sites and deserted farmsteads have developed a literature of their own.[23] The role of turbary has also been traced through Winchester's study of peat storage huts which utilised landscape, oral and documentary evidence for such structures in the Eskdale valley and concluded that low, thatched structures which had predominated in the sixteenth century, were gradually replaced by more substantial, slated 'bank-barn' huts by 1860 (fig. 6.6).[24] Kevin Baverstock and Suzanne Tiplady have highlighted the significant role of gated tracks leading to common land, again combining documentary and landscape evidence.[25]

Fig. 6.5. The bracken harvest in Eskdale in the 1930s. Bracken was a valuable crop for potash and animal bedding, with rules against its cropping on the commons enforced through manor courts, *(photograph: Mary Fair. Image Cumbria County Council, Carlisle Library)*

FARMING

Although surveys of agriculture, like those in the late eighteenth century, have provided valuable snapshots of farming, changes over time in farm output and methods are notoriously difficult to research. Farmers rarely leave any records while official statistical data on crops and livestock have only been collected consistently since 1870 and the results only published on a county basis. Nevertheless, contributions to *Transactions* have provided significant insights into both the domestic economy of the farming household and the nature of farming, particularly in the early modern period.

Francis Grainger used a variety of contemporary sources to trace the nature of the farming year, cropping, livestock and domestic economy in the early modern period,[26] while the polymath Mary Louisa Armitt produced a pioneering and powerful case study as early as 1908 of 'Fullers and freeholders of the parish of Grasmere'. This was a 69-page analysis constructed from an impressive range of local and national sources, all fully referenced, including manuscripts in the Public Record Office, Rydal Hall MSS, ministers' accounts, George Browne's papers, Farrer's Lancashire inquests and Whitaker's history. Armitt propounded the thesis that the late sixteenth century witnessed a major decline in the wool trade.[27] Although some of her general conclusions have been challenged, her article is still consulted today by rural historians of early modern England.[28]

Fig. 6.6. Peat storage huts in Eskdale in the early 1980s (*photograph by courtesy of Angus Winchester*)

Over most of the region arable crops seem to have been relatively unimportant compared to livestock. John Marshall's important analysis of inventories – lists of deceased individuals' assets and debts – has contributed most to our understanding of the nature of change, particularly in Lakeland and Furness, in the late seventeenth century.[29] He portrayed precarious subsistence farming with limited income from the sale of wool or yarn, except possibly around Kendal, disposal of grain surplus and 'markedly larger sums (if he had the initial capital) from the sale or wintering of cattle'. From then on, however, cattle were responsible for increasing prosperity, fuelled by the droving trade and the practice of fattening for urban markets (fig. 6.7). In a later extended study Marshall noted a significant rise in the value of savings at death by the early eighteenth century and calculated an increase in the value of cattle and sheep of between 90 and 100 per cent between 1661-90 and 1721-50.[30] Henry Swainson Cowper's reproduction of a 'A Grasmere farmer's sale schedule in 1710', which he copied verbatim from a document in the hands of local farmer, offers a fascinating insights into the value of a wide range of household goods, utensils and clothes, crops, hay etc. but particularly into the relative importance of cattle and sheep in this period. At nearly £39 the value of his 18 heifers, steers and cows far outstripped the value of other farm produce and was nearly three times the £13 which his 75 lambs, twinters (two year olds) and wethers (castrated rams) raised.[31]

Fig. 6.7. Cattle at Coniston. Cattle were not only important in the farming economy but frequently portrayed as an integral part of Lake District pastoral landscape from the late eighteenth century. Today the farm animals most likely to be depicted are Herdwick sheep. *(Image Cumbria County Council, Carlisle Library)*

This increasing prosperity promoted the rebuilding of farmhouses and the provision of extra shelter for overwintering from the late seventeenth century described by Brunskill and others (see Chapter 5). Although W.G. Hoskins in the 1950s had dated the 'Great Rebuilding' as nearly a century earlier based on researches further south in the country, Machin later showed that the timing, and probably the causes, of Cumbria's developments mirrored those in other parts of the country, particularly the pastoral economies of the North.[32] Peter Roebuck's recent research into the Parkers of Old Town near Penrith has demonstrated how one family took advantage of their location on one of the major cattle-droving routes and near the site of a major cattle fair, to expand grazing for cattle and facilities for the drovers. In the 1720s they substantially reconstructed their modest farmhouse and later built up an industrial empire around Manchester and Stockport before returning to the family's Cumbrian roots and purchasing further estates.[33] A similar expansion took place on the Musgrave estate and is evident in the Flemings' activities at Rydal in the late seventeenth century, including their erection of new farmstead buildings.[34] Appleby fair, associated today exclusively with horses, also developed initially in response to the expanding cattle trade.[35] Even so, as Marshall warned, not all farmers benefited from this, and M.A. Parsons' case study of developments in Troutbeck also concluded that it created 'growing social divergence within the community between those who prospered – even on a modest scale – and those who did not'.[36]

The nature and timing of the 'Agricultural Revolution' have been major themes of agricultural history ever since the late nineteenth century, particularly after the appearance of R.E. Prothero's (later Lord Ernle), *English Farming Past and Present* (1912). Studies of lowland England have also discussed the fluctuating prosperity of farming and its impact on the agricultural worker, on crop rotations and yields, machinery, implements and on the role of prominent agricultural innovators. With a few notable exceptions, however, neither the period nor these aspects have featured significantly in *Transactions*. Nor have estate records been consistently explored for this period, although valuable details about farming in eighteenth-century Cumberland can be reconstructed from the entries in Isaac Fletcher's diary, while the farm accounts and day books of William Fisher of Low Furness and William and John Barrow of Coniston also offer insights into the later period.[37] The only substantial study of Westmorland farming has been Frank Garnett's, *Westmorland Agriculture 1800-1900*, which, although published by Titus Wilson, was not inspired or produced by the Society. Rather it was a by-product of Garnett's contribution to the still-born Victoria County History of Westmorland. As a vet from Windermere he was well positioned to understand the practical operations and development of livestock farming.[38]

Thirty years later a Carlisle school teacher, Newcastle-born Thomas Henry Bainbridge, began to open up many aspects of Cumbria's demographic, maritime, industrial and agricultural history, publishing in national journals such as *Geography, British Geography, Economic Geography,* and *Geographical Journal*. In the early 1940s he placed a number of short articles in *Transactions*, largely based on published sources, and he also explored how tithe schedules could be used to reconstruct land utilisation.[39] More recently, studies by D.J.W. Mawson and David Johnson of the lime-burning industry have demonstrated the importance of this for improving the fertility of acidic soil and facilitating land reclamation from 'the waste', although the industry was held back in some areas by poor access to fuel supplies. Edward and Stella Davis have also produced a definitive survey of the importance of often-overlooked (literally) industry associated with tile manufacture in Cumberland in the mid-nineteenth century which was central to the creation of today's drained landscape; they documented both the rise and fall of the industry and its physical remains (fig. 6.8).[40] Although much more remains to be done, collectively these contributions paint a picture of farming which was very different from that described by Ernle and most subsequent studies of English agriculture, and they challenge the widely-held view that this region was 'backward'.

Fig. 6.8. Newcastle Kiln, Kirkcambeck in 2013 *(photograph by courtesy of Stella Davis)*

Enclosure

A central issue in discussions of agricultural change in lowland England since the late eighteenth century has been the process and consequences of Parliamentary enclosure. Not surprisingly, the experiences which most of these studies have described were very different from those evident in Cumbria.

The extent and distinctive nature of much Parliamentary enclosure in Cumberland were first addressed by W.E. Tate, a science teacher from Nottinghamshire with a passion for local history. From the 1930s he published a series of hand lists of enclosure awards for English counties in local journals.[41] The results of his researches into Cumberland were published in *Transactions* in 1943.[42] His awareness of developments elsewhere in the country allowed him to recognise the distinctive aspects of enclosure in this county:

> The fact that there are but half a dozen acts including open field arable, to some eighty relating to common pasture and waste alone, brings out how largely the enclosure movement locally

> was one of bringing into cultivation – or at any rate into several ownership – waste moorlands, etc. rather than, as in the midlands, for extinguishing village communities.

Tate identified two waves of enclosure – the 1770s and the two decades after 1810 – but he also recognised that much of Cumberland was enclosed after the General Acts of 1836 and 1845: '... there were actually more enclosures (though probably by no means so much acreage enclosed) under the General Acts than under special acts. I think Cumberland is unique among English counties in this respect'. He suggested that the Cumbrian village community was a 'very coherent social entity, and was able to resist attempts at its dissolution until the smaller proprietors were able to make fairly good terms for themselves under the cheap and relatively equitable procedure of the 1836 Act'. This comment anticipated the conclusions of later scholars like Elliott who also recognised the social significance of such enclosures:

> One of the noteworthy features of these changes was that they came from within the township and, unlike so many enclosures in Midland England, were not the enforcement of the will of the lord of the manor or a few wealthy tenants in the village ...

Fig. 6.9. Enclosure landscape near Shap (*photograph by courtesy of Rob David*)

> These changes were neither accompanied by any great social disturbances nor by the creation of a mass of landless labourers, and as such seem to differ greatly from those portrayed in the gloomy picture painted by the Hammonds.[43]

The distinctive nature of much of the Parliamentary enclosure in the region has since received significant attention. Following on from Tate's observations, Christopher Searle has explored in more detail what he labelled 'rural quiescence' or the relative lack of popular opposition to enclosure:

> Apart from a handful of random and unconnected cases of genuine opposition, the great majority of both Parliamentary counter-petitions and non-Parliamentary forms of conflict generated by the division of the commons were either due to a falling out among leading landowners over the spoils of enclosure, or arose from a final settling of accounts between rival groups of customary tenants.[44]

This was not the 'class against class' conflict which had been identified further south, but the consequence of longstanding 'inter-communal conflicts'. He demonstrated how the nature of the customary tenure entitled tenants to have a say in whether Parliamentary enclosure took place in their manor or township, and to receive an allotment in lieu of former common pasture rights. Overall, customary tenants recognised that they benefited, rather than lost, from the expansion of enclosed land. Ian Whyte's detailed study of enclosure in Westmorland, published by the Centre for North-West Regional Studies, has largely confirmed Tate's phasing of distinctive types of enclosure and demonstrated both the processes which influenced them and their lasting impact on the rural landscape (fig. 6.9).[45]

The decline of the yeoman

Customary tenants enjoyed rights equivalent to 'yeomen' or freeholders, at least from the seventeenth century.[46] The importance of this form of tenure in Cumbria has long been recognised. Some insights into its nature and survival followed the implementation of the Law and Property Act in 1922 when Wilson Butler, in his role as a solicitor in Broughton in Furness, was able to gain access to sufficient manorial documents to produce a survey of manorial customs and tenant right in the district. Fines of certain and fixed amounts and descent on intestacy to the eldest daughter or other nearest female relative in default of males were evident in all bar one of the 16 manors he surveyed. Tenant right, he argued, 'never fell into such a slough of servile degradation as the manors of the south of England but retained many of its key elements up to the present day'.[47] As the case of enclosure shows, such tenants were active in preserving their rights and privileges but this was not new. Rawlinson Ford had earlier demonstrated how customary tenants in Yealand successfully preserved their rights and privileges in the seventeenth century, and more recently Joe Scott has explored how a 'very cohesive social community' successfully maintained its rights against disunited and ineffective lords in the Kendal tenant-right dispute of 1619-26.[48] Anne Hillman has explained how well-preserved manorial records in the Barony of Kendal later helped tenants to preserve turbary rights when lands were subject to Parliamentary enclosure.[49]

Despite this emphasis on the resilience of the freeholder and customary tenant one of the longest and liveliest areas of debate in the rural history of the region over the last half-century has been the decline of the 'yeoman'. This has been beset by issues of semantics and sources. Terms like 'customary tenant', 'yeoman', 'gentleman' and 'statesman' have often been used interchangeably but not consistently. John Marshall concluded that 'statesman', for example, was not in widespread local use before the late eighteenth century:[50]

> It is very clear that the word, from being obscured in a mass of provincialisms and colloquialisms, became fashionable in about 1800. ... it was undoubtedly used by the more articulate and educated inhabitants – quite a numerous company – who read what poets and guidebook writers said about them, or who remembered the occasional traditional use of the expression in certain families and localities.

John Walton focused on the difficulties of defining 'yeoman'. The word reflected perceived social status as much as it did actual relationship to the land. He compared entries in directories with those in the census to show how they not only differed but changed over time making the identification of such men from such sources problematic:

> Our understanding of what happens is affected, and sometimes even determined, by the labels we give to the phenomena we are describing; and if we try to chart the decline of a social grouping, our conclusions may be affected by whether we call its members yeomen, peasants or small owner-occupier farmers. ... we are immediately faced with the central question: what is, or was, a yeoman? Unfortunately different historians have different definitions, and this renders comparisons over time and between interpretations difficult, especially as explanations for decline will vary in emphasis according to each historian's perception of the nature of the yeomanry.[51]

The situation was further complicated by the fact that not all customary tenants and yeomen were necessarily occupiers of their land. Individuals who referred to themselves as 'yeomen' might well have been described as 'small proprietors' or 'landlords' elsewhere. Their land could be occupied by a layer of sub-tenants, farming on a commercial lease rather than by the custom of the manor.[52] Therefore, whereas customary tenants were often portrayed by writers like Wordsworth as thrifty and resilient, and even at the end of the eighteenth century as being subsistence-oriented,[53] a number of studies have highlighted the social diversity evident in rural society, ranging from the frugal farming family through to independent, often absentee landowners.[54] Nor were yeomen's activities restricted to farming. The diary of the Quaker yeoman, Isaac Fletcher of Underwood, for example, records his diverse investments in textiles, mining and coastal and overseas trade in the second half of the eighteenth century.[55]

Despite these problems of definition, there has been an enduring fascination with the fluctuating fortunes and long-term potential decline of the 'small owner', whether freeholder or customary tenant. The issue first attracted serious academic study nationally in the 1890s, in part initially inspired by statistics from the census and agricultural returns which supported the view that rural depopulation was largely a consequence of the decline of the smallholder.[56] Interest in the yeomen's fate in Cumbria, however, remained relatively dormant until G.P. Jones' seminal article ignited a debate in the 1960s. He argued that 'whether the fact was connected with enfranchisement or not, it is indisputable that from the 16th century onwards the number of yeomen decreased; and so too did the number of farms'.[57] He saw the decline as being particularly marked in the late eighteenth and early nineteenth centuries, citing evidence from trade directories to support his view. Others have subsequently resorted to arguably more objective sources: land tax, tithe commutation schedules and the Inland Revenue District Valuation Survey of *c.*1909-14. Their conclusions have differed, as have their explanations for changes, but Jones's original thesis has received significant support. John Beckett restated the view that the depression after the Napoleonic Wars witnessed a major collapse in numbers of yeomen, a view supported more recently by David Uttley who suggested that there was a particularly active land market at this time and that a third of the yeoman class, whom he defined as owner-occupiers, disappeared. He also argued that the decline continued throughout the century at a slower rate, although 'it is impossible to say whether this was a gradual or stepwise declension, given the sources available, and the time elapsed'.[58] Ian Whyte's study of Watermillock, however, found no indication of major changes in numbers or turnover of customary tenants suggestive of any agricultural crisis. Instead he argued that any changes were gradual and unspectacular rather than rapid and dramatic.[59] Margaret Shepherd's study of the Eden Valley reached a similar conclusion for the post-1840 period, suggesting that although numbers of landowners fell, the percentage of owner-occupiers remained relatively stable through to the twentieth century.[60]

Rather than attempt to measure these aggregate changes, others have supported Marshall's and Parsons' warnings about social divergence apparent in rural society and have continued to stress the complexities and fluidity of the rural social structure, illustrating how individual yeomen and customary tenants declined while others continued to prosper.[61] Arthur Duxbury's case study of Ravenstonedale concluded:

> Neither were yeomen a static group. The picture of a yeoman cultivating his ancestral plot and handing it down to his eldest son more or less *ad infinitum* is not true. There was an active market in land. Some yeomen prospered and increased their holdings. Some did not, sold out and disappeared. New people from outside the parish bought holdings, some of whom settled in the parish whilst some moved on again after a short time. The picture is one of continual change.[62]

Those like the Parkers who prospered have proved easier to identify and study than those who failed.[63] The debate about the fate of the 'yeoman' will no doubt continue (fig. 6.10).[64]

Fig. 6.10. A 19th-century Lakeland farmer. George Black, tenant farmer of Monk Coniston, photographed aged 92 in 1897. George had farmed at Keen Ground, Attwood and Knipe Fold, all near Hawkshead, during his working life, largely relying on family labour (sons, nephew and latterly grandson). He was always a tenant. *(Image Cumbria County Council, Carlisle Library)*

Other agendas

Studies of field systems, settlement patterns, customary tenants, yeomen and pasture farming may have dominated the Society's contributions to the agrarian history of the region, but other aspects have also received attention.

The significance of place-names in understanding not just local dialect but the development of landscape was highlighted as early as 1880 by Miss Powley of Langwathby (see Chapters 1 and 4) in a series of articles pleading for the 'Old Names'. These were, she argued, 'incontestible [*sic*] as evidence of ethnological, topographical, and historical changes'. She challenged the Society, 'with all the power and scope of a Topographical Society', to record and preserve the old local names of the 'lonely and desert places and of the common fields'.[65] In 1899 Canon Thornley, the vicar of Kirkoswald, also drew attention to the value of field names in tithe surveys, valuation books and estate records as ways of interpreting the past landscape. 'If all the names of places etc. now scattered over the sheets of Ordnance Survey were gathered up and printed in one complete list, county by county, what a roll it would be ... what a history of the colonisation of these islands!' He feared that such names were fast disappearing in his locality as a result of the 'distressingly large turnover of tenants' who were 'not too careful to retain the old names'.[66] In 1915, the Society, jointly with the University of Manchester, published W.J. Sedgefield's *The Place-names of Cumberland and Westmorland*, but subsequent research in terms of recording and publishing them has been largely taken forward by dialect historians and the English Place-Name Society.[67] However, in a pair of linked articles in the 1920s Frank Warriner explored the etymology of place-names in south Cumberland and Revd W.S. Sykes meticulously sought to locate many of the places to which they referred.[68] David Uttley has demonstrated how valuable they can be for landscape studies. He charted a loss of place-names shown on a survey of 1568 for Glassonby but, even so, was able to identify over half of them in 2009, which enabled him to reconstruct the Tudor landscape.[69]

The role of the lakes themselves in sustaining primary industries, such as fishing on Windermere, has been usefully outlined over the long period by Charlotte Kipling but there is scope for exploring further the role of water in the agricultural and industrial economy of the region (fig. 6.11).[70] The importance of woodland management for winter grazing, construction, charcoal burning, mining, metal smelting, bobbin making and other woodland industries has also recently begun to be explored.[71] If the society had been named a 'literary and historical' society, there might have been more contributions concerned with the interface between landscape and literature, images and portrayals of the Lake District, landscape aesthetics and tourism but these aspects have occasionally featured in *Transactions*. In 1932 T.E. Casson read a paper to commemorate the centenary of the death of Sir Walter

Scott in which, *inter alia,* he gave detailed references to places in Cumbria mentioned in his works. In 1976 Marijane Osborn used references in Wordsworth's play, *The Borderers,* to argue that it was set in the Penrith-Stainmore area.[72] In a wide-ranging paper in 2011 Penny Bradshaw challenged the popular view of the 'Lake Poets' and the influence of the landscape on their work. She dismissed several of those usually linked with Wordsworth while drawing attention to other poets whose earlier prominence has been largely overlooked in the established literary canon.[73] Derek Denman's study, however, is one of the few published by the Society on the attractions and implications of the Picturesque and Romantic movements on the Lake District landscape. He demonstrated how the changing attitudes towards the value of woodland affected the landscape around Derwentwater, providing a valuable reminder that it was not just lakes and mountains which were seen as crucial in the creation of the 'ideal' Lakeland landscape.[74]

Other aspects of Cumbria's rural past also remain relatively unexplored. The influence of the agrarian economy on transforming the landscape has received increasing attention in Britain from the 1970s and Angus Winchester and Alan Crosby have presented the

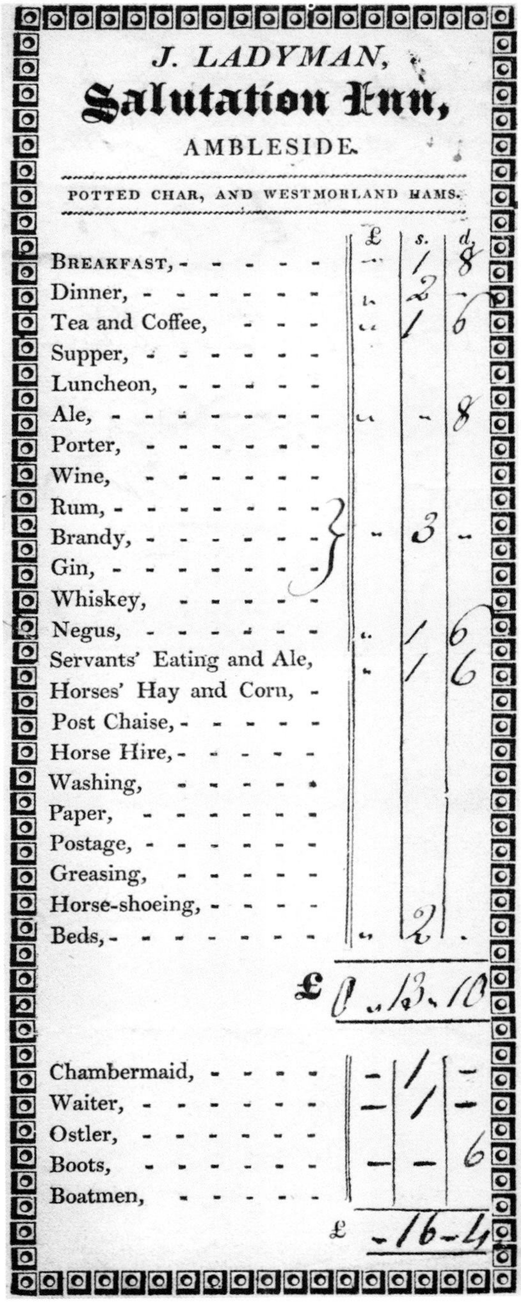
J. LADYMAN,

Salutation Inn,

AMBLESIDE.

POTTED CHAR, AND WESTMORLAND HAMS.

	£	s.	d.
Breakfast,	–	1	8
Dinner,		2	6
Tea and Coffee,		1	6
Supper,			
Luncheon,			
Ale,		–	8
Porter,			
Wine,			
Rum, Brandy, Gin,	–	3	–
Whiskey,			
Negus,		1	6
Servants' Eating and Ale,		1	6
Horses' Hay and Corn,			
Post Chaise,			
Horse Hire,			
Washing,			
Paper,			
Postage,			
Greasing,			
Horse-shoeing,			
Beds,		2	
£	0	13	10
Chambermaid,	–	1	–
Waiter,	–	1	–
Ostler,			
Boots,	–	–	6
Boatmen,			
£	–	16	4

Fig. 6.11. Salutation Inn Ambleside, bill, 1828 highlighting its local specialities: 'Potted Char and Westmorland Hams' (*Image Cumbria County Council, Carlisle Library)*

fruits of much of this research for north-west England, but there is scope for further work on similar lines to Roberts' work in Cumbria.[75] There has also been a lack of research on the expansion of settlement and enclosure in the sixteenth and seventeenth centuries, although the 1:25,000 OS map shows many potentially suitable case-studies. There has been little work on the amalgamation of farms and the abandonment of farmsteads in the later nineteenth and twentieth centuries or the development of agriculture at that time. Although lost medieval villages have attracted some attention,[76] the creation of landscapes of abandonment, as on Tebay Fell, has still to find its chronicler. The roles of women, children, farm servants and migrant labour in the farming economy have also received little attention from the Society, as has the interplay between farming and industrial work, evident in Rob David's study of the slate industry and more widely in John Marshall's detailed study of Furness.[77] The Society has, as yet, not published any contributions on the origins, creation and development of the Lake District National Park or on afforestation and the rise of the Forestry Commission.

Whatever research agenda emerges in the future, however, the Society, which has been central in developing our understanding of many aspects of the region's agrarian economy over the last 150 years, will doubtless continue to do so.

Notes and References

1 For example J. Bailey and G. Culley, *General View of the Agriculture of the County of Cumberland* (London, 1794); A. Pringle, *General View of the Agriculture of the County of Westmorland* (Edinburgh, 1794). For an interesting discussion of a man whose work encompassed both agriculture and identity at this time, see D. Denman, 'The published topographical work of John Housman, from 1793 to 1800 with its relevance to Cumbrian identities', *CW3*, 12 (2012), 217-31.

2 W.G. Hoskins, *The Making of the English Landscape* (London, 1955).

3 F. Seebohm, *The English Village Community* (London, 1883). The American historian H.L. Gray published a massive amount of evidence in *English Field Systems* (Cambridge, 1915) including material on Cumberland, which is still of value.

4 T.H. Hodgson, 'The village community in Cumberland, as instanced at Halltown, near Rocliff' *[sic]*, *CW1*, 12 (1893), 133-40.

5 T.H.B. Graham, 'The common fields of Hayton', *CW2*, 8 (1908), 340-54.

6 Such as A.R.H. Baker and R.A. Butlin (eds.), *Studies of Field Systems in the British Isles* (Cambridge, 1973) and D. Hall, *Open Fields of England* (Oxford, 2014).

7 T.H.B. Graham, 'The townfields of Cumberland Part I', *CW2*, 10 (1910), 118-34; 'The townfields of Cumberland Part II', *CW2*, 13 (1913), 1-32.

8 Miss G.M. Simpson, 'Townfields of Threlkeld, Mardale, Wet Sleddale and Langdale', *CW2*, 29 (1929), 269-72; R.E. Porter, 'The townfields of Coniston', *CW2*, 29 (1929), 273-77; W. Butler, 'Townfields of Broughton and Subberthwaite-in-Furness', *CW2*, 29 (1929), 293-302.

9 Miss M.C. Fair, 'The town fields of Drigg', *CW2*, 34 (1934), 41-42.

10 C.S. and C.S.L. Orwin, *The Open Fields* (Oxford, 1938 and later editions).

11 G.G. Elliott, 'The system of cultivation and evidence of enclosure in the Cumberland open fields in the 16th century', *CW2*, 59 (1959), 85-104, quotation 104. Elliott joined the society in 1961 and gave his address as c/o St John's School, Episkopi, NELF, BFP.

12 G. Elliott, 'Field systems of north-west England', in Baker and Butlin, *Studies of Field Systems*, 41-92. A later confirmatory study is B. Tyson, 'Murton Great Field near Appleby: a case study of the piecemeal enclosure of a common field in the mid-eighteenth century', *CW2*, 95 (1995), 161-82.

13 R.S. Dilley, 'The case of the Stainton, Newbiggin and Blencow enclosure award', *CW2*, 95 (1995), 187-98.

14 G.G. Elliott, 'The enclosure of Aspatria', *CW2*, 60 (1960), 97-108.

15 B.K. Roberts, *Rural Settlement: an historical perspective* (Norwich, 1982); *The Making of the English Village* (London, 1987); B.K. Roberts and S. Wrathmell, *An Atlas of Rural Settlement in England* (London, 2000); B.K. Roberts, 'Five Westmorland settlements: a comparative study', *CW2*, 93 (1993), 131-44; B.K. Roberts 'A field survey of Maulds Meaburn, Westmorland', *CW2*, 96 (1996), 45-50.

16 Miss Powley, 'Past and present among the Northern Fells no.1', and 'Past and present among the Northern Fells No.2', *CW1*, 2 (1876), 171-86 and 354-74. See also Crosby chapter 4 in this volume on sheep markings.

17 W. Hodgson, 'A century of "Paines," or local government in the time of the Stuarts, as illustrated by extracts from "A Paine Book for the Hamlet of Weathermelock"', *CW1*, 7 (1884), 27-47; E. Conder jun., 'Some notes on the manor of Mansergh and Rigmaden formerly in the parish of Kirkby Lonsdale', *CW1*, 14 (1897), 450-59; Revd J. Whiteside, 'Paines made at Shap', *CW2*, 3 (1903), 150-62. See also N.F. Hudleston, 'Elizabethan Paines at Hutton John', *CW2*, 69 (1969), 115-28. For a useful introduction to the general functions of manor courts see, P. Holdsworth, 'Manorial administration in Westmorland 1589-1693', *CW3*, 5 (2005), 137-64. For a comprehensive illustrated guide to using manor court records see Cumbrian Manorial Records, http://www.lancaster.ac.uk/fass/projects/manorialrecords/ compiled by Angus Winchester and Eleanor Straughton. Accessed 31 Jan. 2016.

18 R.S. Dilley, 'The Cumberland court leet and the use of the common lands', *CW2*, 67 (1967), 125-51; C.E. Searle, 'Customary tenants and the enclosures of the Cumbrian commons', *Northern History*, 29 (1993), 126-53.

19 E.A. Straughton, *Common Grazing on the Northern English uplands 1800-1965: a history of national policy and local practice with special attention to the case of Cumbria* (Lampeter, 2008); Common Land Research, http://commons.ncl.ac.uk/ joint project between Lancaster and Newcastle universities. Accessed 7 Dec. 2015.

20 M.A. Atkin, 'The medieval land use of Kentmere', *CW2*, 91 (1991), 69-78.

21 A.J.L. Winchester, 'Demesne livestock farming in the Lake District: the vaccary at Gatesgarth, Buttermere, in the later thirteenth century', *CW3*, 3 (2003), 109-18; *The Harvest of the Hills* (Edinburgh, 2000).

22 P. Matthiessen *et al*, 'A survey of longhouse structures in the Duddon Valley, Cumbria', *CW3*, 15 (2015), 117-38; J. Quartermaine and R. Leech, *Cairns, Fields and Cultivation: archaeological landscapes of the Lake District uplands* (Lancaster, 2012).

23 N.Hair and R. Newman, 'Excavation of medieval settlement remains at Crosedale, Howgill', *CW2*, 99 (1999), 141-58; A.J.L. Winchester. 'Deserted farmstead sites at Miterdale Head, Eskdale', *CW2*, 79 (1979), 150-55; A.J.L. Winchester, 'Shielings in Upper Eskdale', *CW2*, 84 (1984), 267-68; G.G.S. Richardson, 'King's Stables - an early shieling on Black Lyne Common, Bewcastle', *CW2*, 79 (1979), 19-28.

24 A.J.L. Winchester, 'Peat storage huts in Eskdale', *CW2*, 84 (1984), 103-16. See also discussion in chapter 4 in this volume.

25 K. Baverstock and S. Tiplady, 'Gated trackways between common land and in-bye land within Satterthwaite parish', *CW3*, 9 (2009), 91-110.

26 F. Grainger, 'Agriculture in Cumberland in ancient times', *CW2*, 9 (1909), 120-46.
27 M.L. Armitt, 'Fullers and freeholders of the parish of Grasmere', *CW2*, 8 (1908), 136-205.
28 J.Thirsk, *Rural Economy of England* (London, 1984), 226-27; G. Elliott, 'The decline of the woollen trade in Cumberland, Westmorland and Northumberland in the late 16th century', *CW2*, 61 (1961), 112-19.
29 J.D. Marshall, 'The domestic economy of the Lakeland yeoman, 1660-1689', *CW2*, 73 (1973), 190-219. These are the dates on the contents page but the article's title itself refers to 1660-1749. The text makes clear, however, that the main focus is 1660-89 with only illustrative examples from the later period.
30 J.D. Marshall, 'Agrarian wealth and social structure in pre-industrial Cumbria', *Economic History Review*, 33.4 (1980), 503-21.
31 H.S. Cowper, 'A Grasmere farmer's sale schedule in 1710', *CW1*, 13 (1895), 253-69.
32 W.G. Hoskins, 'The rebuilding of rural England, 1570-1640', *Past & Present*, 4 (1953), 44-59; R. Machin, 'The Great Rebuilding: a reassessment, *Past &* Present, 77 (1977), 33-56.
33 P. Roebuck, 'The Parkers of Old Town and district in Cumberland: yeomen farmers, industrialists and landed proprietors, 1630-1900', *CW3*, 10 (2010), 177-96; P. Roebuck, *Cattle Droving, Cotton and Landownership: a Cumbrian family saga* (CWAAS, Extra Series XLIII, 2014).
34 P. Roebuck, 'Cattle droving through Cumbria after the Union: the stances on the Musgrave estate 1707-12', *CW3*, 12 (2012), 143-58; B. Tyson, 'The cattle trading activities of Sir Daniel Fleming of Rydal Hall, 1656-1700', *CW3*, 2 (2002), 183-200.
35 A. Connell, *Appleby Gypsy Horse Fair: mythology, origins, evolution and evaluation* (CWAAS, Extra Series XLIV, 2015).
36 M.A. Parsons, 'Pasture farming in Troutbeck, Westmorland, 1550-1750', *CW2*, 93 (1993), 115-30, quotation 125.
37 A.J.L. Winchester, *The Diary of Isaac Fletcher of Underwood, Cumberland, 1756-1781* (CWAAS, Extra Series XXVII, 1994), succinctly discussed in the introduction, xv-xx; W. Rollinson, 'The diary and farm accounts of William Fisher, a Low Furness yeoman farmer, 1811-1859', *CW2*, 66 (1966), 382-401; H. Harris, 'Farm diversification in mid-Victorian Cumbria: the daybook of William and John Barrow of Coniston 1847-59', *CW3*, 14 (2014), 231-50.
38 F. Garnett, *Westmorland Agriculture, 1800-1900* (Kendal, 1912).
39 T.H. Bainbridge, 'Eighteenth-century agriculture in Cumbria', *CW2*, 42 (1942), 56-66; 'Land utilisation in Cumbria in the mid-nineteenth century as revealed by a study of the tithe returns', *CW2*, 43 (1943), 87-95; 'Some factors in the development of Cumbrian agriculture, especially during the nineteenth century', *CW2*, 44 (1944), 81-92.
40 D.J.W. Mawson, 'Agricultural lime burning: the Netherby example', *CW2*, 80 (1980), 137-52; D.S. Johnson, 'Lime burning and the uses of lime in the historic county of Westmorland and along the Pennine edge of Cumbria', *CW3*, 13 (2013), 191-214; E. Davis. 'Clay drainage tile and pipe manufacture at Johnby Wythes, Greystoke *c.*1851-1909', *CW3*, 2 (2002), 261-76; E. and S.B. Davis, *Draining the Cumbrian Landscape* (CWAAS, Research Series XI, 2013).
41 These surveys laid the groundwork for his later books on *The English Village Community and the Enclosure Movements* (London, 1967) and *A Domesday of English Enclosure Acts and Awards* (Reading, 1978).
42 W.E. Tate, 'A hand list of Enclosure Acts and Awards', *CW2*, 43 (1943), 175-98. R.S. Dilley has since expanded this list and provided more details of the contents: 'The enclosure awards of Cumberland: a statistical list', *CW2*, 100 (2000), 225-40.
43 Elliott, 'The enclosure of Aspatria', 106.

44 C.E. Searle, 'Cumbria's Parliamentary enclosure movement: a comparative study of rural quiescence', *CW2*, 95 (1995), 247-70. Unfortunately he refers to the protagonists as 'peasants', which many of them clearly were not. See also C.E. Searle, 'Custom, class conflict and agrarian capitalism: the Cumbrian customary economy in the eighteenth century', *Past & Present*, 110 (1986), 106-33.

45 I.D. Whyte, *Transforming Fell and Valley: landscape and parliamentary enclosure in north-west England* (Lancaster, 2003). See also I.D. Whyte, '"Wild, barren and frightful": Parliamentary enclosure in an upland county: Westmorland 1767-1890', *Rural History*, 14 (2003), 21-38; R.S. Dilley, 'The case of the Stainton, Newbiggin and Blencow enclosure award', *CW2*, 95 (1995), 187-98.

46 For a wider discussion of tenant right see R.A. Hoyle, 'An ancient right and laudable custom: the definition of tenant right in north-western England in the sixteenth century', *Past & Present* 116 (1987), 22-55.

47 W. Butler, 'The customs and tenant right tenures of the northern counties, with particulars of those in the district of Furness in the county of Lancaster', *CW2*, 26 (1926), 318-35.

48 J. Rawlinson Ford, 'The customary tenant-right of the manors of Yealand', *CW2*, 9 (1909), 47-60; J. Scott, 'The Kendal tenant right dispute, 1619-26', *CW2*, 98 (1998), 169-82.

49 A. Hillman, 'Peat use in the Barony of Kendal, common of turbary and the Levens anomaly', *CW3*, 13 (2013), 139-50.

50 J.D. Marshall, 'Statesmen in Cumbria: the vicissitudes of an expression', *CW2*, 72 (1972), 248-73.

51 J.K. Walton, 'The strange decline of the Lake District yeoman: some thoughts on sources, methods and definitions', *CW2*, 86 (1986), 221-34, quotation 223-24.

52 I.D. Whyte, 'Owners and occupiers: subtenancy and subtenants in Watermillock, Cumberland, *c.*1760-*c.*1840: a case study', *Northern History*, 50 (2013), 77-92.

53 P. Bicknell, *The Illustrated Wordsworth's Guide to the Lakes* (London, 1984), 93-111; I. Thompson, *The English Lakes; a history* (London, 2010), 47-62.

54 Marshall, 'The domestic economy of the Lakeland yeoman'; Parsons, 'Pasture farming in Troutbeck'.

55 Winchester, *Isaac Fletcher of Underwood,* succinctly discussed in the introduction, xxiv-xxvi.

56 G. Slater, *The English Peasantry and the Enclosure of the Common Fields* (London, 1907); A.H. Johnson, *The Disappearance of the Small Landowner* (Oxford, 1909); E.C.K. Gonner, *Common Land and Inclosure* (London, 1912), and John and Barbara Hammond's polemical work, *The Village Labourer, 1780-1832* (London, 1911).

57 G.P. Jones, 'The decline of the yeomanry in the Lake Counties', *CW2*, 62 (1962), 198-223, quotation 211.

58 D. Uttley, 'The decline of the Cumbrian yeoman: fact or fiction?', *CW3*, 7 (2007), 121-34; See also, J.V. Beckett, 'The decline of the small landowner in eighteenth and nineteenth-century England; some regional considerations', *Agricultural History Review*, 30 (1982), 97-111.

59 I.D. Whyte, 'The customary tenants of Watermillock, *c.*1760-*c.*1840: continuity and change in a Lake District township', *CW3*, 9 (2009), 161-74.

60 M. Shepherd, 'The small owner in Cumbria, *c.*1840-1910: a case study from the Upper Eden Valley', *Northern History*, 35 (1999), 161-84.

61 See also, J. Healey, 'Agrarian social structure in the central Lake District *c.*1574-1830: the fall of the 'mountain republic', *Northern History*, 44 (2007), 73-91.

62 A.H. Duxbury, 'The decline of the Cumbrian yeoman: Ravenstonedale: a case study', *CW2*, 94 (1994), 201-13, quotation 209.

63 T.E.A. Verity, J. V. Harrison and C.R. Hudleston, 'The Browns of Burnfoot: the decline and fall of a yeoman family', *CW2*, 68 (1968), 169-91; I.D. Whyte 'The last English peasants? Lake District statesmen and yeoman farmers in the late eighteenth and early nineteenth centuries: the example of Tom Rumney of Mellfell', *Folk Life*, 46 (2007), 120-30; A.W. Rumney (ed.), *Tom Rumney of Mellfell (1764-1835) by Himself as set out in his Letters and Diary* (Kendal, 1936).

64 The extensive contributions to this debate were assessed in D. Uttley, 'The decline of the Cumbrian "yeoman"', *CW3*, 8 (2008), 127-46.

65 Miss Powley, 'A plea for the old names', *CW1*, 4 (1880), 19-22, 280-84; *CW1*, 6 (1883), 272-79.

66 Revd Canon Thornley, 'The field names of the parish of Kirkoswald', *CW1*, 15 (1899), 48-81. Rawnsley wrote a memorial hymn for Thornley's funeral.

67 W.J. Sedgefield, *The Place-Names of Cumberland and Westmorland* (CWAAS, Extra Series XIV, 1915). Sedgefield was Professor of English Language at the University of Manchester. A.H. Smith, *The Place-Names of Westmorland. 2 vols. (Cambridge, 1967);* A.M. Armstrong, A. Mawer, F.M. Stenton and B. Dickens, *The Place-Names of Cumberland* (Cambridge, 1952); D. Whaley, *A Dictionary of Lake District Place-Names* (English Place-Name Society: Nottingham, 2006).

68 F. Warriner, 'Some south Cumberland place names', *CW2*, 26 (1926), 77-102; Revd W.S. Sykes, 'On the identification of some ancient places in south Cumberland', *CW2*, 26 (1926), 103-49.

69 D. Uttley, 'Field-names in a Cumbrian manor: their longevity in Glassonby, 1568-2009', *CW3*, 12 (2012), 171-82. This was published posthumously and edited by A.J.L. Winchester.

70 C. Kipling, 'The commercial fisheries of Windermere', *CW2*, 72 (1972), 156-204; 'The netting sites of Windermere', *CW2*, 73 (1973), 111-19.

71 C. Kipling, 'Some documentary evidence on woodlands in the vicinity of Windermere', *CW2*, 74 (1974), 65-88; M.A. Parsons, 'The woodland of Troutbeck and its exploitation to 1800', *CW2*, 97 (1997), 79-100.

72 T.E. Casson, 'Sir Walter Scott and the antiquities of Cumberland', *CW2*, 33 (1933), 146-62; M. Osborn, 'Wordsworth's "Borderers" and the landscape of Penrith', *CW2*, 76 (1976), 144-58.

73 P. Bradshaw, 'Romantic poetic identity and the English Lake District', *CW3*, 11 (2011), 65-80.

74 D. Denman, 'Lord William Gordon and the picturesque occupation of Derwentwater in the 1780s', *CW3*, 14 (2014), 207-30. See also B.L. Thompson, 'The Greenwich Hospital Woods at Keswick in the eighteenth century', *CW2*, 75 (1975), 293-99; T. Marsh, 'Rooms with a view: the Low Wood Hotel, Windermere *c.*1700-1914', *CW3*, 14 (2014), 251-57.

75 A.J.L. Winchester with A.G. Crosby, *England's Landscape: the North West* (London, 2006).

76 W. Rollinson, 'The lost villages and hamlets of Low Furness', *CW2*, 63 (1963), 160-69.

77 R. David, 'The slate quarrying industry in Westmorland: Part One: the valleys of Troutbeck, Kentmere and Longsleddale', *CW2*, 87 (1987), 216; J.D. Marshall, *Furness in the Industrial Revolution* (Barrow, 1958).

Chapter 7
Industrial and Urban History and Archaeology

Alan G. Crosby and Michael Winstanley[*]

Reviewing the Society's publications on 'industrial history' over the previous century in 2000, John Marshall noted that the term was 'commonly associated with industrial archaeology and the history of technology'. For him, however, it had much wider implications. It was 'a general term for a portmanteau subject derived from economic history and relating to various aspects of social history, population history, the development of banking, commerce and business history, urban history, the history of housing, and the history of transport'.[1]

Different perspectives and approaches have been adopted since the late-nineteenth century to explore this 'portmanteau subject': documentary research; field observation; building survey and excavation; site and object conservation. *Transactions* has carried articles on industrial history ever since the 1870s, often about specific sites, but systematic and wide-ranging exploration of the region's varied industrial and urban past did not really begin until the early 1960s. In part this reflected growing national interest in economic history in the post-war period; more specifically, it developed from the growing interest in 'industrial archaeology' from the 1950s. The first published use of this term has been attributed to Michael Rix in an article in *The Amateur Historian* (now *The Local Historian*) in the autumn of 1955.[2] The Council for British Archaeology established a dedicated committee for it in 1959 and this paralleled the growing national interest in the conservation and preservation of iconic industrial buildings. In 1963, partly in response to the furore over the demolition of the Doric portico to Euston station, the government commissioned a survey of industrial 'monuments' to inform policy on protection and preservation.[3] Since then the concept and purpose of 'industrial archaeology', especially of the more recent past, have been regularly discussed, debated, redefined and extended. Marilyn Palmer, for

---

* Alan Crosby is responsible for the majority of the discussion of the Society's publications but with additional material from Michael Winstanley, who also wrote the introductory and concluding sections and collated the text. The authors are grateful to Warren Allison, Rachel Newman and Richard Newman for providing information but the views expressed here are their own.

example, even posed the question in 1988 whether 'the archaeologist of recent times, then, abandon the title "industrial" and become an historical archaeologist ... The wider question, perhaps, is how far the study of archaeology is relevant at all in a period from which such vast quantities of documentary evidence survive?'[4]

During the 1960s new industrial archaeology groups or societies were formed in many parts of Britain to record potential sites, structures and objects, particularly those deemed to be at risk from urban redevelopment schemes and rural industrial sites such as those associated with lead and metal mining heritage of northern England. For example, in 1960 the Northern Cavern and Mine Research Society was formed – from 1975 termed the Northern Mine Research Society. It has published a tremendous quantity of scholarly research and actively campaigned for the preservation, interpretation and investigation of mining archaeology across northern England. In Cumbria, however, it was CWAAS which took the lead with the formation of a sub-committee specifically to promote such work (fig.7.1). As seen previously

Fig. 7.1. Some of the members of the Committee for Industrial Archaeology in April 1998: front row left to right John Marshall, Anne Hillman, Ron Jackson; back row Jack Lancaster, John Helme, Graham Brooks *(Photograph: John Gavin)*

(see Chapter 1), the question of forming such a committee was raised as early as July 1964 and a Committee for Industrial Archaeology had been established by September 1966. This reflected the Society's commitment to this emerging area of study and its continuance reflects the enduring importance of the subject. For four decades the most influential figures were John Marshall, Reader in History from Lancaster University with a broad interest in the region's economic history and chair of the committee from 1969 until 2004, and Mike Davies-Shiel, a teacher in Windermere with wide-ranging interests in surveying and mapping industrial sites and a committee member until his death in 2009. They bequeathed a rich legacy of activity, publications and, in the case of Mike Davies-Shiel, extensive working notes and photographs.[5]

Since the 1960s members of the Society have been involved in a variety of initiatives. As well as undertaking documentary research, they have promoted the surveying, excavation, conservation, preservation, interpretation and potential re-use of significant industrial sites and buildings. As early as 1968 the committee were requesting information on relevant material in museums, although Denis Perriam responded to Davies-Shiel in December that he found it 'difficult to draw the line between industrial archaeological and folk material' in Carlisle museum (see Chapter 4).[6] In 1969 Marshall and Davies-Shiel published their ground-breaking survey, *Industrial Archaeology of the Lake Counties.*[7] By 1972 the committee had drawn up a list of potential sites for conservation throughout Cumbria and was contacting companies which operated from them. By 1980 it was distinguishing between sites which could, or should be, saved and those which could be merely recorded. While seeking to harness the enthusiasm of amateurs the committee was equally keen to deter random digging and to promote systematic and informed exploration. It also encouraged the publication of findings in *Transactions* and, partly as a result of its activities, more articles on broadly defined 'industrial' subjects have appeared in the last 50 years than in the whole of the previous century. In the 1980s members helped to found the Cumbria Industrial History Society and increasingly cooperated with other volunteers undertaking survey and conservation work.[8]

Coal and Iron

In sharp contrast to most other early county societies, the Cumberland and Westmorland Society has particularly appreciated and welcomed research on early mineral-based industries and has published progressive and innovative articles from its earliest days. 'The archaeology of the West Cumberland coal trade' by Isaac Fletcher, MP for Cockermouth, read to the Society at its Whitehaven meeting in December 1877, would appear to be the first time the term 'archaeology' appeared in print in relation to industrial sites.[9] It was, even by national criteria, a pioneering piece of research which was extraordinarily advanced in its terms of reference and approach. After considering the geology of the coalfield and the role of the Lowthers in the development of Whitehaven and its coal trade, Fletcher described the location and engineering characteristics of early collieries, provided statistics on output, and highlighted the early use of steam power for pumping. He drew attention to the problem of gas, and ways of removing it, to accidents and disasters, and to the early use of wooden railways. Furthermore, he carried his historical perspective into recent times, covering the coal trade at Harrington in the 1840s and discussing the mode of working coal, ventilation methods and transport.[10] The detailed line drawings which accompanied the article illustrated equipment which had been employed locally over the previous century (fig. 7.2).

After this very promising beginning, however, little else appeared on the coal industry for nearly 100 years and, despite some recent studies, it remains one of the relatively under-represented aspects of Cumbria's industrial history in the Society's publications. The most active contributor has been Oliver Wood. In 1971 his detailed account of the Curwen family's collieries

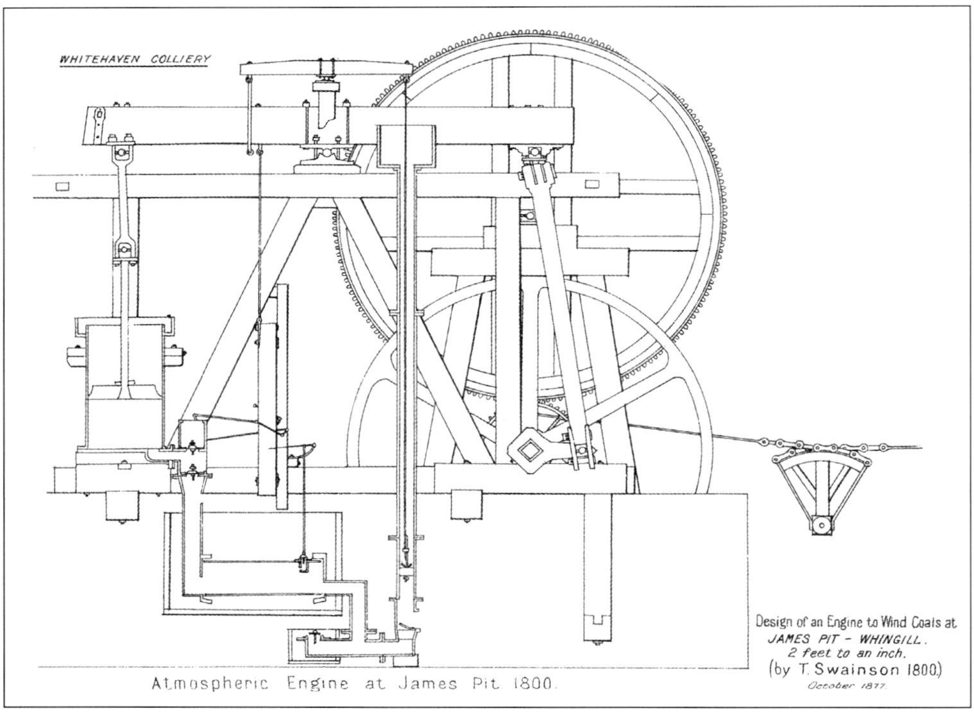

Fig. 7.2. Atmospheric engine by T. Swainson at James Pit, Whingill, Whitehaven, 1800, *CW1*, 3 (1878), opposite 281

in the Broughton area, south of Maryport, between the 1750s and the 1820s, looked at the power and effectiveness of progressive landowners in developing mining enterprises and made special reference to the use of waggonways and steam power. The financial circumstances, with large working profits offset by heavy personal debts, growing operating costs, and steady exhaustion of accessible reserves, contrasted sharply with the accounts of working conditions, including the employment of women and children, the use of the truck system, and the wage levels and piece rates. That theme was revisited in the following year with the same author's valuable article on the workforce at the Howgill Colliery in Whitehaven, based upon a unique 1802 payroll which gives details of output, wages, the gender and age of all the workforce (at 453 people, this was among the largest collieries in Britain at the time). Of special importance because of its rarity, was the information in the original document of 'where they came from', which allowed analysis of in-migration. Wood followed this up with an exploration of a colliery disaster and finally, in 1988, a masterly overview of coal mining in West Cumberland since 1600, the culmination of some four decades of research.[11]

Other studies have since appeared in *Transactions*. Jean Ward discussed the use of horses in the Whitehaven collieries in the early eighteenth century, using the accounts kept by John Spedding, agent to Sir James Lowther and, later, using the same source, she described the sinking of the great Saltom Pit, on the headland south of the town between 1730 and 1732.[12] In 2000, Nick Hair and Julian Cotton combined documentary research and archaeological survey to explore the site of Parton colliery, which closed in 1830. They concluded that one of the waggonways on the site was approximately of a gauge of 1.16m (3'10"), a typical example of a northern English colliery waggonway just prior to the introduction of what would become the standard gauge.[13] One of the minor coalfields of Cumbria, at Reagill and Sleagill near Shap, was investigated in an exemplary paper by Blake Tyson in which he combined very detailed documentary and cartographic evidence with analysis and biographical summaries of the miners and their families, derived especially from parish records, and with thorough field investigation of the surviving remains and surface traces of an industry which had its heyday in the century from the 1730s. East Cumberland collieries provide the backdrop for Alan Harris's study of the communities which worked them (see p. 245), but the most detailed analysis of their operation was by Graham Brooks who analysed an exceptionally rare survival, the detailed account book of a small early eighteenth-century colliery at Hartley above Kirkby Stephen. Covering the period 1729 to 1732, he revealed the costs and logistics of sinking a shaft, the output and production figures, the colliery workers and their working times and employment periods, sales and profit and loss. This was an example of a 'land sales' pit, selling its output purely to the locality, and the article gives an effective picture of the small-scale nature of the industry before the major expansion of the later eighteenth century.[14]

Unlike coal, where interest has been sporadic and often very local, studies of the region's iron industry, including that of the Furness peninsula, have featured regularly in the Society's publications. Indeed, Marshall noted that in the 'industrial archaeology and history of iron making, it has been in the forefront nationally'.[15] Isaac Fletcher had planned to follow his study of the coal industry with one on the west-coast iron industry, but his death meant that his brother Henry Allason Fletcher, managing director of the Lowca ironworks, reluctantly undertook the research on his behalf, Isaac having 'not collected any materials'. Nevertheless his work was equally pioneering for the period. He drew special attention to sites which are now widely acknowledged to be of national significance such as the Duddon Bridge furnace, 'a charcoal blast furnace which was in operation as recently as eight or ten years ago, and was the last in use in Great Britain, with the exception of one still in blast at Newlands and another at Backbarrow' (fig. 7.3). He also described the mid-eighteenth century emergence of the iron industry in the Whitehaven district, with furnaces at Little Clifton, Maryport, Seaton, Frizington, Lowca and Cleator.[16]

Regular contributions on the early iron industry appeared over the next 40 years. In 1886 the indefatigable curate of Torver, Thomas Ellwood, gave a detailed account of bloomeries or ancient iron-smelting hearths in the vicinity of Torver, Nibthwaite, Coniston and Hawkshead, based on field evidence and archaeological investigation, in which he postulated a link with Furness Abbey.[17] In 1897 Thomas Barlow-Massicks, manager of the iron works at Millom, provided a very early, albeit brief statement of the significance of industrial heritage, reminding members of the outstanding importance of the Duddon site: 'Of the many tourists who now visit the beautiful Duddon Valley, but few are aware that ruins of Ironworks of a most interesting character exist ... on the Cumberland side of Wordsworth's "cerulean Duddon"'. Unfortunately, perhaps implying that an interest in industry was rather radical and conflicted with the aims of an antiquarian, he observed that 'Bearing in mind that the objects of this Society are far removed from such mundane operations as iron-making, I will exclude from this paper but the merest technical details'.[18] In marked contrast, at the very end of the nineteenth century no less a luminary than W.G. Collingwood along with the energetic H. Swainson Cowper excavated a bloomery site at Coniston, and published their results in *Transactions* and other appropriate journals.[19] In 1913 J. Wilfred Jackson, Assistant Keeper at Manchester Museum, described the unexpected discovery of a bloomery in the grounds of Lindale church, which was then being extended. He credited a local coach builder, T.R. Wilson, for his prompt action in recording this, and undertook pioneering chemical analysis of the slag which showed that it used the richer red oxide of haematite ore.[20] Charles Parker undertook a similar exercise to Ellwood's for Eskdale.

The leading local historian and archaeologist Mary C. Fair wrote this up and extended it with an investigation of sites in Wasdale.[21]

Interest in the early iron industry revived from the late 1960s. In 1970 Tylecote and Cherry evaluated a bloomery at Muncaster Head producing not only a locational plan, but also detailed building plans and sections, a contour survey, geochemical analysis of the iron, and a brief comment on finds.[22] They concluded with a suggested reconstruction of the site. More recently Ian Miller has surveyed the site of Cunsey forge, 'one of the best surviving examples of a bloomforge/refining forge in the region', which was largely built in the period following 1715 but on the site of earlier workings (fig. 7.4).[23] In the early 1990s a team of volunteers, co-ordinated by John Marshall and the Society's Industrial Archaeology Committee, explored the important physical remains of Newland Furnace and its various adaptations over time.[24] While early researchers were hampered by an inability to date these sites, given the lack of associated cultural material, this is slowly being redressed by the growing number of radiocarbon dates being provided by these structures, largely under the auspices of the Lake District National Park Authority. These dates are demonstrating that the vast majority of such sites can be traced back to the medieval period.[25]

Fig. 7.3. The Backbarrow charcoal store *c.*1920s *(Photograph: Mary Fair. Image Cumbria County Council: Carlisle Library)*

Fig. 7.4. Cunsey Forge: the principal buildings and adjacent structure in the 1980s, prior to their demolition *(photograph: Mike Davies-Shiel)*, *CW3*, 5 (2005), 178

As well as site exploration, documentary studies have continued to provide important insights. Brian Awty meticulously analysed the remarkable seventeenth-century accounts of Force Forge near Colton, held at Lancashire Archives. He was able to explain working arrangements from the late 1650s onwards, cross-referenced with a very valuable inventory of 1663 describing the machinery, and to investigate the employees and owners, the sources of raw materials (iron was mined in Plain Furness, and charcoal gathered very widely from woodland Furness), and the markets. This is a major contribution to the history not only of the Furness iron industry but also to national understanding of the early phases of proto-industrialisation. Blake Tyson similarly analysed forge accounts from Coniston, which survive from 1675 to 1766. In a densely-packed article he traced the building of the forge, the supply of raw materials, the getting of iron ore (which came not from Plain Furness but from the Coniston Fells), repairs and maintenance, the sale and marketing of the iron including transport charges, profits, and the eventual decline and closure of the enterprise. In another article about early metalworking, Richard Spence considered the entrepreneurial activities of the Clifford earls of Cumberland in the seventeenth century, as they developed coalmining on their Stainmore estates and an ironworks at Brougham (near Penrith). The latter, for which detailed accounts survive, was notable for its use of haematite brought overland from Adgarley in Furness, one of the earliest documented examples of this exceptionally rich ore being sent beyond the area.[26]

The expansion of mining and production of iron in south-west Cumberland in the late nineteenth century and the new settlements associated with it (see p. 245) were extensively explored in the 1960s by Alan Harris, lecturer in geography at Hull University. In 1969 he and Ronald Davis provided a powerful account of the great Hodbarrow mine at Millom. They told the dramatic story of the discovery of the richest deposits of haematite in the British Isles, the realisation of its potential scale and the huge profits and dividends made into the early twentieth century, and they recounted the social consequences and the remarkable engineering solutions which allowed exploitation of undersea ore reserves. The article notes the subsequent inexorable decline, observing that 'Hodbarrow today is a strangely empty place, yet no one viewing it from the Outer Barrier, across a great expanse of broken ground, could fail to be moved by the signs of former prosperity', and ends on a deeply poignant note: 'Since this article was written it has been announced that Hodbarrow mine will be closed not later than March 1968' (fig. 7.5).[27]

Despite the attention paid to the industry, there are still issues to be unravelled and sites to identify, such as the short-lived, late- nineteenth century Ellenborough Foundry, described from historical sources by Lancaster and Wattleworth, but whose precise physical and technological details remain unknown.[28]

Fig. 7.5. Hodbarrow Mine *c.*1920s *(Photograph: Mary Fair. Cumbria County Council: Carlisle Library)*

OTHER MINING AND QUARRYING

A transition from purely documentary to archaeological approaches is evident in the study of German miners who were at Keswick, Coniston and elsewhere in the second half of the sixteenth century, with each approach offering contrasting perspectives and insights. The glamorous connection

Fig. 7.6. Silvergill Mine: collection of wooden sleepers and planks associated with a waggonway that was radio-carbon dated to about 1560 *(Photograph by courtesy of Warren Allison)*

with Queen Elizabeth's Society of Mines Royal and copper mining in the region had long been among the most celebrated aspects of the industrial history of Lakeland. As more documentary evidence became available it was possible to go beyond the semi-legendary tales of such men as Daniel Hechstetter [or Hochstetter] and to construct a more reliable account. In 1883 J. Fisher Crosthwaite published documentary evidence for the Germans at Keswick, using published State Papers and unpublished parish registers, leases and title deeds. The story attracted the attention of W.G. Collingwood, and in 1910 he produced an extremely comprehensive account of Coniston families bearing German names who were descendants of the men who came under Elizabeth and James I. He described in detail the circumstances of the original invitation to German miners in the 1560s, used parish registers to identify the miners and their families, and made suggestions as to their origins in Germany. Two years later he published his detailed transcription of records of these German mines held in the Augsburg City Archives. Finally, in 1928 Collingwood transcribed another account of the mines at Keswick and Coniston in the seventeenth and eighteenth centuries using documents discovered in the archives of the Fleming family of Rydal Hall.[29] More recently, in an interesting paper which investigated the practicalities of financing and managing mining operations in the years around 1700, Douglas Grant looked at the Newlands mines, also once worked by the Germans, but in a later phase of their exceptionally long period of operation.[30]

These mines at Newlands, including Goldscope, and at Coniston, and

Fig. 7.7 . Silvergill Mine: radio-carbon analysis showed that this wooden hand-shovel probably dated to the 11th or 12th centuries *(Photograph by courtesy of Warren Allison)*

the presence of German miners in both places, were familiar to historians of mining in the Lake District, but the fact that Germans had also been involved in mining activity in the Caldbeck Fells was scarcely mentioned in earlier works. In 2001 Richard Smith, Warren Allison and Samuel Murphy, through a combination of field work and documentary sources, were able to pinpoint for the first time the location of the principal sixteenth- and seventeenth-century workings on the Caldbeck Fells at Silvergill mines, whereas previously Roughtengill mine had been considered the most probable location. This was followed up in 2010 with Allison and Murphy's particularly important paper presenting the results of further documentary research, fieldwork and archaeology into the workings at Silvergill mine, which has yielded finds of the greatest archaeological significance. The mines are internationally important as examples of the European spread of technology and contained stunning artefacts, including remnants of the earliest known waggonway in Britain, and probably Europe, in the form of small wooden sleepers and planks dated to 1420-1640. This work also demonstrated that a wooden shovel blade found in the workings was dated to between 1020 and 1200, making it clear that mining had been in progress here almost a thousand years ago, long predating the German presence by five centuries. (figs. 7.6 and 7.7).[31]

Lead mining also received early attention. In July 1884 Revd W. Nall, editor of the third edition of Westgarth Forster's classic *A Treatise on a Section of the Strata from Newcastle-upon-Tyne to the Mountain of Cross Fell in Cumberland*, gave a lengthy paper to accompany one of the Society's excursions to Alston. As well as covering the town and parish, he discussed lead mining and methods of extraction, with accounts of the processes involved – this was still an active mining area and recent changes were highlighted. The documentary and archaeological evidence for mining from the Roman period onwards was explained (including the tantalising twelfth-century reference to a silver mine near Carlisle) and, unusually, the social history of the industry including the philanthropic activities of the Quaker owners in the eighteenth and nineteenth centuries which later attracted more attention.[32] In 1940 F.W. Monkhouse adopted an economic history approach focusing on the life and career of George Liddell who, in 1736, obtained a near-monopoly of the 31 working lead mines on Alston Moor when the new owners, Greenwich Hospital, reorganised the leases. He analysed Liddell's personal business notebook, looking at working arrangements, profit and loss in relation to costs and transport expenditure, the promotion of the company and the impact of Liddell's business methods – in short, an analytical, coherent and systematic piece of business history in the style pioneered at Manchester and remaining in vogue there until the 1970s and beyond.[33] With the growing emphasis on industrial archaeology a contrasting approach was offered by Paul Wilson. His article included not only a comprehensive account of the background and genesis of the Nent Force Level, started in 1775 to drain lead mines but not completed until 1842, but also explained its limited surviving physical remains and engineering features.[34] In an intriguing aside he quoted Thomas Sopwith's description of 1832 of the level as a tourist novelty.[35] A more recent article has focused on the little-known lead mines in the manor of Kinniside, south of Ennerdale. This charted the major investment which took place in the first decades of the nineteenth century at a time when industrialisation and urbanisation were generating new demands for lead, and then showed how these ventures suffered in the widespread contraction the industry experienced in the late 1820s and early 1830s.[36]

As well as publishing on south-west Cumbria, Alan Harris had a particular interest in the little-known and highly-evocative abandoned industrial landscapes between Brampton and the South Tyne. In 1977 he undertook a brief analysis of the local lime trade, based on early nineteenth-century accounts of the Earl of Carlisle's staith, or loading place, on the horse-drawn railway at Brampton. Five years earlier he had published a thorough account of the nearby Tindale Fell waggonway, using documents in the Naworth archive at Durham University. The remoteness of the area, its physical challenges and its distance from markets had constrained the exploitation of mineral resources, but in 1799 the waggonway opened and a transformation took place. By 1803 it handled 17,000 tons of coal and 28,000 tons of lime and by the late 1830s almost 70,000 tons of coal. The article described the route and engineering features, as well as analysing the economic impact and eventual decline of the waggonway. In 1978 J.K. Almond extended coverage of this fascinating area with his paper on the almost-forgotten Tindale Fell spelter works, opened in 1845 to smelt zinc ore, hitherto a largely useless waste product of lead mining, for the manufacture of sheet zinc for building purposes and zinc metal for batteries and brass production. He showed how the works, closed in 1895, caused environmental devastation from toxic fumes, and discussed the social conditions of this rough community, developed under the (usually) benevolent patronage of the earls of Carlisle.[37]

More recently work has been done on other mining and quarrying in the Lake District including copper mining at Coniston[38] but particularly on the importance of slate quarrying in several parts of the area. Blake Tyson's 1984 article on the Troutbeck Park quarries used a collection of letters from the 1750s to shed light on the management of the quarries, their markets, and the transportation of slate to the purchaser by coastal shipping. Since then two articles have considered the quarrying industry of Troutbeck, Kentmere and Longsleddale from documentary and archaeological perspectives (fig. 7.8). In 1987 Rob David focused on the eighteenth and nineteenth centuries when booming demand from the industrialising areas transformed the scale of production – although he pointed out that the output from Westmorland

Fig. 7.8. 'Long Sleddale slate quarries' by Thomas Allom from Thomas Rose, *Westmorland, Cumberland, Durham and Northumberland Illustrated* (London, 1832-35)

remained comparatively small by national standards and never matched the expansion of the industry evident in North Wales. A subsequent article with Geoff Brambles in 1992 provided a comprehensive field survey of physical remains. Meanwhile Julian Munby had used documents from the archives at Levens to trace the use of Westmorland slate, quarried in Longsleddale, in prestige building projects in Bath and at Buckland in Berkshire.[39]

OTHER INDUSTRIES

Mining, quarrying and related industries may have attracted the bulk of the Society's attention but other industries have also been the subject of valuable studies. Crocker and Sandbach used a stock book compiled by Harrison Ainslie between 1871 and 1876 to describe the pattern of trade in gunpowder in the region and the methods used to ensure its safe storage.[40] In the last few decades *Transactions* has carried reports of projects on tanneries undertaken by Lancaster University Archaeological Unit, the Lake District National Park Authority and North Pennines Archaeology which have increased our understanding of an industry which was once widespread in the county.[41] Bruce Jones highlighted new evidence about what he considered to be the first factory in Carlisle, a complex of textile and fulling mills and a dyehouse developed on the River Caldew, just below the Citadel in the 1720s.[42] Chaloner's study of cotton mills at Cark-in-Cartmel published in 1964 focused primarily on the owners, while Mawson's discussion of Langthwaite cotton mill near Carlisle 12 years later concentrated on both its owners and its operations in the 100 years from *c.* 1790.[43] A stimulating pair of papers in 2007 considered the history of something so familiar, so commonplace, as to be largely disregarded by historians, though it played a revolutionary part in the transformation of the domestic lives of almost the entire population. Arguing that 'gasworks have not received the attention they deserve' and stating that 'By 1890 there were 30 gasworks in the area of modern Cumbria and a few more followed', Blake Tyson sketched out developments nationally before looking at the incorporation of the Windermere Gasworks in 1862. He traced the history of the company, the technology involved, a major modernisation and extension scheme in 1934, the consumers and financial position of the company, and census evidence for the workforce. The decline following nationalisation was discussed. Tyson had noted that there was a paucity of archival information relating directly to the company and James and Joyce Cherry made the same observation in their article on the undertaking at Seascale which, with Burton-in-Kendal, was one of the two smallest places in Cumbria to have a gasworks. From about 1881 gas and water were supplied by the Furness Railway Company but in 1911 a new company was formed – this was one of the first villages anywhere in the country to enjoy gas lighting. The article covers nationalisation, the impact of Sellafield and its unlimited cheap electricity, and closure in 1957.[44]

Mike Davies-Shiel gave a personal account of his research into an important industry which had been largely forgotten. In 1972, when looking for early iron-smelting sites, Mike, his wife and a friend discovered (by almost falling into it while picnicking) a stone-walled pit near Newby Bridge. Within a few weeks he had identified or been told about seven more in the Rusland area and others from Winster, Ambleside, Dunnerdale and Patterdale. What were they? Checking the back issues of the Society's *Transactions* uncovered intriguing references, especially from Mary C. Fair of Eskdale, who recorded that in Miterdale there were 'the remains of kilns used for burning bracken roots for soap-making'.[45] The result was an article which provided a wealth of information, based on documentary sources and painstaking field investigation, and which single-handedly uncovered what had been a major rural industry of potash production in south Cumbria (fig. 7.9). He surmised on the basis of his fieldwork that 'one would expect at least one per square mile throughout hilly, brackenny Lakeland, with three or four times that number per square mile with the area of the Kendal clothiers' operations.'[46]

In 1942 W.T. McIntire drew attention to another long-forgotten but once widespread trade, the making of salt along the shore from Morecambe Bay to the Solway. He used the description of salt-making given by John Lucas in his history of Warton (1732) and gathered evidence from place-

FIG. 1, a.—Elfhow Pit, Staveley.
Note "chimney" at rear.

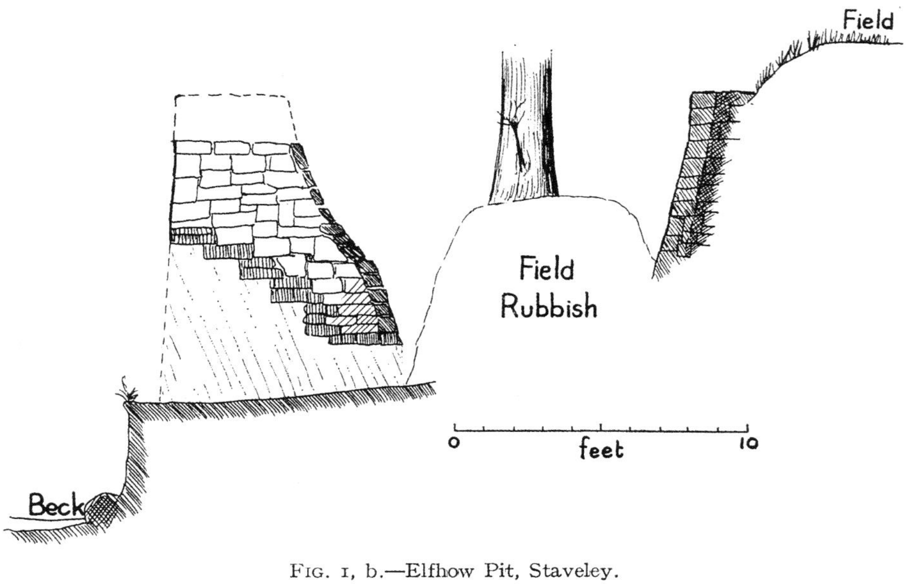

FIG. 1, b.—Elfhow Pit, Staveley.
Cross-section, front to rear.

Fig. 7.9. Elfhow potash kiln, Staveley as drawn by Mike Davies-Shiel, *CW2*, 72 (1972), 87

names, monastic cartularies, and references in grants and leases. Blake Tyson revisited the subject almost 60 years later, gathering more information for the Cumberland coast and focusing on the saltpan at Whitehaven, for which accounts survive from between 1675 and 1677. His very detailed paper explains the technologies of the salt-making process and provides a comprehensive analysis of the operation of the saltworks and its eventual fate.[47]

In 1972 Joseph Hughes listed sites of windmills in the county, finding them largely on the lower-lying ground of Cumberland where the use of water power was less feasible. A later documentary case-study by Blake Tyson explored the construction of two post-mills, and their construction, maintenance, management and operations.[48] Hughes and Tyson have also been responsible for two case-studies of studies of water mills in Wigton and Kendal while as early as 1936 Nicholas Size had drawn attention to an early click mill at Buttermere.[49] Water-powered mills remained important for manufacturing in the Kendal area, where coal continued to be relatively expensive, well into the nineteenth century. D.G. Watts argued that their collective significance on the River Kent amounted to 'an industrial revolution without steam'. Paul Wilson discussed the 1844 Act of Parliament which empowered local commissioners to build reservoirs to ensure an adequate supply of water for both the power and processes involved in the diverse woollen, gunpowder, bobbin, logwood, dyewood, paper and marble works that were located along the banks.[50] Elsworth and Whitehead have recently explored the site of a later steam corn mill at Barrow which relied on coal brought into the region. This remained in operation for almost 100 years and at its peak was part of an international trade in grain and flour.[51]

Craft-based industries and those engaged in them have only occasionally been the subject of papers in *Transactions*, possibly because of the difficulty of finding adequate documentary sources and the relative paucity of obvious physical remains or sites. Most attention, therefore, has been paid to the individuals involved. Clock and watch makers, particularly in Westmorland and North Lonsdale, have exerted an enduring fascination since the 1930s. Thomas Cann Hughes and J.L. Hobbs initially provided valuable surveys of those involved and a series of later articles have focused on individual families and their inter-relationships.[52] Michael Finlay's detailed study of the pewterers of Penrith also used a biographical approach to look at the individual craftsmen and their work during the seventeenth and eighteenth centuries. Blake Tyson has also recently deployed apprentice and charity records to explore the lives and careers of craftsmen in Kendal.[53] Recent popular interest in the craft workshops associated with the Arts and Crafts movement, however, has not yet been reflected in the Society's publications.

Transport

Transport improvements were necessary complements to the development of industry. As with industry, the Society's contribution has been wide-ranging, but with interest focused more on some aspects than others.

The earliest contribution on a transport theme was John Fell's 1884 article on the guides who worked the Morecambe Bay crossings – an article prompted in part by a contemporary debate, and official inquiries, over their responsibilities and terms of employment. The paper was graced by a double-page coloured map showing the routes across the sands (fig. 7.10), and drew upon official records, diaries, journals and parish registers to recount tragic tales of mass drownings and celebrated disasters, as well as more sober stuff. These routes also featured prominently in an anecdotal article on travelling and postal arrangements in eighteenth- and nineteenth-century Furness, published by J. Melville and J.L. Hobbs in 1946, while in 1955 Hobbs gave a more systematic account of the turnpike roads of the area, including the interesting project to build a 'Coach road to Cumberland' or 'Slate road', over the central ridge of Low Furness to link the Ulverston Canal with the Duddon near Grizebeck.[54]

In 1977 Paul Hindle, a geographer at Salford University who has worked extensively on Cumbrian topics, produced an important study of the medieval roads in the diocese of Carlisle. He used the framework of known Roman roads, place-names, documentary references to, among others, *magna strata* [the Roman road from Kendal to Shap], and royal itineraries in an attempt to reconstruct the network. He argued that the routes east to Newcastle and south-east over Stainmore to York were much more important than that south towards Lancashire and Cheshire, but wisely counselled that 'it cannot be stated too strongly that the process of inferring the existence of medieval roads from later written evidence must never be used without contemporary evidence'. His survey included roads which were built for special purposes, and Cumbria has some fine examples of these. In 1902 T.H. Hodgson had given a detailed account of the Military Road from Newcastle to Carlisle, built by the government in the aftermath of the 1745 Jacobite Rising but with Roman forebears. The passage of over a century since he wrote the article is best exemplified by the statement that the road, 'which was doubtless planned by military engineers and chiefly with a view to military exigencies, does not appear to have met the requirements of commercial traffic … for much of its course it traverses a difficult and hilly, and very thinly populated country; and for a long distance is now little used and grass-grown'. Sections of this grass-grown route are now the traffic-laden A69. The construction of the Military Road itself was described by William Lawson in 1979 in an article based on his Durham University MA thesis.[55]

There have been fewer studies of the traffic which used the roads.

However, in 1959 Bruce Jones published a seminal paper on Westmorland pack-horse men who appeared in Southampton records of the late fifteenth and early sixteenth centuries. This demonstrated the long-distance trade in Westmorland (and particularly Kendal) cloth, and its international markets. Jones was unduly modest about what he called his 'sketchy observations', suggesting that 'many questions concerning the trade are still to be answered', but this paper had a significant influence on re-assessments of English economic activity in the first half of the Tudor period, and helped to make plain that the international cloth trade was not limited, as popular history had hitherto suggested, to the Cotswolds and adjacent areas. Here, as in so many other instances, the use of local evidence was instrumental in revising and improving the over-generalised and perhaps southern-centric traditional picture.[56] Rob Vickers' article on carriers provided a more detailed and focused analysis than most studies of the subject (which rely heavily or exclusively on the evidence of trade directories) by exploiting two sets of records of Victorian carriers in Cumbria Archive Centre, Kendal. Normally only the routes and timings can be identified but the businesses of the two carriers involved, Walter Berry of Milnthorpe and Thomas Elwood of Ayside near Cartmel, are carefully described in terms of goods conveyed, prices and rates, clients (including industrial enterprises) and financial arrangements, as well as relationships with the railways and railheads. This is a major contribution to a better understanding of the country carrier in Victorian England.[57]

The Lancaster Canal was the subject of a fine early article by John F. Curwen who analysed the politics of its planning and construction, the choice of route, the engineering and financial aspects, and the vexed relationships between the company and its railway competitors. A model of careful analysis, Paul Wilson's excellent case-study of the canal terminus published in 1968 revealed the morphological and economic impact of transport development. He looked at the canal basin itself, with its warehouses and wharves but, unlike many studies in the field of transport history, he also charted the wider effects, showing how the arrival of the canal helped to create a new industrial quarter. A paper by Andrew White highlighted one of the most distinctive features of the canal – its operation of fast packet boats which offered a swift and reliable means of passenger transport between Preston, Lancaster and Kendal from the mid-1830s and which, but for railway competition from 1840, might have revolutionised the canal network as a whole.[58]

Between the 1920s and 1960s several articles dealt with Cumbrian ports and shipping, with studies of minor ports being particularly prominent. The use of the little river port of Ravenglass from the sixteenth century to the First World War was explored by Caesar Caine as early as 1922, while in 1936 and 1943 W.T. McIntire published articles on the port of Milnthorpe and the 'lost' port of Sandsfield on the Solway. His later paper highlighted the existence of very minor ports on the south shore of the Solway, all eclipsed by the opening of the Carlisle Canal in 1819. In 1973 W.A.J. Prevost focused on one such place, at Alison's Bank where the Carlisle-Gretna road crosses the Sark into Scotland. This was the first tollhouse over the border into Scotland and the article used pre-1707 customs accounts to reveal the nature of Anglo-Scottish trade. Much more recently, Margaret Robinson has shown how the Solway as a whole was relatively underdeveloped in terms of its maritime trade even in the early nineteenth century. Despite Carlisle and its outports developing modest coastal shipping links with North Wales, Ireland and even London, nothing elsewhere in Cumbria could compare with Whitehaven's pre-eminence.[59] Although Whitehaven's primary trade was shipping coal to Ireland, two articles remind us of its global reach. David Richardson edited the manuscript of the late Maurice Schofield on Whitehaven's slave ships, defined as those sailing from or fitted out in the port, which made 69 voyages to Africa between 1710 and 1769 while Rob David has explored the port's connections with the whaling trade.[60]

Earlier, three important articles by Rupert Jarvis had looked at the evidence from port and customs records, a subject on which he was a specialist – he was concurrently undertaking very important work on the eighteenth century records of the port of Liverpool. In 1943 he used the documents produced by revenue officers at the port of Whitehaven to explore unfamiliar aspects of the 1745 rising, including reports about suspicious activity sent by the officers to the authorities in London, the steps taken by local people to organise and arm themselves, and movements of shipping to and from Scotland. Four years later he used the records of Crown appointments (including customs collectors, comptrollers and searchers) to paint an overview from the 1579 survey of Cumberland (which lists as ports Millom, Ravenglass, Calder, St Bees, Whitehaven, Workington, Skinburness and 'the Water of Solway') via the rise of Whitehaven to national importance, to the bounds and jurisdictions of the port of Lancaster and its minor Morecambe Bay associates such as Foudray and Milnthorpe – for which he (in contrast to McIntire) was able to find considerable evidence. In 1954 he turned his attention to the voluminous shipping registers, listing an extraordinary series of 47 questions which he argued should be asked as part of any analysis but never had been and then, frustratingly, though disarmingly, he stated they would be not addressed in detail by him either. Rather he described the principal sources available, providing illuminating examples and extracts from them, and deployed them to chart the growing rivalry between Liverpool and Whitehaven.[61]

Surprisingly, railways have only occasionally featured in the Society's publications, apart from brief sections in articles about more general topics. Nothing substantial appeared before Melville and Hobbs' pioneering study

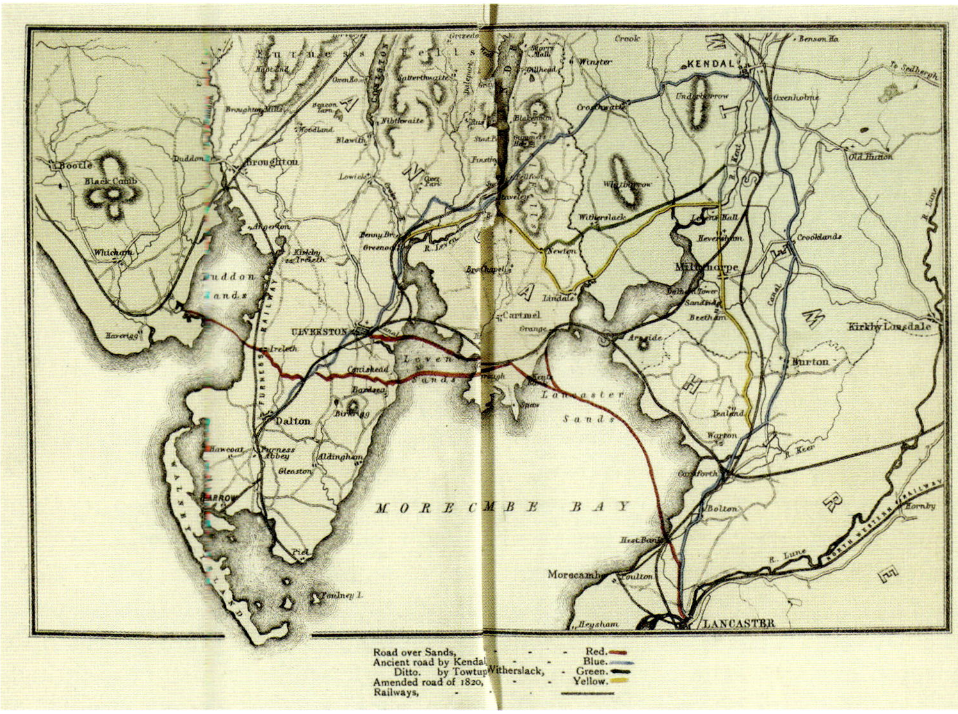

Fig. 7.10. The developing road and rail network connecting Furness peninsula with Westmorland and Lancashire showing ancient roads, later routes, and the 'road' over the Sands, *CW1*, 7 (1884), opposite 1

of the early railway history of Furness, published in the Tract Series in 1951. In 1952 Sidney Pollard analysed the politics of railway promotion in the North West in the 1860s, posing a question: what problems were perceived at the time regarding the idea of unifying short coastal lines to form a new main route to Scotland which would bypass the LNWR between Lancaster and Carlisle? Pollard explained the emergence of the network from the 1830s to the 1860s, and its economic rationale, and analysed the flows of traffic which had to be accommodated, such as coke from the North East to Furness and ore transported to the Durham furnaces. He recounted the complex machinations whereby the LNWR, Furness, Maryport & Carlisle, and Midland companies negotiated with one other and with minor local undertakings, and how the LNWR used skilful tactics to emerge triumphant, and suggested that, despite claims that the Midland Railway sought a new coastal route to Scotland, little evidence of that ambition can be found. Thereafter, apart from the transcription of some correspondence of James Losh related to the Newcastle & Carlisle Railway, nothing further has appeared except an article by T.M. Bell and R.W. Rennison in 2001 which recounted the genesis, planning and construction of the Alston branch of the

North Eastern Railway, detailing the route and the several abortive plans for extensions to Nenthead, Weardale or Teesdale.[62] In this respect the Society has not reflected the burgeoning interest in railway history evident locally, for example, in the activities of the Cumbrian Railways Association.

Urban development

In 1878, the same year as Fletcher's pioneering article on the coal industry, *Transactions* published an equally pioneering paper on urban history. Using primary sources, William Jackson discussed the historical development of Whitehaven and the dominant role played by the Lowther family. He identified many of the public buildings and other features of the townscape, including the engine-house 'used for pumping sewage to its outlet in Saltom Bay' and the notorious slum dwellings clinging to the cliff on the south side of the harbour. This was unconventional fare – the idea of mentioning slum housing and sewage would have been anathema in almost any other county society, and it was almost 100 years before significant attention was again paid in the pages of *Transactions* to such subjects, or indeed to other aspects of relatively recent urban growth and development. Even Carlisle was little covered except in the context of its political and military history, although in 1881 William Nanson had published a paper on the 'cullery tenure' of the city, for at least 300 years a distinctive form of customary tenure. He discussed the specific locations of the properties involved, which he argued from their distribution were once the open places within the city walls. Nanson suggested that these deserved 'at least a passing notice from those who are interested in our local archaeology'.[63]

However, following the publication of an influential 1916 lecture by Professor Thomas Tout of Manchester University on medieval town planning which highlighted the phenomenon of 'planted towns', those established on more or less virgin sites with a least basic principles of formal design and layout, researchers began to explore these possibilities locally.[64] In 1946 Douglas Simpson investigated the twin planted towns of Church Brough and Market Brough in Westmorland, arguing on the basis of their morphology and relationship to the road system of the area below Stainmore that the former was one of the very earliest English new towns, dating from the reign of William II immediately after the conquest of Cumberland, and that the latter, which eventually eclipsed it, was founded perhaps a century later. Three years later Simpson gave an authoritative account of the 'perfect' planned town of Appleby, 'a purposeful transplantation of European urbanism into the "Celtic fringe" of eleventh-century England'.[65] Nearly half a century later Angus Winchester dissected the morphology and topography of medieval Cockermouth, showing the components of the plan and interpreting the complex evolution of its apparently simply layout, including the key question of the pre-urban settlement of the area. This remains the most detailed analysis of the urban morphology of a Cumbrian town, convincingly demonstrating a local example of a series of themes and processes which are familiar in the generalised national literature on the medieval town.[66] These papers by Simpson and Winchester were defined by their modern approach to the subject – rather than relying almost exclusively on the documentary evidence, and especially the legal or constitutional sources, they gave full attention to fieldwork and maps, highlighting the physical form of the settlements in question (as the subtitle of the Appleby paper, 'a morphological study', emphasises).

In 1964, neatly linking the themes of the planned town and the industrial town, Edward Hughes discussed the development of Maryport between 1748 and 1752 by the Senhouse family, and included a complete list of those who purchased plots of land in the new planned town, giving to the financial and commercial dimension the essential human character which might otherwise be ignored or overlooked.[67] More recently Richard Newman has shown that such towns can also disappear. His fascinating study of Harrington explains how the ancient township was transformed by the building of a harbour in about 1760 and its rapid growth as a coal port, just as happened with the new harbour built by the Senhouses at Maryport. A planned town with a formal grid pattern of wide streets was laid out in the late 1770s under the auspices of the lord of the manor, John Christian Curwen, but after industrial decline and dereliction the 'new town' was targeted by Workington Borough Council for slum clearance in the early 1960s and was completely demolished.[68]

A comparably broad perspective characterises a splendid collection of papers which have addressed the fascinating theme of the 'mushroom' industrial communities of Victorian Furness and Cumberland, which were only just emerging when the Society was formed. Their iron industry was then the most productive in the world and new communities were springing up almost overnight. Most studies of these new communities were the work of Alan Harris. His work was specifically singled out by Marshall in 2000 as being a major contribution to the history and morphology of the communities associated with this mining and ironworking. Harris's first paper in 1965 took a post-industrial view of the history and landscape of Askam-in-Furness:

> Although the local iron industry is now almost extinct, its legacy remains in the landscape in the form of spoil heaps, the crumbling stonework of mine buildings, and the embankments and cuttings of abandoned mineral railways ... The tracks of several mineral tramways, the silted beds of reservoirs, and a considerable extent of derelict and semi-derelict land combine to give Askam the appearance of a place that has long outlived the purpose for which

> it was created ... It would be difficult to argue a case for the village as a thing of beauty, but as a product of an important phase in the development of the Furness district Askam is worthy of the attention of local historians.

Using tithe maps and Ordnance Survey maps as its canvas, the article looked at the morphology of the settlement and assessed the intimate physical, social and economic relationship between the community and the iron industry.[69] This successful formula was followed in other articles. In 1966 Harris undertook a similar exercise for Millom, and in 1974 he published a particularly interesting study on the dispersed and straggling colliery settlements in north-east Cumberland, showing how patterns of landownership and leasing, and the relationship between farming and mining, shaped marginal communities such as Hallbankgate and Halton Lea Gate. The paper discussed the housing stock and the settlement forms, including their physical and sanitary condition, and noted how the continuing influence of the earls of Carlisle was manifested in, among other controls, the temperance campaigning of Lady Rosalind Howard.[70]

Harris's study of Millom was reinterpreted 40 years later by Ruth Hughes, who argued that the physical development of the planned town after the early 1860s reflected the urgent need for accommodation for a large number of in-migrant workers, in an area without significant settlement. She suggested that the two iron ore companies vied with each other for political and economic power over the growing community and that only after 1875, and the establishment of the Millom Local Board which coincided with the 'victory' of the Hodbarrow Mining Company, did the real planning of the new town take place – and that it was dictated by the needs of the Hodbarrow Mining Company. Cumberland's other celebrated, or notorious, new town of the industrial age, Cleator Moor, was investigated by John Marshall in 1978, not using a morphological approach but instead focusing on social history and on such key themes as the process of industrialisation and housing construction, railway development, Irish immigration, overcrowding, crime, disorder and drunkenness, paternalism and religion.[71]

John Marshall also undertook a comprehensive and lengthy analysis of late seventeenth- and eighteenth-century Kendal. He emphasised the social structure and its relationship with the commercial, administrative and cultural role of a place which, although not the county town, bore many comparisons with Carlisle, Lancaster and Preston in terms of function, if not religion and politics. In this magisterial essay Marshall demonstrated how evidence drawn from a broad range of inter-related sources could be used to build up a multi-faceted picture of the town and its changing character. He made extensive use of probate records and researched occupations and employment, the wealth and status of individual townsmen and social groups, and local and longer-distance trading links; while the records of churches and chapels allowed him to construct a convincing model of the association between religion, commerce and social class. Julian Munby looked at an earlier period in the town's history, using the text of the borough charter that had been discovered in a volume of seventeenth-century transcripts at Levens Hall. Arguing that 'the economy and settlement of medieval Westmorland still await investigation', he analysed the content and implications of the charter, comparing it with near contemporary examples from Ulverston and Warton, and discussed the topography and economy of medieval Kendal and its extensive rural hinterland. At the other end of the region, David Mawson considered Brampton in the late-eighteenth century, and particularly the increasing diversification of employment and the emergence of weaving in the 1790s, a time of road improvements and dynamic changes such as the enclosure of the commons.[72]

In the mid-1970s the archaeological investigation of Carlisle was in progress, with redevelopment of The Lanes and other major projects. Bruce Jones published a background paper on the topography of medieval Carlisle, in which he drew attention to the problems posed by the very limited documentary evidence and the need to pay close attention to the topography and urban plan. His careful analysis proposed a model of frequent and extensive change to the geography of the city within the walls, as Roman road alignments were abandoned or heavily modified and as strip fields provided the framework within which urban development took place during the medieval period. This work was complemented by Denis Perriam in an article on the demolition of the eastern stretch of the city walls between 1807 and 1821, and the impact of these changes on the street pattern and commercial centre. He quoted the sharp contrasts in contemporary opinion, from Dorothy Wordsworth's hostile comment that they were 'broken down in places and crumbling away and most disgusting from filth' to Walter Scott's lament: 'I have not forgiven them for destroying their quiet old walls'. He also traced the emergence of the heritage movement from the mid-nineteenth century, with its aim of preserving and protecting the stretches of wall which survived.[73]

Alan Harris has also produced a very detailed and exemplary case-study of suburban growth in Carlisle, looking specifically at Denton Holme using a wide range of sources, from census schedules, Carlisle Corporation minute books, title deeds, local newspapers, Board of Health reports, maps and plans, to the physical evidence of architecture and morphology. The article reflected a growing interest in the 'ordinary' aspects of urban history. In a study of what has become known as 'micro-history', Jeremy Godwin contributed a detailed study of Duke Street in the Shaddongate district of Carlisle, tracing its history from the pre-urban estate, via the development of the street in the early nineteenth century, to its demolition under slum clearance programmes between the wars. His central theme was the dominance of handloom weaving in the years from 1820 to 1860, and in describing this he provided valuable insights into that trade in the city as a whole.

Carlisle's housing conditions were also analysed by Jean Turnbull in a paper which described developments prior to the First World War and then, using detailed statistics and mapping, analysed the content of a housing census and survey undertaken by the City Council in 1917. She concluded that the city had working-class housing which was usually significantly smaller than the hardly-generous national average, with a higher proportion of back-to-back and tenement dwellings and very serious levels of overcrowding. There was much to be done to make 'Homes Fit For Heroes'.[74] More recently the Society has woven together a wide range of strands to outline the development of Carlisle over the two millennia in its popular publication, *The Making of Carlisle: from Romans to Railways*.[75] Further south in the region, Andrew Watterson studied the development of working-class housing in Kendal and the associated questions of public health and its reform, the background being the complex relationships between the town council and the Kendal Fell Trustees. He paid special attention to the influential role played by the local social reformer John Whitwell, MP for Kendal 1868-1875 but before then among the most active public figures in the town's history and one with very wide contacts in reformist circles nationally and a founder member of the Society (see Chapter 1). This outstanding study effectively weaves together general issues, the local dimension, and the powerful role played by an individual.[76]

Conclusion

As will be clear from this review the Society has made significant contributions to urban and industrial history, as broadly defined by John Marshall, over the last 150 years and undertaken activities which have helped to establish them as legitimate and thriving subjects for study. In addition, its members have often published important contributions in other journals and publications.[77] The Committee for Industrial Archaeology's ambition that wider public interest and involvement in exploring the industrial archaeology of the Lake Counties could be generated has also been amply realised.

As in other aspects of its activities, however, the context in which the Society has operated has been changing dramatically, particularly from the 1980s since when it has no longer had the field largely to itself. Although the decline of 'traditional' industries, especially evident since the 1980s, has gradually eroded the numbers and experiential knowledge of those who had worked in them, nevertheless, over the last 40 years, various local organisations emerged, often with an interest in a specific industry, site or district such as

North Pennines Heritage Trust, the Cumbria Amenity Trust Mining History Society (CATMHS – a local member of the National Association of Mining History Organisations), West Cumbrian Mines Research Group, Nenthead Mines Conservation Society, Mines of Lakeland Exploration Society, Harrington History Group, Cumbrian Railways Association and the wide-ranging Cumbria Industrial History Society (CIHS). Newland Furnace Trust was formed after preliminary field-survey and documentary research undertaken by members of the Industrial Archaeology Committee in the 1990s. Documentary research, field-surveying and publishing has continued to be attractive to, and feasible for, the lone scholar, male or female, academic or enthusiast and, apart from articles in *Transactions*, the results of their work have appeared in some of the other societies' own journals such as *The Mine Explorer* and, since 1998, the CIHS's *The Cumbrian Industrialist.* Books on coal, copper, lead, iron and steel, tobacco, town and port histories, roads, canals and railways have all appeared and, most notably in more recent years, Ian Tyler's remarkable studies of various mining and related industries of the northern Lake District, published in the 1990s and early 2000s, although none of these was published by the Society.[78]

The last 40 years have also witnessed the increasing involvement of university-based and professional field archaeologists. The rescue archaeology boom of the late 1960s and 1970s led to the appointment of archaeological advisers in planning authorities and the emergence of archaeological field units with paid staffs. These have often undertaken large-scale surveys and excavations whose scale and technical requirements have demanded resources and, increasingly, expertise, which are beyond the scope of the individual or local voluntary society. Present-day industrial archaeological research often arises from development control, planning policies, heritage conservation projects, and initiatives sponsored by local and national agencies. In 1989 English Heritage launched the Monuments Protection Programme organised on an industry-by-industry basis to assist with scheduling and this provided the impetus for more detailed thematic and site-based surveys. The 1990s also witnessed a growth in survey work to assist in establishing priorities for site preservation and management. New planning guidelines from Cumbria County Council in 2002-03 resulted in a growth in the number of planning applications outside the National Park that required archaeological works either as a pre-requisite in order to determine a planning application or as a condition of planning consent. Since applications have tended to be concentrated in towns, and 'brownfield' sites in particular, a considerable proportion of these have not only involved industrial remains but also have required significant resources to explore. Development-control advice from conservation officers has also led to detailed recording work on listed industrial structures. The results have often appeared in what has become known as 'grey literature', reports commissioned as part of the work of local authorities or other organisations.[79] These organisations, along with district councils and various charitable foundations, have often provided funds for industrial heritage conservation.

By the 1990s, therefore, the Society had been joined by a number of voluntary, commercial and public organisations which were undertaking research and offering publication outlets. In view of this the Society's precise role in fostering industrial archaeology was reconsidered in 1999 after Peter Robinson had written to the secretary of the Committee for Industrial Archaeology, raising issues related to its future membership and potential role. In response the committee drew up a formal list of broad objectives and then, under Richard Newman's chairmanship between 2004 and 2008, undertook a fuller appraisal of its membership and purpose as part of the Society's ARA review (see Chapter 1) when it was agreed that a major priority should be the scrutiny of the increasing number of planning applications which affected previous industrial sites. The committee subsequently involved itself in developments at Kendal's Woolpack Yard, the Cockpit at Heversham, and the iron furnaces at Backbarrow and Newland. It has also liaised with other organisations to exchange information and preserve industrial sites and archives.[80] In recognition of Mike Davies-Shiel's many contributions the committee worked with the Cumbria Industrial History Society, of which Mike was a founding member, and with the Cumbria Archive Service, to organise and fund, through the Research and Grants Committee, a project to catalogue, identify and digitise Mike's extensive slide collection with a view to making it available to the public.[81] A new initiative in 2012 saw the first joint meeting between members of the Society and the CATMHS, which was held at Tilberthwaite copper mine near Coniston. An industrial walk has become a regular feature of Society activities – Carrock tungsten mine at Brandy Ghyll in the Caldbeck Fells in 2014, Glenridding in 2015, and Newland Furnace and Cunsey Forge in 2016 (fig. 7.11). These activities and the publication of articles in *Transactions*, including substantial contributions by committee members to the 2010 volume as a tribute to Mike Davies-Shiel, have helped the Society retain a high profile regionally and beyond. Most notably, for example, the discovery of the oldest wooden waggonway in Britain, and possibly Europe, at the Caldbeck mines, referred to earlier (see p. 234) was presented to the fourth Early International Railway Conference at University College London in 2008.

John Marshall and Mike Davies-Shiel had noted in 1969 that 'The English Lake District is not, in the minds of its countless visitors, associated with industry'[82] yet, as they and others have amply demonstrated, it has a rich and varied 'industrial history' which has been documented, surveyed and dug from the earliest days of the Society. This history, however defined, has

Fig. 7.11. The CWAAS visit to Carrock Mine in 2014 *(Photograph: Trevor Grahamslaw)*

helped to mould the landscape and built-heritage seen today, not just within the Lake District but throughout present day Cumbria, and the Society has played its part in ensuring that this has been recognised. The Society has explored both the physical remains of activity and the people associated with them – the investors, speculators, managers, workforces and agents. As Angus Winchester's reproduction of the diary of the eighteenth-century yeoman Isaac Fletcher reminds us, industries should not just be studied in isolation. Entrepreneurs could come from a wide range of backgrounds and did not restrict themselves to specific industries. Over a 30 year period Fletcher variously invested in the importation of corn, yarn and plumbago; brewing; textile manufacture, including a stocking factory producing for the American market; and lead mining locally and in Galloway.[83]

The Society's involvement in this field, and particularly industrial archaeology, has changed significantly during the last 50 years but, as the publication programme and the Society's other activities demonstrate, it remains vibrant. The mining and heavy industries based on Cumbria's mineral wealth, rural industrial sites and the period prior to what is popularly conceived to be the period of the 'classic' Industrial Revolution, have arguably attracted most attention. A major challenge in the next 150 years for historians and archaeologists alike will be to document, survey and evaluate the later history and physical legacies of increasingly complex business structures and industrial processes. The diverse and important industrial, commercial and market functions of Carlisle and Kendal also offer considerable scope for further research.[84] As Britain, and Cumbria, enter a post-industrial era, increasingly dominated by services and consumerism, and with new technologies transforming not just production and distribution but even the ways in which business records are kept, the Society's role, and those of other societies in the region, in taking forward research into Cumbria's fascinating 'portmanteau' industrial past may well become not just more challenging, but even more crucial.

Notes and References

1 J.D. Marshall, 'Retrospective', *CW2,* 100 (2000), 271.

2 M. Rix, 'Industrial archaeology', *The Amateur Historian,* 8 (1955), 225-29.

3 The mood and debate are captured in K. Hudson, *Industrial Archaeology* (London, 1963).

4 M. Palmer, 'Industrial archaeology as historical archaeology', *AIA Bulletin* (Association for Industrial Archaeology) 15.2 (1988), 1. Mike-Davies Shiel kept a copy of this with his committee papers.

5 CAS (Kendal), WDMDS.

6 WDMDS/13.

7 J.D. Marshall and M. Davies-Shiel, *Industrial Archaeology of the Lake Counties* (Newton Abbot, 1969).

8 WDMDS/13.

9 Hudson, *Industrial Archaeology,* 13-15.

10 I. Fletcher, 'The archaeology of the West Cumberland coal trade', *CW1,* 3 (1878), 266-313.

11 O. Wood, 'The collieries of J.C. Curwen', *CW2,* 71 (1971), 199-236; 'A colliery payroll in 1802', *CW2,* 72 (1972), 303-19; 'The Chapel Bank Colliery disaster, 1837', *CW2,* 73 (1973), 317-24; *West Cumberland Coal, 1600-1982/3* (CWAAS, Extra Series XXIV, 1988).

12 J.E. Ward, 'John Spedding's account of horses used in the Whitehaven collieries etc. from 1715 onwards', *CW2,* 89 (1989), 181-86; 'The sinking of Saltom Pit, Whitehaven', *CW2,* 91 (1991), 127-44.

13 N. Hair and J. Cotton, 'Excavations at Parton colliery', *CW2,* 100 (2000), 241-60.

14 B. Tyson, 'Coalmining at Reagill, Sleagill and Newby, 1683-*c.*1837', *CW3,* 4 (2004), 175-200; G. Brooks, 'An eighteenth century Westmorland colliery', *CW3,* 10 (2010), 77-92.

15 Marshall, 'Retrospective', 271.The most wide-ranging early study of Furness, however, was not published by the Society: A. Fell, *The Early Iron Industry of Furness and District* (Ulverston, 1908).

16 H.A. Fletcher, 'The archaeology of the West Cumberland iron trade', *CW1,* 5 (1881), 5-21.

17 Revd T. Ellwood, 'The bloomeries of Furness', *CW1,* 8 (1886), 85-92.

18 T. Barlow-Massicks, 'The old blast furnace at Duddon Bridge', *CW1,* 14 (1897), 448-49.

19 W.G. Collingwood and H.S. Cowper, 'Reports on excavations at Springs bloomery, near Coniston Hall, Lancashire, with notes on the probable age of the Furness bloomeries', *CW1,* 15 (1899), 211-28. Also W.G. Collingwood, 'The ancient ironworks of Coniston Lake', *Historic Society of Lancashire and Cheshire,* 53 (1901), 1-22; H.S.

Cowper, 'Excavations at Springs bloomery (iron smelting hearth) near Coniston Hall, Lancashire, with notes on the probable age of the Furness bloomeries', *Archaeological Journal*, 55 (1898), 88-105.

20 J. Wilfred Jackson, 'On the discovery of a bloomery at Lindale church, near Grange-over-Sands', *CW2*, 14 (1914), 256-61.

21 C.A. Parker and Miss M.C. Fair, 'Bloomery sites in Eskdale and Wasdale, Part I', *CW2*, 22 (1922), 90-97; 'Bloomeries in Eskdale and Wasdale Part 2', *CW2*, 25 (1925), 272-74.

22 R.F. Tylecote and J. Cherry, 'The 17th-century bloomery at Muncaster Head', *CW2*, 70 (1970), 69-109.

23 I. Miller, 'Iron working at Cunsey Forge: the archaeological and documentary evidence from an initial survey', *CW3*, 5 (2005), 173-98.

24 J.D. Marshall *et al*, 'The lineaments of Newland iron furnace, 1747-1903', *CW2*, 96 (1996), 195-214.

25 See, for instance, R. Gregory with E. Kingston, *Windermere Reflections. Reflections on history: exploring the industrial archaeology of the Windermere area* (Lancaster, 2014). We are particularly grateful to Rachel Newman for making this important point.

26 B.G. Awty, 'Force Forge in the seventeenth century', *CW2*, 77 (1977), 97-112; B. Tyson, 'Coniston Forge, 14 January 1675 to 12 May 1766', *CW2*, 89 (1989), 187-206; R.T. Spence, 'Mining and smelting by the Cliffords, earls of Cumberland, in Westmorland in the early seventeenth century', *CW2*, 90 (1990), 101-18.

27 A. Harris and R.B. Davis, 'The Hodbarrow iron mines', *CW2*, 68 (1968), 151-68. Harris's subsequent book on Hodbarrow was not published by the Society: A. Harris, *Cumberland Iron: the story of Hodbarrow mine 1855-1968* (Truro, 1970).

28 J.Y. Lancaster and D.R. Wattleworth, *The Iron and Steel Industry of West Cumberland: an historical survey* (Workington, 1977).

29 J. Fisher Crosthwaite, 'The colony of German miners at Keswick', *CW1*, 6 (1883), 344-54; W.G. Collingwood, 'Germans at Coniston in the seventeenth century', *CW2*, 10 (1910), 369-94; *Elizabethan Keswick: extracts from the original account books, 1564-1577 of the German miners in the archives of Augsburg* (CWAAS, Tract Series VIII, 1912); 'The Keswick and Coniston mines in 1600 and later', *CW2*, 28 (1928), 1-32.

30 D. Grant, 'The sixth duke of Somerset, Thomas Robinson and the Newlands mines', *CW2*, 85 (1985), 143-62.

31 R. Smith, S. Murphy and W. Allison, 'The lost German mines at Caldbeck', *CW3*, 1 (2001), 89-104, carried out by the Mines of Lakeland Exploration Society; W. Allison and S. Murphy, 'The German mines of Caldbeck and the discovery of an early primitive wagonway', *CW3*, 10 (2010), 35-54, carried out by the Cumbria Amenity Trust Mining History Society.

32 Revd W. Nall, 'Alston', *CW1*, 8 (1886), 7-20; A. Raistrick, *Two Centuries of Industrial Welfare: the London (Quaker) Lead Company, 1692–1905* (London, 1938).

33 F.J. Monkhouse, 'An eighteenth century company promoter', *CW2*, 40 (1940), 141-53; 'Pre-Elizabethan mining law, with special reference to Alston Moor', *CW2*, 42 (1942), 43-55.

34 P.N. Wilson, 'The Nent Force Level', *CW2*, 63 (1963), 253-80.

35 T. Sopwith, *An Account of the Mining Districts of Alston Moor etc...* (Alnwick, 1833), 30-32.

36 T.M. Banks, C. Nichol and D.G. Bridge, 'Lead mines in the manor of Kinniside', *CW2*, 94 (1994), 215-48.

37 A. Harris, 'A traffic in lime', *CW2*, 77 (1977), 149-55; 'The Tindale Fell waggonway', *CW2*, 72 (1972), 227-47; J.K. Almond, 'Tindale Fell Spelter Works, east Cumbria, and its closure in 1895', *CW2*, 78 (1978), 177-85.

38 R.H. Middleton, 'A survey of the old copper works, Coppermines Valley, Coniston', *CW2*, 85 (1985), 273-75. This was based on a survey of the site by the Cumbria and Lancashire Archaeological Unit.

39 B. Tyson, 'The Troutbeck Park slate quarries: their management and markets 1753-1760', *CW2,* 84 (1984), 167-90; R. David, 'The slate quarrying industry in Westmorland: Part One: the valleys of Troutbeck, Kentmere and Longsleddale', *CW2,* 87 (1987), 215-36; R. David and G.W. Brambles, 'The slate quarrying industry in Westmorland: Part Two: a field survey of selected sites in Troutbeck and Longsleddale', *CW2,* 92 (1992), 213-28; J. Munby, 'Westmorland slate at Buckland (Berkshire) and Bath, 1754-9', *CW2,* 89 (1989), 233-48.

40 A. Crocker and P. Sandbach, 'A Harrison Ainslie gunpowder stock book of 1871-76', *CW3,* 10 (2010), 17-34.

41 C. Howard-Davis, 'The tannery, Rusland, south Cumbria', *CW2,* 87 (1987), 237-50; J. Reeves, 'Recent archaeological work at Rusland tannery, Cumbria', *CW3,* 2 (2002), 210-16; M. Railton, 'The excavation of the remains of an eighteenth-century tannery on land at Riverside Place, K-Village, Kendal', *CW3,* 10 (2010), 3-16.

42 B.C. Jones, 'Carlisle's first factory', *CW2,* 85 (1985), 187-91.

43 W.H. Chaloner, 'The Stockdale family, the Wilkinson brothers and the cotton mills at Cark-in-Cartmel', *CW2,* 64 (1964), 356-72; D.J W. Mawson, 'Langthwaite cotton mill', *CW2,* 76 (1976), 159-83.

44 B. Tyson, 'The Windermere Gasworks, 1862-2004', *CW3,* 7 (2007), 135-68; J. and J. Cherry, 'Seascale Gasworks', *CW3,* 7 (2007), 169-78.

45 Fair, 'Bloomery sites in Eskdale' (1922), 91.

46 M. Davies-Shiel, 'A little known late medieval industry Part 1: the making of potash for soap in Lakeland', *CW2,* 72 (1972), 85-111; 'A little known late medieval industry Part 2: the ash-burners', *CW2,* 74 (1974), 33-64, quotation 34. See also Chapter 6 for M.L. Armitt, 'Fullers and freeholders of the parish of Grasmere', *CW2,* 2 (1908), 136-205 which brings out the early importance of the cloth trade in the area.

47 W.T. McIntire, 'The salt pans of the Solway', *CW2,* 42 (1942), 1-12; B. Tyson, 'The Whitehaven Pier saltpans 1632-86 and their accounts 1675-77', *CW2,* 99 (1999), 195-220. J.C. Varty Smith at the beginning of the century, describing a medieval jug found near Newton Arlosh, mentioned in passing that it was found in association with an 'old salt pan': 'The Newton Arlosh pitcher', *CW2,* 13 (1913), 122-23.

48 J. Hughes, 'Cumberland windmills', *CW2,* 72 (1972), 112-41; B. Tyson, 'Two post-mills at Whitehaven in the 17th century', *CW2*, 88 (1988), 177-92.

49 J.Hughes, 'Mill management at Wigton', *CW2,* 78 (1978), 141-48; B. Tyson, 'Some mill building work at Kendal, 1581-1600', *CW2,* 97 (1997), 101-18; N. Size, 'Click mill at Buttermere and Buttermere notes', *CW2,* 36 (1936), 192-95. For broader surveys see J. Somervell, *Water-power mills of South Westmorland* (Kendal, 1930) and M. Davies-Shiel, *Watermills of Cumbria* (Dalesman Books, 1978).

50 D.G. Watts, 'Water-power and the Industrial Revolution', *CW2,* 67 (1967), 199-205; P.N. Wilson, 'Kendal reservoirs', *CW2,* 73 (1973), 325-47.

51 D.W. Elsworth and S. Whitehead, 'The Barrow steam corn mill, 1870-1972', *CW3,* 10 (2010), 55-76.

52 T. Cann Hughes, 'Notes on some Westmorland clockmakers', *CW2,* 35 (1935), 42-55; 'Notes on some Westmorland clock-makers (Part II)', *CW2,* 37 (1937), 147-52; 'Notes on some Westmorland clockmakers', *CW2,* 39 (1939), 171-89; J.L. Hobbs, 'Former clock and watch makers of North Lonsdale', *CW2,* 57 (1957), 100-24; 'Former clock-and watch-makers of North Lonsdale', *CW2,* 64 (1964), 391-92; M.J. Watts and C.T. Watts, 'The Burton family of clockmakers', *CW2,* 81 (1981), 83-92; B.E. and M.A. Clark, 'William Clark, clockmaker of Kendal 1716-1763', *CW2,* 92 (1992), 135-60.

53 M. Finlay, 'The pewterers of Penrith', *CW2,* 85 (1985), 163-77; B. Tyson, 'Some craftsmen and their houses on Fellside, Kendal, 1655-1877', *CW3,* 9 (2009), 131-52; 'The William Banck and Christopher Woodburne charities for poor apprentices of Kendal; their origins, management, beneficiaries and problems', *CW3,* 14 (2014), 139-60.

54 J. Fell, 'The guides over the Kent and Levens Sands, Morecambe Bay', *CW1,* 7 (1884), 1-26; J. Melville and J.L. Hobbs, 'Furness travelling and postal arrangements in the 18th and 19th centuries', *CW2,* 46 (1946), 77-107; J.L. Hobbs, 'The turnpike roads of North Lonsdale', *CW2,* 55 (1955), 250-92.

55 B.P. Hindle, 'Medieval roads in the diocese of Carlisle', *CW2,* 77 (1977), 83-96; T.H. Hodgson, 'The Military Road in Cumberland', *CW2,* 2 (1902), 274-81; W. Lawson, 'The construction of the Military Road in Cumberland 1751-58', *CW2,* 79 (1979), 109-19;

56 B.C. Jones, 'Westmorland pack-horse men in Southampton', *CW2,* 59 (1959), 65-84.

57 R. Vickers, 'Country carriers in Victorian Lakeland', *CW2,* 98 (1998), 277-86.

58 J.F. Curwen, 'The Lancaster Canal', *CW2,* 17 (1917), 26-47; P.N. Wilson, 'Canal Head, Kendal', *CW2,* 68 (1968), 132-50; A. White, 'Fast packet boats to Kendal', *CW3,* 6 (2006), 145-62.

59 C. Caine, 'The port of Ravenglass', *CW2,* 22 (1922), 101-7; W.T. McIntire, 'The port of Milnthorpe', *CW2,* 36 (1936), 34-60; 'The old port of Sandsfield', *CW2,* 43 (1943), 71-81; W.A.J. Prevost, 'The turnpike and custom port at Allisonbank', *CW2,* 73 (1973), 282-98; M. Robinson, 'The port of Carlisle: trade and shipping in Cumberland, 1675-1735', *CW3,* 8 (2008), 147-58.

60 D. Richardson and M.M. Schofield, 'Whitehaven and the eighteenth-century British slave trade', *CW2,* 92 (1992), 183-204; R. David, '"A perilous situation": Whitehaven-built ships in the Northern Whale Fishery', *CW3,* 10 (2010), 197-216.

61 R.C. Jarvis, 'Whitehaven port records and the Forty-five', *CW2,* 45 (1945), 1-21; 'The appointment of ports in Cumberland, Westmorland and Lancashire-North-of-the-Sands', *CW2,* 47 (1947), 128-65; 'Cumberland shipping in the eighteenth century', *CW2,* 54 (1954), 212-35.

62 J. Melville and J.L. Hobbs, *Early Railway History in Furness* (CWAAS, Tract Series XIII, 1951); Sidney Pollard, 'North-West coast railway politics in the eighteen-sixties', *CW2,* 52 (1952), 160-77; K.N. Smith, 'Correspondence connected with the Newcastle and Carlisle Railway', *CW2,* 60 (1960), 196-98; T.M. Bell and R.W. Rennison, 'The Alston branch of the Newcastle and Carlisle Railway', *CW3,* 1 (2001), 175-90.

63 W. Jackson, 'Whitehaven; its streets, its principal houses, and their inhabitants', *CW1,* 3 (1878), 348-80; W. Nanson, 'On the customary tenure at Carlisle called "Cullery Tenure"', *CW1,* 5 (1881), 305-18.

64 T.F. Tout, *Medieval Town Planning* (Manchester, 1917).

65 W. Douglas Simpson, 'Brough under Stainmore', *CW2,* 46 (1946), 223-83; 'The town and castle of Appleby: a morphological study', *CW2,* 49 (1949), 118-33.

66 A.J.L. Winchester, 'Medieval Cockermouth', *CW2,* 86 (1986), 109-28.

67 E. Hughes, 'The founding of Maryport', *CW2,* 64 (1964), 306-18.

68 R. Newman, 'Harrington: Cumberland's lost town', *CW3,* 8 (2008), 159-68.

69 A. Harris, 'Askam iron: the development of Askam-in-Furness, 1850-1920', *CW2,* 65 (1965), 381-407, quotations 382, 407.

70 A. Harris, 'Millom: a Victorian new town', *CW2,* 66 (1966), 449-67; 'Colliery settlements in east Cumberland', *CW2,* 74 (1974), 118-46.

71 R. Hughes, 'Millom: an industrial colony 1860-1875', *CW3,* 6 (2006), 163-76; J.D. Marshall, 'Cleator and Cleator Moor: some aspects of their social and urban development in the mid-19th century', *CW2,* 78 (1978), 163-75.

72 J.D. Marshall, 'Kendal in the late seventeenth and eighteenth centuries', *CW2,* 75 (1975), 188-257; J. Munby, 'Medieval Kendal: the first borough charter and its connexions', *CW2,* 85 (1985), 95-114; D.J.W. Mawson, 'Brampton in the 1790s', *CW2,* 73 (1973), 299-316.

73 B.C. Jones, 'The topography of medieval Carlisle', *CW2,* 76 (1976), 77-96; D.R. Perriam, 'The demolition of Carlisle city walls', *CW2,* 76 (1976), 184-98. The Society's

CARR series also reports on surveys of the early development of urban landscapes: R.M. Newman, *Carlisle: excavations at Rickergate, 1998-9 and 53-55 Botchergate* (CWAAS, CARR 2, 2001); R. Leech and R.A. Gregory, *Cockermouth, Cumbria: archaeological investigation of three burgage plots in Main Street* (CWAAS, CARR 3, 2012); J. Zant, *Penrith: the historic core* (CWAAS, CARR 6, 2015).

74 A. Harris, 'Denton Holme, Carlisle: Part II The growth of a suburb', *CW2,* 67 (1967), 206-28; J. Godwin, 'Duke Street, Carlisle, a street of handloom weavers', *CW2,* 88 (1988), 225-38; J. Turnbull, 'Housing conditions in Carlisle in 1917', *CW3,* 5 (2005), 217-34.

75 M. Brennand and K.J. Stringer (eds.), *The Making of Carlisle: from Romans to railways* (CWAAS, Extra Series XXXV, 2011) particularly R. Newman, 'The origins of the modern city', 137-52.

76 A. Watterson, 'Working-class housing and related health policies in mid-nineteenth century Kendal with particular reference to the activities of John Whitwell, MP', *CW2,* 87 (1987), 183-214.

77 J.D. Marshall, *Furness and the Industrial Revolution* (Barrow, 1958, rpt. 1981); Davies-Shiel, *Watermills of Cumbria.* One should not overlook the early contribution by C.M.L. Bouch and G.P. Jones in their wide-ranging, *A Short Economic and Social History of the Lake Counties, 1500 to 1830* (Manchester, 1961). The history was continued by J.D. Marshall and J.K. Walton, *The Lake Counties from 1830 to the mid-twentieth century* (Manchester, 1980).

78 All are available through Cumbria Libraries.

79 Summaries of most projects since 2003 are listed in the *Transactions'* roundup of archaeological projects in Cumbria.

80 CAS (Kendal), WDMDS/13.

81 The images can be accessed through the advanced search in CASCAT, the archive service's online catalogue: CAS (Kendal), WDMDS/PC.

82 Marshall and Davies-Shiel, *The Lake Counties,* 13.

83 A.J.L. Winchester, *The Diary of Isaac Fletcher of Underwood, Cumberland, 1756-81* (CWAAS, Extra Series XXVII, 1994), xxiv-xxvi.

84 See, however the excellent summary of developments by C. Newman, 'The industrial and manufacturing city', in Brennand and Stringer, *The Making of Carlisle,* 153-72.

Chapter 8
Social and Political History

Alan G. Crosby

Throughout its 150 years the Society has promoted local history, from its foundation in the days when 'antiquarian' was used to describe such activities and had not yet become a term of contempt or derision, and continuing to the present when *Transactions* is the leading Cumbrian-based medium for the publication of substantive local history research. In the pages of *Transactions* and in the volumes produced by the Society has been published the work of almost all leading historians of the county, many of them active members of the Society, together with others of renown from beyond its borders.

What often passes for national history frequently masks significant regional variation and diversity with too many books making the assumption that what happened in, say, Oxfordshire was also happening in Cumberland and Westmorland, thereby giving a false picture (see for example Chapter 6). A regional society such as CWAAS provides a medium for local case studies that can inform wider debates and assessments, while conversely allowing issues of national significance to be placed under the magnifying glass of local documentary or field evidence, to test whether or not they share characteristics with other areas. Furthermore, the Society's publications have been instrumental in facilitiating that local research by making many Cumbrian records available in print, long before the establishment of record offices. These activities continue to the present and, in the absence of a separate record or parish register society, the Society has undertaken a variety of roles which elsewhere are often performed by separate organisations (see Chapters 1 and 2).

Editions and Transcripts of Archives

A feature of the first decades of the Society's activities was the concern of members about the local archival heritage and the deplorable conditions in which it was so often kept – witness the comments made in 1877 by G.E. Moser, introducing an article about the parish registers of Kendal:

> if anyone should wish to obtain information as to the contents of the missing register book [1631-1679] a few of the Bishop's

> Transcripts for the period comprised may be found in a mouldy and chaotic heap of documents, which is now lying on the floor of a room in the Archdeaconry of Lancaster, where they came along with other important ecclesiastical documents ... from the vestry of the parish church at Lancaster, having been transmitted there with the assistance of a cart and pitchfork from the Archdeaconry Court at Richmond ... Many of the bonds and other papers in this heap are half moulded away with the damp, and whether the documents will ever be cared for and preserved is not for me to say [but] I do trust that those who feel the importance of preserving these documents will not allow them to remain in the state that they are in.[1]

In the absence of a record society, and long before the creation of county record offices, individual local historians sought to make primary sources more accessible. Much attention focused on parish registers, partly because of their relevance to the genealogy of leading Cumbrian families. Thus, in volume 4 of *Transactions* in 1880 there were substantial articles on the registers of Hawkshead, Dean, Bridekirk, Kirkby Thore and Hayton. These, and most of their numerous successors over the next 40 years, did not purport to be full transcripts but rather described the registers and their survival, discussed the evidence for leading families, and picked out 'curious' entries which were of historical interest or merely quaint. This approach was in many ways unsatisfactory, but fully-fledged transcripts could not be accommodated within the format of a *Transactions* series and the eventual result was the development of the Society's parallel series of parish registers.

Others delved into the archives of local government, looking especially at the period before the mid-eighteenth century and tracing the development of municipal institutions. For example in 1882, when the president, Richard Ferguson, was not only chancellor of the diocese but also served as mayor of Carlisle, he read a paper assessing the content and importance of the 'Dormont Book' (fig. 8.1), the city's assembly minutes (1561-1666), register of deeds (1654-1656) and register of apprenticeship indentures (1672-1844). Ferguson observed that the 800 or so indentures formed 'a most important mass of genealogical material relating to the freemen of Carlisle' and suggested that they should be indexed. He thus explicitly emphasised the prominence of genealogical research in the thinking of antiquarians of the period,[2] but Ferguson was not simply an antiquarian, for in the same volume he contributed an analytical paper which for the first time identified the coat of arms in the initial letter of the charter granted to the city by Edward II. He showed that it belonged to Sir Andrew de Harcla and that the dramatic drawing of a besieged city which forms the initial was therefore a representation of the defence of Carlisle against the Scots by Sir Andrew in

1315, the knight who is prominently portrayed presumably being the man himself.[3] Later the Society went on to publish substantial volumes of the early records of Carlisle and Kendal in a number of volumes of the Extra and Record Series.[4]

Fig. 8.1. The Dormont Book, *CW1*, 6 (1883), opposite 334

Although the work of the Record Commission (1800-37) had led to the establishment of the Public Record Office and the publication of transcripts of some key groups of national archives, very much more remained largely inaccessible in distant London repositories. Some members of the Society began to explore these almost unknown resources, delivering papers and publishing extracts and calendars in *Transactions*. In 1877, for example, Sir George Duckett produced an interesting summary of evidence from the Cottonian manuscripts in the British Museum relating to the administration of the Anglo-Scottish border in the early-sixteenth century. He included transcripts of the pensions lists of the gentry of the West March liable to border service, the device (or government strategy) for safeguarding the West March, and lists of the names of deputy wardens and pensioners in the East and Middle Marches, the council and household of the warden, and all the gentlemen in Westmorland, in the period 1515-1526.[5] A comparable exercise was undertaken by T.H. Hodgson in 1894 when he provided extracts of numerous references to Cumberland and Westmorland from the published register of the Privy Council in the reigns of Henry VIII, Edward VI and Mary I.[6] Some years later Hodgson published extracts from the legislation and enactments of Elizabeth I relating to Cumbria, including letters to the wardens of the marches.[7] Such work was of great value, both in providing information and also in stimulating ideas for research – Hodgson himself contributed other work on, for example, the military routes between Carlisle and Newcastle from the Roman period to the late eighteenth century. An examination of surviving pipe rolls led to a volume in the Extra Series.[8]

We should recognise the tremendous potential impact of such comparatively modest exercises. For the first time local historians in Cumberland and Westmorland could make use of definitive evidence, drawn from primary sources, about, for example, the experience of the two counties in the troubled years of the early Tudor period. No longer must they rely solely on doubtful hearsay, unreliable anecdote or the unsupported statements of earlier antiquarians. An interesting example of the growing emphasis on historical accuracy, and of scepticism about the work of those earlier antiquarians, was given in 1922 when Sir Samuel Haslam Scott contributed a note concerning the persistent belief that the Kendal cloth industry was founded by Flemish weavers – a story also found in many other textile towns. He firmly refuted the claim, pointing out that there was no evidence whatsoever from documentary sources and that all the stories apparently derive from an unsupported statement in Nicolson and Burn's *History* of 1777.[9]

But it was essential for the reader to be discerning, since it was usually unclear as to what criteria had been employed in selecting extracts, and some sense of the reliability of the researcher was also needed. In the mid-1890s the Revd James Wilson contributed what might have seemed a promising piece of innovative research on the victims of 'the Tudor Disestablishment' in

Cumberland and Westmorland. His lack of objectivity was quickly revealed: referring to Edward VI, he observed that 'The religious persons ejected from the monasteries were in no envious circumstances when the youthful son of the Royal exterminator ascended his father's throne'. Wilson claimed that in trying to trace the pensions paid to former monks he had 'searched in the Public Record Office for the documents connected with these ... for Cumberland and Westmorland, but for the reign of Edward VI have met with only partial success'. Our sympathy is soon undermined by his casual admission that 'It is only fair to say that my search was neither very careful nor very extensive'. The article includes a full transcript of the commission carried out under Mary to determine the circumstances of former monks in Westmorland and Cumberland, but overall the value of the exercise is clearly questionable.[10] In a similar vein, the Revd Henry Whitehead of Lanercost provided a catalogue of Westmorland parish registers, admitting that he had personally only ever looked at one parish register from the county and would have done the exercise for Cumberland were it not for the fact that Westmorland offered 'less occasion for digression' (presumably because he thought it was rather dull) and in any case had fewer parishes.[11]

The publication of edited transcripts continued into the 1960s. In 1960 J.L. Hobbs, in his transcript of the 1847 journal of the schoolboy John Wilson Soulby of Rampside Academy, considered that although the work was

> of small literary importance the writings are interesting, describing the passing mid-19th century scene in a small Furness village and its immediate district, and have some value in assisting to advance knowledge of several minor points of local history [but]many entries include repetitious formal observations. To avoid undue length, and tedium in reading, a number of these, and other non-informative dates and remarks are omitted, but the most interesting excerpts are quoted *in extenso*. Although perhaps some of the original schoolboy naivety has been lost by this necessary editing, it is thought that nothing of historical value has been sacrificed.

The accuracy of transcripts was another cause for concern: in 1957 Hobbs co-authored an article with F.L. Barnes concerning the 'Four and Twenty' of Dalton-in-Furness, which was essentially a transcript of the vestry minutes covering 1573-1721. It had been made by the late Edward Walker of Ulverston, deputy steward of ten manors in Furness, but the original was now presumed lost and unfortunately, as they acknowledged, Walker's transcript was not entirely accurate, particularly in the translation of Latin entries.[12]

The treasures that lay hidden in private archives were highlighted by a talk given to the Society in 1918 by Daniel Scott, who explained that three weeks before he had been given 'by the courtesy of Lord Hothfield, one of our patrons, an opportunity of examining at Appleby Castle a very large number of parchments, books, and other documents, most of which had been found recently among his muniments'. Lord Hothfield had 'entered heartily into a proposal that the whole of his muniments at Appleby Castle, Skipton Castle, and in the strong rooms of his bankers and legal advisers in London and Appleby, should be carefully examined and properly calendared' by Miss Dorothy Shilton of the PRO, 'one of the leading palaeographers of the day'. Among her discoveries were the original wills of George, Earl of Cumberland, and of Lady Anne Clifford herself; medieval deeds; the original 1330 charter for the market and fair at Brough; books belonging to the 'Shepherd Lord'; Lady Anne's book containing her claim to the tithes of Clifford, Westmorland and Vescy (1616) with her own handwritten notes; and her account books for 1665, 1667 and 1668.[13] The sense of excitement, of gazing for the first time upon 'these wonderful records of antiquity' which would help to rewrite key aspects of Cumbrian history, was palpable. Other contributors drew attention to the major problems posed by lack of access to key records. For example, in his 1924 article on the history of Barrow, based on the remarkable work of the local historian William Barrow Kendall (d. 1919) but including much pioneering research of his own, Paul Kelly commented that 'The court rolls of the Manor after the grant to the Duke of Albemarle in 1660 are in private hands and inaccessible. The Dalton Registers only give bare lists of names and I have not had an opportunity of seeing any of the Richmond wills'.[14]

Much of this early work on primary sources is disappointing in terms of its real historical value. The absence of analysis is problematic, and the thinness of content, selectivity of the extracts (without evidence of the criteria used) and uncertainties over the academic rigour of the work mean that what seems promising often fails to satisfy. Sometimes articles were published for flimsy reasons. Perhaps the most ostentatious name-dropping in the Society's history was in 1921, when Colonel Oliver North published an edition of the travel diary of the fifteenth-century French soldier and diplomat Sir Gilbert de Launoy: 'After the Armistice', wrote Colonel North, 'I was quartered at the Chateau d'Auvaing, Hainault, Belgium, the residence of the Comte de Launoy, Master of the Household of H.M. the Queen of the Belgians'. De Launoy showed him the diary of his ancestor (1386-1462) and North transcribed it. The only rationale for its inclusion in *Transactions* was that the medieval de Launoy passed through Carlisle, on which there are five lines of text. Almost all the article is a biographical account of the man in question.[15] No less unsatisfactory was Francis Grainger's article on the diary of James Jackson (1650-1683) which had been discovered in the Holm Cultram parish chest. He transcribed the diary in full, but the 1½ page introduction did not give any background at all and made no attempt even to identify who James Jackson was.[16]

Other writers had no hesitation in expressing personal opinions, in a way which would now be regarded as inappropriate in an academic publication. T.E. Casson, introducing the diary of William Fleming of Rowhead in Pennington, observed that Fleming was

> perhaps a rather coarse and illiterate man; but his narrative has the virtue of fidelity, joined to some vigour of expression. His handwriting is, at its best, most legible and even fine. Unfortunately his spelling and punctuation are far from the same excellence. The description Fleming furnishes of country life at that period is of a backward community, where drunkenness seems to be prevalent and hygiene imperfectly understood. The diary, however, has raciness and a good native pith.

It is hard to disagree with that judgment: on 6 May 1852 Fleming recorded that he had 'attended the Funeral of John Postlethwaite Late of Greenmoorhouse. He was not taken into the Church owing to being so far decomposed and the smell being so intollerable and the whole service was read over him at the Grave side. He was 61 years old and very corpulent'. Casson was no less scathing about another diarist, Margaret Ashburner of Ireleth, whose writing covered the years from 1814 to 1819. This is in fact a very rare and important instance of a young countrywoman's personal testimony from the early nineteenth century, but he was far from impressed: 'It is, in the last degree, homely and unpretentious. The spelling is extremely archaic, and might have passed muster in Tudor times. Indeed, not to put too fine a point on it, the orthography is shocking, and may possibly be barely intelligible. The poor girl, from our view of things, seems to have been very ill-educated'.[17]

Ecclesiastical and religious history

Given that so many of the active early members of the Society were clergymen, it is unsurprising that churches featured prominently in the programmes of visits and in contributions to *Transactions*. Until the Second World War almost every volume included at least one article, and some had several, 'profiling' a parish church, giving an architectural history and description, and an account of the parish from the perspective of the church and the incumbents. Many also included a brief account of the registers, church plate and any outstanding monuments. In most cases these papers had been read *in situ* during a Society visit to the church. More analytical papers on ecclesiastical history were, and indeed continue to be, much less frequent. Nonetheless, some pioneering work was undertaken in the late nineteenth century.

Thus, in 1884 the Revd Edmund Venables, canon residentiary and precentor of Lincoln Cathedral, published the fruits of his research into church dedications in the diocese of Carlisle, giving a full list and setting out reasons to be sceptical about claims that some local dedications originated in what was then called the 'British period'. He discussed the dedications to British saints, such as Patrick, Bridget, Begha, Kentigern, Cuthbert, and Oswald, and identified the distinctively Cumbrian problems not only that in many instances the dedications were unknown, especially those in small remote chapels, but also that in consequence recent adoptions were particularly numerous. The theme was revisited in 1925 in a joint paper by T.H.B. Graham, a prolific writer on the medieval history of Cumberland, and W.G. Collingwood. They reviewed the dedications of all churches, chapels and religious houses, together with holy wells, in the diocese of Carlisle and attempted a systematic chronology and analysis of origins and patterns, focusing on the pre-Conquest and immediate post-Conquest periods. An unusual aspect of diocesan history was investigated by Richard Ferguson in 1885, when he asked why Alston was in the diocese of Durham but also in the county of Cumberland, while T.H.B. Graham, in a somewhat unstructured contribution in 1925, looked at the history of the diocese of Carlisle from the perspective of its organisation, condition and administration, pointing out serious problems including absentee incumbents and poverty, but eventually losing his way in discourses about ecclesiastical vestments and the forms of service used in medieval churches.[18]

The theme of chapels and their significance was extended in 1885 by the Revd Canon Henry Ware, who discussed the one at Killington near Kirkby Lonsdale in the context of a 1696 lawsuit concerning the curate's salary. His colleague Canon Simpson then explored the medieval origins of the same chapel, widening the scope to include those elsewhere in Westmorland, their status and relationship with mother churches and their financial basis including dues and burial rights. Twenty years later, when Henry Ware had become bishop of Barrow-in-Furness and was president of the Society, he gave a scholarly, wide-ranging account of another little-considered aspect of ecclesiastical history, the use of lay readers, noting that because of the miserable poverty of livings and the lack of endowments, lesser chapels in the Lake Counties were usually served by such men, who were often schoolmasters. Few became priests, and since formal consecration of chapels was not a major consideration, the widespread use of readers remained typical until the mid-eighteenth century.[19]

More recently, Margaret Clark published a superb and richly-researched paper on the Church of England in Kendal between the Reformation and the civil wars, vividly illustrated with quotations from a wide range of contemporary sources to support her contention, set out in an arresting opening sentence, that 'sixteenth century Kendal appeared a Protestant island in an unreformed sea, providing a parallel with Manchester in Lancashire, or, at the other end of the country, Lewes in Sussex'.[20] Alongside Margaret Clark's paper there has been a renewed interest in the various nineteenth-century descriptions of churches in the diocese of Carlisle which has resulted in the Society publishing edited volumes by Lawrence Butler and by Jane Platt. Rose Castle, the future of which remains uncertain, has been the subject of another timely volume published by the Society.[21] Taken together studies such as these have provided important new perspectives on the nature and organisation of the Church of England in the Lake Counties, as well as emphasising regional and local distinctiveness, countering the generalities which were so prevalent in the published literature by drawing attention to the quite different circumstances which so often prevailed in Cumbria.

Nonconformity and religious dissent were the subject of many articles in the 'middle years' of the Society, and recently there has been a major revival of interest in the subject. The concentration of dissent in the Brampton area of north-east Cumberland was the subject of a particularly impressive early article by the Revd Henry Whitehead, published in 1885. It begins by noting that in 1854 the Revd P.R. Crole, minister of the Brampton Presbyterian congregation, provided a completely incorrect account of its history when he gave an address on laying the foundation stone of the present church. Whitehead tartly commented that his source was an indenture of 1649: 'Mr. Crole, however, though he seems to have read no further than the first line ... did manage to read that aright; which is more than can be said of some who came after him'. He then discusses, in forensic detail, the history of the church during the seventeenth and eighteenth centuries, the ministers, evidence for their tenure and links with other congregations, and their roles in preaching. His work was supplemented in 1903 with further exemplary research undertaken by Henry Penfold, making use of sources such as accounts, briefs, baptism and burial registers and private papers to place the chapel in the context of the wider community of the Brampton area.[22]

Nonconformity was also investigated by Norman Wilson, who transcribed part of a volume of minutes kept in the early 1660s by the Committee for Ejected Ministers in Cumberland and Westmorland, and discovered inside a volume at Kendal parish church. Dissent of a different sort was considered by Roy Hudleston in his analysis based on the registers of the Commissioners for Forfeited Estates; he listed the estates of eleven leading Catholic recusants in Cumberland in 1723-24 and gave extensive biographical details. Janet Martin painstakingly reconstructed the genealogies of a series of inter-related Baptist families from the Hawkshead area between the late-seventeenth and mid-nineteenth centuries, reminding us of the importance of kinship and social networks and the opportunities afforded by family reconstruction techniques. She also emphasised how nonconformist congregations, unconstrained by parish and chapelry boundaries, might draw members from considerable distances.[23] Ian Moonie's work on the Abbey Street Dissenting Meeting in Carlisle included analysis of the social class, occupations and place of residence of the congregation, and emphasised how the role of an individual – in this case the minister George Thomson – could be crucial. In later articles Moonie analysed other dissenting groups and meetings in the city, and collectively his work provides a uniquely detailed picture of nonconformity in a medium-sized urban area from the late seventeenth to the mid-nineteenth centuries. The Society's recent publication of R.B. Wordsworth's *The Cockermouth Congregational Church Book (1651-c1765)* has provided a scholarly edition of a rare surviving manuscript from that era.[24]

In 1947 T.H. Bainbridge recounted the travels of John Wesley in Cumberland, derived from his published diaries and setting out a table of itineraries and dates of visits to specific places. More recently Lydia Gray has looked in fine detail at Methodism in the area between the Eden and Cross Fell, focusing on the meeting at Hunsonby which emerged in the 1820s and by 1871 was one of the largest in the Kirkoswald Circuit, at a time when Methodism had become the largest religious denomination in the district (fig. 8.2). Using membership lists, census returns and registers she was able to reconstruct key aspects of the Methodist community in the half-century from 1821.[25]

Fig. 8.2. Hunsonby Chapel (*photograph by courtesy of Lydia Gray*)

Nevertheless, there is much that is not covered; in particular, the Society has published little on the Quakers, despite their importance to Cumbria and the significance of Cumbria in Quaker history. It is also apparent that after 1939 there was a rapid lessening of interest in religious history and church history in general, and only in recent decades has work revived. However, in 1949 a very comprehensive and detailed article on the history and architecture of Carlisle Cathedral, by C.G. Bulman, included some of the most lyrical writing in the history of *Transactions*, worth quoting as a reminder that local history is in part about a sense of place, and to demonstrate that the aspects of antiquarianism still flourished after the Second World War:

> We have at Carlisle, in our eastern façade, a supreme achievement; it is a masterpiece, and has been well called a piece of poetry in stone ... To see [the choir] on a morning in summer, when the early sun throws a radiance through the great east window and revitalises the slumbering splendours of the painted glass and fills the east end with a shimmering light, is a sight not easily forgotten; or on an afternoon in late autumn, when the mellow sun throws long shafts of mote-filled, melancholy gold, slanting from the clerestory windows. Best of all, perhaps, is to stand in a dark aisle on a winter's evening, when the faint lights throw masses of mysterious shadow through the aisles and along the roof, while the young voices in the choir rise and soar and die away.[26]

Demography and medical history

Church and parish records provided the raw material for early analyses of population history. Their use for population analysis can be traced back to the late-eighteenth century, when the growing interest in statistics demanded the exploitation of reasonably reliable and systematic sets of data collected over long periods. The first census in 1801 included the requirement that data derived from parish registers should be tabulated to show population trends over the previous century. From that point onwards local historians, including the clergymen who were so prominent in this field and who themselves had custody of the registers, began to investigate the content of parish records, looking both at the systematic data and at the non-statistical evidence provided by register entries, churchwardens' accounts and other papers. In 1886, for example, Charles Parker gave a narrative account of the content of the Gosforth registers from their beginning in 1571, looking at such themes as plague (or periods of high mortality), suicide, marriage rates and surnames. Five years later Henry Barnes, author of several important papers on local medical history, published the first detailed account of the great mortality crisis which affected the north-western counties in 1623-24. He began with an account of plague in general, and then used parish register evidence (with detailed statistical analysis) to focus on the sickness of 1597-98 and the great mortality of the mid-1620s. Linking this with contemporary comment in, for example, the State Papers, he examined register evidence from Cumberland and Westmorland and southern and central Scotland. In line with contemporary opinion he attributed the great mortality to plague but included observations relating to famine, an explanation which has more recently found greater, though by no means unanimous, favour.[27]

A more recent study of the outbreak of plague in Carlisle in December 1597, by J. Hughes, used documents in the Mounsey-Heysham papers, deposited at the record office in the late 1960s. These including a list of 323 householders and their approximate place of residence, and the names of 242 households who were 'visited'. The article was constructed around conjectural statistics based on this evidence, but context was provided by letters from the Council of the North, the city chamberlain's accounts showing reliefs granted, and emergency measures put in place including barricades, the opening of pesthouses and cabins, and regulations for nursing. Colin Phillips assessed comparable new evidence relating to the outbreak of plague in Kendal in 1598. Two lists, apparently produced by the Corporation, gave the numbers and names of those who died, listed under headings for different parts of the town, and suggesting the terrifying scale of mortality. Having carefully cross-checked with parish register evidence, and with a scrupulous comparison with the evidence from other places in Cumbria, Phillips concluded that some 1471 deaths could certainly be attributed to plague (that is, perhaps half the population of the town) and that the impact of the devastation is supported by abundant circumstantial evidence.[28]

Henry Barnes investigated evidence for the hospitals of medieval Cumbria, considering in particular leper hospitals, and with praiseworthy scepticism noted that much mythology surrounded the subject. He pointed out that the place-name 'Spital' has a more general meaning but noted incontrovertible documentary evidence for such establishments at Carlisle, Appleby and Kendal. A century later, in 1987, Bill Wiseman extended Barnes' work; he looked at the general role and function of hospitals in the medieval period and provided a detailed gazetteer of seventeen definite and three doubtful Cumbrian examples. A subsequent pair of papers looked in great detail at the hospital of St Nicholas, Carlisle, and its masters, giving a definitive account of a major urban institution. Hospitals in more recent centuries have rarely been considered by local historians in the region. Barbara Copeland provided an authoritative article on the establishment of the Westmorland Sanatorium, for the treatment of tuberculosis patients, which opened at

Meathop near Grange-over-Sands in 1900, while Graham Brooks discussed the building of the Cumberland and Westmorland Joint Lunatic Asylum at Carleton near Carlisle (better known as Garlands Hospital) in the 1850s (fig. 8.3). Paul Cheesebrough looked at the Ethel Hadley Orthopaedic Hospital for Crippled Children at Calgarth Park on Windermere, opened in 1920 and closed in 1970. This was founded following major epidemics of polio in Westmorland and adjacent counties, at a time when there was a realisation that this and related diseases were not only treatable but also preventable. It is, however, notable that Cumbrian local historians have apparently only looked at hospitals which were unusual and distinctive – nothing has yet appeared on any aspect of public health in general in the later nineteenth or twentieth centuries.[29]

Susan Scott and C.J. Duncan used parish registers to look at mortality peaks at Penrith in the seventeenth and eighteenth centuries, arguing (by means of statistical calculations and tabulations) that the identifiable patterns correlate most satisfactorily with the known behaviour of smallpox epidemics. They suggested that this disease recurred at roughly five-year intervals and had a particular impact upon children. Continuing their analysis of the particularly good set of registers from Penrith, they also analysed patterns of marital fertility in the parish between 1557 and 1812. They made numerous comparisons with similar demographic calculations undertaken in other English towns and argued persuasively that under-nutrition or malnutrition played a powerful role in reducing fertility until the

Fig. 8.3. Cumberland and Westmorland Joint Lunatic Asylum (Garlands Hospital) *(reproduced by permission of Cumbria County Council, Carlisle Library)*

mid-eighteenth century. Between 1751 and 1781 the burial registers of Holy Trinity, Whitehaven, recorded cause of death in many cases, and provided ancillary detail about the deceased including place of residence. Jean Ward analysed these to give a picture of mortality in the town, ranging from the unhelpful generic descriptions such as 'decline' to the medically-specific (for example, inflammation of the bowels) and the too-numerous instances of accidental death in the pits or in the maritime trades, as well as noting the prevalence of epidemic diseases.[30]

In 1915 the parish records of Holm Cultram were used by Francis Grainger in a short article on poor relief in Cumberland during the seventeenth and eighteenth centuries. This work, though modest, was the first contribution to the question of poverty and its social history to be published by the Society and is significant because it exploited a scarcely-used source – the quarter sessions petitions which would later emerge as a crucial quarry of evidence on the operation of the Old Poor Law. More sophisticated is the 1953 article by Gwilym Jones on the eighteenth-century population of Broughton-in-Furness. He provided a wide-ranging demographic analysis based on the parish registers and manor court tenant lists, and used multipliers to calculate the likely size of the population and assessed evidence for rapid growth and the locations within the parish where (using architectural evidence) it could be shown that development was taking place. The review also considered illness and mortality, and tried to approach the vexed question of in-migration by identifying distinctive surnames (eleven of the 35 'outside' names were Manx, Welsh, Scottish or Irish).[31]

Two years earlier Francis James had assessed the population of the diocese of Carlisle in 1676, using documents in the Bodleian Library, Oxford, which 'contain a list of the parishes in the diocese of Carlisle with the number of inhabitants old enough to communicate, the number of Roman Catholics (including reputed Catholics) and the number of Quakers and other Dissenters'. These were the local returns for what is generally known as the Compton Census, a national statistical survey of religious observance, but there was no indication in the article that the author was aware of its wider context.[32] Other exercises were undertaken by Edward Conder, who in 1919 provided a transcript of the 1671 hearth tax returns for the barony of Kendal – a notably early instance of the use of a source which more recently has become of outstanding importance in demographic analysis, studies of housing and the distribution of wealth – and by J.L. and A.D. Kirby in their 1958 transcript of the Carlisle poll tax for 1377. Also in 1958, Gwilym Jones published a wide-ranging overview of the demography of Cumberland and Westmorland in the eighteenth century, using as its starting point Thomas Denton's 1688 population estimates for each parish in the diocese. He then used parish registers and census evidence, to analyse regional variations, urban growth and rural depopulation, mortality crises, baptism and burial ratios and, importantly, the sharp differences between the experiences of Cumberland and Westmorland.[33]

This highlights an important change in perspective during the previous 40 years. Traditionally, the majority of material published in *Transactions* had been parochial in both the literal and metaphorical senses. By the late 1950s, however, there was both a powerful awareness of the regional distinctiveness of Cumbria and also an appreciation of the often profound variations within the region. An increasing number of articles looked at the Lake Counties in their entirety, charting the varying experiences of this extraordinarily diverse area and demonstrating that, for example, the fringes of Morecambe Bay did not necessarily share the same historical processes and trends as the southern shores of the Solway. This change was superbly exemplified in 1969 in the first article published by a great historian of Cumbria, John Marshall of Lancaster University who, after observing that 'We in the north-west are fortunate in that important pioneering work in both industrial and regional social history has already been performed', analysed out-migration using census returns and argued that 'the Lake Counties, in the 19th century and much earlier, were suppliers of people to other regions: indeed, it is probably true to say that much of the basic social history of our region must be concerned with its emigrants'. He assessed internal migration, seasonal migration, and the impact of improving communications, access to the outside world and the expansion of horizons, and emigration to London, Northumberland and Durham, 'to say nothing about the Cumbrians who went overseas during the 19th century'. Marshall concluded his article with a typically wry observation: 'One rather piquant piece of information emerges from the 1891 [census]; Scandinavians no longer favoured the Lake Counties, and the enumerators of that year could find only six Norwegian-born people in Cumberland, and one in Westmorland! Thus had the great movements of history altered in character'. W.R. Sellick's original piece on the lack of a permanent Jewish community in Whitehaven, as opposed to short-term migrants, added to this impression; there were simply not enough business opportunities to retain them in contrast to the rapidly-developing cities of Liverpool, Manchester and Glasgow. The significant exception to this pattern of events, was the major migration of Scots, Irish, Cornish and Devonians in the later nineteenth century, attracted by the mushrooming of mining and heavy industry along the west coast in particular (see p. 286).[34]

Political and military history

Traditionally, coverage of political and military history in *Transactions* was largely confined to four key topics: medieval officials and military events;

the Debatable Lands and the Scottish border; the Civil Wars of the 1640s; and the second Jacobite Rising of 1745-46. In 1962 David Kirby set out a sophisticated analysis of Strathclyde and Cumbria in the period from *c*.450 to the English conquest of Carlisle in 1092,[35] but although these seven centuries have been dealt with in articles on archaeological themes little else has appeared which looks at them from a historical perspective. One fundamental difficulty is the great scarcity of early documentary evidence from the region, which means that until the quantity of archival sources increased in the thirteenth century historians in the past had little on which to base their analyses.

The sense of relief which access to archives represented for professional historians is conveyed in the words of John Morris of Magdalen College, Oxford, who in 1903 gave a paper on Cumberland and Westmorland military levies in the reigns of Edward I and Edward II:

> The fascination of history is most powerfully felt when we enter into detail; such detail can only be got from the public records. Mr Bain did splendid work in his four volumes of Documents relating to Scottish History ... I have found that it has been useful to study at more length certain documents which he calendared somewhat shortly; and, moreover, the new catalogue in the Record Office is so well arranged that I have been able to examine documents which he could not find.

He discussed, among other sources, payrolls, horse lists, contracts to serve the king, writs of summons to war, and registers of feudal service, and explained their limitations against the background of the Scottish Wars and their impact on Cumberland.[36] Editions of other medieval documents have also been published, including two fourteenth-century accounts of Robert Bruce's 1322 raid in Furness and Lonsdale, reproduced as a full transcript. Colm McNamee published a transcript of a document from the Exchequer Records, which recorded in detail the amounts paid by Cumberland communities to buy off the Scots under Robert and Edward Bruce in 1313-1314, and gave a thorough and accessible account of the raids which so badly affected Cumbria in the second decade of the fourteenth century. Katherine Longley's complete and scholarly transcript of the 1328-1329 accounts of John de Preston of Wigton, which are almost certainly the oldest surviving churchwarden's accounts for anywhere in England, included references to the losses sustained during the raids. However, it is striking, in the light of current debates about the publication of texts only in Latin, that even in 1983 no attempt was made to provide either an English translation or even an English summary. Over 20 years later Jeremy Godwin, one of the archivists at Carlisle, rectified this omission, noting that Longley's article was a valuable contribution but one 'that for most readers [is] now diminished in its effects by being wholly in Latin, and medieval technical Latin at that'. Godwin's clear and fluent translation provides a splendidly accessible route to this remarkable document.[37]

In 1919 John Richard Magrath, provost of Queen's College, Oxford (which has a very close connection with Cumbria, its original endowment of 1341 being the manor of Renwick) published a fine biographical study of Sir Robert Parvyng, MP for Cumberland and chancellor of England from 1341 until his death in 1343. The article identified him as a Carlisle man, traced his family connections and role as a Cumbrian landowner, and teased out his networks of political linkages and roles. An article such as this, which would have been eminently suitable for publication in a major national journal such as the *English Historical Review*, points to the growing involvement of professional historians in the work of county societies, although at this stage most were active only in the fields of ecclesiastical, political and constitutional history.

Another biographical essay was by Marjorie Rowling, author of several best-selling popular books on everyday life in medieval England. She had researched the life of William de Parr (*c.*1350-1404), knight to Henry IV, and proposed that 'by looking at the life of one man, we can consider the rise and fall in family fortunes as exemplified by that of the Parrs of Kendal Castle through a period of great political upheaval and transition', pointing to patronage, marriage alliances, and the ability of the head of the household to avail himself of opportunities for advancement. The first half of her paper focused on Parr's political career in the retinue of John of Gaunt, and the latter's European activities, but the second looked at his local influence and role in Westmorland and adjacent counties as commissioner of the peace. Her scholarly and sober account contrasted with the gushing and highly unreliable story of Queen Katherine Parr given in 1895 by Frederick Garnett, in which he referred to 'the fair Westmorland Dame who became the first Protestant Queen of England'. Susan James demonstrated convincingly, in her 1988 article, that in fact 'Queen Kateryn Parr' (as she rather self-consciously terms the lady) had no connections with Kendal at all apart from her ancestry.[38]

The romantic and intense story of the Debatable Lands and the Anglo-Scottish border rivalry, particularly of the fifteenth to the seventeenth centuries, and its legacy in terms of landscape, architecture and society, have been perennially popular topics among historians and writers in the area. As noted earlier, the publication of extracts from State Papers and other central government sources allowed local historians to look at more reliable evidence for the period. In 1912 the prolific and enthusiastic T.H.B. Graham published a lengthy article about the Debatable Lands, using the evidence of charters and boundary claims to reconstruct aspects of the topography and landscape, before assessing the contemporary evidence for lawlessness, the role of landowners, the partition agreement of 1552, and the subsequent history of the area. A second article, in 1914, focused on the Border families including the Grahams and the Armstrongs, and Graham also wrote extensively on other families from the area north-east of Carlisle, as well as churches, parishes and baronies in the area. Joseph Gavin later analysed the 1597 negotiations between England and Scotland, which led to the Treaty of Carlisle and a significant reduction in border tensions. He set his detailed account in the context of the numerous domestic feuds and the complex religious problems of the West March, and the decay of churches such as those at Bewcastle and Arthuret. Gwilym Jones took up the same theme in 1969, moving away from a purely military and political perspective to consider the social and economic conditions of the western borderlands at the end of the sixteenth century. He looked at questions of lordship and social structure, emphasising the highly unstable nature of local society in the reign of James VI and I, and showing how the king and his commissioners devised sometimes drastic strategies for pacification which included resettlement and transportation of local families to the Roscommon plantations in Ireland.[39]

Interest in the Civil War focused particularly on the siege of Carlisle in 1644-45 since there was little other military action in the county and this major episode is reasonably well documented in local sources. As early as 1884 William Nanson published an article which included a transcript of a selection of key documents concerning efforts by the city authorities to raise money for the war, and the melting-down of Corporation plate for emergency coinage. Seven years later Richard Ferguson wrote a detailed narrative account of the siege itself, using contemporary sources and a coloured plan showing General Leslie's positions on the roads into the town. Denis Perriam, in an important paper which made a valuable contribution to studies of Carlisle Cathedral, investigated the impact of the Civil War siege and the despoiling and demolition of the former priory buildings, including portions of the nave, after the siege had ended.[40]

In contrast, some writers have looked at the wars more generally and at their aftermath. Clark Colman considered what he called 'the paralysis of the Cumberland and Westmorland army' during the war, and exposed the 'crippling split among its gentry officers' that he concluded was the cause of this. He suggested that bitter personal animosities between the Musgrave and Lowther families were at the root of it all, but in setting out the background he provided the best available summary of the military and political position of the two counties at the outbreak of war and during its early years. William Farrer, the great historian of Lancashire, produced transcripts of documents which he had found in the papers of Sir Roger Bradshaigh, deputy lieutenant of Lancashire after the Restoration. They concerned the watchful eye which

Bradshaigh maintained over North Lonsdale and included evidence of disaffection because of religious issues, reported rumours of a rising against Catholics, the organisation of the militia, and petitions from the inhabitants of Dalton-in-Furness regarding the burdensome cost of contributing to militia expenditure. Peter Clarke, a pupil at St Aidan's School, Carlisle, contributed a remarkable article on the fears of political and religious subversion, and the real or imaginary plotting of risings in Restoration Cumbria including the almost forgotten (but very real) risings in the Mallerstang area in the autumn of 1663.[41]

Equally enduring as a popular theme was the 1745-46 Jacobite Rising, including the last 'battle' on English soil (the skirmish at Clifton Moor near Penrith) and the romantic events of Prince Charles Edward Stuart's (Bonnie Prince Charlie's) arrival in Carlisle and sojourn in the city. Richard Ferguson compiled a comprehensive account of the battle, based on a contemporary plan which he discovered in the museum of the Society of Antiquaries of Newcastle upon Tyne and which he described in vivid terms: 'its limits were defined by a broad margin of red paint, within which a vast tartan boa constrictor seemed to be endeavouring to swallow a church and sundry red and black blocks'. Ferguson wrote his paper and sent it to the Society of Antiquaries in London, who returned it with the plans unopened, by the next post, on the grounds that they did not have anything to do with 'matters later than 1700'. Publication in *Transactions* was clearly second best, but the article was impressive and detailed, using all available contemporary sources and plans drawn shortly after the battle. Jonathan Oates described the siege of Carlisle in December 1745, immediately following the skirmish at Clifton Moor, and observed that most writers have been sympathetic to the rebels and their cause. Noting that this was the last siege on English soil, he described the events both inside and outside the city in great detail and concluded with a summary of the aftermath, when the prisoners were imprisoned and tried. Those events were discussed at much greater length by Rupert Jarvis in an article about the trials of Jacobite prisoners and the impact of the trials on the city itself, using the papers of the mayor and corporation, the sheriff of Cumberland, the governor of Carlisle, and the Crown Solicitor. The paper detailed the planning and arrangements for the trials, including the personnel involved and the major problems over accommodation, and also considered the overcrowding and the alarming political tensions within the city. It gave detailed statistics, and Jarvis observed that 91 men were sentenced out of an original 315 who were imprisoned, and that 30 were executed in the ensuing four weeks.[42]

Attention was also given to the response of Westmorland and Cumberland to the approach of the Jacobite forces in November 1745 and, more widely, local military organisation. Taking that broader perspective, Jarvis contributed an imaginative paper which analysed the coupling of Cumberland and Westmorland in a joint lord lieutenancy in the century from 1660; he looked at examples of other joint counties or arrangements such as separate lieutenancies held by same person, and at the work of successive lord lieutenants during times of political and military activity, with special emphasis on the militia and its mustering. This was followed up by an article on the Westmorland militia during the 1715 Jacobite rising, including its local organisation and the emergency arrangements which were made. The 1715 was considered in more detail by Jonathan Oates, who noted that its local impact in Cumbria had been almost completely ignored by previous historians, in marked contrast to the great attention given to its successor. The main theme of his paper was the wide variety of responses within the two counties: Carlisle was bypassed by the rebels and their southward march was opposed only by a posse which gathered near Penrith and ran away as the Jacobites approached. Providing another perspective, Alison Wright examined how Anglican gentry in the North West during the second half of the seventeenth century shared many interests and common causes with their Catholic fellow-gentry, whom they shielded and protected during times of repression. In the 1690s and early 1700s they maintained common ground, with implicit or sometimes explicit Jacobite sympathies, but these relationships tended to break down after 1715. She also analysed the powerful influence of networking among the Catholic gentry during this period, showing (using a case study of the Layburne family) how links of faith, kinship, politics and friendship extended not only to the wider Catholic community in Britain and northern Europe but also to significant numbers of influential Anglicans.[43]

The effects of more recent wars on Cumbria have been given sporadic attention (see the article by June Barnes on the period of the French wars referred to below). An opportunity has been taken in the year of the Society's 150th anniversary, which coincides with the centenary of the Battle of the Somme, to dedicate a greater part of a volume of *Transactions* to a range of studies focusing on the First World War's impact on the county.[44]

Parliamentary politics has likewise been of little interest until recently. Roy Hudleston's 1946 article on the Cumberland election of 1768 was simply a transcript of papers found among the Whelpdale records at Hutton John, and not until 1975 was there a substantive contribution, when J.A. Downie published a paper on the political battle in Carlisle in 1692. This was triggered when Christopher Musgrave, MP for the city, was on duty at the castle as clerk of the ordnance and violently assaulted a wayward recruit, a gunner who arrived late. Unfortunately the not-so-innocent victim was John How, an alderman and son of the mayor, and as a result Musgrave was 'disfranchised' that very evening, turning a petty local dispute into an affair with national political implications. Two recent volumes by Michael Mullett on Restoration politics, one on the development of two-party politics in Cockermouth, and the other on the political influence of Lady Anne Clifford in Appleby have significantly increased understanding of seventeenth-century political life in parts of the county.[45]

Two centuries later, other political rivalries and scheming machinations surfaced at Barrow-in-Furness in the mid-1880s. Recently created as a separate borough constituency, it was notable for the unseating of the victor, the Liberal candidate David Duncan, by his Tory opponent H.W. Schneider (the dominant figure in the town's industrial and business community) on the grounds of malpractice. The only detailed longer-term study of electoral politics in a specific constituency has been Andrew Connell's work on North Westmorland in the later nineteenth century. The constituency was created in 1885, coinciding with the arrival of male household suffrage, and included not only the upper Eden valley and the Appleby area but also Ambleside, Windermere and Bowness. The Liberals, representing the commercial middle class, vied for control against the established Conservative interest which was embodied by the Lowther family. The article charted the battles fought at each of the nine general elections and by-elections between 1885 and 1910, and especially those of 1900, 1905 and 1906 when Liberals were returned despite fierce Conservative opposition. Connell also looked in more detail at the hard-fought Westmorland election of 1880, noting that there had not been a contested election for the two county seats since December 1832, and only two contests for the single-member seat for Kendal borough in the same period. Aristocratic and clergy control of the county electoral 'machine', and the dominant Liberal commercial interests in Kendal, ensured that with those two exceptions all candidates were returned unopposed – and the 1880 election resulted in a predictable Conservative victory, following massive expenditure by both sides. The career of an individual MP, John Robinson (1727-1802) was highlighted by Connell in another article which showed how this Appleby-born middle-class man became the immensely skilful manager of the Lowther interest, ensuring their total domination of Westmorland's parliamentary representation in the 1750s and 1760s. He rose socially to become deputy lord lieutenant of the county, sitting in parliament for Westmorland (1764-74), but then breaking with the Lowthers and representing Harwich (1774-1802). A very different perspective on Westmorland's electoral politics has been given by Roger Smalley both in his book on political dissent in Westmorland and in his account of the formation of female suffrage organisations in the county, and their often vigorous and effective campaigning. He drew upon the papers of the suffragist Catherine Marshall, held at the archive centre in Carlisle, and made extensive use of the coverage of these issues in the local press.[46]

Despite the industrialisation of Cumbria in the first half of the nineteenth century little has been published in *Transactions* on working-class politics, except for Carlisle which has featured in three articles by June Barnes. In 1978, in an important contribution, she looked at the trade union and Radical political activities of the city's handloom weavers from the late 1770s onwards, using local newspapers, memorials and addresses to demonstrate the gradual emergence of organised rather than spontaneous activity and revealing the major problems faced by handloom weavers from the 1830s onwards. She noted that histories of the city have largely ignored them and their plight. Six years later she discussed the red flag which was given to Tullie House Museum by the Caldewgate Working Men's Association in 1932, and used it as an introduction to the historical context of working-class radicalism in Carlisle from 1819 onwards. Among her themes were the formation of political unions, the holding of protest meetings, government espionage and infiltration, and the experience of Chartism in the city. More generally, she also investigated how people in Cumberland and the Borders were affected by, and responded to, the events of the French Revolution between 1789 and 1802, looking at popular unrest, the government's response and its military precautions, the evidence of private correspondence, and the underlying reasons for the discontent including food shortages and price increases. Other than that there is only Donald MacRaild's investigation of the growing sectarian tension in the boom town of Barrow-in-Furness, and the pressures that led up to the anti-Irish riots of 1864, which he placed in the context of widespread industrial unrest, strikes and wage disputes in northern England during the 1850s and 1860s.[47]

Social history

Finally, consideration must be given to that very important but somewhat amorphous subject known loosely as 'social history'. As elitism began to wane in the period between the wars, and as the history and experience of 'the common people' challenged and stimulated historical researchers, so the attention given to social history grew. There were pioneers even before the First World War – for example, Francis Grainger's early consideration of quarter sessions as a source of evidence about poverty (1915) has already been mentioned – but only in the 1950s did the social history of ordinary people and of everyday communities begin to assume greater significance. In 1955 Gwilym Jones, a regular contributor to *Transactions* on a wide variety of topics, set himself an intriguing challenge – he sought reliable evidence to assess Macaulay's claim, made a century earlier, that the northern counties were 'in a state of barbarism' until the mid-eighteenth century and that 'physical and moral causes had concurred to prevent civilisation from spreading to that region', of which poverty was the greatest. He used probate inventories from the period 1686 to 1738 (although he did not look in detail at the original documents), together with deeds, journals, taxation returns, ship money demands of the 1630s, and somewhat random evidence from business papers, and concluded that the poverty of Cumberland and Westmorland was overstated. Rather, he felt, the two counties had evaded or avoided tax quite successfully.[48]

Pursuing this theme, he then investigated the nature of wealth and finance in Cumbria in the period before the mid-eighteenth century, looking at a range of personal documentary sources to gain an impression of the credit and loan systems which operated within and between communities, and within networks shaped by social class. The exceptionally early surviving financial accounts kept by Sir John Pennington of Muncaster between 1491 and 1511 provided an invaluable starting point, while the records of debts due and owing in probate inventories revealed rich detail about lesser folk. Individuals such as Margaret Lancaster of Crosthwaite cum Lyth who, in the 1740s, lent over £200 each, at high interest rates, to selected individuals, were revealed as moneylenders on a grand scale, while the celebrated shop accounts of Abraham Dent of Kirkby Stephen showed how the private networks of loans and credits interlocked with those of traders and small businessmen.[49] More recently Peter Roebuck has examined the fortunes of the Parker family from the area south of Carlisle and their financial stake in the droving trade which led to investments in Manchester and beyond.[50] Two papers from 1982 looked at other dimensions to the world of local and personal finance. John Beckett analysed the varying fortunes of Cumbrians known to have invested in the South Sea Company, which was founded in 1711 and collapsed in 1720. He charted the sorry tale of corruption, manipulation, fraud and naivety to tell a story which has alarmingly clear resonances three centuries on. Robert Homan looked at the Kendal Union Building Societies in the 1820s, showing how their financial affairs were managed and their building activities organised, and assessing their impact upon the growth and development of the town (fig. 8.4).[51]

R.F. Dickinson had earlier investigated self-help of a different sort, with his research on the Lamplugh Friendly Society, founded in 1788 and by 1948, when it was wound up, the oldest friendly society in the country. He traced its history, finances, regulations and impact upon the people of this scattered community, and added a personal note: 'the writer regards it as an honour to be included as the very last name in the list of subscribers'. In nearby Eskdale the minute and account book of the select vestry survives from 1827 to 1837, and Mary Hall discussed the evidence it provides for the administration of the Poor Law, its effectiveness and the extent of pragmatic humanity displayed by the vestry and its overseers. A similar approach, though with a much longer perspective and greater relationship to the framework of national and regional patterns and processes, was demonstrated by Margaret Parsons' fine

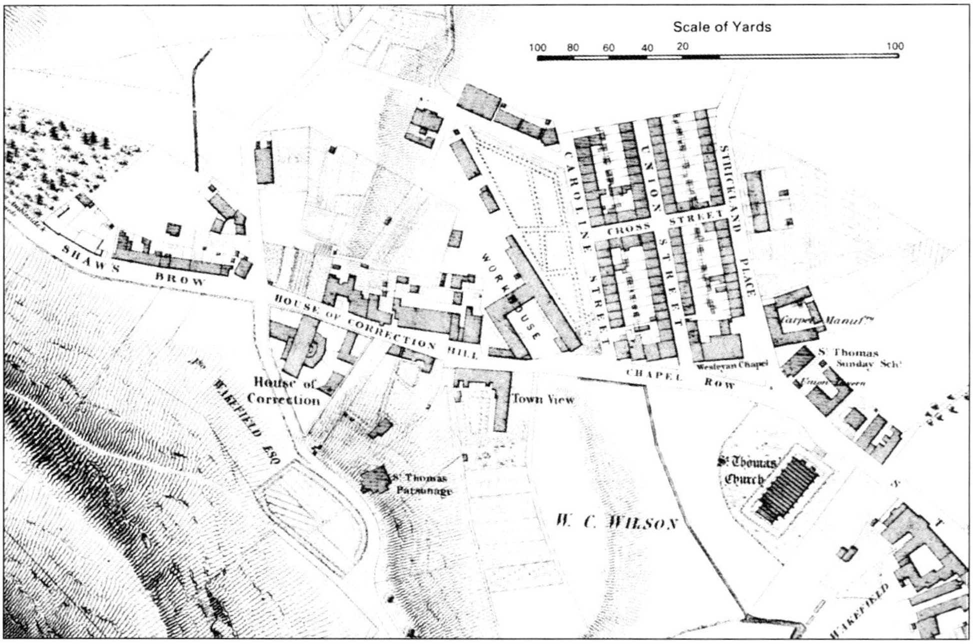

Fig. 8.4. The Kendal Union Building Societies' housing development in Kendal, *CW2*, 82 (1982), 185

analysis of poor relief in Troutbeck (Ambleside) between 1640 and 1836. While giving many specific examples, her essay painted a broad picture, and was all the more powerful for that – especially as she used calculations of the amount raised from the poor rate, year by year from 1700 to the mid-1830s, to demonstrate the truth of the contemporary perception that from the 1780s onwards the cost of the system rose very rapidly (fig. 8.5). Blake Tyson also adopted a local focus in a paper on the paupers of Windermere 1749-1862, looking at the sharply-rising trend of annual expenditure and giving special attention to the building of a workhouse in Undermillbeck in 1829, a uniquely well-documented, and very late, Cumbrian example of a local workhouse of the sort more familiar from other parts of England before the Poor Law Amendment Act of 1834. All such analyses, if they rely only on overseers' papers and other official records, risk omitting the personal perspectives of those on the receiving end, the paupers themselves. John R. Walton helped to redress this imbalance with an important paper on the experiences and life stories of the Cumbrian poor, based on the testimony set out in settlement examinations. Covering the period 1770-1830, it was a persuasive exercise in adding the human dimension to a subject which can all too readily be reduced to statistics and sums of money. His paper was illustrated with simple but effective maps which reveal the geographical movements and horizons of the poor.[52]

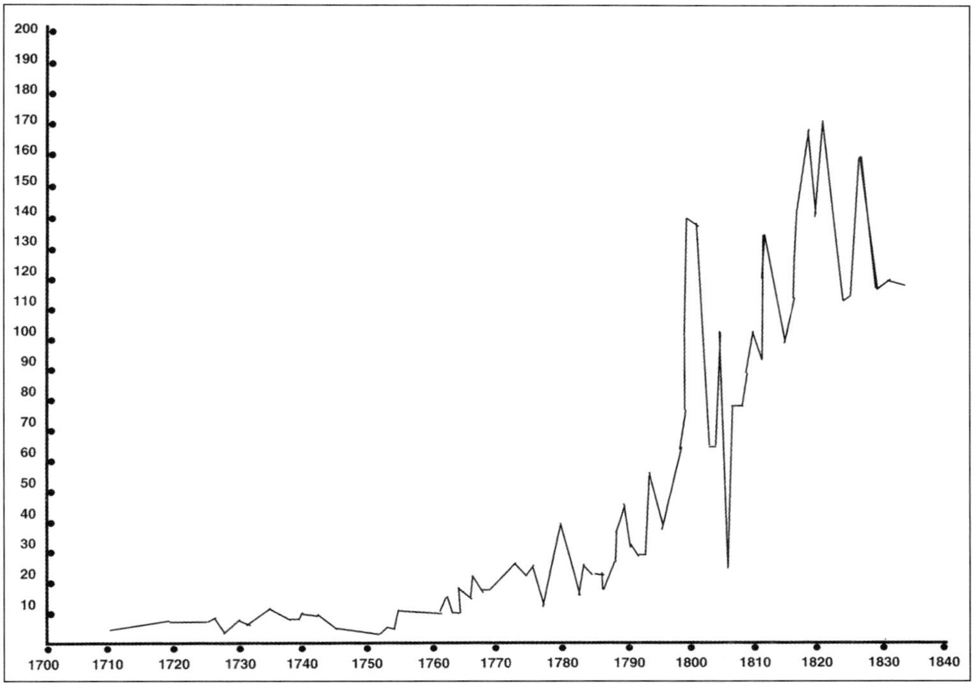

Fig. 8.5. The rising cost of poor rates in Troutbeck, *CW2*, 95 (1995), 174

Money, or the lack of it, is often linked (at least in the popular imagination) with crime and misdemeanour. The study of crime as a branch of social history emerged in the 1960s and several articles have looked at the subject in Cumbria. Henry Summerson, whose work on medieval Carlisle is of national importance, ranged beyond the bounds of the city to consider crime and society in medieval Cumberland; he suggested the scale of the challenge by observing that 'it is not easy for us to imagine an age in which the day-to-day life of nearly the whole of society went almost entirely unrecorded'. He analysed all the surviving eyre and gaol delivery rolls held at the Public Record Office, a total of 19 sets of data for the period 1335-1457, recording 522 suspects of whom a mere 36 (or seven per cent) were convicted. These criminal activities were discussed against a background of emerging systems of justice, the relationship with Scotland, and the social structure of Cumberland itself. Summerson later described in detail a specific and exceptionally brutal crime – the strangling of young William, heir of the recently-deceased John de la Cressoner of Hutton-in-the-Forest, at the instigation of his 'wicked' uncle Thomas in 1260. This was followed by an extraordinary and protracted series of legal processes and manoeuvres which lasted until the early 1290s. Summerson's analysis emphasised the growing power of law enforcement and legal control exercised by the Crown even in distant Cumberland. Robert Dilley drew upon the court books and other papers of no fewer than 126 Cumbrian manors in the 150 years before 1750 to produce a delightful synthesis of the evidence for malediction, or speaking ill, of neighbours. In what must surely be the most entertaining and colourful paper ever published in *Transactions*, he quoted extensively from contemporary sources to investigate the nature of slander and assesses the circumstances of social conflict, moral condemnation, sexual wanderings and financial opportunism which gave rise to the abuse. The article concludes with a wonderful list of 'imaginative invective', drawn from the courts of Millom where people were apparently, for reasons that remain unclear, unusually productive of 'inventive turns of phrase'.[53]

Previously, John Marshall had investigated 'crime, morals and the countryman' in nineteenth-century Cumbria. In a characteristically information-laden contribution, full of stimulating insights, he showed how Cumberland and Westmorland were not only among the most literate of English counties in the mid-nineteenth century but also among the least criminal. In 1841 Westmorland, with one committal to every 1711 inhabitants, was lowest, while Cumberland had 1:1178, compared with dramatically higher rates in, for example, Lancashire (1:481) and Gloucestershire (1:348). Marshall discussed a range of social tensions, from railway-building and the opening up of mining areas, to food price increases, and highlighted the very limited policing: in 1852 there was only one policeman each at Keswick, Whitehaven and Maryport. Developing his researches on Cleator Moor, he detailed the question of Irish migrants from the 1840s to the 1870s and showed how they were blamed for virtually all local problems. More generally, the context of crime was explained in discussion of vagrancy and the astonishingly high illegitimacy rates in the Lake Counties – this being the point where the question of morality (or its absence) raised its head. Bill Wiseman looked at crime from an opposite perspective, investigating the history of the Kendal Petty Sessions and showing how these courts were preceded by borough courts going back to the medieval period and crystallised in function and jurisdiction by the 1575 charter of incorporation. The post-1575 court was considered in detail, together with others which functioned within the borough, and the often hostile or uncomfortable relationships between the borough and the Westmorland quarter sessions were explained. The story was brought forward to the present with the reorganisation of the petty sessions in Cumbria in 1987.[54]

Audrey Eccles picked up the theme of vagrancy in a detailed study of Westmorland from 1748 to 1800, analysing the 299 cases for which papers survive among the quarter session records and assessing the 'social profile' of the individuals involved, with a wealth of personal biographical detail as well as summaries of their origins and place of apprehension and the nature of the punishment (if any) which they received. Her argument was that most of those concerned were victims of the failure of the system and that in Westmorland, as elsewhere, the central government view – that vagrancy was a matter of choice – was superseded at local level by a more flexible, pragmatic and realistic perception. As befits a social geographer, Colin Pooley included extensive statistical tables and numerical analysis when he assessed crime in Westmorland in the late nineteenth and early twentieth centuries – it is perhaps ironic that this, the most law-abiding of English counties, should have its criminality analysed in such depth. In fact, despite its title, the paper focused almost exclusively on Kendal, since it was based on the prisoners' photograph book kept by the borough constabulary (fig. 8.6). Pooley concluded that contemporary assertions that vagrants and outsiders were the main cause of crime did not stand up to statistical testing, and that instead the evidence supported the contention that criminals represented 'a cross section of wider society'.[55]

And who were the 'Cumbrians'? Several authors addressed aspects of this theme, looking at individuals and communities in the eighteenth and nineteenth centuries. Robert Dilley drew upon a somewhat unexpected

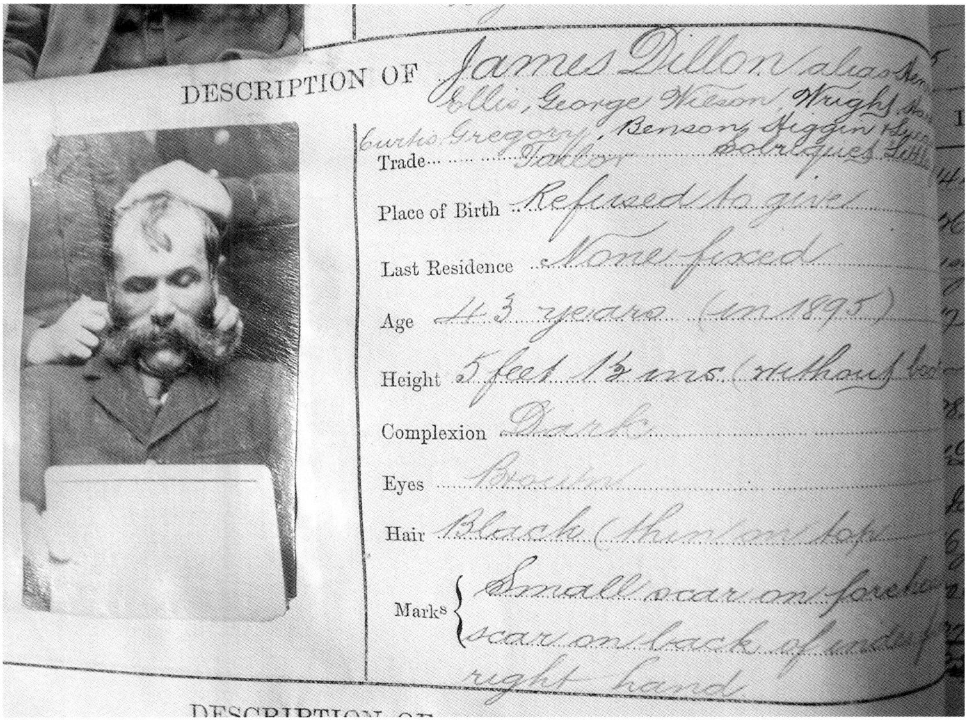

Fig. 8.6. James Dillon and aliases from Kendal Borough Constabulary Prisoners' Photograph Book, (WSCONS10/2) *(image: Cumbria County Council: Kendal Archive Centre)*

source – the 169 Cumberland enclosure awards between 1742 and 1893 – for the forenames of Cumbrians in that period. He compiled a list of those individuals who received allotments of enclosed land – a total of 4925 males and 896 females – and ranked their names. While admitting that this was not fully representative, because it excluded the landless and the smaller tenants and most urban dwellers, he felt it gave a good base for analysis. Unsurprisingly, four names (John, William, Thomas and Joseph) together accounted for almost 60 per cent of the males, while Mary, Ann, Elizabeth and Jane together represented the same proportion of women. A more sophisticated approach to the same subject was taken by Angus Winchester in his analysis of the personal names recorded in the 1642 Protestation Returns for Cumberland. He sought to test claims made by Housman in the late eighteenth century that there were three distinct local 'societies', those of the Borders, the lowlands and the Lake District fells. Winchester demonstrated that there were indeed self-contained patterns of surnames, suggesting that the three areas were significantly separate, and that – more unexpectedly – forenames also demonstrated clear localisation below the level of the usual 'top' names such as John and Thomas. At Carleton near Carlisle, for example, there were 51 oath-takers, of whom five were called Randal and five Barnard. This paper suggested that there is much potential for further detailed regional and sub-regional analyses of names.[56]

Peter Lucas discussed the megalomaniac James Ramsden, creator of Barrow-in-Furness, who in the first half of the 1870s published a daily newspaper, the *Barrow Times*, and employed agents to distribute it as a publicity vehicle throughout the North West and the West Riding. Using a keyword search (an early instance of this methodology) Lucas revealed the extravagant style of its advertising of the town and its industries, noting the prevalence of such words as progress, rapid, unique, increasing, unequalled, remarkable, enormous, and extensive. Many of these might equally have applied to the losses made by the newspaper and it became a weekly from 1875 (fig. 8.7). Continuing the theme of newspapers and their influence, Lucas researched the career of Mrs Roseanne Hart Bigg, for 32 years from 1865 the sole proprietor of the *Ulverston Advertiser*. Under the provocative title 'The regional roots of feminism', he placed his study firmly in the context of wider historical debates about the role of women in late Victorian society, the politicisation of the question of women's rights, and the power of the provincial press. He later developed his researches on the Bigg family beyond their newspaper proprietorship to consider the role of John Stanyan Bigg (husband of Roseanne) in the 'striking burst of curiosity about the old ways of talking', a boom in the study of, and reverence for, dialect and vernacular speech. This took place in the 1860s, and Lucas provided insight into why Bigg used dialect in his newspapers – as a means of linking readers with 'the everyday world' and showed how in the small town of Ulverston a wealth of poetry, novels and newspaper prose was published in dialect during this period. Local and other historians make much use of newspapers as source material, the more cautious being conscious that newspapers do not always tell the truth, and that bias is perhaps inherent in reporting. Lucas discussed some of these issues in the context of the same small town when he looked at the sometimes vitriolic rivalry between Joseph Alexis Bernard,

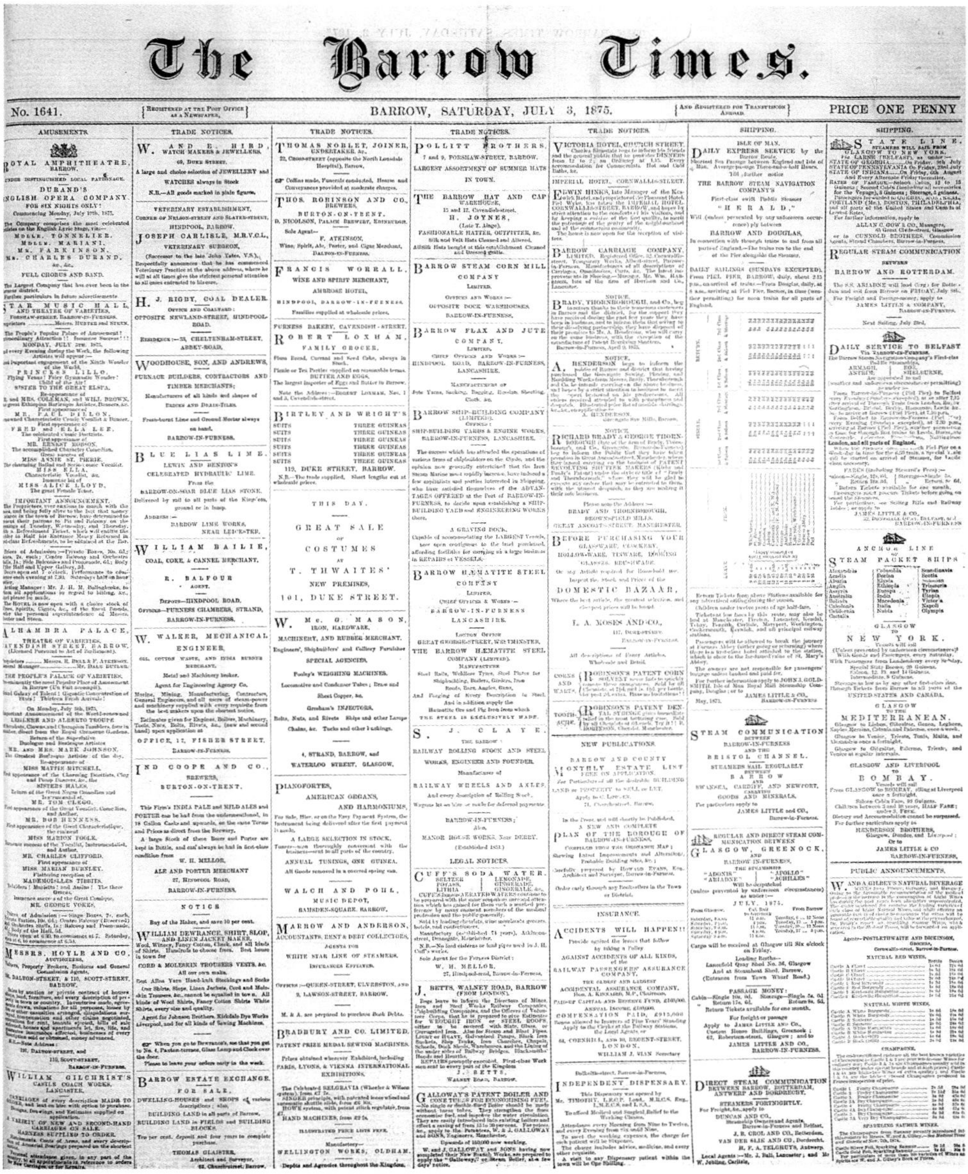
The Barrow Times.

No. 1641. | REGISTERED AT THE POST OFFICE AS A NEWSPAPER. | BARROW, SATURDAY, JULY 3, 1875. | AND REGISTERED FOR TRANSMISSION ABROAD. | PRICE ONE PENNY

Fig. 8.7. *The Barrow Times*, 3 July 1875 *(image: Cumbria County Council: Barrow Archive Centre)*

editor of the magnificently-titled *Ulverston Mirror and Furness Reflector*, and our friend John Stanyan Bigg of the *Ulverston Advertiser*, as they reflected the contemporary debate over the role, morality, ethics and prejudices of journalists and their craft.[57]

Until recently Roseanne Hart Bigg was one of the few Cumbrian women to have been given prominence in the Society's publications. In the last few years, however, Jennifer Holt has rescued the daughters of an eighteenth-century Kendal attorney from obscurity through her article on their generous gifts to the town, while Blake Tyson has used the Kendal apprenticeship indenture records to recover the largely seventeenth-century histories of three women apprentices, and six widows of tradesman who became 'masters' in their own right. As noted above Michael Mullett has provided new insights into Lady Anne Clifford's patronage and political authority in Appleby, and Roger Smalley has used the papers of the suffragist Catherine Marshall in his article on that movement.[58]

Demography lends itself to – indeed, is focused on – statistical analysis, and census returns are essential raw material for this. Mark Saunders used the returns from 1841 to 1871 to chart the rise of Barrow and the many and varied origins of the new Barrovians. A comparable exercise was undertaken by D.I. Smith in a comprehensive analysis of migration into Workington using the 1861, 1881 and 1891 census enumerators' books. During the period 1841-1891 the town's population grew from just under 6500 to almost 24,000, and Smith analysed the incomers in terms of their geographical origins, occupational structure, roles in the workforce of the iron and steel industry, and as domestic servants. A notable feature is that he provided comparative analysis by looking at other studies, including Saunders' on Barrow.[59]

While these papers considered migration to Cumbria, John Marshall looked at the opposite process – the local and regional patriotism and sense of Cumbrian identity among the many who had moved to London, there setting up Cumberland and Westmorland societies, which were active in political activities, the promotion of Cumbrian sports and, as a cultural icon emerged, popularising the song "John Peel". The question of 'identity' was one which attracted much attention among historians in the early twenty-first century, and in 2011 a special 'themed' issue of *Transactions* included papers presented at a recent conference on Cumbrian identities. It began with a characteristically provocative piece by John K. Walton, arguing that Cumbria did not really have an identity, and included papers on the identity of medieval Cumbria, romantic poetry and the idea of the Lake District, sport and local identity, and ways in which archaeology provides an approach to the identities consequent upon industrialisation. The most accessible of the papers was perhaps that noted above, by Angus Winchester on names and local identities, reminding us that history, in this region, as elsewhere, is ultimately about people.[60]

Notes and References

1 G.E. Moser,' Kendal parish church registers', *CW1,* 3 (1878), 49-63, quotation 52.
2 R.S. Ferguson, 'An account of the "Dormont Book" belonging to the Corporation of Carlisle', *CW1,* 6 (1883), 297-304.
3 R.S. Ferguson, 'Notes on the initial letter of a charter of Edward II to the City of Carlisle', *CW1,* 6 (1883), 319-27.
4 See for example: R.S. Ferguson, *The Royal Charters of the City of Carlisle* (CWAAS, Extra Series X, 1892), and W. Farrer *Records Relating to the Barony of Kendale* (CWAAS, Record Series IV, V, VI, 1923-26).
5 Sir G. Duckett, 'Extracts from the Cottonian MSS. relating to the Border Service', *CW1,* 4 (1880), 206-14.
6 T.H. Hodgson, 'Cumberland and Westmorland under the Tudors, being extracts from the Register of the Privy Council in the reigns of Henry VIII and Edward VI', *CW1,* 13 (1895), 69-85; and '... in the reign of Queen Mary', 227-50.
7 T.H. Hodgson, 'Extracts from Acts of the first ten years of the reign of Elizabeth relating to Cumberland and Westmorland', *CW2,* 3 (1903), 126-49.
8 F.H.M. Parker, *Pipe Rolls of Cumberland and Westmorland, 1222-1260* (CWAAS, Extra Series XII, 1905).
9 Sir S.H. Scott, 'A footnote on the Flemish tradition at Kendal', *CW2,* 22 (1922), 85-89.
10 J. Wilson 'Victims of the Tudor Disestablishment in Cumberland and Westmorland during the reigns of Edward VI and Mary', *CW1,* 13 (1895), 364-88.
11 H. Whitehead, 'Westmorland parish registers', *CW1,* 13 (1895), 125-41.
12 J.L. Hobbs, 'The journal of John Wilson Soulby of Rampside Academy, August-December 1847', *CW2,* 60 (1960), 156-86; F. Barnes and J.L. Hobbs, 'Some early Furness records', *CW2,* 57 (1957), 44-71, esp. 46.
13 D. Scott, 'Recent discoveries in the muniment rooms of Appleby Castle and Skipton Castle', *CW2,* 18 (1918), 189-210.
14 P.V. Kelly, 'Muchland and its owners and Newbarns', *CW2,* 24 (1924), 260-70 (the manor court rolls are now held at Cumbria Archive and Local Studies Centre Barrow, and the Richmond wills at Lancashire Archives).
15 O. North, 'The travels of Sir Gilbert de Launoy in the North of England and elsewhere, 1430', *CW2,* 21 (1921), 43-48.
16 F. Grainger, 'James Jackson's diary, 1650-1683', *CW2,* 21 (1921), 96-129.
17 T.E. Casson, 'The diary of William Fleming of Rowe Head, Pennington, 1848-1856', *CW2,* 42 (1942), 132-48; 'The diary of Margaret Ashburner of Ireleth, 1814-19', *CW2,* 43 (1943), 55-69.
18 E. Venables, 'The dedications of the parochial churches and chapels of the modern diocese of Carlisle', *CW1,* 7 (1884), 118-49; T.H.B. Graham and W.G. Collingwood, 'Patron saints of the diocese of Carlisle, *CW2,* 25 (1925), 1-27; R.S. Ferguson, 'Why Alston is in the Diocese of Durham, and in the County of Cumberland', *CW1,* 8 (1886), 21-28; T.H.B. Graham, 'The medieval diocese of Carlisle', *CW2,* 25 (1925), 96-114.
19 Revd Canon [Henry] Ware and Revd Canon Simpson, 'Killington, Kirkby Lonsdale, its chapel salary', *CW1,* 8 (1886), 93-119; [Ware], 'On the readers in the chapelries of the Lake District', *CW2,* 5 (1905), 89-105.
20 M.A. Clark, 'Kendal: the Protestant exception', *CW2,* 95 (1995), 137-52.
21 L.A.S. Butler (ed.), *The Church Notes of Sir Stephen Glynne for Cumbria, 1833-1872* (CWAAS, Extra Series XXXVI, 2011); J. Platt (ed.), *The Diocese of Carlisle, 1814-1855* (CWAAS, Record Series XXII, 2015); D.W.V. Weston, *Rose Castle and the Bishops of Carlisle, 1133-2012* (CWAAS, Extra Series XL, 2013).
22 H. Whitehead, 'Brampton XVIIth century Presbyterians', *CW1,* 8 (1886), 348-72; H. Penfold, 'Early Brampton Presbyterianism 1662-1780', *CW2,* 3 (1903), 94-125.

23 N. Wilson, 'Ejected Ministers in Westmorland and Cumberland: minutes of proceedings of the Committee', *CW2,* 24 (1924), 66-77; C. Roy Hudleston, 'Cumberland recusants of 1723-24', *CW2,* 59 (1959), 115-38; J.D. Martin, 'The Hawkshead Connexion: some Cumbrian Baptists', *CW2,* 91 (1991), 213-36.

24 R.B. Wordsworth (ed.), *The Cockermouth Congregational Church Book, 1651-c.1765* (CWAAS, Record Series XXI, 2012); I. Moonie, 'The Abbey Street Dissenting Meeting, Carlisle *c.*1773-*c.*1810', *CW3,* 2 (2002), 217-30; 'Annetwell Street Protestant Dissenting Meeting, Carlisle *c.*1778-1843', *CW3,* 4 (2004), 201-20; 'The English Presbyterian Meeting, Fisher Street, Carlisle, 1736-1809', *CW3,* 12 (2012), 199-216; 'Presbyterians and Independents or Congregationalists in Carlisle, 1648-1736', *CW3,* 9 (2009), 111-30.

25 T.H. Bainbridge, 'John Wesley's travels in Cumberland', *CW2,* 47 (1947), 183-98; L. Gray, '"Efficient members": the early years of Methodism in Hunsonby and Winskill, 1821-1871', *CW3,* 12 (2012), 231-48; '"And who is my neighbour?": the Methodists of Hunsonby and Winskill in their local context 1821-1871', *CW3,* 13 (2013), 171-90.

26 C.G. Bulman, 'Carlisle Cathedral and its development in the thirteenth and fourteenth centuries', *CW2,* 49 (1949), 87-177, quotation 117.

27 C.A. Parker, 'Gosforth Registers', *CW1,* 8 (1886), 70-81; H. Barnes, 'Visitations of the plague in Cumberland and Westmorland', *CW1,* 11 (1891), 158-86.

28 J. Hughes, 'The plague in Carlisle 1597/98', *CW2,* 71 (1971), 52-63; C.B. Phillips, 'The plague in Kendal in 1598: some new evidence', *CW2,* 94 (1994), 135-42.

29 H. Barnes, 'Leprosy and leper hospitals', *CW1,* 10 (1890), 95-123; W.G. Wiseman, 'The medieval hospitals of Cumbria', *CW2,* 87 (1987), 83-100; 'The hospital of St Nicholas, Carlisle, and its masters: Part 1 – The period up to 1333', *CW2,* 95 (1995), 93-110; 'The hospital of St Nicholas, Carlisle, and its masters: Part 2 – The period from 1333', *CW2,* 96 (1996), 51-70; B. Copeland, 'The Westmorland Sanatorium at Meathop', *CW2,* 97 (1997), 239-52; G.Brooks, 'The building of the Cumberland and Westmorland Joint Lunatic Asylum (Garlands Hospital), *CW3,* 4 (2004), 229-44; P. Cheesbrough, 'The Ethel Hedley Orthopaedic Hospital for Crippled Children, Calgarth Park, Windermere', *CW3,* 13 (2013), 215-31.

30 S. Scott and C.J. Duncan, 'Smallpox epidemics at Penrith in the 17th and 18th centuries', *CW2,* 93 (1993), 155-60; 'Marital fertility at Penrith, 1557-1812: evidence for a malnourished community?', *CW2,* 96 (1996), 105-14; J.E. Ward, 'Death in 18th century Whitehaven: the mortality records from Holy Trinity Church', *CW2,* 98 (1998), 249-62.

31 F. Grainger, 'Poor relief in Cumberland in the seventeenth and eighteenth centuries', *CW2,* 15 (1915), 90-6; G.P. Jones, 'The population of Broughton-in-Furness in the eighteenth century', *CW2,* 53 (1953), 136-48.

32 F.G. James, 'The population of the diocese of Carlisle in 1676', *CW2,* 51 (1951), 137-41.

33 E. Conder, 'The Hearth Tax return, 22 Charles II, Kendal Barony', *CW2,* 19 (1919), 140-50; J.L. Kirby and A.D. Kirby, 'The poll-tax of 1377 for Carlisle', *CW2,* 58 (1958), 110-7; G.P. Jones, 'Some population problems relating to Cumberland and Westmorland in the 18th century', *CW2,* 58 (1958), 123-39.

34 J.D. Marshall, 'Some aspects of the social history of 19th-century Cumbria: (I) migration and literacy', *CW2,* 69 (1969), 280-307; W.R. Sellick. 'Whitehaven and its Jews, 1774-1850', *CW2,* 93 (1993), 215-36.

35 D.P. Kirby, 'Strathclyde and Cumbria: a survey of historical development to 1092', *CW2,* 62 (1962), 77-94.

36 J.E. Morris, 'Cumberland and Westmorland military levies in the time of Edward I and Edward II', *CW2,* 3 (1903), 307-27, quotation 307.

37 H.G. Pearson, 'Two fourteenth-century documents illustrating Robert Bruce's raid in Furness and Lonsdale, 1322', *CW2,* 16 (1916), 205-20; C. McNamee, 'Buying off Robert Bruce: an account of monies paid to the Scots by Cumberland communities in 1313-14', *CW2,* 92 (1992), 77-90; K.M. Longley, 'The Scottish incursions of 1327: a glimpse of the aftermath', *CW2,* 83 (1983), 63-72; J. Godwin, 'The Wigton church accounts 1328-9: a translation into English', *CW3,* 7 (2007), 85-94.

38 J.R. Magrath, 'Sir Robert Parvyng, Knight of the Shire for Cumberland, and Chancellor of England', *CW2,* 19 (1919), 30-91; M.A. Rowling, 'William de Parr, King's Knight to Henry IV (*c.*1350-1404)', *CW2,* 56 (1956), 87-103; F.B. Garnett, 'Queen Katherine Parr and Sudeley Castle', *CW1,* 13 (1895), 9-19; S.E. James, 'Queen Kateryn Parr (1512-1548)', *CW2,* 88 (1988), 107-20.

39 T.H.B. Graham, 'The Debatable Land', *CW2,* 12 (1912), 33-58; Revd J.B. Gavin, 'The Bishop of Durham, the West March Border Negotiations, and the Treaty of Carlisle 1597', *CW2,* 73 (1973), 120-42; G.P. Jones, 'King James I and the western Border', *CW2,* 69 (1969), 129-51.

40 W. Nanson, 'Carlisle during the Siege of 1644-45', *CW1,* 7 (1884), 48-63; R.S. Ferguson, 'The Siege of Carlisle, in 1644-5', *CW1,* 11 (1891), 104-16; D. Perriam, 'The demolition of the priory of St Mary, Carlisle', *CW2,* 87 (1987), 127-58.

41 C.S. Colman, 'The paralysis of the Cumberland and Westmorland Army in the first Civil War, *c.*1642-44', *CW3,* 1 (2001), 123-38; W. Farrer, 'North Lonsdale after the Restoration', *CW1,* 10 (1890), 202-15; P.D. Clarke, 'The Sectarian "Threat" and its impact in Restoration Cumbria', *CW2,* 88 (1988), 161-76.

42 R.S. Ferguson, 'The retreat of the Highlanders through Westmorland in 1745', *CW1,* 10 (1889), 186-228; J. Oates, 'The last siege on English soil: Carlisle, December 1745', *CW3,* 3 (2003), 169-84; R.C. Jarvis, 'The Carlisle Jacobite Trials, 1746', *CW2,* 61 (1961), 249-74.

43 R.C. Jarvis, 'Westmorland in the "Forty Five" – three manuscripts', *CW2,* 45 (1945), 179-86; 'The lieutenancy in Cumberland and Westmorland 1660-1760', *CW2,* 64 (1964), 219-39; 'The militia in Westmorland in 1715', *CW2,* 64 (1964), 240-55; J. Oates, 'Cumberland and Westmorland in the Jacobite Rebellion of 1715', *CW3,* 6 (2006), 89-102; A. Wright, 'Loyalty and tradition: Jacobitism amongst the gentry of north-west England, 1640-1720', *CW3,* 10 (2010), 147-62; A. Wright, 'Loyalty and tradition Part II: networking among the north-western Catholic gentry in England and abroad 1640-1720: the case of the Layburnes', *CW3,* 14 (2014), 103-24.

44 *CW3,* 16 (2016), 5-144.

45 C. Roy Hudleston, 'Papers relating to the Cumberland election of 1768', *CW2,* 49 (1949), 166-79; J.A. Downie, 'The disfranchisement of Christopher Musgrave MP by Carlisle Corporation in 1692', *CW2,* 75 (1975), 174-87; M.A. Mullett, *Politics and Relgion in Restoration Cockermouth* (CWAAS, Tract Series XXIV, 2013); M.A. Mullett, *Patronage, Power and Politics in the Era of Lady Anne Clifford 1649-1689* (CWAAS, Tract Series 25, 2015).

46 B. Trescatheric, 'The parliamentary elections at Barrow-in-Furness, 1885-1886', *CW2,* 84 (1984), 227-37; A.N. Connell, 'Blue sky over North Westmorland: Appleby's Liberal decade', *CW3,* 6 (1906), 195-216; A.N. Connell, '"Ice in the centre of a glowing fire": the Westmorland election of 1880', *CW3,* 8 (2008), 219-40; A.N. Connell, 'Appleby in Westminster: John Robinson MP (1727-1802)', *CW3,* 10 (2010), 217-36; R. Smalley, *Agitate! Educate! Organise!: Political Dissent in Westmorland from 1880-1930* (CWAAS, Extra Series XXXVIII, 2013); R. Smalley, 'The Westmorland suffragists', *CW3,* 10 (2010), 237-52.

47 J.C.F. Barnes, 'The trade union and Radical activities of the Carlisle handloom weavers', *CW2*, 78 (1978), 149-61; 'Liberty or Death', *CW2*, 84 (1984), 203-13; 'Freedom and

liberty: Cumbria and the Borders during the period of the French Revolution 1789-1802', *CW2*, 90 (1990), 253-66; D.M. MacRaild, 'A case of undercutting wages? Sectarian tension and the Barrow anti-Irish riot of 1864', *CW2*, 96 (1996), 215-22.

48 G.P. Jones, 'The poverty of Cumberland and Westmorland', *CW2*, 55 (1955), 198-208. See also Chapter 6 for a discussion of increasing agrarian wealth in the late 17th century.

49 G.P. Jones, 'Some sources of loans and credit in Cumbria before the rise of banks', *CW2*, 75 (1975), 275-92.

50 P. Roebuck, *Cattle Droving, Cotton and Landownership: a Cumbrian family saga* (CWAAS, Extra Series XLIII, 2014).

51 J.V. Beckett, 'Cumbrians and the South Sea Bubble', *CW2*, 82 (1982), 141-50; R. Homan, 'The Kendal Union Building Societies', *CW2*, 82 (1982), 183-90.

52 R.F. Dickinson, 'The Friendly Society of the inhabitants of the parish of Lamplugh and its neighbourhood', *CW2*, 66 (1966), 418-31; M. Hall, 'Poor relief in Eskdale in the early 1800s', *CW2*, 92 (1992), 205-12; M.A. Parsons, 'Poor relief in Troutbeck 1640-1836', *CW2*, 95 (1995), 169-86; B. Tyson, 'Windermere paupers 1749-1862 and the Undermillbeck workhouse (1829)', *CW3*, 6 (2006), 113-38; J.R. Walton, 'Some Cumbrian pauper narratives 1770-1830', *CW2*, 99 (1999), 237-50.

53 H. Summerson, 'Crime and society in medieval Cumberland', *CW2*, 82 (1982), 111-24; 'Murder at Hutton-in-the-Forest: a study in the government of thirteenth-century Cumberland', *CW2*, 91 (1991), 59-68; R.S. Dilley, 'Rogues, Raskells and Turkie Faced Jades: malediction in the Cumbrian manorial courts', *CW2*, 97 (1997), 143-52.

54 J.D. Marshall, 'Some aspects of the social history of 19th-century Cumbria: (II) crime, police, morals and the countryman', *CW2*, 70 (1970), 221-46; W.G. Wiseman, 'A brief history of Kendal Petty Sessions', *CW3*, 1 (2001), 105-22.

55 A. Eccles, 'Vagrancy in later eighteenth-century Westmorland: a social profile', *CW2*, 89 (1989), 249-62; C.G. Pooley, 'Contours of crime in Westmorland, *c.*1880-1910', *CW2*, 92 (1992), 213-28.

56 R.S. Dilley, 'The personal names of Cumberland 1740-1890', *CW2*, 98 (1998), 263-26; A.J.L. Winchester, 'Personal names and local identities in early-modern Cumbria', *CW3*, 3 (2011), 29-49.

57 P. Lucas, 'Publicity and power: James Ramsden's experiment with daily journalism', *CW2*, 75 (1975), 352-75; 'The regional roots of feminism: a Victorian woman newspaper owner', *CW3*, 2 (2002), 277-300; 'The dialect boom in Victorian Furness', *CW3*, 5 (2005), 199-216; 'J.A. Bernard's challenge: journalists on journalism in a Victorian country town', *CW3*, 7 (2007), 193-214.

58 J.S. Holt, 'James Dowker's daughters: benefactors of Kendal', *CW3*, 14 (2014), 187-206; B. Tyson, 'Women in a man's world: some female apprentices and masters in Kendal, 1595-1731', *CW3*, 15 (2015), 155-182; Mullett, *Patronage, Power and Politics*; Smalley, 'The Westmorland suffragists'.

59 M.N.K. Saunders, 'Migration to 19th-century Barrow-in-Furness: an examination of the census enumerators' books 1841-1871', *CW2*, 84 (1984), 215-25; D.I. Smith, 'Worker migration into Workington, Cumbria, based on the census enumerators' books for 1861, 1881 and 1891', *CW2*, 94 (1994), 249-76.

60 J.D. Marshall, 'Cumberland and Westmorland Societies in London 1734-1914', *CW2*, 84 (1984), 239-54; *CW3*, 11 (2011), special section on 'Cumbrian identities': C. Phythian-Adams, 'From peoples to regional societies: the problem of early medieval Cumbrian identities', 51-64; J.K. Walton, 'Cumbrian identities: some historical contexts', 15-27; P. Bradshaw, 'Romantic poetic identity and the English Lake District', 65-80; M. Huggins, '"Sport helps make us what we are": the shaping of regional and local sporting identities in Cumbria *c.*1800-1960', 81-96; R. Newman, 'Manufacturing identities: an archaeological approach to industrialisation and the formation of modern Cumbria', 97-111; Winchester, 'Personal names and local identities'.

Part 3

Conclusion

Chapter 9
Anniversary Reflections

Angus J. L. Winchester

In drawing the book together, this final chapter attempts to stand back from the history of the Society and its activities and to describe out some of the themes running through a century and a half of 'investigating, describing and preserving' the antiquities of Cumbria. It takes the form of a contemplation built around the elements of the Society's name: The Cumberland and Westmorland Antiquarian and Archaeological Society. This somewhat cumbersome handle sets out its stall clearly, capturing the many facets of the Society's history. The following pages play with the name, disarticulating it as a means of reflecting on the Society's geographical perspective, the approaches to the past in which it has been active, and its nature as an organisation.

'Cumberland and Westmorland': changing perspectives

The Society's name defines its geographical scope as the two historic counties of Cumberland and Westmorland, sister counties which have been yoked together in antiquarian study since the seventeenth century. Yet a wider entity, 'the Lake Counties', had become well established several decades before the Society came into being in 1866. It is not surprising, therefore, that from the Society's early days the Furness and Cartmel peninsulas of Lancashire North of the Sands, the third constituent of the Lake Counties (and of modern Cumbria), were treated as an integral part of its remit, unofficially at first but after 1911 with the agreement of the neighbouring county society in Lancashire. The final building block, the Sedbergh area, was also formally brought within the Society's purview when the modern county came into being in 1974. As the modern strap-line, 'Cumbria Past', indicates, the Society's area of interest now covers the whole of the modern county.

However, Cumbria is an entity without a central focus and this poses problems for any organisation contributing to the county's cultural life. At one level a focus is provided by the iconic tourist honeypot of the Lake District but, despite the increasingly common conflation of the county with the national park (as in estate agents' literature or where the road sign on the M6 informs drivers that they are entering 'Cumbria: the Lake District'), the bulk of the region's population (and hence many of its major antiquities) were and are in the lowlands surrounding the mountainous core. This centrifugal geography, in which towns (and their hinterlands) are separated from each other by the hilly interior, has affected the Society and the study of Cumbria's past, as so much else. Unlike other county societies, the Cumberland and Westmorland does not have a single county town in which to focus its activities. From the very beginning, Council sought to rotate meetings and excursions around the two counties to ensure that the Society was not perceived to favour one area. The fragmented geography led directly to the establishment of 'regional groups' after the Second World War and the acceptance that no single centre could provide a winter lecture programme, the staple fare of many county societies. Membership has always been fragmented, with concentrations at the opposite ends of the region, in the urban centres of Carlisle and Kendal, from the beginning so that most individual members view the county from one of the edges looking in. Professional and academic perspectives have also been peripheral, with the location of county offices reinforcing the twin dominance of Carlisle and Kendal and with the absence (until 2007) of a university in the county meaning that the academic viewpoint has tended to be from outside.

Some patterns can be picked out in these peripheral perspectives. The closest the Society came to having a physical base was in the late-nineteenth century when the diocesan centre, city and county town of Carlisle filled that role. The foundation of Tullie House as library, museum and art gallery – and, particularly, the close association between it and the forceful leading light of the Society in the 1890s, Chancellor R.S. Ferguson – made that institution almost synonymous with the Society, despite the distance from its counterweight in Kendal, in which the Society's administrative officers (secretary and treasurer) were based. So close was the link that, when the library and museum at Tullie House split into separate institutions, there was continuing uncertainty over the ownership of some of the Society's possessions housed there. Although the Society's library has remained in the city throughout its history, Carlisle lost its central role in the life of the Society in the twentieth century. The void left by Ferguson's death in 1900 was filled by W.G. Collingwood, whose perspective was firmly from the south, from a base in Coniston. The balance gradually shifted as the Society's officers increasingly tended to view the county from homes on its southern side, a process accentuated as de-industrialisation left Carlisle the poorer, while increasing numbers of retired people settled in the Kendal area and the Lake District. Both the treasurership and the secretaryship of the Society have been Kendal- or Lancashire-based for its entire history. From the 1960s almost all of the presidents who lived in Cumbria dwelt in the southern half of the county (the notable exception being John Todd). At the time of writing, the President, Treasurer, General Secretary and Editor of *Transactions* are all based outside (and south of) the Society's territory, in Lancashire. Residence outside the county does not preclude either interest in Cumbria or loyalty to the Society.

The Society's links to neighbouring counties have also witnessed marked shifts of emphasis. The line of Hadrian's Wall, the most renowned ancient monument in Cumbria, runs as a thread through the Society's story, not least as a cord binding it to its elder sibling, the Society of Antiquaries of Newcastle upon Tyne, the oldest antiquarian society in the North. From its inception, the Society looked to the North East, seeking inspiration and advice from Collingwood Bruce in Newcastle and Greenwell in Durham. The two societies' shared Roman heritage has been renewed regularly by the decennial pilgrimages to Hadrian's Wall, led across the twentieth century by a chain of scholars linked in a series of tutor-pupil relationships from Francis Haverfield to Robin Collingwood, to Eric Birley and to David Breeze. Durham, the North of England's oldest university and seat of archaeological learning, provided much of the academic grounding for the Society's endeavours in the middle and later decades of the twentieth century, notably through the committed involvement of Eric Birley, Roy Hudleston and Rosemary Cramp. The connection continues, both in the Society's ongoing collaboration with the Surtees Society in the field of record publishing, and in that several recent presidents and the current General Secretary are proud to be alumni of Durham University.

However, that north-eastern perspective has increasingly been balanced by – and to some extent eclipsed by – a southern one from Lancashire, the county most accessible to Cumbria through the north-south railway and motorway links. The older universities of Manchester and Liverpool played a part in this (particularly as the Furness and Cartmel areas fell within the extra-mural territory of Liverpool University in the second half of the twentieth century) but it was the foundation of Lancaster University in 1964 which gave the Society a seat of learning on its doorstep. Through its (comparatively short-lived) Department of Classics and Archaeology (established as a Department of Classics in 1965 and closed in 1989), its Centre for North-West Regional Studies (founded in 1973) and the Cumbria & Lancashire Archaeological Unit (established in 1979) the University began to engage directly with the Society's areas of interest. From the late 1960s individual scholars (pioneered by John Marshall and David Shotter) became closely involved in the Society's affairs and have made an increasingly prominent contribution to its life and work.

The continuation of different geographical perspectives on Cumbria's past has ensured that, unlike some other county societies, the Cumberland and Westmorland has not fallen into the pocket of any one university. It could be said that balancing competing geographical interests – both within the centrifugal topography of its region and from outside – have helped to strengthen the Society's independence.

'Antiquarian and Archaeological': creative tension

The dual aspects of academic endeavour encapsulated in the Society's name – and the attempts to foster both and to balance their competing interests – run as a second theme through the Society's history. The potential tensions between the two sides of the Society's interest were visible from the very beginning when, at the inaugural meeting, Richard S. Ferguson pleaded that the new society should not devote itself exclusively to archaeological remains but should also work on the region's documentary heritage.

The Society appears to have been the only one of the Victorian county societies to have used the pairing 'antiquarian and archaeological' in its title. Many combined the study of the past with the study of natural history: 'Natural History and Antiquarian' were paired in Bath, Dorset and Penzance, for example, but 'Natural History and Archaeological' was a more frequent pairing, as in Burton-on-Trent, Derbyshire, Shropshire, Somerset, Suffolk, Warwickshire, Wiltshire and, closer to home, in Dumfries & Galloway.[1] Where the focus was intended to be squarely on the human past, the name of the society not infrequently combined archaeology with architecture, as in the Durham and Northumberland Architectural and Archaeological Society. Such societies tended to give particular attention to church architecture, mirroring the partisan ecclesiological societies associated with Tractarianism which championed medieval architecture and which tended to be dominated by the clergy. The 27 per cent of the Society's founding members who were clergy pales into insignificance beside the high proportions of clerics in some other counties.[2] By choosing to focus on the antiquarian and the archaeological, the Society avoided becoming embroiled in its early days in clergy-dominated battles over architectural styles.

From the very beginning, archaeological enquiry lay at the heart of the Society's activities. James Simpson, the founding chairman, was passionate about digging prehistoric barrows and the Society's archaeological role was formalised when the Cumberland Excavation Committee was established in 1894. A succession of archaeological pioneers (Francis Haverfield, W.G. and R.G. Collingwood, F.G. Simpson, Kate Hodgson and Eric Birley) stood at the Society's helm across the early- and mid-twentieth century, to the extent that archaeological exploration dominated much of the Society's activities by the 1930s. Archaeology is now a fully-fledged, highly technical academic discipline with a proud history, confident and soundly established in universities across the world. It also enjoys an enthusiastic following among non-professionals, the strength of which is visible in the enduring fascination for the material remains of the past which characterises the membership of societies like the Cumberland and Westmorland. Academic archaeology and the Society have developed to the mutual advantage of both.

The Society's relationship to the academic study of history has been more problematic. The professionalisation of history in universities from the later nineteenth century resulted in a distancing of the discipline from the traditions of antiquarian study. Indeed, the predominance of archaeological study in the Society has as much to do with the disdain with which professional historians have viewed 'antiquarianism' for much of the Society's 150 years as with the enduring attraction of archaeological discovery among the Society's membership. To describe research as 'antiquarian' is one of the worst terms of abuse that can be hurled at an academic historian and parts of mainstream history have had an enduring suspicion of local history, seeing it as essentially 'antiquarian' in character. If history is the interpretation of evidence in order to further our understanding of the past, 'mere antiquarianism' (note the dismissive tone of this frequent word-pairing) is the collection of data for its own sake, a focus on the particular without considering the wider context.

Why, then, has the Society retained 'Antiquarian' in its title? The word order of the Society's name is instructive: antiquarianism was born before its younger sibling, archaeology. Antiquarianism has a noble heritage, stretching back to the sixteenth century. Its essence was, and is, what David Starkey has termed 'thingyness': the study of the 'remnants of history which have casually escaped the shipwreck of time' in the words of Francis Bacon, writing in 1605.[3] The great burst of antiquarian activity associated with William Camden and others in the late Elizabethan period was a celebration of national and regional identity, rediscovering the past at county level, so that, in Camden's words, people should not be 'strangers in their owne soile'.[4] 'Thingyness' grounds the past in particular localities, so that, even if we rarely talk in such terms, antiquarian interests are intimately linked with trying to capture the 'spirit of place'.

The triumphs of past antiquaries lay in collecting, cataloguing, recording and hence preserving the 'remnants of history'. What is the role of 'mere antiquarians' in the modern world, now that so much of the study of the past is in the hands of professionals, whether archaeologists or historians? It can be argued that societies such as the Cumberland and Westmorland still have an important role to play in collecting, recording, putting in order and presenting the raw materials of history. The Society's activities in record publishing, the systematic study of even minor 'things', such as milestones, coin finds, or date stones, for example, and newer pursuits such as recording vernacular buildings or gathering oral testimony can all be thought of as modern manifestations of the antiquarian impulse. For the conception of which 'remnants of history' are worthy of study has changed as the social character of the Society has changed: the gentleman antiquaries' preoccupation with gentry genealogies and manor houses has faded in the face of the 'democratisation' of the past and the rise of economic history, social history, industrial archaeology and family history. The field of enquiry has widened and there is no shortage of subjects for study.

Without the burst of antiquarian activity from the sixteenth century, the modern science of archaeology would not have been born; without the continuing antiquarian – as opposed to historical – endeavour of individuals and societies like the Cumberland and Westmorland, the raw materials for future historians may perish, making the past more difficult to recapture. The Society need not feel diffident about celebrating the local, and valuing the things that make our 'two sister counties' distinctive in a world in which places increasingly look the same.

'Society': a shared passion

At the heart of the antiquarian impulse lies a passion for the past and it is this which has resonated down the generations, binding the members into a community with a strong sense of shared interest. From the earliest meetings of the Society to the present, a persistent questioning and desire to understand the past, whether at the level of an individual find or archaeological site or in the broader sweep of societal change, have drawn members together and often led to stimulating debate as ideas have taken flight and been batted back and forth. But the life of groups such as the Society is also sustained by other forces. The importance of the social aspect of meeting like-minded people and, often, old friends ought not to be underplayed, nor should a sense of awe and wonder. Such societies thrive on the experiential, on enabling their members to encounter the tangible legacies of the past. Whether this is standing in the Neolithic circle of Long Meg's daughters, or on the ramparts at Hardknott Roman fort, or tracing out the pagan Norse mythology in the carvings of the Gosforth cross, or the excitement of handling a document written centuries ago, the activities of the Society have helped successive generations to make that leap of the imagination which is necessary if we are really going to understand past worlds.

For much of the first century of its existence membership of the Society was to a large extent socially exclusive, restricted to the educated and leisured sector of Cumbrian society and sustained by subtle distinctions of dress and speech, networks of shared acquaintance and other cultural whispers. Within those restricted social boundaries the enjoyment of meeting, trudging to visit sites (often, it seems, in the rain!) and eating together is palpable from the accounts of the Society's 'Proceedings' reported in early volumes of *Transactions*. Within the more open membership of the modern Society the social aspect is similarly important. Sustaining the communal life of the Society has been fostered by a succession of leaders whose commitment to the Society has engendered strong affection from their fellow members:

W.G. Collingwood appears to have acted as such a magnet in the early decades of the twentieth century, as Kate Hodgson and Clare Fell did in the middle and later decades of the century, respectively.

If that makes the Society sound like a cosy club, it gives the wrong impression. Many of those with a passion for the past were strong personalities and some could be crusty, if not outright difficult. As in many other organisations, a cautious and conservative Council sometimes collided with a new broom, seeking to do things differently. Clashes of opinion and personality, combined with the inherent tensions discussed earlier and a relentless search for true historical and archaeological understanding, could lead to friction and disagreement. Feelings might be hurt (as when Roy Hudleston felt that his editorial independence was being undermined)[5] or frustrations might surface. A subversive alternative expansion of the initials 'CWAAS', circulating by the 1960s,[6] captures some of the Society's perceived shortcomings: the 'Cumbersome and Wearisome Antique and Arcane Society' neatly expresses that combination of exasperation and affection with which some of its leading members experienced CWAAS.

Yet the Society has not only survived to celebrate its sesquicentennial but has also evolved and thrived. Despite perennial expressions of concern about the need to attract new (and younger) members, the Society's membership remains healthy, standing at 666 individuals and 137 institutions in January 2016.[7] What has been the secret of the Society's success? Three factors may perhaps be identified.

First is the introduction of fixed-term presidencies after the Second World War. Vesting the leadership of a society in a single individual over many years, as had been the case until then, could have positive results by allowing a committed and vigorous president a long reign and (to some extent) a free rein, as was the case with W.G. Collingwood's presidency. But, as the experience of some other societies has shown, a constitution which allows one person to dominate can have a stultifying effect, in worst cases converting the society into a personal fiefdom and discouraging potential successors from becoming involved. The Society has been able to avoid this by limiting its presidential term to three years. As a result, new blood and fresh thinking are regularly brought into the leadership of the Society. A balance has been provided both by the happy longevity of service which has characterised the other key offices of General Secretary and Treasurer, and by the rule that Past Presidents remain members of Council for life. The combination of new ideas and long experience has served the Society well. A second element of the Society's recipe for success has been its ability to maintain involvement by both amateurs and professionals. Despite the increasing professionalisation of the study of the past, the Society's officers and members of Council have regularly included 'amateurs'. Most importantly, unlike the journals of some other societies, *Transactions* has never become the exclusive preserve of professional archaeologists and university academics. In most years it contains a remarkable range of papers, enabling serious amateurs to disseminate the fruits of their research in an internationally respected, (lightly) refereed journal. In a very real sense, 'ownership' of *Transactions* rests with the membership; it has not become a distant academic journal, run from a university.

Finally, the Society has benefited from the checks and balances implicit in the dualities expressed in its name. The decentralised character of its area of interest ('Cumberland and Westmorland' but in reality the whole of Cumbria) has demanded a conscious attempt across 15 decades to cater for a dispersed population and has meant that no one town or city has dominated the Society's affairs (even if Carlisle almost did so in the later nineteenth century and as Kendal did during the Second World War). Geography has also prevented the Society from declining into a mere lecture society, inactive in research and enquiry. Similarly, the tension between 'Antiquarian and Archaeological' has never lain far below the surface and has presented a perennial challenge, in view of the way that the historical and archaeological professions have developed and diverged across the century and a half since the Society was founded. It has never quite become the 'Cumberland and Westmorland Archaeological Society', even if outsiders sometimes mis-name it such.

In reporting the Society's inaugural meeting in September 1866, the local press summarised the function of the new body as being to

> explore and investigate from time to time the numerous interesting antiquities of these two counties and, meeting at different places, to give the public, either in the shape of written papers or printed pamphlets, the results of their explorations and discoveries.[8]

One hundred and fifty years later, members continue to explore and investigate Cumbria's past and the Society's financial resources continue to be directed towards furthering such study in the much more complex world of archaeology and history in the twenty-first century. The Society continues to meet in different places, to enable its members to develop their understanding of the past on-site, and, through its increasingly impressive publication programme and its developing web presence, to make the fruits of research available globally, to the widest possible audience. By moving with the times, it continues to honour the intentions of those enthusiastic Victorians who met in Penrith that September Tuesday a century and a half ago.

Notes and References

1 County societies in England are listed in P. Levine, *The Amateur and the Professional: antiquarians, historians and archaeologists in Victorian England, 1838*-1886 (Cambridge, 1986), 182-83.

2 Levine, *Amateur and Professional*, 46-48.

3 D. Starkey, 'Making History', introduction to *Making History: antiquaries in Britain 1707-2007* (London, Royal Academy of Arts, 2007), 12-13; F. Bacon, *The Advancement of Learning*, Book II, f. 10v (London, 1605).

4 W. Camden, *Britain or a chorographical description* ... (London, 1610), 'To the Reader'.

5 CAS (Carlisle), DSO/1/18, Council minutes, 1 Sept. 1967; DSO/1/102, Council minutes 7 Sept. 1972, minute 7. See also R. Hall, 'Obituary: Christopher Roy Hudleston', *Newsletter*, 16 (Summer, 2014), 8.

6 As remembered by Council members in 2015. Several longstanding members associated the phrase with Barbara Harbottle and/or John Gillam.

7 Figures courtesy of Adrian Allan, membership secretary, 24 Jan. 2016.

8 Press cutting in DSO/1/1.

Appendix 1
Presidents of the Society

Compiled by I.D. Caruana

William Lowther, 2nd Earl of Lonsdale, PC, FRS, 21/7/1787-4/3/1872, President 1866-72.
Educated Harrow and Trinity College, Cambridge. Conservative politician who represented various Cumbrian seats between 1808 and 1841. Government minister under Wellington, Peel and Derby. Privy Counsellor 1818; Lord Lieutenant of Cumberland and Westmorland 1844-68. Founder of *Westmorland Gazette*. Unmarried. H. Owen, *The Lowther Family* (1990), 390-92.

Henry Lowther, 3rd Earl of Lonsdale, 27/3/1818-15/8/1876, President 1872-76.
Educated Westminster and Trinity College, Cambridge. Nephew of 2nd Earl. Officer in 1st Life Guards, 1841-52. MP for West Cumberland 1847-72. Lord Lieutenant of Cumberland and Westmorland 1868-76. Owen, *Lowther Family*, 400-01.

St George Lowther, 4th Earl of Lonsdale, 4/10/1855-8/2/1882, President 1876-82.
Educated at Eton. Deputy Lieutenant of Cumberland. Colonel in Royal Cumberland Militia. Owen, *Lowther Family*, 401.

Canon James Simpson, MA, LLD, FSA, Aug. 1819-8/3/1886, President 1882-86.
Born Lyth. Educated at Crosthwaite School (Westmorland) and University College, Durham. After school he first became a teacher at Shap (1839) and then trained for the ministry. Curate at Chester-le-Street, then Morland; vicar of Shap 1857, and Kirkby Stephen 1863. Canon of Carlisle 1874. Retained an interest in education, Poor Law administration and Freemasonry. Magistrate for Westmorland, Chairman of Quarter Sessions, Mayor of Appleby. Founder member of the Society, Editor 1866-67; Chair of Council 1866-82. Contributed several papers to *Transactions* on the antiquities of Westmorland. Obituary: *CW1,* 8 (1886), 532-35.

Richard Saul Ferguson, MA, LLM, JP, FSA, FSA Scot., 28/6 or 7/1837-3/3/1900, President 1886-1900.
From Carlisle family of cotton spinners. Educated Carlisle GS, Shrewsbury, and St John's College, Cambridge. Attended Lincoln's Inn and called to bar 1862. Returned to Carlisle 1874. JP (1872), Chairman of Cumberland Quarter Sessions (1886); Chancellor of Diocese of Carlisle (1887); Carlisle Town Council (1878), alderman, mayor twice (1881, 1882). Founder member of the Society, Editor 1867-1900. He edited six major and five lesser publications for the Society and was editor of the entire first series of *Transactions* from 1867-1900. Other publications include: *Early Cumberland and Westmorland Friends*; *Cumberland and Westmorland MPs*; *History of Cumberland*; *History of Westmorland.* The list of articles published in *Transactions* runs to four pages in his obituary. Outside Cumbria he was active in the Royal Archaeological Institute and Surtees Society. He was an active promoter of the links between the county and the wider archaeological community as exemplified in his paper 'An archaeological survey of Cumberland and Westmorland', *Archaeologia*, 53 (1893). Obituary: *CW1,* 16 (1900), vii-x. *Oxford DNB.*

Henry Ware, Bishop of Barrow, MA, DD, 22/6/1830-16/4/1909, President 1900-09.
Educated Trinity, Cambridge. Ordained deacon 1860, priest 1862, Vicar of Kirkby Lonsdale 1862-88, Canon of Carlisle 1870, and first suffragan Bishop of Barrow-in-Furness 1889 until his death. Married (2) to Ellen, daughter of Harvey Goodwin, Bishop of Carlisle, 1887. Died in Rome. Founder member of the Society and an active member as member of Council, Vice-President and then President. Published papers in *Transactions* on Kirkby Lonsdale and edited Bishop Nicolson's Diaries in five parts in the New Series. Obituary: *CW2*, 9 (1909), 338.

Thomas Hesketh Hodgson, JP, FSA, 14/11/1841-18/10/1917, President 1909-15.
Born Warwickshire. Educated Marlborough & Jesus College, Cambridge. Admiralty civil servant, retired to Newby Grange inherited from W.N. Hodgson, uncle, 1876. Joined Society in 1883, member of Council 1891, Chairman of Council 1900. Retired as President through ill health and made Honorary Member. Contributed papers, particularly on Crosby-on-Eden. and was leading local figure in Cumberland Excavation Committee, 1894-1903 involved with Roman Wall excavations. Edited *Marriages of Crosby-on-Eden 1665-1836* (1912). Married 1888 Elizabeth Cookson whose drawings for the Cumberland Excavation Committee are in *CW1*, 14 (1895) and who published in her own right. Obituary: *CW2,* 17 (1917), 262-64.

Professor Francis John Haverfield, MA, LLD, DLitt, FSA, Hon. FSA Scot., FBA, 8/11/1860-1/10/1919, President 1915-19.
Born Shipston-on-Stour. Educated Winchester and New College, Oxford. Schoolmaster at Lancing (1884) during which time he met Mommsen who invited him to help with updating *Corpus Inscriptionum Latinarum* (Vol. 7), forerunner of *RIB*. Returned to Oxford as tutor at Christ Church 1892, Camden Professor of Ancient History 1907-19, FSA 1891, FBA 1904. Joined SANT 1889 – Vice-President 1906. First President of the Society for Promotion of Roman Studies 1910. Widely regarded as the creator of Romano-British archaeology. Joined Society 1890, Vice-President 1899, member of Cumberland Excavation Committee 1894-1903. Obituary: *CW2,* 20 (1920), 255-57. See also: P.W.M. Freeman, *The Best Training Ground for Archaeologists: Francis Haverfield and the Invention of Romano-British Archaeology* (Oxford, 2007). *Oxford DNB.*

William Gershom Collingwood, MA, FSA, 6/8/1854-1/10/1932, President 1920-32.
Born Liverpool, son of an artist. Educated University College, Oxford where he met John Ruskin. Became Ruskin's secretary at Brantwood and wrote his biography. Studied at Slade 1876-78. Moved to University College, Reading in 1905 serving as Professor of Fine Art 1907-11. Served in Naval Intelligence during Great War. Developed an interest in pre-Norman art in collaboration with W.S. Calverley which led to the publication of *Northumbrian Crosses of the pre-Norman Age* (London, 1927). This and his interest in Iceland and its sagas formed the backdrop to his novels. President of Viking Club. Joined Society 1887, Editor 1900-25 and also oversaw production of ten additional volumes. As editor he created the 2nd series of *Transactions* and designed the Society's seal. Obituary: *CW2,* 33 (1933), 308-12. See also M. Townend, *Vikings and Victorian Lakeland* (2009) and *W.G. Collingwood's Letters from Iceland,* eds. M. and K. Lea, (R.G. Collingwood Society, 2012). *Oxford DNB.*

Robin George Collingwood, MA, FSA, FRHS, FBA, 22/2/1889-9/1/1943, President 1932-38.
Son of W.G. Collingwood (q.v.). Born Cartmel, educated Rugby and University College, Oxford, where he was a pupil of Haverfield (q.v.). Fellow of Pembroke College, Oxford 1912, and Waynflete Professor of Metaphysical Philosophy 1935-41. His academic work covered philosophy and Roman archaeology. On the latter, three works stand out: *The Archaeology of Roman Britain* (1930), later editions of which, edited by Ian Richmond (1969), are still in print; his joint contribution (with J.N.L. Myers) to the *Oxford History of England* (1936); and the *Roman Inscriptions of Britain* (a project inherited from Haverfield, and eventually published 1965). His *An Autobiography* (1939) and *The Idea of History* (1946) are widely influential among historians. His contributions to *Transactions* cover a wide range of sites and

finds. One particularly noteworthy creation was the invention of the numbering system for Hadrian's Wall, *CW2,* 30 (1930), 108-15. Joined Society 1909. Joint Editor with his father 1920-25 and with T.H.B. Graham and Mcintire 1925-33. Obituary: *CW2,* 43 (1943), 211-14; D. Boucher and T. Smith, *R.G. Collingwood: an autobiography and other writings with essays on Collingwood's life and work* (2013). See also British Idealism and Collingwood Centre at Cardiff University. *Oxford DNB.*

Walter Travers McIntire, BA, FSA, FRHS, FSA Scot., 23/4/1870-24/8/1944, President 1938-44.
Born Yorkshire. Educated Giggleswick and Bedford GS. Uncompleted medical studies at Edinburgh were followed by an external arts degree at London University. After several teaching posts, latterly at Kendal GS, he became Director of Technical Education & Principal of Tullie House in 1904. After re-organisation of Tullie House he retired to Milnthorpe in 1924 from where he continued to read and lecture. A leading member of the Historical Association. He joined the Society in 1904, Editor 1926-44. His ten articles in *Transactions* covered topics on the Solway and Furness areas; he contributed a regular column to the *Cumberland News* (1930-44) collected in *Lakeland and the Borders of Long Ago* (1948), but it was said his publications do little justice to the immense breadth of his learning. Obituary: *CW2,* 44 (1944), 166-68.

Lt.-Col. Oliver Henry North, DSO, FSA, 28/4/1874-21/7/1954, President 1945-47.
Family from Newton Hall, Lancashire. Plans to become a tea-planter in Ceylon were disrupted by the Boer War when he was commissioned into the Lancashire Fusiliers with whom he served until 1925, winning a DSO and three Mentions in Despatches during the Great War. Was District Remount Officer from 1933 and in Home Guard during the Second World War. Joined Society 1908, member of Council 1930, Vice-President 1935, member of Cumberland Excavation Committee and Committee for Prehistoric Studies. Elected FSA 1921. Published archaeological papers on prehistoric and Roman finds, particularly on Burrow-in-Lonsdale, Watercrook and Old Penrith. *Obituary: CW2,* 54 (1954), 305-07.

Frank Gerald Simpson, CBE, MA, Hon. FSA Scot., 31/10/1882-14/5/1955, President 1947-48.
Born Boston Spa. Educated Rydal School. Eschewed Oxford and became a marine engineer with Hawthorne, Leslie & Co. in Newcastle 1899. Joined SANT in 1905 and was on 1906 Pilgrimage. His first major excavation was at Haltwhistle Burn fortlet 1907 and this was followed by a long series of excavations on Hadrian's Wall in collaboration with J.P. Gibson, Eric Birley, and Ian Richmond in which they addressed the major problems in Wall studies. Joined Society 1909, member of Council 1920,

Vice-President 1924. Awarded MA by University of Durham 1924 and led its field excavation activities 1924-30. His term of office as President was curtailed by ill health. His CBE was for services to archaeology (1949). From 1938 he lived by the fort at Stanwix and is buried at Nether Denton, within another Roman fort. Obituaries: *CW2*, 55 (1955), 359-65; *AA4*, 34 (1956), 219-21. See G. Simpson, *Watermills and Military Works on Hadrian's Wall* (1976), 1-23, for an assessment by his daughter.

Katherine Sophia Hodgson, FSA, Sept.1889-27/3/1974, President 1948-51.
Daughter of T.H. Hodgson of Newby Grange (q.v.). Studied at Institute of Archaeology, London. Joined Society 1918, member of Excavation and Prehistoric Studies Committees, member of Council 1936, Chairman of Council 1955-65, Honorary Member 1962. Lived at Brampton. Founder member of Carlisle Regional Group and Chairman 1949-66. FSA 1949. Said to have worked on her first excavation aged five. First paper in *Transactions* 1910. Worked and published with the Cumberland Excavation Committee on Hadrian's Wall in the 1930s and excavated a number of prehistoric barrows in the North East of the county (published in *Transactions* up to 1953). Publication of her final excavations at Broomrigg and in the White Lyne Valley were completed by her collaborators, *CW2*, 75 (1975), 17-29. Bequeathed half her estate to the Society including moiety of the manor of Crosby-on-Eden. Obituary: *Cumberland News* 5 April 1974; *The Times* 2 April 1974. Photo and tribute in *CW2*, 74 (1974), frontis.; *Cumberland Families and Heraldry* (1978), 161.

Joseph Edward Spence, MB, ChB, DPH, FSA, 1885-27/2/1962, President 1951-54.
Medical Officer of Health in Eccles (Lancashire) 1922. Returned to Cumbria after retirement but moved to Weymouth for his health in 1955 when he withdrew from Society affairs. FSA 1939. Joined Society 1916, member of Council 1931, Secretary of Prehistoric Studies Committee 1932 and Chairman 1948, Excursion Secretary 1945, Vice-President 1947-51, Chairman of Council 1951-55. Apart from several archaeological papers and reports of the Prehistoric Studies Committee in *Transactions* he compiled the 'Author and Subject Index to Transactions... 1-45' which appeared in *CW2*, 46 (1946), 1-66. His obituarist credits him with reviving the excursion programme after the war. Obituary: *CW2*, 62 (1962), 356-57.

Canon Charles Murray Lowther Bouch, MA, FSA, 29/5/1890-22/7/1959, President 1954-57.
Born London, educated Radley College. Joined Civil Service and served in World War I where he was severely wounded. Christ Church College, Oxford, BA 1921; ordained to curacy of St John's, Workington in 1922, then served at Maryport, Barrow and St

Barnabas, Carlisle 1932-46. Rector of Clifton and Brougham 1946-59, Hon. Canon of Carlisle 1955. Joined Society 1913, member of Council 1946, Editor of Parish Register Section 1946, Joint Secretary 1947, Joint Editor 1951-57. FSA 1952. Contributed widely to *Transactions* from 1927-55. His *Prelates and Peoples of the Lake Counties* (1948) remains a fundamental source for the religious history of the county. Obituary: *CW2,* 59 (1959), 175-57; *Cumberland Families and Heraldry* 32.

Professor Eric Barff Birley, MBE, MA, FBA, FSA, 12/1/1906-20/10/1995, President 1957-60.

Born Eccles, Lancs. Educated Clifton College and Brasenose College, Oxford. Archaeological career begin on Hadrian's Wall with F.G. Simpson (q.v.) in 1927. Discovery of two inscriptions at Birdoswald led to the creation of his theory of Wall Periods. Lecturer at Durham 1931, Reader 1943, Vice-Master 1947 and Master of Hatfield College 1949, Professor of Romano-British History and Archaeology 1956-71. Founded the Congress of Roman Frontier Studies 1949 and organised three Hadrian's Wall Pilgrimages 1930, 1949, 1959. His war service was in military intelligence, having joined the TA in 1939, retiring as major in 1956, with rank of honorary lieutenant-colonel. Awarded MBE in 1943 and Polish and American decorations for his war work. His academic specialisms were the Roman army, Roman epigraphy and samian pottery. In 1929 he bought the Chesterholm estate (with the fort of Vindolanda) starting his family's long association with the site. Joined Society 1926, Editor 1948-57, member of Excavation Committee 1930-73, Committee for Prehistoric Studies 1932-69, Committee for the Parish Register Section 1948-80. Obituaries: *CW2,* 96 (1996), 243-44; *AA5*, 24 (1996), 218-20; *Oxford DNB*.

Christopher Roy Hudleston, MA, BLitt, FSA, FSA Scot., FRHS, 13/10/1905-8/2/1992, President 1960-63.

Born Stroud, with ancestors from Millom and Hutton John. Educated Wycliffe College. Worked as a journalist in Bristol from 1923. Wartime forestry work in Cumbria and in 1945 he became Editor of *Penrith Observer*. Bursar of Hatfield College, Durham 1955-65 and initially part-time lecturer in palaeography and later full-time until 1970, taking an in-service MA in 1960. In Durham he catalogued the Howard of Naworth papers and Durham Diocesan records, the first leading to *Naworth Estate and Household Accounts 1648-1660* (1959). President of Bristol & Gloucestershire Archaeological Society, FSA 1949, Editor of Surtees Society 1968-79, first President of Cumbria Family History Society 1976. Joined Society 1930, Editor Parish Register Section 1955, Vice-President 1955-60, Editor 1956-74, a period which saw a revival in series publications. Besides numerous articles in *Transactions*, he co-authored *An Armorial for Westmorland* (1975) and *Cumberland Families and Heraldry* (1978). *Obituary: CW2,* 92 (1992), 95-98; CWAAS, *Newsletter* 16.

Clare Isobel Fell, MA, FSA, 10/10/1912-17/7/2002, President 1963-66.
Younger daughter of Lt-Gen Sir Matthew Fell of Flan How, Ulverston, a leading figure in the RAMC and creator of the RAF medical services. Educated Harrogate College and Newnham College, Cambridge. Took second part of her degree in Archaeology & Anthropology gaining 1st class, but not awarded her degree until 1948. In 1933 awarded Sparkes Scholarship by her college and began to publish. During the war she drove ambulances with the ATS. After the war joined the staff of the Museum of Archaeology and Anthropology in Cambridge and worked with many of the leading prehistorians of her era such as Christopher Hawkes and Grahame Clark at Star Carr. FSA 1951. Member of Council of Prehistoric Society. Returned to Cumbria in 1953. Joined Society 1937, member of Council 1945, Vice-President 1957-63, variously member and Chairman of Prehistoric and Excavation Committees from 1937-82. Left her archaeological papers to Society (CAS, [Kendal], WDX 1408) as well as her library. Obituary: *CW3*, 2 (2002), 317-19; K.E. Sharpe, 'The Lady of the Lakes' in P.J. Cherry (ed.), *Studies in Northern Prehistory: essays in memory of Clare Fell* (2007).

Sir Roger Thomas Baldwin Fulford, CVO, MA, 24/11/1902-18/5/1983, President 1966-68.
Son of a vicar. Educated Lancing and Worcester College, Oxford. Qualified barrister (1931) but never practised. Journalist on *The Times* and part-time lecturer at King's College, London 1937-48. Leading Liberal politician and party President 1964-65. Lived at Barbon Manor. As an historian he specialised in 18th and 19th centuries. Major works included a ten-volume edition of Charles Greville's Diaries. CVO 1970, knighted 1980. Joined Society 1946. Obituary: *The Times*, 19 May 1983; *Oxford DNB.*

John Charlton LVO, MA, FSA, 7/6/1909-29/10/2004, President 1968-71.
Born Gateshead. Read English and History at Durham University. Began working in archaeology under the influence of Eric Birley (q.v.) and was at Birdoswald in 1929. Became an Inspector for the RCHM(E), became a specialist in medieval buildings, and was responsible for its volume on Westmorland (1936). Played a significant role in preventing destruction of Hadrian's Wall by wartime quarrying. Early excavations included Waltham Abbey and Clarendon Palace 1933-39. Principal Inspector of Ancient Monuments and the Royal Palaces. He wrote many of the Ministry of Works guidebooks to sites in Cumbria such as Carlisle and Brougham Castles. FSA 1947. President of Royal Archaeological Institute 1975-78. The Society's volume on Brougham Castle (1998) was dedicated to him and he was present on site at the launch. Joined Society 1947, member of Council 1948, Vice-President 1959-68. Obituary: *CW3,* 5 (2005), 305-07; *Society for Medieval Archaeology Newsletter,* 35, 10-11.

Revd John Compton Dickinson, MA, DLitt, FSA, FRHS, 1913-23/7/1991, President 1971-74.

Born into a horse-racing family at Cark-in-Cartmel. Educated Ulverston GS and Keble College, Oxford. Lecturer in History, Leeds University 1936, war service in the navy, followed by research in France and Italy. Fellow of Emmanuel College, Cambridge 1947, ordained 1949; Assistant Lecturer in History, Cambridge 1949-54, Fellow and Chaplain of Pembroke College, Cambridge 1950-60. Department of Theology, Birmingham University 1960, then Senior Lecturer 1962-73. Hon. Canon of Peterborough 1970-73. Joined Society 1933, member of Council 1938, Editor 1945-48, Vice-President 1952-71. Besides papers in *Transactions* he produced two books on Cartmel, *The Land of Cartmel* (1980) and *The Priory of Cartmel* (1991), following his authoritative *The Origins of the Austin Canons and their Introduction to England* (1950). Obituary: CWAAS, *Newsletter*, 15.

Paul Norman Wilson, Baron Wilson of High Wray, OBE, DSC, KStJ, JP, MA, FSA, 24/10/1908-24/2/1980, President 1974-78.

Educated Gresham's and Clare College, Cambridge. Worked as engineer in South Africa 1930-34 then joined Gilbert, Gilkes and Gordon Ltd. of Kendal as Managing Director, becoming Chairman in 1954. Served with RNVR in World War II, winning DSC. Awarded OBE 1959. Lord Lieutenant of Westmorland 1965-74 and of Cumbria 1974-80. Life peer 1976. Various public offices included Governor of BBC, Chairman of Lake District Museum Trust and Vice-President and President of Newcomen Society. Joined Society 1952. Patron before becoming President. Published on watermills. *Armorial for Westmorland and Lonsdale* (1978), 325; http://en.wikipedia.org/wiki/Paul_Wilson,_Baron_Wilson_of_High_Wray.

Dorothy Charlesworth, MA, FSA, 17/9/1927-7/6/1981, President 1978-81.

Born Tynemouth but raised in Hexham. Educated Cheltenham Ladies College and Somerville College, Oxford where she read History. Developed her interest in Roman glass as research assistant to Donald Harden at the Ashmolean. Assistant Inspector of Ancient Monuments for Ministry of Works, 1956. Later had responsibility for Hadrian's Wall and from 1974 rescue archaeology in the North where she oversaw the creation of various regional rescue units. First President of re-founded Council for British Archaeology Group 3 1972. FSA 1962. Lead organiser for 1979 Pilgrimage and participant in Roman Frontier Congress. Research interests centred on the Roman military and on ancient glass on which she was a leading authority. Secretary of the Association for the History of Glass 1977-81. Many of her publications appeared as glass reports for other excavators but significant articles on 'Roman glass in the Northern Britain' appeared in *AA4*, 37 (1959) and 'Roman square bottles' in *Journal. of Glass Studies*, 8 (1966). Excavated widely on Roman forts in Cumbria: Kirkby Thore, Papcastle, Brougham, Hardknott (published as CWAAS, Research Series IX), Piper Sike (T51a on Hadrian's Wall). On Hadrian's Wall she excavated at Housesteads and Carrawburgh. Her paper 'Roman Carlisle', *Arch. J.* 135 (1978), summarised our knowledge at the time and formed platform for subsequent work. Her excavations at Annetwell Street, Carlisle finally established the correct position of the Roman fort. Joined Society 1957, member of Council 1962-65, 1968-70, 1975-77 (co-opted); member of Excavation Committee 1974 and Chairman 1977. Tribute in *J. Glass Studies*, 24 (1982), 119-20.

Joseph (Fred) Hughes, FSA, 27/7/1916-18/3/2000, President 1981-84.
Born Ireleth, educated Ulverston GS. Articled to architectural firm in Kendal. Joined Office of Works in London, then Cumberland County Architects Department, Carlisle 1938. Served with Royal Engineers during war being Mentioned in Despatches. Returned to Carlisle becoming Chief Building Inspector. In 1974 he transferred to Kendal as Historic Buildings Officer, retiring 1981. FSA 1977. Joined Society 1956, Excursions Secretary 1962-73, Committee for Industrial Archaeology 1969-82, Committee for Prehistoric Studies 1970-73, Assistant Editor 1970-75, Joint Editor 1975-82, Vice-President 1972-81, Hon. Member 1996. Contributor to *Armorial for Westmorland* and *Cumberland Families and Heraldry* (1975) and to *The New History of Freemasonry in the Province of Cumberland & Westmorland* (1994). Obituary: *CW2*, 100 (2000), 295-97.

Professor Dame Rosemary Jean Cramp, DBE, MA, BLitt, FSA, FBA, Born 6/5/1929, President 1984-87.
From farming family of Glooston, Leicestershire. Educated Market Harborough GS and St Anne's College, Oxford. Lecturer St Anne's College 1950-55, lecturer Durham 1955, Professor 1971-90. Commissioner RCHAMS 1974-99 and RCHME 1984-89, Trustee of British Museum 1978-98, President of Society of Antiquaries 2001-04. CBE 1987, DBE 2011, FSA 1959, FBA 2006. Leading scholar in Anglo-Saxon studies, conducted major excavations on the monasteries of Jarrow and Monkwearmouth, and The Hirsel. Co-author of three volumes of *Corpus of Anglo Saxon Stone Sculpture,* including vol. 2 on Cumberland and Westmorland with Richard Bailey (1988). Joined Society 1962, member of Council 1973, Vice-President 1978.

James (Jim) Cherry, BSc, FSA, 25/11/1920-20/7/2008, President 1987-90.
Born and educated in Blackburn. External degree in chemistry from London University. Worked for UKAEA, later BNFL, at which time he moved to Seascale in 1950 where he began to fieldwalk in the coastal dunes – work recorded in many articles in *Transactions.*

After moving to Kendal in 1980, he (with his family) transferred their attention to the uplands in the east of the county, resulting in *Prehistoric Habitation Sites on the Limestone Uplands of Eastern Cumbria* (1987). FSA 1989. Joined Society 1959, member of Council 1965, Committee for Industrial Archaeology 1969-83, Secretary of Committee for Prehistoric Studies 1970-73, Fieldwork and Excavation Committee 1973-88. Chairman of South-West Regional Group. Married to Joyce, General Secretary (1974-85) and together they compiled indexes to Old Series *Transactions* and the 1960-89 volumes. Obituary *CW3*, 8 (2008), 301-02.

Professor Ronald William Brunskill, OBE, MA, PhD, ARIBA, FSA, 3/1/1929-9/10/2015, President 1990-93.
Educated Bury High School and Manchester University where he trained as an architect. ARIBA 1951. 2nd Lt. Royal Engineers 1953-55. Lecturer Manchester University 1960, Reader 1984, Professor De Montfort University 1995-2001. FSA 1975, OBE for services to conservation 1990. Published widely on vernacular architecture including *Vernacular Architecture of the Lake Counties* (1974 and later editions) and *Traditional Buildings of Cumbria* (2002). President of the Vernacular Architecture Group, Vice-Chairman of the Weald and Downland Museum, and was a member of the Royal Commission on Ancient and Historical Monuments of Wales, the Heritage Lottery Fund, and the Friends of Friendless Churches. Patron of the Cumbria Vernacular Buildings Group 2013. Joined Society 1955, member of Council 1965, Vice-President 1975-90. Obituary *CW3*, 16 (2016), 1-4.

Ruth Barbara Harbottle, MA, FSA, 23/8/1931-18/2/2012, President 1993-96.
Born Gosforth (Newcastle), educated Girton College, Cambridge. After graduating worked on the Far East section of the *Official History* of the Second World War. Returned to work in the archive section of Newcastle Corporation and took part in a number of excavations in the North East. In Cumbria she excavated at Kendal Castle and in Penrith. In 1975 she became the first county archaeologist for Tyne & Wear, retiring 1997. FSA 1970-99. Joined Society in 1962, Vice-President 1991-93, then President and always an active participant in Society activities. She was President of SANT 1996-68, Editor of *Transactions of Durham & Northumberland Archaeological & Architectural Society* 1968-70, supporter of Newcastle Lit. & Phil. and CBA. Obituary *CW3*, 12 (2012), 1-2.

John Macnair Todd, MA, PhD, FRHS, 2/5/1934-20/1/2009, President 1996-99.
Born Wilmslow. Educated Manchester GS and Balliol College, Oxford. Civil servant in Ministry of Labour 1955, Married Mary Tyson, daughter of Whitehaven solicitor. Moved to St Bees 1966 and joined her family's law firm. Qualified as solicitor 1970 and became

partner. Retired 1996. Historical scholarship began with various contributions to the history of St Bees, including his involvement with the 'St Bees man'. PhD awarded at Lancaster in 1991. He subsequently lectured on medieval history. He edited *The Lanercost Cartulary* (1997) and *A Window on to Late Medieval Cumbria* (2000). Deeply involved with lay readership of the diocese since 1974. Founder member and first Chairman of FOCAS 1991-94. Joined Society 1975, member of Council 1982-85, 1988-91, Chairman of Research Committee 1994-97 and Editorial Committee 1999-2004 where he systematised its procedures, Vice-President 1994-96. Revised constitution of the Society. Obituary: *CW3*, 9 (2009), vii-ix. See also K. Stringer (ed.), *North-West England from the Romans to the Tudors: essays in memory of John MacNair Todd* (CWAAS, Extra Series XLI, 2014).

Geoffrey Haward Martin, CBE, MA, DPhil, FSA, FRHS, 27/9/1928-20/12/2007, President 1999-2002.
Educated Colchester RGS and Merton College, Oxford, with whom he had a long association and wrote its official history (1997). Lecturer in Economic History at Leicester University, later Professor 1973-82 and Pro-Vice-Chancellor 1979-82. His specialist area was medieval urban history, stemming from his doctoral study of Ipswich and *The Story of Colchester* (1959). Appointed Keeper of the Public Records 1982 and oversaw the Domesday Book 900th anniversary exhibition and celebrations culminating in publication of the facsimile edition in 2003. Bought house at Finsthwaite 1969. Joined Society 1982, Vice-President 1988-99, Chairman of Editorial Committee 1996-99. Obituary: *CW3*, 8 (2008), 294-98; *The Times* 31 Jan. 2008.

Professor Angus James Logie Winchester, BA, PhD, FSA, Born 16/07/1951, President 2002-05.
Educated Cockermouth GS, Bootham School, York, and Durham University. Lecturer in Historical Geography, Department of Continuing Education, Liverpool University 1981; Lecturer 1990 and Professor 2012, Department of History, University of Lancaster. Director of the Centre for North-West Regional Studies (2012-14) and the Regional Heritage Centre (2014-15). Vice-President and Joint General Editor, Surtees Society since 2011. Member of Victoria County History National Advisory Board and Director of the VCH Cumbria project. FSA 2004. Research interests include medieval landscape and Cumbrian local history. Major publications include: *Landscape and Society in Medieval Cumbria* (1987);*The Harvest of the Hills: rural life in Northern England and the Scottish borders, 1400-1700* (2000); *Contested Common Land: environmental governance past and present* (2011) plus editions of *John Denton's History of Cumberland* (2010), *Thomas Denton: A Perambulation of Cumberland* (2003) and *The Diary of Isaac Fletcher* (1994) for the Society. Joined Society 1966, member of Council 1981, Vice-President 1997-2003. Initiator and first Editor of Newsletter, 1983.

Professor David Colin Arthur Shotter, BA, PhD, FSA, Born 1/3/1939, President 2005-08.
Born Raynes Park (London). Educated King's College School, Wimbledon and Southampton University. Assistant Lecturer in Greek and Latin at Magee University College, Londonderry 1964-66, Lecturer in Classics, University of Lancaster, 1966, Senior Lecturer 1973-89 when he transferred to Department of History, Personal Chair in Roman Imperial History, 2003. Retired 2004. Published commentaries on Tacitus (1989), Suetonius (1993), and a biography of Nero (2008), plus various Lancaster Pamphlets. Research turned to Romano-British Archaeology (especially numismatics), publishing *The Roman Frontier in Britain* (1996), a number of Occasional Papers for the Centre for North-West Regional Studies, and four volumes of *Roman Coins from North-West England* (1990-2011). Co-founder of the Lancaster Archaeological and Historical Society in 1973, and Chairman over a number of years. FSA 1978. Chair of annual Lancaster Archaeology conferences 1974-2013. Joined Society 1971, Vice-President 1991-2005. Chaired a working-party which produced a wide-ranging report on the role the Society should have in the twenty-first century. Numismatic adviser to Portable Antiquities Scheme in this area.

Richard Newman, BA, PhD, MIFA, FSA, Born 10/5/1958, President 2008-11.
Born Dinas Powys. Educated Newent Comprehensive School and University College, Cardiff 1976-82. Assistant Director Wessex Archaeology 1991-94. Director of Lancaster University Archaeology Unit 1994-2000. Set up private consultancy 2001-02. County Archaeologist for Cumbria 2002-07, then Historic and Natural Environment Manager 2007-13 where he managed the Cumbria Historic Landscape Characterisation programme and the North West Research Frameworks. Now pursuing personal research interests and from April 2014 working for English Heritage as the North West's Heritage at Risk Project Officer. FSA 1996. Member of Listed Building Advisory Committee for Methodist Church 2005-11, Milnthorpe parish councillor 2009-11. Research interests in historic landscapes, medieval settlement and post-medieval archaeology. Edited *The Archaeology of Lancashire* (1996); co-authored *The Historical Archaeology of Britain 1540-1900* (2001). Joined Society 1995, member of Council 2004, Chair of Committee for Industrial Archaeology, 2004-08.

David John Breeze, OBE, BA, PhD, FSA, FRSE, Hon. FSA Scot., Hon. MIFA, Born 25/7/1944, President 2011-14.
Educated Blackpool GS and University College, Durham, where he was a pupil of Eric Birley (q.v.). Awarded PhD 1970. Joined Ministry of Public Building and Works rising to be Chief Inspector for Historic Scotland 1989-2005. Specialist interest in Roman army and frontiers co-authoring (with Brian Dobson) *Hadrian's Wall* (1976) and

editing the 14th edition of *John Collingwood Bruce's Handbook to the Roman Wall* (2006), plus many other books and papers. President of Society of Antiquaries of Scotland 1987-90, SANT 2008-11, Royal Archaeological Institute 2009-12 and Chairman of the Roman Frontier Studies Congress 2000-, and Trustee Senhouse Museum 1985-. Presided over Hadrian's Wall Pilgrimages 1989, 1999, 2009. Honorary Professor at Universities of Durham, Edinburgh and Newcastle upon Tyne. Joined Society 1967, Vice-President 2002-11, Chairman of Research & Grants Committee 2004-08 and 2014-16, Charlesworth lecturer 1987, 2008.

Rachel Margaret Newman, BA, FSA, Born 2/8/1957, President 2014-
Born Gosforth, Newcastle upon Tyne. Educated Heathfield School for Girls, Harrow and Durham University, taking BA in Archaeology & Anthropology, as student of Rosemary Cramp (q.v.). Specialist interest in early medieval period. Joined Lancaster University Archaeological Unit 1983, currently Senior Executive Officer, Research and Publications at Oxford Archaeology North. Series Editor for the *Lancaster Imprints* monographs and has overseen the development of the Greater Manchester's *Past Revealed* series (2010-). Period co-ordinator for the early medieval aspects of the North West Regional Archaeological Research Framework and member of the working party of the Hadrian's Wall Research Framework. Joined Society 1980, member of Council 1987-89, 1993-96, Vice-President 2003-14, Member of Research Committee 1990-, Chairman of Research & Grants Committee 2008-14, first Chairman of Activities Committee 1995-98, Charlesworth lecturer 2011. Trustee Senhouse Museum 2005-, Committee Hadrian's Wall Pilgrimages 1999, 2009 and the International Limes Congress, Newcastle 2009, Trustee Mouswald Trust 2014-. Chairman Lancaster Archaeological and Historical Society 2016-. FSA 2004.

Acknowledgements
The Society is grateful to the following for permission to reproduce photographs: Lothian Health Service Archives at Edinburgh University Library (Joseph Spence); Westmorland Gazette (Paul Wilson); *Cumberland News* (Roger Fulford and Roy Hudleston).

I would like to thank all the people who contributed information for the presidential biographies and who helped to locate images. I am particularly grateful to David Breeze, Stephen White, Janet Martin and Tom Beaumont Jones.

A note on sources
Where possible these notes are based on obituaries published in *Transactions* or, latterly, the Society's Newsletter. Websites have provided biographical information for several presidents. *Times* obituaries are noted in some cases, but have not always been consulted. The two armorials published by the Society have supplied some information.

Appendix 2
The Society's Publications listed by Series

I.D. Caruana

See Chapter 2 for the objectives and history of each type of publication.

Extra series

I R.S. Ferguson (ed.), *Miscellany Accounts of the Diocese of Carlile with the Terriers Delivered in to me at my Primary Visitation by William Nicolson, late Bishop of Carlile* (1877).

II W. Jackson (ed.), *Memoirs of Dr. Richard Gilpin of Scaleby Castle in Cumberland and of his Posterity in the two Succeeding Generations; Written in the Year 1701 by the Rev. W. M. Gilpin, Vicar of Boldre: together with an Account of the Author by himself and a Pedigree of the Gilpin Family* (1879).

III R.S. Ferguson (ed.), *The Old Church Plate in the Diocese of Carlisle* (1882): 2nd.ed. supplement by Mrs Ware (1908).

IV R.S. Ferguson and W.S. Nanson (eds.), *Some Municipal Records of the City of Carlisle* (1887).

V W. Jackson (Mrs Jackson ed.), *Papers and Pedigrees Mainly Relating to Cumberland and Westmorland, Vol. 1* (1891).

VI W. Jackson (Mrs Jackson ed.), *Papers and Pedigrees Mainly Relating to Cumberland and Westmorland, Vol. 2* (1892).

VII R.S. Ferguson (ed.), *The Boke Off Recorde of the Burgh of Kirkbie Kendall* (1892); reprint with new introduction by C.B. Phillips (2001).

VIII M.W. Taylor, *The Old Manorial Halls of Westmorland and Cumberland* (1892).

IX R.S. Ferguson (ed.), *Testamenta Karleolensia: the Series of Wills from the Prae-Reformation Register of the Bishop of Carlisle, 1353-1386* (1893).

X R.S. Ferguson (ed.), *The Royal Charters of the City of Carlisle* (1894).

XI W.S. Calverley (W.G. Collingwood ed.), *Notes on the Early Sculptured Crosses, Shrines and Monuments in the present Diocese of Carlisle* (1899).

XII F.H.M. Parker (ed.), *The Pipe Rolls of Cumberland and Westmorland, 1222-1260* (1905).

XIII J.F. Curwen, *The Castles and Fortified Towers of Cumberland, Westmorland and Lancashire North of the Sands together with a brief Historical Account of Border Warfare* (1913).

XIV W.J. Sedgefield, *The Place-names of Cumberland and Westmorland* (1915); joint publication with University of Manchester.

XV C.A. Parker, *The Gosforth District: Its Antiquities and Places of Interest,* 2nd. revised edition by W.G. Collingwood (1926). [The first edition, (1904) was published by Titus Wilson].
XVI T.H.B. Graham, *The Barony of Gilsland: Lord William Howard's Survey taken in 1603* (1934).
XVII D. Scott (H. Hornyold-Strickland ed.), *Index to Nicholson and Burn's History and Antiquities of Westmorland and Cumberland* (1934); reprinted (2011).
XVIII F.J. Field, *An Armorial for Cumberland* (1937).
XIX J.M. Ewbank (ed.), *Antiquary on Horseback: the First Publication of the Collections of the Rev. Thos. Machell Chaplain to King Charles II Towards a History of the Barony of Kendal* (1963).
XX C.E. Stevens, *The Building of Hadrian's Wall* (1966).
XXI R.S. Boumphrey, C.R. Hudleston, and J. Hughes, *An Armorial for Westmorland and Lonsdale* (1975).
XXII M.G. Jarrett, *Maryport, Cumbria: a Roman Fort and its Garrison* (1976).
XXIII C.R. Hudleston and R.S. Boumphrey, *Cumberland Families and Heraldry with a supplement to 'An Armorial for Westmorland and Lonsdale'* (1978).
XXIV O. Wood, *West Cumberland Coal, 1600-1982/3* (1988).
XXV H.R.T. Summerson, *Medieval Carlisle: the City and the Border from the Late Eleventh to the mid-Sixteenth Century* (1993).
XXVI L.N.S. Smith (ed.), *The Stained Glass in the Churches of the Anglican Diocese of Carlisle: a Catalogue & Gazetteer* (1994).
XXVII A.J.L. Winchester (ed.), *The Diary of Isaac Fletcher of Underwood, Cumberland 1756-1781* (1994).
XXVIII R.J.A. Wilson (ed.), *Roman Maryport and its Setting : Essays in Memory of Michael G. Jarrett* (1997), published on behalf of the Trustees of the Senhouse Roman Museum.
XXIX D.R. Perriam and J. Robinson (eds.), *The Medieval Fortified Buildings of Cumbria: an Illustrated Study Guide and Gazetteer* (1998).
XXX N. Jennings, *Clay Dabbins: Vernacular Buildings of the Solway Plain* (2003).
XXXI R.J.A. Wilson and I.D. Caruana (eds.), *Romans on the Solway: Essays in Honour of Richard Bellhouse* (2004).
XXXII P. Ryder, *The Medieval Cross Slab Grave Covers in Cumbria* (2005).
XXXIII P.J. Cherry (ed.), *Studies in Northern Prehistory: Essays in Memory of Clare Fell* (2007).
XXXIV M. Townend, *The Vikings and Victorian Lakeland: the Norse Medievalism of W.G. Collingwood and his Contemporaries* (2009).
XXXV M. Brennand and K.J. Stringer (eds.), *The Making of Carlisle: From Romans to Railways* (2011).
XXXVI L.A.S. Butler (ed.), *The Church Notes of Sir Stephen Glynne for Cumbria (1833-1872)* (2011).
XXXVII D.J. Breeze (ed.), *The First Souvenirs: Enamelled Vessels from Hadrian's Wall* (2012).

XXXVIII R. Smalley, *Agitate! Educate! Organise!: Political Dissent in Westmorland from 1880-1930* (2013).

XXXIX R.G. David, *In Search of Arctic Wonders: Cumbria and the Arctic in the Eighteenth and Nineteenth Centuries* (2013).

XL D.V.W. Weston, *Rose Castle and the Bishops of Carlisle 1133-2012* (2013).

XLI K.J. Stringer (ed.), *North-West England from the Romans to the Tudors: Essays in Memory of John Macnair Todd* (2014).

XLII D.J. Breeze, *Hadrian's Wall: a History of Archaeological Thought* (2014).

XLIII P. Roebuck, *Cattle Droving, Cotton and Landownership: a Cumbrian Family Saga* (2014).

XLIV A. Connell, *Appleby Gypsy Horse Fair: Mythology, Origins, Evolution and Evaluation* (2015).

Tract series

I G.F. Duckett (ed.), *Description of the County of Westmorland by Sir Daniel Fleming of Rydal A.D. 1671* (1882).

II R.S. Ferguson (ed.), *An Accompt of the Most Considerable Estates and Families of the County of Cumberland from the Conquest unto the Beginning of the Reign of K. James (the First) by John Denton of Cardew* (1887).

III R.S. Ferguson (ed.), *Description of the County of Cumberland by Sir Daniel Fleming of Rydal, A.D. 1671* (1889).

IV R.S. Ferguson (ed.), *A Cursory Relation of all the Antiquities & Familyes in Cumberland by Edmund Sandford circa 1675* (1890).

V R.S. Ferguson (ed.), *Account of the City and Diocese of Carlisle by Hugh Todd D.D.* (1891).

VI H. Todd (R.S. Ferguson ed.), *Notitia Ecclesiae Cathedralis Carliolensis: et Notitia Priorate de Wedderhal* (1891).

VII J.R. Ford (ed.), *The Beetham Repository 1770 by the Rev. William Hutton, Vicar of Beetham 1760-1811* (1906).

VIII W.G. Collingwood, *Elizabethan Keswick: extracts from the original account books, 1564-1577, of the German miners, in the archives of Augsburg* (1912).

IX A. Sparks, *A Bibliography of the Dialect Literature of Cumberland and Westmorland and Lancashire North-of-the-Sands* (1907).

X P.H. Reaney, *The Records of Queen Elizabeth Grammar School, Penrith* (1915).

XI R.E. Porter and W.G. Collingwood (eds.), *The Memoirs of Sir Daniel Fleming* (1928).

XII P. Brown, *Edward Wilson of Nether Levens, 1557-1653, and his Kin* (1930).

XIII J. Melville and J.L. Hobbs, *Early Railway History in Furness* (1951).

XIV F. Barnes and J.L. Hobbs, *A Hand-list of Newspapers Published in Cumberland, Westmorland & North Lancashire* (1951).

XV G.S.H.L. Washington, *Early Westmorland MPs 1258-1327* (1959).

XVI H.B. Stout, *The Monumental Inscriptions in the Church and Churchyard of St James, Whitehaven* (1963).

XVII M.A. Faraday (ed.), *Westmorland Protestation Returns 1641-2* (1971).
XVIII G.P. Jones, *A Short History of the Manor of Witherslack to 1850* (1971).
XIX R. and F. Dickinson, *Monumental Inscriptions at Ulverston* (1973).
XX J.M. Todd, *A Window onto Late Medieval Cumbria: the Drawings in the Lanercost Cartulary* (2000). Reprinted 2011.
XXI R. Sharpe, *Norman Rule in Cumbria 1092-1136* (2006).
XXII W.D. Shannon, *Murus ille famosus (that famous wall): depictions and descriptions of Hadrian's Wall before Camden* (2007).
XXIII H.R.T. Summerson, *Edward I at Carlisle: King and Parliament in 1307* (2011)
XXIV M.A. Mullett, *Politics and Religion in Restoration Cockermouth* (2013).
25 M.A. Mullett, *Patronage, Power and Politics in Appleby in the Era of Lady Anne Clifford, 1649-1689* (2015).

Record series

I J.E. Prescott (ed.), *The Register of the Priory of Wetheral* (1897).
II W.N. Thompson (trans.), *The Episcopal Registers of Carlisle*: *the Register of John de Halton, Bishop of Carlisle, A.D. 1292-1324* (3 volumes, 1906-1913); joint publication with Canterbury and York Society.
III J. Wilson (ed.), *The Register of the Priory of St Bees* (1915); joint publication with Surtees Society.
IV W. Farrer (J.F. Curwen ed.), *Records Relating to the Barony of Kendale (Vol. 1)* (1923); (reprinted 1998).
V W. Farrer (J.F. Curwen ed.), *Records Relating to the Barony of Kendale (Vol. 2)* (1924); (reprinted 1999).
VI J.F. Curwen, *Records Relating to the Barony of Kendale (Vol. 3)* (1926); joint publication with Westmorland County Council.
VII F. Grainger, (W.G. Collingwood ed.), *The Register and Records of Holm Cultram* (1929).
VIII J.F. Curwen, *The Later Records of North Westmorland or the Barony of Appleby* (1932); joint publication with Westmorland County Council.
IX C.R. Hudleston, *Naworth Estate and Household Accounts 1648-1660* (1959); joint publication with Surtees Society.
X A. Bagot and J. Munby (eds.), *'All Things is Well Here', Letters from Hugh James of Levens to James Grahme, 1692-95* (1988).
XI J.M. Todd (ed.), *The Lanercost Cartulary* (1997); joint publication with Surtees Society.
XII L.A.S. Butler (ed.), *The Cumbria Parishes 1714-1725 from Bishop Gastrell's Notitia with additions by Bishop Porteus 1778-1779* (1998).
XIII B. Tyson (ed.), *The Estate and Household Accounts of Sir Daniel Fleming of Rydal Hall, Westmorland from 1688-1701* (2001).
XIV P. Hindle, *Thomas Jefferys Historic Map of Westmorland 1770:* reproduced in four sections from the original engravings with introduction (2001).

XV P. Hindle, *Historic Map of Cumberland (1774)* by Thomas Donald; reproduced in six sections from the original engravings, with introduction (2002).

XVI A.J.L. Winchester (ed.), *Thomas Denton: a Perambulation of Cumberland 1687-8* (2003); joint publication with Surtees Society.

XVII A.Taylor, (J.D. Martin ed.), *The Websters of Kendal: a North-Western Architectural Dynasty* (2004).

XVIII P. Gaskins (ed.), *Parish Registers of St James, Burton in Kendal 1653-1837* (2004).

XIX C. Phillips, C. Ferguson and A. Wareham (eds.), *Westmorland Hearth Tax Michaelmas 1670 & surveys 1674-5* (2009); joint publication with British Record Society.

XX A.J.L. Winchester (ed.), *John Denton's 'History of Cumberland'* (2010); joint publication with Surtees Society.

XXI R.B. Wordsworth (ed.), *The Cockermouth Congregational Church Book (1651-c.1765)* (2012).

XXII J. Platt (ed.), *The Diocese of Carlisle 1814-1855: Chancellor Walter Fletcher's 'Diocesan Book', with additional material from Bishop Percy's parish notebooks* (2015); joint publication with Surtees Society.

Research series

I T.W. Potter, *Romans in North-West England: excavations at the Roman forts of Ravenglass, Watercrook and Bowness on Solway (*1979).

II J. and P.J. Cherry, *Prehistoric Habitation Sites on the Limestone Uplands of Eastern Cumbria: a survey of the area between Shap and Kirkby Stephen* (1987).

III R.L. Bellhouse, *Roman Sites on the Cumberland Coast: a new schedule of coastal sites*(1989).

IV M.R. McCarthy, *A Roman, Anglian and Medieval Site at Blackfriars Street, Carlisle: Excavations 1978-9 (*1990).

V M.R. McCarthy, *The Roman Waterlogged Remains and Later Features at Castle Street, Carlisle 1981-2* (1991).

VI P.S. Austen, *Bewcastle and Old Penrith: a Roman outpost fort and a frontier vicus; excavations, 1977-78* (1991).

VII J.P. Gillam, I.M. Jobey and D.A. Welsby, *The Roman Bath-house at Bewcastle, Cumbria (*1993).

VIII H.R.T. Summerson, M. Trueman and S. Harrison, *Brougham Castle, Cumbria: a survey and documentary history* (1998).

IX P. Bidwell, M. Snape and A.T. Croom, *Hardknott Roman Fort including an account of the excavations by the late Dorothy Charlesworth* (1999).

X H.R.T. Summerson and S. Harrison, *Lanercost Priory, Cumbria: a survey and documentary history* (2000).

XI E. and S. B. Davis, *Draining the Cumbrian Landscape: a revolution in underdraining with tiles; with a Gazetteer of Sites and Manufacturers* (on a CD) (2013).

CUMBRIA ARCHAEOLOGICAL RESEARCH REPORTS

1 D.J. Breeze and D.J. Woolliscroft (eds.), *Excavation and Survey at Roman Burgh-by-Sands* (2009).

2 R.M. Newman, *Carlisle: Excavations at Rickergate, 1998-9 and 53-55 Botchergate 2001* (2011).

3 R.H. Leech and R.A. Gregory, *Cockermouth, Cumbria: Archaeological Investigation of Three Burgage Plots in Main Street* (2012).

4 J. Walker and M. Graham, *St Mary's Abbey, Holme Cultram, Abbeytown, Cumbria: Archaeological and Historical Investigations* (2013).

5. D. Elsworth and T. Mace (eds.), *Aldingham Motte, Cumbria and its Environs in the Medieval Period* (2015).

6. J. Zant, *Penrith: the Historic Core: Excavations and Building Surveys* (2015).

INDEXES

Index to Transactions of the Cumberland and Westmorland Antiquarian and Archaeological Society, Vols. I-VII Inclusive. Compiled by W.B. Arnison (1885).

Catalogue-Index to the Transactions of the Cumberland and Westmorland Antiquarian and Archaeological Society, Vol. I, 1866 – Vol. XVI., 1900. Compiled by A. Sparke (1901).

Catalogue-Index to the Transactions (New Series) of the Cumberland and Westmorland Antiquarian and Archaeological Society, Vol. I, 1901 to Vol. XII, 1912. Compiled by D. Scott (1915).

Index to the Transactions (New Series) of the Cumberland and Westmorland Antiquarian and Archaeological Society, Vol. XIII, 1913 to Vol. XV, 1925. Compiled by W.G. Collingwood. (1928).

'Author and Subject Index to the Transactions of the Cumberland and Westmorland Antiquarian and Archaeological Society, New Series, Volumes 1-45', compiled by C. Spence and J.E. Spence, *CW2*, 46 (1946), 1-66.

'Subject Index to Transactions, New Series, Volumes 46-72', compiled by J. Melville, *CW2*, 73 (1973), 1-24.

Index to the Transactions, Old Series Vol. I to Vol. XVI. Compiled by Joyce Cherry (1981).

Index to New Series Transactions (1960-89). Compiled by J. & J. Cherry (n.d.).

Parish registers

(Places and periods covered with names of transcribers)

1 Dacre 1559-1716, H. Brierley (1912).
2 Milburn 1679-1812, H. Brierley (1913).
3 Warcop 1597-1744, J. Abercrombie (1914).
4 Great Orton 1568-1812, W.F. Gilbanks (1915).
5 Barton 1668-1750, H. Brierley (1917).
6 Skelton 1580-1812, H. Brierley (1918).
7 Kendal, Part I: 1558-1587(Baptisms), H. Brierley (1921).
8 Kendal, Part II: 1558-1587 (Marriages & burials), 1591-1595 (Baptisms), H. Brierley (1922).
9 Brough Under Stainmore, Part I: 1556-1706, H. Brierley (1923).
10 Brough Under Stainmore, Part II: 1707-1812, H. Brierley (1924).
11 Millom 1591-1812, J.F. Haswell (1925).
12 Middleton in Lonsdale 1670-1812, J.F. Haswell (1925).
13 Whicham 1569-1812, J.F. Haswell (1926).
14 Bridekirk 1584-1812, J.F. Haswell (1927).
15 Newbiggin, Westmorland 1571-1812, J.F. Haswell (1928).
16 Crosthwaite, Part I: 1562-1600, H. Brierley (1929).
17 Crosthwaite, Part II: 1600-1670, H. Brierley (1930).
18 Crosthwaite, Part III: 1670-1812 (Baptisms & Marriages), H. Brierley (1930).
19 Crosthwaite, Part IV: 1670-1812 (Burials), J.F. Haswell (1931).
20 Cliburn 1565-1812, J.F. Haswell (1932).
21 Lowther 1539-1812, H. Brierley (1933).
22 Newton Reigny 1571-1812, J.F. Haswell (1934).
23 Crosthwaite Cum Lyth 1569-1812, J.F. Haswell (1935).
24 Lamplugh 1581-1812, J.F. Haswell (1936).
25 Crosby Ravensworth 1570-1812, J. F. Haswell (1937).
26 Penrith, Part I: 1556-1604, J.F. Haswell (1938).
27 Penrith, Part II: 1605-1660, J.F. Haswell (1939).
28 Penrith, Part III: 1661-1713, J.F. Haswell (1940).
29 Penrith, Part IV: 1714-1769, J.F. Haswell (1941).
30 Penrith, Part V: 1770-1812, J.F. Haswell (1942).
31 Brougham 1645-1812, J.F. Haswell (1943).
32 Bolton, Westmorland 1647-1812, J.F. Haswell (1944).
33 Crosby Garrett 1559-1812, J.F. Haswell (1945).
34 Holm Cultram, Part I: 1580-1597, F.B. Swift (1948).
35 Wigton, Part I: 1604-1727, F.B. Swift (1950).
36 Kendal, Part III: 1596-1631 (Baptisms), 1591-1599 (Marriages & Burials), R.N. Birley (1952).
37 Wigton, Part II: 1728-1797 (Baptisms), 1728-1781 (Marriages) & 1728-1779 (Burials), F.B. Swift (1955).
38 Morland, Part I: 1538-1742, transcriber unknown (1957).

39 Kendal, Part IV: 1606-1631 (Marriages & Burials), R.N. Birley (1960).
40 Whitehaven, St James, Part I : 1753-1837 (Baptisms), W.B. Stout (1964).
41 St Bees, Part I: Baptisms 1538-1837; Part II: Burials 1538-1837; Part III: Marriages 1538-1837, W.B. Stout (1968).
42 Index to Kendal Parish Registers, Parts III & IV, 1591-1631, R. Dickinson (1973).

Other

E. Birley (compiler), *The Centenary Pilgrimage of Hadrian's Wall, 4th-9th July 1949* (1949); joint publication with SANT.

Paul Bidwell (ed.), *Hadrian's Wall 1989-1999: a summary of recent excavation and research* (1999); joint publication with SANT.

B.J.N. Edwards and D.J. Breeze, *The Twelfth Pilgrimage of Hadrian's Wall, 1999: a report* (2000); joint publication with SANT.

N. Hodgson (ed.), *Hadrian's Wall 1999-2009: a summary of excavation and research prepared for the thirteenth Pilgrimage of Hadrian's Wall, 8-14 August 2009* (2009); joint publication with SANT.

G. Avery (M. Lea and K. Lea eds.), *The Collingwood Icelandic Pilgrimage, 2012* (2013).

Appendix 3
The Society's Library

I.D. Caruana

The library began about 1880 with the Victorian practice of exchanging journals. A journal library would have been of particular benefit to the early members of the Society as many journals were difficult to access. Gentlemen members of the Society would have had their own collections of books and could also have accessed a range of existing libraries. For example, members who lived in the Carlisle area could take advantage of subscription libraries, aimed at the more affluent reader, such as the Carlisle Library (founded 1831) and the library at The Athenaeum (1840), as well as the library belonging to the Dean and Chapter, which was perhaps of particular interest to the large number of clergy who were also members of the Society. The borrowing rules for the last library were published in one of the early volumes of *Transactions*, and early loans by Society members included books on general history, particularly church history, including Calendars of State Papers and the local monastic cartularies (St Bees, Lanercost and Wetheral), as well as key works on local history and the Society's own *Transactions*. Subscription libraries existed in most of the major towns (e.g. in Kendal from 1794), and these were supplemented towards the end of the nineteenth century by public libraries. In Carlisle a free public library came into existence with the creation of Tullie House in 1893, and in Kendal one was established in 1891, the basis of the Carnegie Free Library which was opened in 1909. Through the society's registration with the Society of Antiquaries in 1889 members of the Society were able to access its library in London.

In 1880 *Transactions* recorded that the Oxford Archaeological Society and the Lincoln Architectural Society had deposited their journals with the Society. Three years later the Kent Archaeological Society journal (*Archaeologia Cantiana*) was added and there followed a small but steady increase in journal exchanges with other county societies largely in the North of England through the rest of nineteenth century and into the twentieth. The first foreign exchange was *Heidelberger Historischer Verein* in 1895, closely followed by the journal of the Nordic Museum (Nordiska Museet), Stockholm in 1899. The former was probably of interest to Society members because of its Roman content, and the latter because of the Scandinavian links between Sweden and Cumbria. A few national journals such as *Journal of the British Archaeological Association*, *Archaeological Journal* and *Proceedings of the Society of Antiquaries of London* were housed in the library in the late nineteenth century. In 1907 it seems that the exchange system was not working as well as it should and five exchanges, including the original two, were ended. *Archaeologia Cantiana* now represents the earliest surviving exchange journal.

A collection policy based on the exchange of journals is not in itself systematic. The limitations of such a policy were recognised in 1980 by Dorothy Charlesworth who noted its random nature and observed that the Society lacked important national journals which were not part of exchange arrangements. During the 1990s the Society's librarian, Colin Richardson, made a concerted effort to contact our exchange partners to obtain missing volumes, including early volumes that predated the foundation of the Society. By this time the covers of some of the Society's own journals were in a poor state because of the unsuitable climatic conditions in the cellars of Tullie House where they had been stored. However, since they were largely inaccessible, even to Society members, rebinding was not considered a priority. More recently an attempt has been made to remedy deficiencies in the holdings of national journals by initiating subscriptions to the most important archaeological period journals (*Proceedings of the Prehistoric Society*, *Medieval Archaeology*, and *Post-Medieval Archaeology*) and by adding the important regional historical series, *Northern History*, while at the same time acquiring back numbers to make the sets as complete and useful as possible.

The book collection has largely developed from donations by Society members. Richard Read of Whitehaven and Harold Duff of Aspatria donated useful collections of basic classics and archaeology texts. William Calvert of Bardsea bequeathed to the Society an important collection of books on the Furness and Cartmel region in 1998. Through her legacy, Clare Fell probably donated the most important of the society's collections. Her bequest gave the library a substantial archaeological collection which was particularly strong in prehistory and the early medieval periods. Brian Ashmore's library of Roman archaeology books has substantially enhanced that section of the library. The occasional gift of a significant work of reference has always been welcomed. The ten volumes of the *Topographical Dictionary of England and Wales* by Samuel Lewis, published in 1845, was donated by G.B. Kenyon of Coniston and is on deposit in Kendal Archive Centre. Occasionally the value of maintaining our exchange journals scheme has been extended by additional exchanges such as the various parts of the *Corpus Signorum Imperii Romani* for Germany.

As well as these donations and bequests the Society has had opportunities to select items identified for dispersal by other private libraries. This has enabled it to acquire important texts for the history of Cumbria as well as augment its collections of its own publications. Recent donations have included a number of items from the collections of John Todd and Ben Edwards. It has been through the efforts of the current librarian, Ian Caruana, that the Society has a policy of creating a complete set of its own publications, including *Transactions*. Most deficiencies have now been remedied, and the Society has near-complete collections of all series except the Parish Registers where many of the earliest volumes are still missing. The Society does not have a policy of purchasing books but the 11 volumes of the *Register of the Great Seal of Scotland* proved irresistible when it became available for a pittance.

There have only been five holders of the post of Honorary Librarian since the post was instituted in 1924. The first three holders were the principal librarians in the Carlisle City Library – Tom Gray (1924-1949), Kenneth Smith (1949-73) and Henry W. Hodgson (1974-87). When the County Library Service and Tullie House Museum split physically in 1987, Colin Richardson, Keeper of Archaeology in the museum, assumed control of the Society's library. He retired in 1996 and in the following year the current post-holder, Ian Caruana, became Honorary Librarian.

The Society's library has always been hosted by other institutions. By 1902 the Exchange Library was in the care of Tullie House. For many years it was administered by the staff of Carlisle Library as part of the reference library and the journals were made available to all library users. Latterly some journals were stored in the cellars of Tullie House. It was with Carlisle Library's move into The Lanes, that the Society's library came into the care of Colin Richardson at Tullie House. When the old Tullie House museum was enlarged in 1990 it was hoped that a local history room might be included which could house the Society's library. To this end contact had been made with Carlisle City Council as early as 1986. Despite a sympathetic response from the council officers, no dedicated facility materialised. Around this time Colin Richardson was able to relocate the collection within Tullie House – moving it from the climatically unsuitable cellars to the archaeology curator's room and the upper corridors of the museum. Initially Ian Caruana continued to oversee the library in Tullie House, but the situation was not satisfactory to either Tullie House or the Society, as access for members was difficult and the museum was concerned about safety. When the Cumbria College of Art and Design, later Cumbria Institute of the Arts, expanded its range of academic courses and introduced an archaeology degree, it was felt that moving the library there would provide an opportunity to enhance the college's resources and to give Society members proper access to their library. Here the British journals collection was located in a dedicated room, but the foreign journals were placed in the Library reserve store, and the book collection was available for borrowing on open stacks in the main library. An advantage of the link with the Cumbria Institute of the Arts was that a professional librarian, Clare Daniel, supervised the collection and there was an opportunity to tackle the problems of re-binding and conservation with a small budget supplied by the college which allowed a programme of work to be undertaken.

When the Cumbria Institute of the Arts became part of the University of Cumbria, the university sought to rationalise its library provision in Carlisle. Its main library on the Fusehill Street campus did not have the space to accommodate the Society's collection, and consequently it was put in store at a number of sites around the city. During this time only very limited access to the collection was possible. In 2015 the Society's library was returned to the Brampton Road campus and access to it can now be made via the University library in Fusehill Street, where books and journals will be made available for consultation or loan. Details of the library collection and how to access it can be found on the society's website – www.cumbriapast.com. This site also includes a list of the earliest exchange journals as well as a list of all the journals in the collection.

Appendix 4
Archives

Adrian Allan

When the Society was founded at a meeting at the Crown Hotel, Penrith on 11 September 1866 'for the purpose of investigating, describing and preserving the Antiquities of Cumberland and Westmorland', its founders were no less concerned to ensure publicity for, and an adequate record of, its own activities and proceedings. The first minute book of the Society, 1866-73, includes printed circulars, members' tickets, accounts, and extensive press reports of its meetings and excursions (the Society covered the expenses of reporters), besides minutes of its meetings.

The two succeeding minute books (1873-1907) were recorded in 1932 as missing, but it is fortunate that the reports in the Proceedings sections of *Transactions* and reports in the local press help fill in some of this gap. From July 1907 onwards, the sequence of minutes of the Society's Council and AGM is complete; from 1962 onwards the minutes and lists of agenda items are supplemented by the agenda papers themselves. Besides the copies of the programmes of meetings and excursions, 1907-58 and 1972-74, which were included in the minute books, there are the separate volumes of such programmes, 1886-2006, amongst the records of the Excursions Secretary. The only sound recordings currently held amongst the Society's archives are the cassette recordings made on the excursions held in September 1966 as part of the Society's centenary celebrations; the speakers included Eric Birley at Birdoswald, John Charlton at Carlisle Castle, the Revd John Dickinson at Carlisle Cathedral, the Earl of Carlisle at Naworth Castle, and Barbara Harbottle at Lanercost Priory.

As the Society has evolved, so have its committees, responding to new challenges and opportunities. For the majority of the period before the mid-1980s, the three principal committees were the Excavation (later the Fieldwork and Excavation) Committee; the Committee for the Parish Register Section; and the Committee for Prehistoric Studies. The Excavation Committee was founded in 1894 to investigate the Cumberland end of Hadrian's Wall; its scope was widened in 1958 to include all excavations in the Society's area. Besides its reports for 1894-1903, 1932-38, and 1947-49, which were published in *Transactions*, its minutes and agenda papers survive for its last years, 1970-87. The Committee for the Parish Register Section, which was in existence from 1911 until its functions were absorbed into those of the Editorial Committee (now the Publications Committee) in 1991, has left little trace in the archives besides a subscription book, 1912-45, and some correspondence, 1982-92. On the other hand, the Committee for Prehistoric Studies, established by R.G. Collingwood in 1932, is well represented in the archives. Supplementing the Committee's reports for 1933-39 in *Transactions*, its minutes, extensive correspondence, photographs, plans and press cuttings 1934-88 were deposited by Clare Fell, with a later deposit of the Committee's record cards. Meanwhile the Committee for Industrial Archaeology, established in 1966, was active in recording sites; its minutes survive from 1985 onwards, as well as the record cards created by John Marshall and Mike Davies-Shiel. Reflecting the increasing importance attached to fostering research and to publications, the Research (now the Research and Grants) and the Editorial Committees were established in 1987; their minutes, agenda papers and correspondence from this date form an integral part of the Society's archives, alongside those of the Outreach Committee, established in 2007. Representative of the Hadrian's Wall Pilgrimages, organised jointly with the Society of Antiquaries of Newcastle upon Tyne, are minutes and other papers of the Organising Committee for the 8th (1959), 11th (1989), 12th (1999) and 13th (2009) Pilgrimages.

Supplementing the minute books are the extensive papers of the General Secretary dating from the mid-1980s, including correspondence (with Council and other members, local museums and libraries, the regional groups, etc.), agenda papers of the Society and its committees, copies of agenda papers and publications of the various trusts and other bodies on which the Society has been represented, and copies of publications of local societies and groups. The archives of the Society continue to grow and to reflect its activities.

Although the Society's balance sheet for 1871-73 records expenditure on 'photographing Dacre Castle etc'. and although sepia photographs of Yanwath Hall and Dacre Castle, which accompanied papers by Dr Michael Taylor, were included in the first volume of *Transactions,* few original photographs survive prior to the 1920s, other than those reproduced in *Transactions*. In 1907, it was recorded that photographs of the tower [of Shap Abbey] were returned to 'the Society's Chest at Tullie House', by Dr Haswell, to whom they had been loaned. Tullie House Museum and Library, which opened in 1893, served as the principal repository for the Society's archives, as well as artefacts from excavations associated with the Society and its members, until the opening of the Record Office at Carlisle Castle in 1963 and the transfer of the Library to new premises in Globe Lane, Carlisle, in 1985. The Society had long taken an interest in archives, their preservation and exploitation, establishing a short-lived Committee for Records and Publications, supporting the publication of finding-aids through its Tract Series, and promoting the projects for establishing record offices for Cumberland and Westmorland. It was appropriate that the first deposit of Society archives at Carlisle Record Office in 1965 should have been made by Roy Hudleston, editor of *Transactions* and a former President, who himself was a Lecturer in Palaeography and Diplomatic at Durham University. In advance of the move of the library from Tullie House to Globe Lane, the Society agreed that Tullie House Museum should continue to hold 'all excavation papers, photographs etc. together with the actual finds'. In the accession registers of Tullie House are recorded the deposits made by Society members, beginning with those antiquities collected by Robert Ferguson of Morton and the large collection of books, prints and manuscripts assembled by William Jackson of St Bees, followed by later deposits made by the Society's Excavation Committee; more recent deposits include the excavation archives of George Richardson (d. 1982).

Transferred to Carlisle Library in 1985 and forming part of the local history collection were archives which had been donated by members to the Society and papers of former Society officers. They include the extensive papers of Chancellor Richard S. Ferguson (d. 1900), including his 'waste books' (working papers) as editor of *Transactions;* his scrap books; and his copy of William Hutchinson's *History of the County of Cumberland* (1794) into which are inserted copious additional notes, illustrations, etc. The Society has also received gifts such as Mr C.W. Dymond's 'various plans' (1912), a diary of the Vicar of Colton for 1775, and the Revd W.S. Sykes's notes for a history of Eskdale which were received as part of Mary Fair's bequest in 1956. It is unfortunate that, with the migration of archives, it is not always possible to trace the current whereabouts of some of the deposits made with the Society prior to the mid-1960s.

At its foundation, the Society's Council was empowered 'to authorize the formation of Committees for local purposes, in connexion with the central body', but it was not until 1949, largely through the advocacy of Eric Birley, then Chairman of Council, that the Carlisle Regional Group was established, with further affiliated groups being established at Penrith (1950), Kendal (1952) and South-West Cumberland (1957). Though the minutes of the Society's Council refer to the groups, it is principally to record their membership totals and general progress. However, their annual reports to the parent Society since the mid-1980s survive amongst Council's agenda papers. Best documented are the Carlisle and Kendal groups: Carlisle's records include minutes and programme cards from 1949 onwards, and Kendal's (deposited at Kendal Archive Centre) include minutes 1963-96, programme cards 1952/3-1999/2000, and correspondence 1967-2003.

Although not always deposited with the Society, the surviving papers of individual members are extensive, ranging from Dr Amos Beardsley's illustrated accounts of Society excursions 1878-93 to the research and other papers of Clare Fell (1912-2002) (including her papers as member of Council and its committees); the research papers, slides and photographs of Mike Davies-Shiel relating to industrial archaeology; and the building reports written by the late Nina Jennings (author of *Clay Dabbins: Vernacular Buildings of the Solway Plain*, Extra Series XXX, 2003). Reflecting the Society's response to ever-growing threats to objects of historical interest in the area are the files created between 1971-84 by Michael Bunney, the Society's Correspondent for Buildings of Architectural and Historical Interest, and those relating to Carlisle's conservation areas, 1968-96, created on behalf of the Society by Bill Dent. Unexpected deposits include the

Inclosure Award and Map of Crosby, 1772, and deeds relating to the manor of Crosby, a moiety of which Kate Hodgson (d. 1974) left to the Society; her bequest also included the fieldwork notebooks relating to the Hadrian's Wall research undertaken by her father (also a former President of the Society) and her mother, dating from 1896-1904.

Detailed lists of the archives of the Society, the majority of which are held by the Carlisle Archive Centre, its affiliated groups, and those of members may be accessed on the Society's webpages at www.cumbriapast.com. The intention is that these lists will be periodically updated to reflect future accessions. Readers are invited to inform the Society about archives which are not included in the lists and to suggest additions or corrections.

As an end note, the Society is conscious of the challenges presented by born-digital records which exist only in electronic form, of which there will be a growing number subsidiary to the core minutes and agenda papers. Monitored, backed-up, secure storage will need to be sought to support the long-term preservation and access of those born-digital records of ongoing value.

Index